THE ARDEN SHAKESPEARE

GENERAL EDITORS: HAROLD F. BROOKS
AND HAROLD JENKINS

KING HENRY VIII

THE ARDEN EDITION OF THE
WORKS OF WILLIAM SHAKESPEARE

KING HENRY VIII

Edited by

R. A. FOAKES

LONDON

METHUEN & CO LTD

11 NEW FETTER LANE EC4

The general editors of the Arden Shakespeare have been
W. J. Craig (1899–1906), succeeded by R. H. Case (1909–44)
and Una Ellis-Fermor (1946–58).
Present general editors: Harold F. Brooks and Harold Jenkins.
Charles Knox Pooler's edition of *King Henry VIII* first published in 1915
Second edition 1936

Third edition (R. A. Foakes), revised and reset, 1957
Reprinted with minor corrections 1964

Reprinted 1966

First published in this series 1968

Printed and bound in Great Britain
by Richard Clay (The Chaucer Press), Ltd, Bungay, Suffolk
Type set by the Broadwater Press

For Barbara

CONTENTS

PREFACE

In the present work I have departed in many respects from C. Knox Pooler's edition of 1915, and arrived at very different conclusions from his regarding the nature and authorship of *King Henry VIII*. What debt remains is confined to the commentary, where acknowledgement is made.

I am indebted to the General Editor for her unfailing courteous help, and to Professor Allardyce Nicoll, Dr J. G. McManaway, and Miss Waveney Payne for assistance of various kinds. Professor C. J. Sisson kindly allowed me to consult the typescript of his forthcoming *New Readings in Shakespeare*. To Dr H. F. Brooks I owe a wealth of useful suggestions as well as the detection of a number of errors and obscurities. The detailed advice and criticism of Professor Clifford Leech, Mr J. R. Brown, and Mr E. A. J. Honigmann have been invaluable to me, especially in shaping the Introduction. This is not the extent of my obligations, which are too numerous to particularize, and I am grateful to many friends, colleagues, and librarians who have helped to solve difficulties.

R. A. Foakes

University of Durham
April 1955

The preparation of a new impression of this edition has given me the opportunity to make some corrections and revisions. I have made a few changes in the Introduction, adding a postscript to the section on authorship, and bringing the sections on the sources and on the stage history up to date. A few alterations have also been made in the punctuation of the text, in order to clarify some passages where the light pointing of this edition seemed possibly obscure or misleading to a modern reader.

R. A. F.

December 1962

ABBREVIATIONS AND USAGES

1. *Editions:* (This list contains only those modern editions of *Henry VIII* frequently referred to in the commentary.)

Clarendon Ed.	W. A. Wright, Clarendon Press Shakespeare (1891).
Deighton	K. Deighton, MacMillan English Classics (1895).
Nichol Smith	D. Nichol Smith, Warwick Shakespeare (1899).
Pooler	Arden Edition (1915, revised 1936).
Yale	J. M. Berdan and C. F. Tucker Brooke, Yale Shakespeare (1925).

2. *Works cited:*

Abbott	E. A. Abbott, *A Shakespearian Grammar* (1869, etc.). (References are to paragraph numbers, not to pages.)
B. and F., *Works*	Francis Beaumont and John Fletcher, *Works*, ed. A. Glover and A. R. Waller (10 vols., 1905–12).
Boswell-Stone	W. G. Boswell-Stone, *Shakspere's Holinshed. The Chronicle and the Historical Plays Compared* (1896; 1907).
Cavendish	George Cavendish, *The Life of Cardinal Wolsey*, ed. Henry Morley (1885).
Chamberlain	*The Letters of John Chamberlain*, ed. N. E. McClure (2 vols., Philadelphia, 1939).
Chambers, *E.S.*	Sir E. K. Chambers, *The Elizabethan Stage* (4 vols., 1923).
Chambers, *W.S.*	Sir E. K. Chambers, *William Shakespeare. A Study of Facts and Problems* (2 vols., 1930).
Dekker, Grosart	Thomas Dekker, *The Non-Dramatic Works*, ed. A. B. Grosart (5 vols., 1884–6).
Dekker, Pearson	Thomas Dekker, *Dramatic Works* (4 vols., Pearson Reprint, 1873).
Foxe	John Foxe, *Acts and Monuments* (1563 and vol. II of 1597).
Greene, Grosart	R. Greene, *The Life and Complete Works in Prose and Verse*, ed. A. B. Grosart (15 vols., 1881–6).
Halle	Edward Halle, *Henry VIII*, reprinted from *The Union of the Two Noble...Families* (1550), by C. Whibley (2 vols., 1904).
Heywood, Pearson	Thomas Heywood, *Dramatic Works* (6 vols., Pearson Reprint, 1874).
Holinshed	Raphael Holinshed, *Chronicles of England Scotland and Ireland* (vol. III, 1587).

Kellner	L. Kellner, *Restoring Shakespeare* (1925).
Marston, Wood	John Marston, *Plays*, ed. H. Harvey Wood (3 vols., 1934–9).
Massinger, Gifford	Philip Massinger, *Plays*, ed. W. Gifford (4 vols., 1805).
Middleton, Bullen	Thomas Middleton, *Works*, ed. A. H. Bullen (8 vols., 1885–6).
Noble	R. Noble, *Shakespeare's Biblical Knowledge* (1935).
O.E.D.	*A New English Dictionary*, ed. J. A. Murray, H. Bradley, W. A. Craigie and C. T. Onions (13 vols., 1888–1933).
Onions	C. T. Onions, *A Shakespeare Glossary* (1911; revised 1946).
Schmidt	A. Schmidt, *Shakespeare-Lexicon*, ed. G. Sarrazin (2 vols. Berlin, 1902).
Sugden, *Top. Dict.*	E. H. Sugden, *A Topographical Dictionary to the Works of Shakespeare and his Fellow-Dramatists* (1925).
Tilley	M. P. Tilley, *A Dictionary of Proverbs in England in the Sixteenth and Seventeenth Centuries* (Ann Arbor, 1950). (References are to the numbers by which proverbs are listed, not to pages.)
W. S. Walker	W. S. Walker, *A Critical Examination of the Text of Shakespeare* (3 vols., 1860).

3. *Periodicals and other abbreviations:*

C.S.P.	Calendar of State Papers.
D.U.J.	*Durham University Journal.*
F, F2, F3, F4	The four seventeenth-century folio editions of Shakespeare's plays (1623, 1632, 1664, 1685).
J.E.G.P.	*Journal of English and Germanic Philology.*
M.L.R.	*Modern Language Review.*
M.S.R.	Malone Society Reprint.
N.S.S.	New Shakespeare Society.
P.M.L.A.	*Publications of the Modern Language Association of America.*
R.E.S.	*Review of English Studies.*
S.D.; S.H.	Stage Direction; Speech Heading.
T.F.T.	Tudor Facsimile Texts.
T.L.S.	*Times Literary Supplement.*

4. *Line References:*

Quotations from a few authors are given simply by line reference; the following are the editions cited.

Ben Jonson, *Works*, ed. C. H. Herford and Percy Simpson (10 vols., 1925–52).

William Shakespeare, *Works*, ed. W. G. Clark and W. Aldis Wright (Globe Edition, 1864).

John Webster, *Complete Works*, ed. F. L. Lucas (4 vols., 1927).

5. *Early Books:*

The date of publication, or of the edition used where the first was not available, is given for early books cited, with the exception of plays. If the date of acting of a play is known, and preceded the date of publication, the earlier date is given. If a definite acting date is not known, but publication, as of many of the plays by Shakespeare and Beaumont and Fletcher, was very late, an approximate acting date is given. (The chronology of the Jacobean drama has still to be worked out in detail, and the dates assigned to some plays are little more than guesses: for further evidence Chambers, *E.S.*, III and IV, and *The Annals of English Drama 975–1700* A. Harbage, revised S. Schoenbaum (1964), may be consulted.) If printing followed quickly on composition or acting, the date of printing is given.

In all quotations from early books *u*, *v*, and *i* are modernized, where appropriate, to *v*, *u*, and *j*. Titles are generally modernized and abbreviated.

6. *Text and Collation:*

The text returns in many readings to the First Folio, and has been freshly punctuated and collated. The Folio punctuation sometimes makes nonsense, and may in any case not be Shakespeare's, as a scribe or editor or compositor may have intervened. But for this play it is the only authority, and has been followed as far as possible; the alterations that have been made are generally reductions from rather than additions to the Folio's heavy pointing.

In the collation, a number after an editor's name (e.g. *Rowe 1, Collier 3*) indicates the edition referred to (first, second, third, etc.). *Rowe 2* refers to the second edition of 1709, distinguished from the first by R. B. McKerrow (*T.L.S.*, 8 March 1934). The edition of 1714, formerly known as Rowe's second edition, becomes *Rowe 3*. A brief account of the more important editions of Shakespeare up to 1930 may be found in Chambers, *W.S.*, I. 275–7.

The very full stage directions of the Folio are kept, with a number of additions, which are enclosed in square brackets. The Folio Act and Scene divisions are also preserved, and the headings collated. Locations of scenes are not given in the Folio.

Literals and turned letters are not collated unless significant in some way.

Throughout the commentary the titles of Shakespeare's plays are abbreviated in accordance with the usage of Onions, *Shakespeare Glossary*, p. x.

INTRODUCTION

I. TECHNICAL INTRODUCTION

I. THE TEXT AND AUTHORSHIP

"The Famous History of the Life of King Henry the Eight" was first printed at the end of the section of history plays in the First Folio edition of Shakespeare's plays in 1623. The text is a very good one, with act and scene divisions and full, very often elaborate stage directions, which are necessary to set out the play's pageantry. The language of *Henry VIII* is sometimes complicated, and offers many difficulties of interpretation, but few that can be attributed to corruption.

The origin of the Folio text is closely bound up with the question of authorship. It seems to have been taken from a fair copy, possibly made by a meticulous scribe, of the author's manuscript.[1] There are several indications that the printed version stems from author's rather than prompt copy; the most important are the stage-directions and the speech-prefixes. It has been claimed that the more circumstantial directions originated in the theatre, largely because of such details as appear for instance in "The Order of the Coronation" (IV. i. 36), where Garter King of Arms enters, "in his coat of arms, and on his head he wore a gilt copper crown". Although the order of this and other processional entries differs from that given in Holinshed in some respects, this particular description,[2] and many more, are quoted directly from the historian, and show the author at work, not the prompter. While processional entries may usually be traced to a source, many shorter directions are of that nondescript variety which carry no specific mark of origin: where they are at all suggestive, it is again of the author, as in the use of descriptive adverbs , "gracefully salute him" (I. iv. 63),

1. This is the accepted opinion; see W. W. Greg, *The Editorial Problem in Shakespeare* (1942), p. 152, and E. K. Chambers, *W.S.*, I. 495–8.

2. Holinshed, iii. 933: this was pointed out by P. Alexander (*Times Literary Supplement*, 1 January 1931), in reply to W. J. Lawrence and R. Crompton Rhodes (*ibid.*, 18 December 1930 and 1 January 1931), who claimed respectively a scholarly and prompt origin for this direction.

"sits reading pensively" (II. i. 61), or a permissive entry such as "two or three of the Guard" (I. i. 197). There are no directions that anticipate by more than a line or two, and a few, like the entry for Dr Butts at v. ii. 6, may come a little late. Occasionally a character appears in the middle of a scene where no entry has been provided for him, as for instance Lovell in v. i. 169, and the Secretary of I. ii. 102, who, however, has no speaking part.[1]

Some regular variations in speech prefixes are due to the habits of the compositors who set up the text of *Henry VIII*,[2] but several irregular variations were probably in the manuscript. In IV. ii Katherine appears as *Kath.*, but elsewhere as *Que(en)* or *Qu.*; the *Old L(ady)* of II. iii becomes simply *Lady* in v. i; the Lord Chamberlain is introduced as *L. Ch.*, but in v. ii becomes *Cham.*, as a result of which there is confusion between him and *Chan.* (Lord Chancellor).[3] The Queen's Gentleman Usher of II. iv is not named until IV. ii, where he is called Griffith. The Lord Sands who figures in I. iv re-appears in II. i, the next scene, as Sir Walter Sands, a mistake due to the author's compression of chronology.[4] In addition certain pages contain what seems to be an indiscriminate use of *Wol(s).* and *Car(d).* as speech prefixes for Wolsey, which cannot all be accounted for by a shortage of italic capitals[5] or transference from his name as it has just appeared in the text. This occurs notably in III. i, in which scene there are two cardinals on the stage, and the use of the prefix *Car(d).* here is in any case ambiguous. These differences in the speech-prefixes allotted to a character, which could easily lead to confusion in the theatre, again suggest the author's hand,[6] rather

1. Most of the directions could have served in the theatre, and occasional brief orders like "Choose ladies. King and An[ne] Bullen" (I. iv. 74) may show prompt additions to author's copy. The direction "chambers discharged" in this scene was certainly put into practice, for it caused the burning down of the Globe theatre; see below, p. xxvii.

2. Charlton Hinman has found evidence of three compositors. One was B (well known from his characteristic spellings, such as *do*, *go*, etc.; see Alice Walker, *Textual Problems of the First Folio*, 1953, p. 9), who set 13 pages; one was A (known to prefer *doe*, *goe*, etc.), who set 2 pages; the third, whose habits were close to those of A, set 16 pages; see Cyrus Hoy, 'Fletcher and his Collaborators in the Beaumont and Fletcher Canon (VII)', *Studies in Bibliography*, XV (1962), p. 77, n. 6. The table setting out the shares of the compositors in R. A. Foakes, 'On the First Folio Text of *Henry VIII*', *Studies in Bibliography*, XI (1955), p. 55, needs to be corrected; compositor A set only 2 pages, x4^r and x4^v, which are not listed there.

3. See v. ii. 119, 121, 136, 141.   4. See II. i. 53, S.D. and note.

5. This variation occurs on Sigs. V2^v, V3^v–V4^r, and V5^v. See R. A. Foakes, 'On the First Folio Text of *Henry VIII*', pp. 58–9.

6. See R. B. McKerrow, 'A Suggestion regarding Shakespeare's Manuscripts', *R.E.S.*, XI (1935), 459–65; Greg, *Editorial Problem*, p. 103; Chambers, *W.S.*, I. 120.

than prompt copy, which needs to have clear and unambiguous speech headings.

The evidence to suggest that the copy was prepared by a scribe is slight. It should be possible eventually to determine whether a transcript was used for the Folio text, but much more needs to be known about the habits of the compositors and Shakespeare's own usages before a definite answer can be given. The play shows an extensive, but by no means thorough, use of contractions such as are found in other late plays or plays of late transcription. They are distributed fairly evenly, and no significant contraction is confined to a single compositor, or, within the usual division[1] by authors, to a single author. There are no notable variations in spelling apart from compositorial changes. In general the copy for the text must have been very orderly and well set out, and as W. W. Greg[2] says, "If the play was the work of two authors, no doubt it was carefully edited in preparing a fair copy." If, on the other hand, it was Shakespeare's autograph, we might expect a sprinkling of the odd spellings which are found in the "good" quartos. These do not occur, so that a theory that a fair copy written by a scribe was the source of the Folio text satisfies either hypothesis of authorship.

Henry VIII was printed as Shakespeare's by the editors of the Folio, and its authorship remained unquestioned until the middle of the nineteenth century. The theory that two authors were concerned in writing it was first seriously developed in J. Spedding's article 'Who Wrote Shakespeare's *Henry VIII*?' in 1850.[3] He found two different styles in it, one involved, and thick with imagery, the other showing a small "proportion of thought and fancy to words and images". He counted the frequency of end-stopped lines and redundant syllables at the end of lines, and claimed that the proportion in parts of the play corresponded to Fletcher's usual style. On this basis he divided it, with the exception of Act IV, which he felt was too vigorous for Fletcher and too weak for Shakespeare, between these two authors. In the same year Samuel Hickson, working independently, made a similar division of *Henry VIII*, but allocated Act IV also to Fletcher, and Spedding gave his approval to this.[4]

---

1. See below, p. xxii.   2. *Op. cit.*, p. 152.

3. *Gentleman's Magazine*, clxxviii (August–October 1850), 115–24 and 381–2. R. Roderick had earlier noted some peculiarities of style in v. iv (T. Edwards., *Canons of Criticism*, 6th edn, 1758, pp. 225–8), and Farmer, Steevens, and Malone explained some as interpolations of 1613, by Ben Jonson, in an old play written in 1601 (Variorum Edition, 1821, i. 283 ff.).

4. 'Who Wrote Shakespeare's *Henry VIII*?', *Notes and Queries* (24 August 1850), 198; see also pp. 306–7 (12 October), 401 (16 November), 33–4 (18 January 1851).

Spedding's main argument was from his feeling that two very different styles representing two writers could explain what he saw as an incoherence of design. Many others have seen in the play rhythms and cadences characteristic of Fletcher,[1] particularly in the pathetic scenes in which falling rhythms occasionally predominate. Some editors of standing accepted the view that Fletcher had a major share in it, and, by emphasizing this in their introductions and commentaries, gave currency and lent a kind of authority to Hickson's division,[2] which, helped by this editorial sanction, has become established as an orthodoxy amongst those who find Fletcher's hand in *Henry VIII*. His division is as follows:

Prologue	Fletcher	III. ii. 1–203	Shakespeare
I. i and ii	Shakespeare	III. ii. 204–459	Fletcher
I. iii and iv	Fletcher	IV. i and ii	Fletcher
II. i and ii	Fletcher	V. i	Shakespeare
II. iii and iv	Shakespeare	V. ii, iii, iv	Fletcher
III. i	Fletcher	Epilogue	Fletcher

A variety of internal evidence has been brought forward to strengthen the case for Fletcher. Some expressions common in this dramatist's work have been found in the scenes ascribed to him,[3] and while nearly all of them can be paralleled elsewhere, they cannot be altogether ignored. The most characteristic are perhaps "else" at the end of a clause (as at I. iii. 65); the phrase "and a [adjective] one" (e.g. "supper and a great one", I. iii. 52); and "sink" meaning ruin (II. i. 131). An attempt has been made to show that in the use of the contractions *'t, i'th (o'th,* etc.), and *'s* there is a difference between the two parts corresponding in one to the practice of Fletcher, in the other to that of Shakespeare in his last plays.[4] This is of doubtful importance, for the range of evidence

1. Various other divisions have been made, notably by R. Boyle ('*Henry VIII*. An Investigation into the Origin and Authorship of the Play', *New Shakespeare Society Transactions*, 1880–5, 443–87), and H. Dugdale Sykes (*Sidelights on Shakespeare*, 1919, pp. 19–47), who both rejected Shakespeare's authorship entirely and shared the play out, in quite different proportions, between Fletcher and Massinger. For a summary of the criticism prior to 1910 advocating dual-authorship, see W. Poel, 'The Authors of King Henry the Eighth', in *Shakespeare in the Theatre* (1913), pp. 85–98.

2. Among these editors were W. A. Wright (Clarendon Press, 1891); D. Nichol Smith (Warwick Shakespeare, 1899); K. Deighton (1895), and C. K. Pooler (Arden, 1915).

3. Hickson, *op. cit.*, and C. K. Pooler, *King Henry VIII* (Arden edition, 1915), pp. xxiv–xxviii, where a longish list is given.

4. Willard Farnham 'Colloquial Contractions in Beaumont, Fletcher, Massinger and Shakesp are as a test of Authorship', *PMLA*, xxxi (1916), 326–58.

presented is so narrow as to establish little more than that both authors were inconsistent in their usage. Further emphasis has also been laid on the frequency of extra weighted monosyllables and repeated effects at the end of lines. A high proportion of these has been noted in the scenes said to be Fletcher's, but they occur occasionally in Shakespeare's other work.[1]

The most formidable evidence produced in support of Fletcher's workmanship is in the variation between the two sections in the occurrence of certain forms of words. His preference for *'em* and *ye* can be demonstrated from his known plays, while Shakespeare generally seems to use *them* and *you*. The expletive *do* is confined in Fletcher's writing almost entirely to certain formulas, such as the begging phrase, "I do beseech", whereas Shakespeare seems to have retained an affection for it throughout his career. Similarly, the forms *hath* and *doth*, which are uncommon in Fletcher's writing, remained in use with Shakespeare until the end. The habits of the two writers in these respects appear to be reflected in the commonly accepted division of *Henry VIII*, as may be illustrated in the following table:[2]

	Expletive *do*	*doth*	*does*	*hath*	*has*	*them*	*'em*	*ye*
Shakespeare's part	45	2	10	22	14	23	5	1
Fletcher's part	5	0	6	2	33	7	59	72

These statistics reinforce the arguments from style, phraseology, rhythm, and the frequency of double-endings and end-stopped lines. There is nothing suspicious about claiming collaboration between Fletcher and Shakespeare, for *The Two Noble Kinsmen* (1634) has their names on the title-page, and the lost *Cardenio* is entered as by them in the Stationers' Register on 9 September 1653.[3] The case

1. Ants Oras, 'Extra Monosyllables in *Henry VIII* and the Problem of Authorship', *J.E.G.P.*, lii (1935), 198–213. The weight he lays on many extra syllables, e.g. vocatives like "sir" or "lord", is surely all his own; the refrain-like effect of some repetitions, as at v. iv. 28 ff., "nurse her ... counsel her ... bless her ... grows with her ... about her", is not common in Shakespeare, but occurs once or twice for special effects, see *Tempest*, II. ii. 3 ff., "hear me ... upon me ... at me ... torment me."

2. Reduced from the table on p. 22 of A. C. Partridge, *The Problem of Henry VIII Re-opened* (Cambridge, 1949); the fullest and most compelling argument yet put forward on Fletcher's behalf may be found in this book. The occurrence of *'em* and *them* was used as an authorship test by A. H. Thorndike, *The Influence of Beaumont and Fletcher on Shakspere* (Worcester, Mass., 1901), pp. 24–44.

3. Chambers, *W.S.*, I. 528, 538.

then for Fletcher's participation in the writing of *Henry VIII* seems to be a strong one, even though the evidence is all internal.[1]

Most of the evidence for Fletcher is, however, suspect on one ground or another, as a few scholars writing in defence of Shakespeare's authorship have sought to demonstrate. The statistics relating to tricks of style have been shown to mean little. Double-endings become increasingly common in Shakespeare's later plays, and vary in frequency from scene to scene. An increase in double-endings necessarily tends to increase the number of end-stopped lines, and it has been pointed out that these features are not exclusive to Fletcher, but are found in the Shakespearian portions of *Henry VIII*.[2] There are many differences between the style recognized as Fletcher's and that in the scenes assigned to him; in particular, the frequency of parentheses, run-over lines, and proverbs or general truths is much greater than in his known work, and repetitions occur much less frequently.[3] On a wider examination of texts, words and phrases said to be characteristic of Fletcher usually turn out to be fairly common in the period. In addition, it has been observed how strangely appropriate the different styles are to the scenes in which they are found, that

> The scenes reserved for Shakespeare in the mechanical pattern applied are the ones which call for formal, relatively stately, old-fashioned style, and the ones denied him are those of greater emotional appeal.[4]

The strongest statistical evidence of Fletcher's manner is the frequent occurrence of the forms *ye* and *'em* in parts of the play; perhaps together with these the variations in the use of contractions should be taken into account. It may be argued of these usages, as of other features that seem reminiscent of him, that they are not Fletcherian enough. For example, to show seventy-two appearances of *ye* in the Fletcherian portion as against one in Shakespeare's seems at first sight devastating, but this still does not correspond to Fletcher's practice as represented in *Bonduca* (?1610–13).[5] In the

1. The argument that *Henry VIII* is not a good play and therefore cannot be entirely by Shakespeare begs the question: see pp. xlv ff. for a discussion of critical views on the play.

2. P. Alexander, 'Conjectural History, or Shakespeare's *Henry VIII*', *Essays and Studies*, xvi (1930), 85–120. This is the best and most spirited reply to the advocates of Fletcher's part-authorship.

3. See Baldwin Maxwell, *Studies in Beaumont, Fletcher and Massinger* (Chapel Hill, 1939), pp. 54–73.

4. Hardin Craig, *An Interpretation of Shakespeare* (New York, 1948), p. 368; and see below, pp. lv ff.

5. This play is cited by A. C. Partridge in references to Fletcher's usages.

1647 Folio version this has 349 instances of *ye*, while *you* appears very rarely indeed. No parallel can be found in it for a scene like IV. i of *Henry VIII*, which has twelve instances of *you* as against three of *ye*, and these three concentrated into four lines of farewell.

The occurrence of all of these forms may in any case have been affected by scribal or compositorial interference. A manuscript of *Bonduca* which is extant, and differs considerably from the Folio text, offers an illustration of the former: it is a copy apparently prepared for a private collector by the King's Men's book-keeper, or prompter, and in as many as 172 instances *you* is written where the Folio has *ye*.[1] We do not know whether there was any such interference in the copy for *Henry VIII*; the signs are that the manuscript was carefully prepared, and probably written in one hand.[2] Sophistication of the text by the compositors who set up the type in the 1623 Folio, and through editorial interference, is known to have taken place. It has been shown that the compositors in printing *Richard III* introduced contractions into the text, and other forms which were not in the quarto used by them as their copy.[3] In particular there is evidence that Compositor B was capable of altering *ye* to *you*, as in *Troilus and Cressida*, and his preference for *you* seems to be confirmed by his work in *Henry VIII*, where his part of the text shows proportionately fewer occurrences of *ye* than that set by the other compositors.[4]

Other changes might easily have been made in the forms cited as evidence, as again Alice Walker found in the case of *King Lear*,

> where the quarto has 'hath' or 'doth' the Folio often substitutes 'has' or 'does'. Contrariwise, when the *Othello* quarto . . . was collated with a more authoritative manuscript, the opposite change took place.[5]

These considerations show that such evidence cannot be taken at its face value, since several kinds of intervention were possible before what the author wrote reached the printed page: in order to evaluate it properly, much more needs to be known about the text and the nature of the copy on which it was based.

The division of work among the compositors who set up the text of *Henry VIII* does not correspond to the commonly

1. The MS has been edited by W. W. Greg and F. P. Wilson, *M.S.R.*, 1951; and see R. C. Bald, *Bibliographical Studies in the Beaumont and Fletcher Folio* (1938), p. 99, whose figures for *Bonduca* are slightly different from mine.

2. In relation to this and the remarks on compositors, see above, pp. xvi–xvii.

3. See Alice Walker, *Textual Problems of the First Folio* (1953), pp. 29 ff.

4. See Philip Williams, Junior, 'New Approaches to Textual Problems in Shakespeare', *Studies in Bibliography*, VIII (1956), 3–14.   5. *Walker*, p. 62.

accepted authorship division,[1] so that it can be argued that the peculiarities assigned to different authors existed in the copy on which the Folio text is based. However, we do not know very much about the ways in which these compositors altered their copy for this particular play, or who was responsible for that copy. The division between compositors indirectly reveals further evidence of importance to the authorship question, for the variation between *Wol(s)*. and *Car(d)*. in the speech prefixes for Cardinal Wolsey in II. iv, III. i, and III. ii cuts right across it. This variation also cuts across the usual partition between authors, and it must have been in the manuscript from which the Folio text was taken. It suggests a single author, unless two writers are postulated who both chose to vary these, and probably other speech prefixes,[2] in an identical way, and were consistent in an identical way in their use of many more.

Contractions also may have been subject to interference from scribe, editor, or compositor. In any case the evidence is unreliable, for we do not know enough about Shakespeare's practice. The figures drawn up for *Henry VIII* show 39 contractions in the part assigned to Fletcher, 77 in Shakespeare's;[3] but if one group of these same contractions in *Coriolanus* (*i'th*, *o'th*, *to'th*, *by'th*) is examined, a very similar division of this play could be made, showing 65 on fourteen pages, and only 37 on the remaining sixteen.[4] Such contractions are usually thought to be the author's, but it is notable that *a'th*, which appears 26 times in *Coriolanus*, occurs not at all in *The Tempest, Cymbeline*, or *Antony and Cleopatra*, which, like *Coriolanus*, is considered to be based on Shakespeare's autograph.[5]

Perhaps the argument for Fletcher's part-authorship that is most difficult to answer is the most intangible one, based on the feeling that some scenes are un-Shakespearian. But when once a lead had been given, as it was by Spedding, his successors found it comparatively easy to see the same peculiarities. It is significant that support for Fletcher has nearly always been associated with condemnation of *Henry VIII* as bad or lacking unity, and belief in Shakespeare's authorship with approval of the play. In any case stylistic evidence is notoriously unreliable; as recently as 1947 it

1. See R. A. Foakes, 'On the First Folio Text of *Henry VIII*', p. 58 and n. The assignment of lines to compositors there given in note 9 is incorrect, but the careless workman compositor B did set a relatively high proportion (635 out of 1165) of the lines generally ascribed to Shakespeare; cf. p. xvi, n. 2 above.

2. See above, p. xvi. 3. Farnham, *loc. cit.*

4. Pp. 1–2, 7; pp. 3–12, 24 (none at all of *o'th*); pp. 13–24, 58 (including 14 of *o'th*); pp. 25–30, 13.

5. Greg, *Editorial Problem*, p. 148.

was proved that a poem long accepted within the canon of Marlowe's work, and considered to be characteristic of him, was in fact
written by Gervase Markham.[1]

The reply to the case for Fletcher has produced some positive
arguments for Shakespeare's sole authorship, and there are more
to be considered. *Henry VIII* was included in the First Folio of 1623,
and there is no reason to doubt the good faith of Heminge and
Condell, who affirm to the reader that they present Shakespeare's
plays "absolute in their numbers, as he conceived thē". Its presence
there is some assurance that Shakespeare wrote it;[2] both *Cardenio*
and *The Two Noble Kinsmen*, for which there is early evidence of
joint authorship, were excluded from the Folio. No early ascription
of *Henry VIII* in part to Fletcher exists, and the textual peculiarities
suggest a single writer.

Another factor of considerable importance is the evidence from
the use of sources. In almost every scene there are indications of a
very close and careful reading of the historians Holinshed and
Foxe, with occasional references to Halle's chronicle: if two authors
wrote the play, they read the same parts of these authorities with a
strangely similar attention to detail. Passages many pages away
from those of immediate relevance to the text are used, and
throughout there is a constant re-shaping of the material and compression of chronology.[3] In addition, widely scattered extracts from
the sources are brought together into one scene in the play. Such an
extensive and detailed study of source-material as is shown here is
not easily fitted into a theory of collaborative writing: it would
have to be assumed that each author read independently not merely
the sections in the histories relevant to the scenes he wrote, but all
the material on the reign of Henry. These sources are often followed
very closely, and what is known of Fletcher's habits suggests a different method of working. He wrote no other history play of this
kind, and on the other occasion when he used Holinshed as a
source, in writing *Bonduca*, he did not make any literal borrowings,
of which there are many in *Henry VIII*.[4] The alternative theory that
Shakespeare left an unfinished play which was handed over to
Fletcher to finish as he wished, and modify or ruin the original

1. John Crow, *Times Literary Supplement*, 4 January 1947.
2. Of the other doubtful plays, many now think *Titus Andronicus* wholly
Shakespeare's (see the Arden edition by J. C. Maxwell, 1953, p. xxxiii), and
Timon an unfinished draft by him. *1 Henry VI* may have been included in the
Folio to complete the trilogy of plays on the reign, and *Pericles* excluded because
no copy of it "absolute" in its "numbers" was available.
3. The handling of the sources is discussed at length below, pp. xxxiii ff.
4. Baldwin Maxwell, *op. cit.*, pp. 58-9.

plan,[1] is still less acceptable in view of the careful selection and re-arrangement of source-material throughout.

There are other important considerations. The play shows a unified, if special, conception and spirit: all the main characters are introduced in the scenes allowed to Shakespeare, which also establish the plot-structure, but have cross-reference to or antici-pate scenes said to be by Fletcher.[2] Many of the peculiarities of style may well represent a further development of characteristics that had already appeared in Shakespeare's later plays. Several of the scenes allotted to Fletcher present gossiping gentlemen, or fes-tive occasions like I. iv (Wolsey's banquet), and v. iv (the christen-ing of Elizabeth), which demand a treatment different from that called for in, say, presenting the trial of Katherine; the undoubted differences in texture between these scenes may have arisen in this way.[3] The accusations of Spedding and others that *Henry VIII* is incoherent in design have been opposed by strong claims that it is an organic whole.[4] More importantly, it has been shown that the spread of thematic material, like the spread of stylistic peculiarities, cuts

> right across any division that might be indicated, as he [Sped-ding] also suggests, by divided minds on the subject-matter.[5]

One further testimony to the unity of the play is its structure of imagery,[6] which also cuts across the proposed authorship division and suggests a single mind at work. Throughout *Henry VIII* imagery of bodily movement, often violent as if to give a dynamic quality to the language of a play which has little physical action, is especially prominent. The interaction of the characters, the machinations of

1. This is the theory favoured by A. C. Partridge, *op. cit.*, p. 34, who suggests that Fletcher worked hurriedly. It might be possible to argue on the basis of the distribution of *ye* and *'em* that *Henry VIII* is a text touched up here and there, sometimes for a whole scene, by Fletcher, for these expressions often occur bunched together, e.g. of six in IV. ii, four appear in four lines; the three in IV. i occur in four lines (114–17); eight of the twelve in v. iii are concentrated into two speeches (ll. 113 and 142–7); three of four in II. i are in three lines (130–2). In the remainder of these scenes *you* is used consistently, and this is unlike Fletcher's normal practice.

2. So for instance the birth of Elizabeth is hinted at already in II. iii. 77 ff.

3. This is discussed below, see p. lv.

4. The earliest of these were by A. C. Swinburne in *A Study of Shakespeare* (1879; 4th edn, 1902), pp. 81–103, and N. Delius, 'Fletchers angebliche Betheiligung an Shakespeares *Henry VIII*', *Shakespeare-Jahrbuch*, xiv (1879), 180 ff.

5. Peter Alexander, *loc. cit.*, p. 114.

6. Caroline Spurgeon drew attention to this in her fine analysis of imagery of bodily movement in the play; see her *Shakespeare's Imagery* (1935), pp. 253–8.

Wolsey, the trials and falls are all presented in terms of movement, or more particularly of carrying and release from a burden, or of the motion of falling. What begins in the opening scenes, "set the body and the limbs Of this great sport together", "interview . . . break i' th wrenching", "rend our subjects from our laws", "crept too near his conscience", carries on throughout and is often very striking in scenes said to be Fletcher's, as in II. ii, where Wolsey's machinations are described.

> now he has crack'd the league
> Between us and the emperor (the queen's great nephew)
> He dives into the king's soul, and there scatters
> Dangers, doubts, wringing of the conscience . . .
>
> (II. ii. 24–7)

This imagery has connections with the imagery of sickness which runs likewise through the play and suggests wrong-doing or mental suffering, as Buckingham is sick of choler, Wolsey's deeds "pestilent to th' hearing", and Henry sick in conscience over his marriage with Katherine. Two other important threads of imagery relate one to the sun and light, which has a special relevance to Henry, as the sun is often in Shakespeare associated with regality,[1] the other to the sea, storms, and shipwrecks, the most vivid imagery in the play, which seems to be reserved for highlighting certain especially dramatic moments.[2]

Perhaps after all what points most strongly to Shakespeare is the similarity in compassionate tone and outlook between *Henry VIII* and the other late plays.[3] The spirit of Fletcher's known work is completely alien to this, so that there seem very good grounds for leaving the play where Heminge and Condell put it, amongst Shakespeare's works. If Fletcher has to be introduced, then I think his share must have been considerably less than the usual division ascribes to him, and that he worked only as an occasional reviser or toucher-up, who perhaps contributed one or two scenes. It is tempting to claim good poetry for Shakespeare, and certainly there is nothing else in Fletcher's work so good as Wolsey's famous speeches of farewell (III. ii. 204–27 and 350–72): but there are other passages in the "Fletcherian" part of *Henry VIII* that, in their strength of character-creation, tone, and handling of language, seem to proclaim themselves still more loudly as Shakespeare's. I would nstance in particular II. ii, IV. ii, and V. iii; for I doubt if Fletcher

1. See I. i. 6, 20, 56, 226; II. ii. 31; II. iii. 6, 78; III. ii. 410, 415; V. iv. 46 etc.
2. See I. i. 92; I. ii. 79; II. iv. 197; III. i. 149, 164; III. ii. 196, 360, 436; IV. i. 71 etc.

3. This and other connections between *Henry VIII* and *The Winter's Tale*, *The Tempest*, etc., are discussed more fully below, pp. xliii ff., lxi–lxii.

was ever capable of, say, Katherine's last flourish of strength in her rebuke to the messenger (IV. ii. 107), or of such bold verse as

> He was a man
> Of an unbounded stomach, ever ranking
> Himself with princes; one that by suggestion
> Tied all the kingdom; simony was fair-play;
> His own opinion was his law: i'th'presence
> He would say untruths, and be ever double
> Both in his words and meaning. He was never
> (But where he meant to ruin) pitiful.
>
> (IV. ii. 33–40)

Finally, it should be noted that these considerations of authorship do not affect the intrinsic worth of the play: they are therefore not allowed to intrude into the commentary on the text, except at one or two points, e.g. II. iii. 78 n., where attention is drawn to links between scenes. Parallels with Shakespeare are generally preferred to parallels with other authors, and no special reference is made to Fletcher's works.[1] Throughout the remainder of this introduction Shakespeare is assumed to be the author.

Postscript, 1962

In my discussion of the authorship of the play, I hoped to do three things: to present fairly the case for Fletcher as part-author; to emphasize the strength of the case for Shakespeare as sole author, or author of most of the text; and to dismiss the whole matter, so that in the remainder of the Introduction and in the commentary the play might be viewed as a whole, and appreciated for what it is. It seemed to me important to ask what the structure of *Henry VIII* is, to appreciate rather than to judge it, because so often in the past critics had attacked it as a "collaboration of such a kind that no unity of conception and design ought to be expected of it".[2] My approach to the play was a sympathetic one, and this no doubt influenced my attitude to the authorship question. The supporters of Fletcher have not let the matter rest, but it should be noted that they tend to begin from the assumption that the play is a poor piece of work, lacking a unified design.[3] This is R. A. Law's

---

1. Where parallels exist (Pooler noted many), they are cited, but often with a parallel also from another author, in order to show that a usage is not confined to Fletcher.

2. See below, p. xlv.

3. Critical hostility to *Henry VIII* and support for Fletcher as author of much of it usually go together, but not always; Irving Ribner, *The English History Play in the Age of Shakespeare* (1957), pp. 289 ff., finds little reason to assign part of it to Fletcher, but also regards the play as a bad one.

point of departure in two essays; in one he argues that there is much
greater dependence on Holinshed, and less exercise of the dramatist's fancy, in the parts ascribed to Fletcher than in the rest of the
play; in the other he sums up again all the stylistic and other
evidence for Fletcher's participation in writing *Henry VIII*.[1]

The statistics concerning what he calls "objective differences of
style and metre" have also been set out again, with some new
emphases, by Marco Mincoff;[2] he thinks that Fletcher had a main
part in writing the play, and worked with Shakespeare, who
influenced his style, and brought about a certain "veiling" of his
stylistic peculiarities. Mincoff's vehement partisanship is evident
throughout his essay, and he does not observe that the interpretation of internal evidence is subjective, depending on a personal
reaction to style and rhythm, that

> external evidence can and often does provide incontestable
> proof; internal evidence can only support hypotheses or
> corroborate external evidence.[3]

The latest study of the evidence, by Cyrus Hoy, carries more
weight, for it is based on a linguistic analysis of the entire canon of
Fletcher's plays, and on a recognition of the way the compositors
worked in setting up the Folio text of *Henry VIII*. He believes that
in some scenes usually attributed to him, namely II. i, II. ii, III. ii.
203 to the end, IV. i, and IV. ii, Fletcher did "nothing more than
touch up a Shakespearean passage, or insert a passage of his own
in a Shakespearean context".[4] He finds consistent strong evidence
of Fletcher's linguistic habits in I. iii, I. iv, III. i, and in V. ii, iii, and
iv. He would thus reduce Fletcher's share in the play considerably
from the usual ascription of ten and a half scenes to six, or, in terms
of lines, by rather more than half. It would be pleasant if the whole
debate could be brought to a halt with his sane conclusion that,

> the truth about Fletcher's share in *Henry VIII* is to be found where
> truth generally is: midway between the extreme views that have

1. 'Holinshed and *Henry the Eighth*', *Texas Studies in English*, XXXVI (1957),
3–11; 'The Double Authorship of *Henry VIII*', *Studies in Philology*, LVI (1959),
471–88.

2. '*Henry VIII* and Fletcher', *Shakespeare Quarterly*, XII (1960), 239–60. Made-
leine Doran, in *J.E.G.P.*, LIX (1960), 289 ff., suggests that Shakespeare may have
imitated Fletcher's style in the play, experimenting with the elegiac effect of
falling rhythms.

3. Samuel Schoenbaum, 'Internal Evidence and the Attribution of Elizabethan Plays', *Bulletin of the New York Public Library*, LXV (1961), 102–24; the
quotation is from p. 105.

4. 'The Shares of Fletcher and his Collaborators in the Beaumont and Fletcher
Canon (VII)', *Studies in Bibliography*, XV (1962), 71–88; the quotation is from p. 79.

traditionally been held regarding it. Those who would deny his presence in the play altogether are wrong to do so, for he is assuredly there. Those who award him ten and one-half of the play's sixteen scenes (the usual ascription) claim too much.[1]

II. THE DATE

On 29 June 1613 the first Globe Theatre was burned down during the performance of a play by the King's Men on the reign of Henry VIII. In the contemporary account that is now best known, Sir Henry Wotton wrote to Sir Edmund Bacon on 2 July that

The Kings Players had a new Play called *All is True*, representing some principal pieces of the Reign of *Henry* 8. which was set forth with many extraordinary Circumstances of Pomp and Majesty, even to the matting of the Stage; the Knights of the Order, with their Georges and Garter, the Guards with their embroidered Coats, and the like. . . Now, King *Henry* making a Masque at Cardinal *Wolseys* House, and certain Canons being shot off at his entry, some of the Paper, or other stuff wherewith one of them was stopped, did light on the Thatch, where . . . it kindled inwardly, and ran round like a train, consuming within less than an hour the whole House to the very grounds . . .[2]

Although less specific, other reports of the event support Wotton's story in two important respects, in describing the play as *Henry VIII* (Thomas Lorkin and Edmund Howes), and in stating that the cause of the fire was the rash discharge of ordnance, or "a peale of Chambers" (John Chamberlain). There can be little doubt that the origin of the destruction of the Globe was the carrying out of that stage direction (I. iv. 49) which heralds the arrival of the king at Wolsey's banquet, "chambers discharged". The date of the fire may be taken at least as the upper limit for the production of *Henry VIII*; it is the date to which the play is usually assigned.[3]

Two points in Wotton's letter do not seem quite to fit the play as we have it. One is his reference to the "Knights of the Order, with their Georges and Garter, the Guards with their embroidered coats", for which the play provides no evidence. But Wotton was apparently not present himself, and this may be the embroidery of hearsay upon what was certainly a play of lavish pageantry. The other detail is the title he gives it, *All is True*. This might well have been an alternative title, for the prologue stresses that the play is

1. *Studies in Bibliography*, xv (1962), 79.

2. *Reliquiae Wottonianae* (3rd edn, 1672), pp. 425–6; ed. L. Pearsall Smith, *Letters of Sir Henry Wotton* (2 vols., 1907), II. 32. This and other accounts of the fire which relate to *Henry VIII* are given in full in Appendix I.

3. See Chambers, *W.S.*, I. 495–8.

presenting truth (ll. 18, 21), and Cranmer's prophecy at the end is spoken as truth (v. iv. 16). Possibly such a title would have had point if it were directed against Samuel Rowley's rambling play on the reign of Henry, *When You See Me, You Know Me* (1605), which was re-issued in 1613 and, probably revived on the stage by a different company, the Princes' Men, who became the Elector Palatine's Men in January of this year.[1] Half of this play is concerned with the famous fools of Wolsey and Henry, Patch and Will Summers, and a long section in it, which is devoted to a tour of inspection Henry makes in disguise to check the London watches, ends with a fight between him and a swaggering ruffian, Black Will, as a result of which they are both thrown into gaol. The prologue of *Henry VIII* may well glance at it in the lines

> Only they
> That come to hear a merry bawdy play,
> A noise of targets, or to see a fellow
> In a long motley coat guarded with yellow
> Will be deceiv'd.   (ll. 13–17)

A ballad on the burning of the Globe theatre which was printed as from a manuscript in the *Gentleman's Magazine* in 1816,[2] has the refrain "Oh sorrow, pittifull sorrow, and yet all this is true", and may be additional evidence that *Henry VIII* had a second title. The authenticity of this ballad has not been proved or disproved.[3]

It remains to consider whether we can arrive at a lower date-limit for the play. Wotton called it a "new play" on the occasion of the fire, but not too much reliance may be placed on this. It is possible that an earlier play was being performed under a new title, or simply revived, as when it was played again after the Restoration in December 1663, Pepys reported how "By and by comes in Captain Ferrers to see us, and among other talk, tells us of the goodness of the new play of *Henry VIII*".[4] No other contemporary report of the fire refers to a new play, and in his letter of 30 June 1613, the nearest in time, Lorkin speaks familiarly of "the play of Hen. 8", as if his correspondent would have heard of it. The indication of admission price of a shilling (l. 12) in the Prologue does not help, for there were certainly twelvepenny rooms at public theatres prior to 1613, and there is no sure chronology of price changes at the theatres. At the same time, it is pointless to seek, with Chambers, to identify the

---

1. The title-pages of 1605 and 1613 have "As it was playd by the ... Prince of *Wales* his servants". For the company, see Chambers, *E.S.*, II. 186–92.
2. Given in full in Appendix I.
3. See Appendix I, p. 181, for a further note on the ballad's authenticity.
4. 26 December 1663; this was noted by Pooler.

play as a revision of an earlier play on the same theme,[1] even if it be allowed that "The reversion to the epic chronicle at the very end of Shakespeare's career is odd."[2] For the language, prosody, treatment of the theme, and all the external evidence point to a late date.

Other indications of date do, however, suggest a time of composition and performance two or three months before the date of the fire, and incidentally a reason why Shakespeare should have set his hand to another history play. On 14 February 1613 Princess Elizabeth, King James's daughter, was married to Prince Frederick, the Elector Palatine, a leader of the protestant union in Germany. The contract for the marriage had been signed in May 1612, and in September Frederick came to England to visit Elizabeth; but though he was welcomed with pleasure, the death in November of Prince Henry, the heir to the throne, who had raised great hopes and inspired general love and admiration, put a halt for a time to any projected rejoicings. Perhaps the great celebrations which accompanied the wedding were made so splendid to mark the general relief after a period of mourning. Certainly no expense was spared on masques, banquets, plays, pageants, and fireworks on the river.[3] To most Englishmen it must have seemed an auspicious event, creating a firm protestant alliance between Britain and an influential German power, and it is not surprising that popular rejoicing seems to have been as marked as court festivities. One of many who celebrated the marriage in print claimed that

> By it great *Brittaine*, and the *Palsgraues* Land,
> Shall checke the *Popish* pride with fierce Alarme,
> And make it in much trepidation stand.[4]

The Prince received considerable acclaim, for what it was hoped he might be rather than what he was,

> Behold that Prince, the Empires prime Elector,
> Of the religious Protestants protector.[5]

1. E.g. the *Buckingham* performed by Sussex's Men, December 1593 (W. W. Greg, *Henslowe's Diary* (3 vols., 1904–8), 11. 158, and Chambers *W.S.*, 1. 497); or the *Cardinal Wolsey* and *The Rising of* or *The First Part of Cardinal Wolsey*, for which Henslowe paid Chettle, Munday, Drayton, and Smith in 1601, and lavished nearly £40 on splendid costumes (Greg, *ibid.*, 11. 218; Malone chose to assign *Henry VIII* to this date). Rowley's *When You See Me, You Know Me* was entered in S.R. 12 February 1605 as "the interlude of *King* HENRY *the* 8th".
2. *W.S.*, 1. 497.
3. On 10 February 1613, Chamberlain reports that the preparations for the mock-battles and fireworks on the Thames had already cost £6,000 (i. 418); the Inns of Court, he says, spent £4,000 and more on two masques (*ibid.*, i. 430–1).
4. Antony Nixon, *Great Brittaines Generall Joyes* (1613), A4v.
5. Thomas Heywood, *A Marriage Triumphe Solemnized* (1613), C4v.

A play on the downfall of Wolsey, the last great Catholic statesman of England, on the rise of Cranmer, and the birth of "that now triumphant Saint our late Queene *Elizabeth*"[1] would have been very appropriate at such a time.

To good patriots the anti-Catholic implications of the marriage offered the best of reasons for great rejoicing, for at the very least it was an affirmation of faith, and might prove a bulwark against what appeared to be strong Popish threats. Chamberlain noted how the Catholics maligned the marriage, "and do what they can to disgrace yt as beeing the ruine of theyr hopes".[2] But it was not quite the ruin, for what George Wither had feared in his lament on the death of Prince Henry,

> But more *Romes Locusts* doe begin to swarme . . .
> Yea Hell to double this, our sorrowes weight,
> Is new contriving of old *Eighty-eight*. . .[3]

seemed to be coming to pass in the threat of a new armada. In March 1613 Chamberlain recorded "a flieng report . . . that the Pope prepares forces both in Italie and Spaine for Ireland".[4] The Venetian ambassador was returning alarming reports to the Doge, of plots in February on the lives of James and Frederick, as a result of which "weapons are removed from houses that are under the Jesuits and those who had a share in the Gunpowder Plot".[5] In March he saw the Archbishop of Canterbury, who told him

> that beacons had been prepared all round the coast to be lighted should an armada appear, and orders given that all the musters are to be filled up by the first of next month, both foot and horse, the men to be armed and ready to march.[6]

Everyone was to be provided with arms, "the times require this and the growing audacity of the recusants."[7] The Archbishop may have been unduly worried, but the *Calendar of State Papers Domestic* bears him out to some extent in recording general musters and the renewing of beacons.[8]

Not only was the theme of *Henry VIII* appropriate to the time, but the play may have had a more specific connection with the triumphs of the wedding, in its pageantry and its celebration of peace, its processions, perhaps reflecting the progress of Princess Elizabeth to the bridal ceremony;

1. G. Webbe, *The Bride Royall* (1613), A6ʳ.
2. 23 and 25 February 1613; *Letters*, I. 427, 430.
3. *Prince Henries Obsequies* (1612), D4ᵛ.   4. *Letters*, I. 440.
5. *C.S.P. Venetian, 1610–13*, edited H. F. Brown (1905), p. 491.
6. *Ibid.*, p. 507.   7. *Ibid.*, p. 508 (15 March 1613).
8. *C.S.P. Domestic 1611–18*, edited Mary Green (1858), pp. 169, 177.

Then came the Bride, apparrelled also in *white* (Cloth of Silver also) with a Coronet on her head of Pearle, and her *haire* disheveled, and hanging downe over her shoulders. . . And her traine borne by eight or nine *Ladyes of Honor*.[1]

The masque at Wolsey's house, the scene of the Porter and his man striving to keep the crowd out of the court, and the Gentlemen commenting on the pageant they are watching in IV. i,[2] all may have been effective in relation to the similar displays which accompanied the marriage. In particular, the climax to which the play leads, the birth of the princess who was to become Queen Elizabeth I, affords a link with this event. For many, the occasion revived memories of the palmy days of the great Queen: Princess Elizabeth was following her namesake in her support of the true religion if not in getting married, and a comparison or identification of the two is common in the marriage tracts:

How much are we, the inhabitants of this whole Ile, bound unto our good God, that hath lent us such a Princesse, & in her hath renued & revived the name and nature of our late deceased, ever to be remembred, happie Queene *Elizabeth*.[3]

Indeed, two authors seized the opportunity to publish under Queen Elizabeth's name a volume of sermons and a tract on good behaviour, and in both there is a dedication to Princess Elizabeth equating her with the Queen.[4]

The last scene of *Henry VIII* probably pays a compliment not only to Queen Elizabeth and to James, but to Princess Elizabeth as well. It begins with Garter King of Arms crying out a blessing on the young Princess Elizabeth, daughter of Henry,

Heaven, from thy endless goodness, send prosperous life, long and ever happy, to the high and mighty princess of England, Elizabeth.   (v. iv. 1–3)

This passage, taken from Holinshed, is, of course, a formula, but to an audience of 1613 it is likely to have recalled the wedding, for after the ceremony and sermon which followed, in the words of Henry Peacham, a witness,

1. Henry Peacham, *The Period of Mourning . . . together with Nuptiall Hymnes* (1613), H2ʳ; cf. IV. i. 36, The Order of the Coronation.

2. This scene was especially successful in the Old Vic production after the coronation of Elizabeth II in 1953.

3. G. Webbe, *The Bride Royall*, F5ᵛ–F6ʳ.

4. J. Maxwell, *Queene Elizabeths Looking-Glasse of Grace* (1612); William Leigh, *Queen Elizabeth, Paraleld in her Princely Vertues, with David, Josua and Hezekia . . . in three Sermons* (1612).

Mr. *Garter* Principall *King of Armes*, published the stile of the Prince and Princesse to this effect. *All Health, Happinesse and Honour be to the High and Mightie Princes*, Frederick . . . *and* Elizabeth.[1]

There follows Cranmer's prophecy of peace and prosperity in the reigns of Queen Elizabeth and James, which resembles in its biblical echoes and stock complimentary imagery what was being said in many of the books celebrating the wedding. For example, the idea expressed in the lines

> Wherever the bright sun of heaven shall shine,
> His honour and the greatness of his name
> Shall be, and make new nations. He shall flourish,
> And like a mountain cedar, reach his branches
> To all the plains about him . . .   (v. iv. 50–4)

is derived from Genesis xvii, as the sermons alluding to the marriage make clear, which call for blessings on Elizabeth in such terms as these:

> that she be not beaten with the weather of adversity . . . nor nipt with the frost of an untimely death: *that shee may take roote in an Honorable people . . . and be set up as a Cedar in Libanus . . . and as a terebinth stretch forth her branches . . . that she may be the mother of nations, and kings of the people may come of her.*[2]

The biblical allusion at v. iv. 33 ff., "every man shall eat in safety Under his own vine . . .", was a favourite reference in relation to the peace of James's reign, "Establisher of Perpetual Peace", as John Speed called him.[3] The comparison of Elizabeth to a phoenix (v. iv. 40) was likewise a common compliment, made specifically to Princess Elizabeth in, for instance, Robert Allen's *Teares of Joy shed At the . . . departure . . . of Fredericke and Elizabeth* (1613),

1. *The Period of Mourning*, H2ᵛ.

2. John King, *A Sermon . . . at Whitehall upon the Tuesday after the mariage of the Ladie Elizabeth* (1614), E2ʳ–E2ᵛ; this same passage is cited in G. Webbe's marriage sermon, *The Bride Royall*, A5ʳ, of Frederick, "That your Highnesse may be . . . a Father of many Nations". The passage in *Henry VIII* has usually been associated with the colonization of Virginia, which was much in the news from 1608 on, and a double allusion may be intended.

3. *Theatre of the Empire of Great Britaine* (1611), Sig. ¶1. The biblical citation is made, for example, in Thomas Adams's sermon, *The Gallants Burden* (1613), D2ʳ, in Daniel Price, *Lamentations for the Death of . . . Prince Henry* (1613), E3ʳ, "Gentlemen, who . . . lived under the *Branches* of our *Princely Cedar*: . . . *you* onely returne to your owne *Families* to drinke of your own *Vines*, and to eate of your owne *fig-trees*," and in the official *A Publication of his Maⁱᵉˢ Edict . . . against Private Combats* (1613), F2ᵛ.

> As *Phoenix* burnes herselfe against the Sunne,
> That from her dust may spring another one . . .
> So now, raise up a world of royall seed,
> That may adorne the earth when ye are dead.[1]

The whole peroration would in fact have been very appropriate for a time when Queen Elizabeth seemed reborn in the princess, another champion of the protestant cause,

> Shee a kings daughter, so are you: shee a maiden *Queene*, you a Virgin *Prince*: her name is yours, her blood is yours, her carriage is yours, her countenance yours, like pietie towards God, like pittie towards men: onely the difference stands in this; that the faire flower of her youth is fallen; yours flourisheth like a Rose of *Saram*, and a Lilly of the *Valley*.[2]

There is extant a record of payments made to John Heminges, presumably on behalf of the King's Men, for plays performed before Princess Elizabeth and Frederick:[3] the fourteen titles include six identifiable as Shakespeare's, but not *Henry VIII*. For this reason it has been denied that there was any connection between the wedding festivities and the play,[4] but it seems to me very difficult not to believe that there was one. The play may not have been acted at court, or it may possibly have been that play which raised expectation on 16 February, but because of the greater attractions of a masque, was not performed,

> Much expectation was made of a stage play to be acted in the Great Hall by the King's players, where many hundred of people stood attending the same; but it lapsed contrarie, for greater pleasures were preparing.[5]

Whatever the reason for its not appearing in the accounts, there is evidence of other kinds to suggest a probable date of composition and first performance, within a short period after the wedding of 14 February. The indications are that the play would have a strong appeal to a London audience soon after the wedding, and I

---

1. B2ʳ; for an application of this idea to James and Queen Elizabeth, see Sylvester's translation of Du Bartas, *Divine Weeks and Works* (1608 edn), A3ᵛ, in the dedication to King James, "From spicie Ashes of the sacred URNE Of our dead Phoenix (dear ELIZABETH). *A new true* PHOENIX lively flourisheth . . . JAMES, thou just Heire".

2. William Leigh, *Queene Elizabeth, Paraleld*, A6ᵛ.

3. *Chamber Accounts*, cited in Chambers, *W.S.*, II. 343. The payment is dated 20 May 1613 and the married couple left London on their slow progress to Germany on 10 April 1613.

4. So Pooler says, "the argument from silence seems conclusive."

5. *The Magnificent Marriage of the Two Great Princes* (1613), cited in Chambers, *W.S.*, II. 342.

am inclined not to accept literally Wotton's description of the play at the Globe fire as "new". At least the likely date limits of first production may be fixed as between 14 February and 29 June 1613.

III. THE SOURCES[1]

The great chronicle histories of England published in the six-teenth and seventeenth centuries borrow extensively one from another, and accounts of some events appear in several of them in almost identical words. Some passages in *Henry VIII* might have been taken from one of several histories, but there are so many detailed connections between the text of the play and Holinshed's *Chronicles* (1587), as to leave no doubt that this was the primary source of the first four acts. It is equally certain that the story of Cranmer in Act v was taken from Foxe's *Acts and Monuments* (1597, etc.). There is good evidence that at least two other authorities were consulted in addition to these. At several points in the text the phrasing is very close to that of passages in Halle's account of the reign of Henry VIII, and certain lines in Wolsey's farewell speeches (III. ii. 223 and 358 ff.), which owe little to Holinshed, were probably developed from passages in John Speed's *The History of Great Britain* (1611).[2] There is nothing to show that the dramatist had independent access to a manuscript of George Cavendish's *Life of Wolsey*,[3] which was used by John Stow in his *Chronicles* (1565, etc.), which in turn formed a source-book for Holinshed.

There is plenty of evidence that the sources were read carefully and fully, including the marginal comments in Holinshed which occasionally provided a striking phrase for the text of *Henry VIII*, as for example at II. iv. 108, where the unusual word "arrogancy" was imported into a speech of Katherine. At some points incidents are introduced from historical events unrelated to the story told in the play. For instance, the immediate cause of Wolsey's downfall is shown as his mistake in sending the King an inventory of his goods, accidentally placed amongst papers of state (III. ii. 120 ff.). In fact Holinshed reports that Wolsey himself brought about the death of Thomas Ruthall, Bishop of Durham, through a similar accident on this bishop's part in 1508.[4] Another example of the

1. The main sources are reprinted, with a substantial essay on them and their relation to the play, in ed. Geoffrey Bullough, *Narrative and Dramatic Sources of Shakespeare*, IV. Later English History Plays (1962), pp. 435 ff.

2. This has not been noted before to my knowledge: see commentary on these lines.

3. This account by a follower of Wolsey's was not printed until 1641.

4. P. 796.

transference of material from an historical event to suit the dramatist's purpose is a passage put in the mouth of the Chancellor in his
attack on Cranmer. This is borrowed from the report by Halle or
Foxe of a speech by the Bishop of London in 1530–1 calling upon
the priests of his diocese to subscribe to a sum of a hundred thousand
pounds in order to be pardoned for their share in the *praemunire* on
which Wolsey was convicted.[1] This kind of transference occurs
elsewhere, and the way in which passages many pages apart in
Holinshed, or events unconnected by the historian, are brought
together and dovetailed in the dramatic shaping of the play, may be
seen in Appendix II, which cites the main borrowings in the order
of their occurrence in the chronicle.

Not only did Shakespeare transfer material from one time and
person to another, he also amalgamated stories from different
sources, or took a phrase or an idea from a source not otherwise
followed in the particular context. So in the account of Wolsey's
downfall, which is clearly based on the story of Ruthall's inventory,
the addition of further damning evidence against the Cardinal, in
the form of an intercepted letter,[2] was no doubt an idea developed
from an undated story told by Foxe, who relates that some of
Wolsey's letters fell into the King's hands, and from that time forward Henry "never trusted him more".[3] Many passages in the text
give an impression that Shakespeare was reading two or three historians at the same time, and taking ideas from more than one. It
cannot categorically be said that Halle's chronicle formed a source
for *Henry VIII*, but not infrequently phrases or ideas are closer
to Halle than to Holinshed.[4] Although Holinshed supplies most of
the material for Acts III and IV, the dramatist evidently had Foxe's
account not only of Cranmer, but also of Wolsey, in mind while
writing the last three acts.[5] It seems certain from the use of the
source-material that Shakespeare read, remembered, or perhaps
even collated, at least three chronicles, besides glancing at Speed's
history; and that he did not confine his attention to the material
immediately relevant to a particular scene of the play, but browsed
widely, and took or combined scraps from scattered pages in
several books.

These indications of a careful reading of source material suggest
a deliberate workmanship in *Henry VIII*. Although contradictions
or loose ends can be found in unimportant details, as when the
"Lord Sands" of i. iii and iv becomes "Sir Walter Sands" in ii. i,

1. See below, v. ii. 44–9 and n.   2. See III. ii. 201–21.
3. *Acts and Monuments* (1597), p. 901.
4. See for example i. i. 97, 120; II. iv. 87, 135; III. ii. 56 and notes.
5. See III. ii. 56–60, 64–7, 99, 212, and notes.

there is generally a skilful compression or distortion of history to serve dramatic ends. This is especially marked in the radical alterations of the historical chronology of events.[1] The trial of Buckingham (1521) is placed in close proximity in the play to Henry's meeting with Anne (1527?) at a masque which she apparently did not attend. The marriage of Henry with Anne Boleyn (1532) is brought forward before the fall of Wolsey, which occurred in 1529 (see III. ii. 42). The death of Katherine (1536) is similarly brought forward by several years, and is made to precede the birth of Elizabeth (1533). In such ways the events of twenty-five years are re-arranged to give a sense of uninterrupted continuity of time in the play's action.

In places, the sources were very closely followed, and some speeches are little more than Holinshed or Foxe versified. What differences there are, however, show characteristic emphases or additions that make a dramatic point or give shape to the material. This can be seen even in the details of the processional entries which are mostly borrowed from the sources: in the entry to II. iv, for instance, the pride of the Cardinals is given stress by the pomp that ushers them in, two priests bearing crosses, a sergeant with a mace, and "two Gentlemen bearing two great silver Pillars". These are not mentioned by Holinshed in relation to Katherine's trial, but are borrowed from the set description of Wolsey which follows the account of his downfall.[2] In this scene the cardinals appear more magnificent than the King, perhaps indicating the ascendancy Wolsey still has over him. In the same scene, the long speech of Katherine in her own defence (ll. 11–55) is almost as reported by Holinshed, but reveals two small, yet most significant changes. One is an additional proof of her loyalty (ll. 29–32), the other her passionate cry,

> in God's name
> Turn me away, and let the foul'st contempt
> Shut door upon me, and so give me up
> To the sharp'st kind of justice . . . (II. iv. 39–42)

These changes give the character of the Queen here a strength lacking in the chronicle.[3]

Other instances might be given of such careful touching-up of source-material for dramatic purposes. No fundamental alterations are made in presenting Henry and his court; the Tudor conception of history was too prevalent and the period of the play too

1. See App. II, pp. 183 ff.
2. For these passages relating to II. iv, Entry (Holinshed, pp. 907–8 and 921), see App. II, pp. 194–5, 204.
3. See II. iv. 11 and n.

near to Shakespeare's own for this to happen. But there are considerable changes from the chronicles, and elaborations of detail in the portrayal of character. This is true especially of the presentation of Katherine, who is much more powerfully drawn than in Holinshed. The historian shows her as sweet and possessing some firmness, but without the fire or the pathos she is given in the play: her vision of heavenly spirits, her regal dismissal of the messenger in her last fit of grandeur before her death (IV. ii. 100 ff.), the faithful attentions of her maid Patience and her gentleman-usher Griffith, are all additions to the material in Holinshed which enlarge these aspects of her character. The vision is especially interesting, for a dream, said by Charles de Sainte Marthe in his funeral oration to have been experienced by Margaret of Navarre on her deathbed, is transferred in the play to Katherine.[1] Margaret of Navarre was the Duchess of Alençon, Wolsey's choice as a partner for Henry instead of Anne,

> It shall be to the Duchess of Alençon,
> The French king's sister; he shall marry her.
> (III. ii. 85–6)

It it not known by what means the dramatist came to know the story of Margaret's dream.

In their falls Wolsey and Buckingham exhibit a patient endurance and forgiveness for which there are only hints in the chronicles: their farewell speeches are much elaborated, and in addition Wolsey, like Katherine, is provided with a faithful servant in Cromwell. The dramatic enlargement of these characters is mainly directed towards emphasizing their initial pride and hot-headedness, and then, in contrast, increasing the pathos of their falls and our sympathy for them. They are both nobler and more sympathetically drawn than in Holinshed.[2] The portrait of Cranmer is given spirit by his firm defence of himself (v. ii. 66 ff.), but otherwise follows the sympathetic portrayal of him in Foxe. Henry himself is continually extolled or defended in the chronicles as one of England's greatest kings, and the play too presents him as a strong, vigorous figure, the centre of the action in the sense that the course of events confirms him in nobility and authority as he throws off the domination of Wolsey, and assumes control of his country. His character passes through no marked development in the play, but is given variety and interest in various ways, by his moodiness, his fits of anger, his majestic entrances, all of which help to suggest life and

---

1. See E. E. Duncan-Jones, 'Queen Katherine's Vision and Queen Margaret's Dream', *Notes and Queries*, new series, VIII (1961), 142–3.
2. This is discussed more fully below, see p. lviii.

sincerity. Some hints for this portrayal, such as the King's repeated ejaculation "Ha" and his anger at being interrupted, may have been borrowed from Rowley's *When You See Me, You Know Me*.[1]

Like her companion the Old Lady, Anne is very much the dramatist's creation, and her humility, sweetness, and beauty, so lightly but skilfully sketched, form probably the only kind of foil possible to the strong and subtle characterization of Katherine. But perhaps the most notable innovation is the group of gentlemen who converse on the topics of the moment, comment on the action, or provide background information. By means of their talk, linkages between widely spaced events are easily made, and their dialogue supplies an essential accompaniment to the main action. One further addition to the source-material is the little scene of the Porter and his man fighting back the crowd (v. iii), which probably owes more to current events than to history.[2]

The handling of the sources, then, produced a dramatic reshaping of history. There are important alterations and additions in the play, and the selection of materials reflects a conscious purpose. It would, of course, have been impossible for an Elizabethan dramatist to present Wolsey in a heroic or a tragic light, as many modern historians see him, since to the protestant chroniclers he was one of the arch-villains of the Tudor period. But *Henry VIII* does present him in a much more sympathetic way than Holinshed, and the general emphasis in his fall and throughout the play on peace and forgiveness is entirely the author's contribution. The perspective of the play's action is individual, even though the sources were attentively read, and sometimes meticulously followed.

2. CRITICAL INTRODUCTION

I

In order to understand Shakespeare's purpose in *Henry VIII*, perhaps his last play, it is important to have in mind the way in which his art had developed. His latest plays seem to work in a different mode, to be striving towards a different end, from the comedies, tragedies, and histories he had written earlier. In the comedies and

1. G. Bullough, in his commentary on the sources, *op. cit.*, pp. 435–51, lays much emphasis on Rowley's play, following K. Elze, in his edition of 1874, and D. Nichol Smith, in his preface, pp. xiv–xvi, to the Warwick Shakespeare edition of *Henry VIII*. Bullough finds enough similarity between the plays "to prove positive influence" (p. 442), and he prints substantial extracts from *When You See Me, You Know Me*. The connection between the plays does not seem very strong to me.

2. See above, p. xxx.

tragedies there is a concentration of interest on two of the exciting and mysterious events of life: falling in love, and death; creation and destruction. In the comedies love is presented in an ideal form in which other values—for instance, the pursuits of hindering fathers—are seen as impertinent intrusions, and are invariably thwarted. The end is the achievement and satisfaction of love in marriage, or at any rate, in the assurance of marriage, in the acceptance of the bond. The youth of lovers, their irrationality, their fierce devotion to qualities in the loved one that cannot be seen by the rest of the world, their joy in beauty and transference of this joy to all creation, and the latent sense of fruition, of the fulfilment of a necessary function in continuing the human race, all go to make their situation immediately appealing and sympathetic. The process of falling in love is capable of transforming very ordinary people into temporary visionaries, and its presentation in comedy in the form of an inevitably successful courtship affords a concentration of all that is good and joyous.

The tragedies deal with the mystery of death and the motives and actions that lead to the destruction of life. Attention is focused on the terrible consequences that may attend on a trivial mistake, an unguarded word, a mistaken trust, or on the ever greater embroilment in crime to which a first yielding to temptation may lead. The tragic hero is entangled in sordid actions and motives, and the calamity that ensues is so huge as to involve nations; the whole universe seems to be concerned, and storms or eclipses occur while "the heavens, as troubled with man's act, Threaten his bloody stage". The motives—greed, jealousy, ambition, and the like—are common enough, but the consequences are magnified; what in life is often grotesque and horrible or simply petty becomes transformed into what is terrible or pitiful on the stage, in the grandeur of the hero's afflictions.

As in comedy the main interest is in the lovers, so in tragedy interest is concentrated on the hero, and much of the best criticism of these plays is in terms of character. This cannot be said of the other modes in which Shakespeare had written before he came to write his last plays. Some of the histories, like *Richard III*, may, it is true, be regarded as tragedies in their concentration of interest in the hero; but in others the idea of a king outweighs the character, and a diffusion of interest through the nation, from noble to commoner, is directed towards amplifying a concept of an ideal king and an ideal commonwealth. Here the argument seems to be more important than the individual characters, and when, as occasionally happens, a character assumes an independent life, a play may become unbalanced and leave many dissatisfied with it. The most notable instance of this is in *2 Henry IV*, where the rejection of Falstaff, although necessary and correct from the point of view of theme, is not so easily justified in terms of character. In the 'dark' comedies, in which certain concepts, sin and pride, love and futility, seem to override the drama, there is also a diffusion of interest. Many critics have felt that Shakespeare was presenting a point of view in them, was concerned more with a problem than with his characters, and the profundity found in them has consisted in the exploration of the nature of, say, chastity, rather than the nature of women.

The last plays show neither concentration of interest on one or two central characters, nor concentration on a problem. As in some of the histories and dark comedies, there is no central character, and several, perhaps six or more, share an equally important status. But it is not a sense of argument or inquiry, so much as a sense of range that is operative here, as though Shakespeare set out to present simply a prospect of life, which should show the beneficent predominating over the evil or unfortunate, and the sins of one generation cancelled out in the blessing of the next. The total effect, the almost visionary whole, is more important than what happens to the individual, or the development of character: for it is not character that is communicated, or a moment of intense action and its consequences, or the working out of an idea, but a sweep of life shaped in a restorative pattern, where the young in their innocence rejuvenate the old, and make restitution for the bitterness of the past.

The presentation in dramatic form of such a prospect of life in its continuance through two generations, involving a great range of time and characters, set for Shakespeare one particularly important problem, that of structure. Each of the last plays offers a different solution, and it is questionable whether any of them is truly successful. *Pericles* is unwieldy and sprawling in following the main figure's adventures from youth to old age. In *Cymbeline* the ingenious convolutions of the plot, culminating in a series of discoveries, and necessitating the odd death of Cloten, emphasize the mechanism of the play unduly; Jupiter's descent and the overt magic and myth-making are distracting because such spectacular unreality seems at odds with the very realistically presented human problems and political situation at the end of the play.[1] *The Winter's Tale*

1. See J. M. Nosworthy's discussion of the disproportion between the realistic and romance elements in his Introduction to *Cymbeline* (Arden Shakespeare, 1955), pp. xlviii–lix.

is more successful, because of the strength of Hermione and Paulina, and the vigour of Autolycus, but still there is that strange perversity of fate which leads Antigonus to a grotesque death, and which is followed by an awkward gap of sixteen years in the action. *The Tempest* overcomes the dramatic difficulties involved in such a long lapse of time by the device of Prospero's tedious narrative of what has passed; but although the apparent strength of the play's construction is greater, it loses in other ways. For to keep the action going in one almost uninhabited small island, so much magic is needed that the audience tends to be left with an impression of the force of charms rather than the overcoming of sin and restitution for ancient misdeeds. Mythology overlays the play to such an extent that some of it—the obscure allusions to Widow Dido for instance—has never been satisfactorily disentangled.

Perhaps this accounts for the comparative unpopularity of these plays in the theatre; the earlier two, *Pericles* and *Cymbeline*, are now rarely performed, and the others, which are difficult to stage successfully, are not among Shakespeare's most frequently acted plays. They have nothing like the dramatic power of, say, the tragedies. Yet the critics are agreed that the last plays are profound, although this profundity is not easily revealed in action: in the theatre they tend to remain what the title *The Winter's Tale* indicated to its first audience, droll whimsical stories to pass the time away. In the study they assume greater power, where the often tortuous syntax may be analysed, the references noted, and the associations of legend and magic explored, until these plays are shown to contain a complex scheme of thought. It is unfortunate that to understand this it seems to be necessary to identify and pursue fleeting allusions which are not dramatically prominent, and may pass unnoticed on the stage.

In seeking to show a perspective of life, Shakespeare seems to have relied on myth and magic to knit together the many strands, the great distances and time-spans of these plays, especially the last two, perhaps after a greater reliance on intricacies of plot in the earlier two had not proved successful. In doing this, providing an allegorical frame of reference, he made use of extra-dramatic themes and values. The plays were written at a time when masques had developed into a sophisticated and complex art under the genius of Ben Jonson and Inigo Jones, and courtly audiences were accustomed to symbolism in these, in which all the scenery and all the characters were likely to be emblematic. Possibly in this wholesale use of symbolism, rather than in the increase of scenic effects and pageantry, may lie the most crucial influence of this new development in courtly entertainments on Shakespeare. But in a mask symbolism is the natural vehicle, for scenery and dance and movement are primary, whereas in a stage-play the interaction of characters and the dialogue are of primary importance, and symbolic values secondary, liable to go unnoticed, or if observed, to mystify an audience unfamiliar with their particular frame of reference. In their time these plays of Shakespeare's were perhaps highly successful (it is on record[1] that *Pericles* was a great 'hit'), but by the introduction of extra-dramatic values, the likelihood of their permanent popularity on the stage was reduced. On the stage now, the symbolism, the fertility pattern in *The Winter's Tale* for instance, the correspondence between Perdita and Proserpine, and the restoration of summer when each is found, or the conflict between Art and Nature which has recently been detected in *The Tempest*,[2] tend to remain unrealized, or obtrude to spoil the action. Most of these correspondences or interpretations belong to the former category, and are only found at all after close pursuit in the study; yet here the secret of these plays is said to lie.

Possibly one reason for the similarity of substance and variety of structures in these plays is that Shakespeare was seeking a dramatic form that would resolve this dichotomy. The opposed views of the plays, ranging from a belief that Shakespeare was bored when he wrote them to something approaching idolatry, reflect their character. They are at once the most mellow in tone, the most richly involved in language, and the most depersonalized of his plays, the most difficult to bring to life in the theatre. In their wide span of time and types of character, the individual too often has to be compressed into an idea, as some of the heroes or heroines are little more than abstractions of purity, or, to speed the action, the motives and decisions of a Leontes have to be compressed into a series of exclamation marks. The remote and the ideal are not always brought quite into focus, not made sufficiently alive to establish a flesh and blood connection, so that an audience does not participate enough. They watch a ritual that is only partly comprehensible, because its terms are not wholly dramatic; they suspect a philosophy of life, recognizing tolerance, benediction, the joy of restitution, but are not given the key to it all.

There is a danger of losing perspective in accepting too readily

---

1. The prologue to R. Tailor's *The Hog Hath Lost His Pearl* (1614) says that if the play is a success, "Weele say 'tis fortunate like *Pericles*"; for this and a further allusion see *The Shakspere Allusion-Book, 1591–1700*, 2 vols. (1909), 1. 209, 248.

2. See Frank Kermode, *The Tempest* (Arden Shakespeare, 1954), pp. li ff.

the high valuation which has been placed by many on these later plays, a valuation which tends to see in *The Tempest* the culmination of the poet's (if not the dramatist's) achievement, even to the extent of identifying him with Prospero, whose farewell to his magic becomes Shakespeare's final leavetaking of his art. It is partly because of this estimate that *Henry VIII* is still ignored in nearly all criticism of the last plays.[1] If, however, *The Tempest* is one of a series of experiments, and not a completely successful one, to find the right vehicle for a new kind of material, then the breaking of Prospero's staff may have another significance. Perhaps after abjuring magic as a means to his end, the dramatist turned to real life again, to fact in the form of a history play.

It was an appropriate time for him to do so, when the great protestant wedding of Princess Elizabeth to Prince Frederick was taking place, and recalling for many, with some nostalgia, the days of Queen Elizabeth; the history of the nation always has an appeal on such occasions, and *Henry VIII* has frequently been revived, most recently in 1953, at times of festival, particularly at coronations. The time was perhaps propitious for another reason, for as the first armada in 1588 precipitated the flood of history plays produced in the following ten years, as long as any danger of Spanish invasion seemed to remain, so now the echo, however faint, of that great alarm, may help to account for the resurrection of a number of history plays in 1613. There is some evidence of continued popularity of several of Shakespeare's histories, in reissues of the quartos, but the great vogue of the history play in the 1590s was not repeated. The plays written after 1600 on themes taken from English history tend to be of a different kind, not so much glorifying England or presenting an idea of history with lessons for the present, as making use of stories from the past for effective theatre. Rowley's *When You See Me You Know Me* (1605) is an example. Although it crowds in many more events and sticks closer to the true chronology of Henry VIII's reign than Shakespeare's play, half of it is devoted to the famous clowns of Wolsey and the King, Patch and Will Summers Here light entertainment is the keynote, and the seriousness of purpose that had earlier made great drama out of history is quite lacking. This is perhaps the more noticeable after 1600 because, for

1. Not all; it receives noble tribute in G. Wilson Knight's *The Crown of Life* (1947). But it is not mentioned in E. M. W. Tillyard's *Shakespeare's Last Plays* (1938) or in Derek Traversi's *Shakespeare: The Last Phase* (1954), and is virtually ignored in much general criticism of Shakespeare's plays. It is worth noting that it cannot be fitted into the scheme of the earlier histories, and is not discussed in Tillyard's *Shakespeare's History Plays* (1944), or in Lily B. Campbell's *Shakespeare's "Histories"* (San Marino, California, 1947).

many years, if Shakespeare wrote on English historical themes, as in *Lear* and *Cymbeline*, he chose remote periods and did not attempt to draw analogies with the current reign.[1] In any case there was no call to perpetuate a Tudor dogma in a time of comparative peace, and after the glory had waned. There was also, after 1603, a new dynasty on the throne.

The wedding and threatened trouble in 1612–13 perhaps provided a new occasion for seriousness. Many old history plays were reissued at this time, and the reissues probably indicate revivals in the theatre.[2] In addition, *Henry VIII* was written.[3] If it was inspired by events of the time, and glorified the protestant heritage of Princess Elizabeth, paying a compliment to her and to James with its stress on "peace and plenty" for a King who

> lived in peace, dyed in peace, and left all his kingdomes in a peaceable condition, with his owne Motto: *Beati Pacifici*;[4]

at the same time it transcended the occasion.[5] The play is a wide departure from Shakespeare's earlier histories and a natural continuation from *The Tempest*. In choosing for his plot the peaceful aspects of a reign Shakespeare was doing something new for him, and was enabled to present in more purely dramatic terms something of that perspective of life which is largely overlaid by myth and symbol in the other late plays.[6]

This vision of life is expressed through several themes. One is the restoration of what has been lost, or compensation, in the winning of self-knowledge, for suffering caused or undergone. So Leontes, having suffered and caused suffering as a result of his own ground-

1. He may have paid a compliment to King James in *Macbeth* [see J. Dover Wilson, *Macbeth* (New Cambridge Shakespeare, 1947), pp. xliv ff., and H. N. Paul, *The Royal Play of Macbeth* (1950)], but this is another matter.

2. These include Marlowe's *Edward II* (1592–3?), Shakespeare's *Richard III* (1592–3?), and *The Famous History of Sir Thomas Wyat* (1607), reprinted in 1612; Shakespeare's *1 Henry IV* (1598), *1* and *2 Edward IV* (1599), *Thomas Lord Cromwell* (1602), Heywood's *If You Know Not Me, You Know Nobody* (1605), on the reign of Queen Elizabeth, and Rowley's *When You See Me, You Know Me* (1605), reprinted in 1613.

3. It should perhaps be noted that it inspired at least one other play, Wentworth Smith's *The Hector of Germanie . . . an Honourable Hystorie*, performed at the Red Bull Theatre and published in 1615.

4. Sir Anthony Weldon, *The Court and Character of King James* (1650), cited in ed. D. Nichol Smith, *Characters from the Histories & Memoirs of the Seventeenth Century* (Oxford, 1918), p. 9.

5. As did Shakespeare's other "occasional" plays; amongst them may be included the earlier histories, *A Midsummer Night's Dream*, probably written to celebrate a wedding, and *Love's Labour's Lost*.

6. This is not to say that there is no use of symbolism in *Henry VIII*; but what there is grows naturally out of the action; see below, pp. xlvii ff.

less jealousy, has Perdita and Hermione restored to him, and himself learns humility; so Gonzalo cries at the end of *The Tempest* for rejoicing "Beyond a common joy", for

> In one voyage
> Did Claribel her husband find at Tunis,
> And Ferdinand, her brother, found a wife
> Where he himself was lost, Prospero his dukedom
> In a poor isle, and all of us ourselves,
> When no man was his own.   (v. i. 208–13)

Another theme is that of justice and injustice, which are involved in the trial of Hermione and the original expulsion of Prospero from his duchy. Another is a kind of rectifying of the mistakes and sufferings of an older generation in the joy and vitality of the next: the movement of the plays is from the former to the latter, from a dark past to a bright present, with the suggestion of a brighter future. This seems assured through yet another theme, that of forgiveness, which, together with the love and beauty of youth, contrasts with former excesses of passion, or failures to forgive. One other very important theme is that of patience in adversity, the quality displayed by Hermione in her long retirement.

All these are present in *Henry VIII*. The first is exemplified in Wolsey's discovery of peace in his downfall:

> Never so truly happy, my good Cromwell;
> I know myself now, and I feel within me
> A peace above all earthly dignities,
> A still and quiet conscience.   (III. ii. 377–80)

The second, that of justice, is one of the major preoccupations in *Henry VIII*, in which four trials are involved. The youth and beauty of Anne, and the promise of a golden future in the birth of Elizabeth, afford a compensation for the falls of Buckingham and Katherine, both of whom show forgiveness and patience. Where this play differs from the others is in its closeness to actuality, and in the greater embodiment of the themes in the characters. In the other late plays there is some sort of abrogation of the ordinary laws of movement, of causation, of time and space, and of social intercourse. Time is compressed, movement expanded, and events are organized in a range of coincidences rather than in an ordered succession. A machinery of the supernatural—the oracle at Delphos, Jupiter on his golden eagle, and Ariel—or of whimsy—"Exit pursued by a bear"—is needed to bring this about. Human, fallible justice is overridden by accident, by the interference of the gods, or by the improbable survival of a Belarius or a Hermione.

The nature of *Henry VIII* becomes clearer in the light of these con-trivances, as an attempt to create a similar total effect within the ordinary terms of causality and succession, terms which the material of history helped to impose; and it is the play's structure, its most neglected aspect, which deserves most careful study.

II

In Wolsey and Katherine *Henry VIII* offers two superb roles which have always tempted actors and actresses. Perhaps because of this, critics have generally given what space they could spare from the authorship question to a study of these characters. The result has been a dissatisfaction with the structure of a play which, according to Spedding, "falls away utterly, and leaves us in the last act among persons we scarcely know, and events for which we do not care".[1] But in so far as it is like the other late plays, the structure of *Henry VIII* is more important than the characters, and to examine the play in terms of character alone is not likely to be rewarding. Its structure deserves careful study for another reason; it has been allowed coherence or shape so rarely that recently a critic, remark-ing the general preoccupation with authorship, has bitterly and justly complained,

> this assumption of Spedding's [i.e. of dual authorship] underlies the dearth of critical comment on the play itself; it is assumed to be of interest only in that it was a collaboration of such a kind that no unity of conception and design ought to be expected of it.[2]

Much adverse criticism has resulted from a comparison of *Henry VIII* with various ideas of what a play by Shakespeare ought to be, or of what this play was intended to be before Fletcher, Massinger, or others stepped in to ruin a projected masterpiece. The most notable argument has been that Wolsey was meant to be Shake-speare's greatest villain after Iago,[3] that in this play,

> the *disiecta membra* of what might have been a great tragedy are hardly to be recognised in the stream of declamation.[4]

Alternatively, the play has been condemned as failing in its general

1. *Loc. cit.*, p. 116.
2. Frank Kermode, 'What is Shakespeare's *Henry VIII* about?', *D.U.J.* New Ser., ix (March 1948), p. 48. His answer to the question is not very satisfactory; like Pooler, he sees the play as "an anthology of falls", a return to the medieval conception of history represented in *The Mirror for Magistrates*.
3. Marjorie Nicolson, 'The Authorship of Henry the Eighth', *P.M.L.A.*, xxxvii (September 1922), p. 500.
4. Pooler, *op. cit.*, p. xxxii.

design through the influence of Fletcher, who is said to have "sentimentalized" each major character in turn, so that each in his or her final appearance is shown behaving in a manner quite different from what might have been expected. In consequence, it is said, interest is not maintained.

It is only a short step from this to a round condemnation of *Henry VIII* as

> Without plot, without development, without any character on which the interest can be concentrated throughout.[1]

Three main strictures on the play have emerged from this onslaught. One is that the characters are inconsistent, that Buckingham, Wolsey, and Katherine become weak at their falls. From this a moral ambiguity is said to result, in as much as the fall of Katherine, who is innocent, is placed on the same level as the fall of Wolsey, who is guilty. The second is a corollary to this, that the major effects are gained by rhetoric, in the great patches of declamation, like Wolsey's farewell speeches. In consequence, such speeches are dissociated from the characters who speak them, and generalized "to the vanishing point of personal responsibility".[2] Both of these criticisms, that character is distorted by being sentimentalized, and that the logical response of the audience is distorted by means of rhetoric, stem from the third stricture, basic to hostile criticism of the play, that *Henry VIII* has no controlling and unifying plan, but is only a series of loosely connected scenes strung together to offer an attractive stage spectacle.

One or two early nineteenth-century writers on *Henry VIII* gave way to idolatry in claiming not only that it is an organic whole, but that

> there is no play of Shakspere's which has a more decided character of unity—no one from which any passages could be less easily struck out,[3]

Few have been prepared to assert so much since Spedding wrote,

1. W. A. Wright, *Henry VIII* (1891; Clarendon Ed.), p. xxii: for similar views see D. Nichol Smith, *Henry VIII* (1899; Warwick Shakespeare), p. xxxi; A. A. Parker, 'Henry VIII in Shakespeare and Calderon', *M.L.R.* (1948), 328 ff.; Eugene M. Waith, *The Pattern of Tragicomedy in Beaumont and Fletcher* (Yale, 1952), p. 118. R. Boyle felt so angry with the play that, more out of wilfulness than with any reason, he threw it out of the canon completely as a degradation of Shakespeare's art, 'Henry VIII. An Investigation into the Origin and Authorship of the Play', *N.S.S. Transactions* (1880–5), 443 ff.

2. Waith, *op. cit.*, p. 121.

3. Charles Knight, *Shakspere's Works* (1840), Histories, II. 398, and cf. W. Watkiss Lloyd, 'Critical Essay on *King Henry VIII*' in ed. S. W. Singer, *Shakespeare's Works* (1856), VII. 150.

but there have been two notable sympathetic interpretations in recent years. One has stressed the need to define a history play as a play with no given, rigid structure, but one controlled, in Shakespeare's time, by an overriding philosophy of history, that God directs all. If seen thus, and not as an abortive tragedy, "from the point of view of form it is one of his [Shakespeare's] greatest achievements."[1] The other views the play as epic rather than dramatic in structure, the three falls of Buckingham, Wolsey, and Katherine gathering all Shakespeare's human sympathies as each one passes away on a note of universal forgiveness.[2] In developing this line of approach, G. Wilson Knight, whose essays on *Henry VIII* are very valuable, has pointed out how the series of falls is countered by the gaiety of the banquet, the coronation, and the final christening scene, how, throughout, the oppositions are deliberate;

> the tragic and religious as opposed by the warm, sex-impelled, blood; the eternities of death as against the glow and thrill of incarnate life.[3]

It is notable that once the play is allowed to be a unity, the inconsistency so often perceived in the characters tends to disappear, and the use of rhetoric takes on a functional aspect.

Structurally *Henry VIII* grows through a series of contrasts and oppositions. The opening description of the splendour of the Field of the Cloth of Gold, where Henry and Francis met to inaugurate peace between England and France, sets the keynote for a play of spectacle and establishes the importance of peace. There follows a bitter characterization of Wolsey, until he enters suddenly, in the first of the processional entries, to confound Buckingham with his very look. Before he is arrested Buckingham foreshadows in his accusations the later downfall of Wolsey, whose present power is shown immediately afterwards in Henry's appearance "leaning on the Cardinal's shoulder". Straightway a dramatic opposition is set up between him and Katherine, who suggests the infirm basis of his ascendancy over the king in her initial victory in the matter of taxation (I. ii. 90 ff.). But towards the end of this scene the tables are turned when her defence of Buckingham fails. After the stress and threat of tragedy of the initial scenes, the next two offer a complete

1. Hardin Craig, *An Interpretation of Shakespeare* (New York, 1948), p. 357; another interesting and sympathetic view of the play is presented by E. I. Fripp, *Shakespeare, Man and Artist* (1938), II. 770–81.

2. G. Wilson Knight, 'A Note on *Henry VIII*', *Criterion* (January 1936), 228–36, and *The Crown of Life* (1947), pp. 256–336. He was perhaps following up a hint dropped by Chambers, *W.S.*, I. 497, that the play shows "an epic, rather than a tragic scheme".

3. *The Crown of Life*, p. 306.

contrast; all is bounty and gaiety in the preparations for and presentation of Wolsey's banquet, and in Henry's entry into it in a
masque of shepherds, showing a king youthful (in heart at least),
active and vigorous, ravished by the beauty of his partner, Anne
Bullen.

The interlude is brief, and the sombre tones return in the description of Buckingham's trial, of the commons' love for him and hatred
for Wolsey. Then the Duke enters on the way to the scaffold; here
is a grim pageant after the lively dancing of the previous scene with
its pastoral costumes suggesting a carefree atmosphere. The Duke
speaks his long farewell, not to complain or curse, but to avow his
innocence, to bless the King, and to forgive,

> But those that sought it I could wish more Christians:
> Be what they will, I heartily forgive 'em . . .   (II. i. 64–5)

The trial and fall of Buckingham set the tone for the trials undergone by Katherine, Wolsey, and Cranmer; but whereas these other
trials are enacted, at least in part, on the stage, that of Buckingham
is merely reported, so although he is tried by his peers and found
guilty, the audience sees only the malicious accusations made
against him at the prompting of Wolsey in I. ii. In addition, the
cardinal's vindictiveness has been demonstrated in action, throwing into special relief the contrast between the fall of Buckingham,
betrayed by a false servant, in II. i and the next scene which presents Wolsey, himself a false servant, at the height of his power and
influence with the King, plotting the divorce of Katherine, and
rousing the anger of the nobles who are spurned for his sake.[1]

The simple reporting of Buckingham's trial prepares for, without
diminishing the dramatic impact of, the full panoply and ceremony
of the crowded court into which Katherine is called in II. iv to make
her noble plea against the divorce proceedings. The 'unqueening'
of Katherine here is also thrown into sharp relief by what precedes
and what follows. For her divorce follows the brief scene between
Anne and an Old Lady—the only scene in the play devoted to
Anne—in which Anne is, as it were, 'queened': it is a scene of rich
and complex meaning, of bawdry and high spirits, in which Anne's
promotion as Marchioness of Pembroke foreshadows her further

1. Dr H. F. Brooks has drawn my attention to the importance of the master-
servant relationship in the play: the relationships of false servant and master
(the Surveyor and Buckingham; Wolsey and the King) are set off against the
relationships of master and good servant (Wolsey and Cromwell; the King and
Cranmer); and as the play begins with the triumph of the false servants, so it
ends with the vindication of the good ones. Wolsey, in his counsel to Cromwell,
and Katherine, in her final message to Henry, take thought for their faithful
servants, as they prepare to die.

elevation. Out of Anne's pity for Katherine grows the Old Lady's series of quibbles, playing always on the idea of Anne becoming queen (or "quean"),

> *Anne.*   By my troth and maidenhead,
> I would not be a queen.
> *Old L.*   Beshrew me, I would,
> And venture maidenhead for't, and so would you
> For all this spice of your hypocrisy.   (II. iii. 23–6)

The placing of this gay little scene of Anne's rise before the trial lends added poignancy to Katherine's refusal to yield. Her stubbornness already by the end of II. iv produces its unexpected consequence in the King's rejection of Wolsey and call for Cranmer to return: and this is particularly ironic since the responsibility for initiating the divorce is largely, in the play's terms, the Cardinal's,

> This is the cardinal's doing: the king-cardinal,
> That blind priest, like the eldest son of fortune,
> Turns what he list.   (II. ii. 19–21)

By the next scene, III. i, the divorce seems assured, but the "two great cardinals" visit Katherine to plead with her, to beg that she will abandon her stubborn attitude and obey the King's wishes. Already the King had gone beyond Wolsey, and so has Katherine, unwittingly, by her refusal to yield. In the trial scene Wolsey and Campeius had sat under the King "as judges", but now the divorce has become more imperative for Henry than for Wolsey, whose inability, because of Katherine's firmness, to bring the proceedings to a quick finish, helps to bring him out of the King's favour. Now, in III. i, the positions are reversed, and it is Katherine who judges Wolsey and Campeius,

> holy men I thought ye,
> Upon my soul two reverend cardinal virtues;
> But cardinal sins and hollow hearts I fear ye:
> Mend 'em for shame my lords.   (III. i. 102–5)

The cardinals are reduced to the character of suitors, with their "Pray hear me," and "I would your grace Would leave your griefs," and although by the end of this scene the queen accepts their offer and begs counsel, it is, for Wolsey, too late. The decline culminates in his fall in III. ii. Here his dignity under the taunting of the lords, their final sympathy ("My heart weeps to see him So little of his great self"), and his display of patience, newly-acquired self-knowledge, and forgiveness, rescue for Wolsey nobility in spite of all the wrong he has done.

Between the downfall of Wolsey and the death of Katherine in

IV. ii is placed the gay coronation procession of Anne accompanied
by the splendour of coronets, crowns, sceptres, and rich costumes,
and the clever running commentary of the gentlemen, with its
dominant note of joy. The dramatic effect of the juxtaposition of
the coronation of Anne and the end of Katherine is more subtle and
complicated than a simple contrast. Anne's earthly coronation is
set against the spiritual coronation of Katherine—in which lies the
importance of her vision, so often omitted from modern productions of the play. The "six personages, clad in white robes, wearing
on their heads garlands of bays, and golden vizards on their
faces" who dance round Katherine and hold "a spare garland over
her head", have the symbolic value of angels, "Spirits of peace",
who promise "eternal happiness"; and their action in the dance is
to crown her with a heavenly garland. In her death she wins this
personal gain, the riches of the soul, the reward of heaven; which is
more than sufficient compensation for her loss of the earth's dignities. Anne's coronation, on the other hand, is depersonalized in
the sense that Anne never speaks: she is seen passing over the stage
and the event itself is reported in terms not of her satisfaction, but of
the joy of the people,

> which when the people
> Had the full view of, such a noise arose
> As the shrouds make at sea in a stiff tempest,
> As loud, and to as many tunes ...   (IV. i. 70–3)

This is for her no personal triumph to match or diminish the
spiritual triumph of Katherine, and the interplay through connection (the two queens, the two coronations), and contrast, of
these two scenes of Act IV is most subtle.

   In the fifth act the mood of gaiety or joy which has appeared
only at intervals in the earlier part of the play gradually assumes
dominance, as it becomes apparent that the machinations of
Gardiner, the successor to and follower of Wolsey in inclination and
religion, are not going to be successful; that through the intervention of the King, Cranmer, in place the successor to Wolsey, in
spirit succeeding Katherine, will emerge unharmed from the
attack on him. The reconciliation between him and his enemies,
the general atmosphere of peace and forgiveness, are crowned in
the final scene, with the christening of the young princess. Again,
as with the coronation of Anne in IV. i, Anne herself has no part,
and is excluded altogether from the act, and the princess has of
course no speaking part; the joy is a nation's joy, represented in the
crowds that afflict the Porter and his man in v. iii and in the prophecy of Cranmer in v. iv with its conventional compliments to

royalty, its vision in familiar language of what was already history to the play's first audience. The nation triumphs here, but the prophecy and glory surrounding the infant reflect also on Henry and on Cranmer, and enhance their prestige in the eyes of the audience.

In this triumphant ending to *Henry VIII* the rise of the "virtuous" Cranmer compensates for the evil of Wolsey, and the glory and promise of a golden future in an age of peace, as represented in the infant princess, compensate for the death of Katherine. The contrasts between scenes of sombreness and scenes of gaiety, the juxtapositions of the rise of Wolsey and Anne against the falls of Buckingham and Katherine, culminate in joy. But the structure of the play is more complex than this. Its keystones are the four trials, each of which is presented in an individual way. Buckingham's trial by his peers is reported, but he is allowed his long farewell and his protestations of innocence, so that there remains with the audience the sense of an earthly and fallible justice at work in the fall of this good man; yet his fall is not tragic, and his guilt under the law of the realm, if exacerbated by Wolsey, is not disproved, rather is it assured in his trial by his peers who sentence him. Katherine is shown defending herself in full trial against her judges, Wolsey and Campeius, and again there is the sense of wrong done against her by Wolsey in fostering the King's impulse and turning the knife in his "wounded conscience"; a sense too, there is, of the force of circumstances operating against a guiltless creature. For the two later trials there is a vital dramatic shift, in that the King intervenes directly, and now right is done; Wolsey is brought low by the King, and the attack of the nobles on Cranmer is foiled by his appearing to reconcile them.

Katherine and Buckingham, the first two, suffer more than they deserve, whereas Wolsey and Cranmer are treated justly. In no case is there any recrimination, or blame attached to Henry; the law operates in its normal course, and against it is always posed the justice of heaven. For Buckingham there is a trust in the future,

> Make of your prayers one sweet sacrifice
> And lift my soul to heaven;   (II. i. 78–9)

for Katherine there is a heavenly vision to assure her of "eternal happiness"; for Wolsey, the thought

> Had I but serv'd my God with half the zeal
> I serv'd my king, he would not in mine age
> Have left me naked to mine enemies.   (III. ii. 455–7)

Where earthly justice fails, all will be made right in heaven; where it does right, as for Wolsey and Cranmer, it corresponds to heavenly justice; and since in the play earthly justice corresponds to heavenly justice only when Henry acts directly, the dramatic effect is to enhance the stature of Henry as God's deputy.

The character of these trials which form the groundwork of the plot is at once public, as they affect the state, and personal, as they affect the protagonists. The conflict they present between the public interest and private joy and suffering is indeed at the heart of the play, and all the contrasts already discussed between neighbouring scenes relate to it. Two other aspects of the structure of *Henry VIII* play a vital part in establishing this general conflict. One is its pageantry, which represents elements of this general conflict visually. So while Buckingham makes his last plea for sympathy, and for our belief in his goodness, which he win, the "tipstaves before him, the axe with the edge towards him, halberds on each side", stand grimly on stage as a silent but public affirmation of his guilt and sentence. The pageantry of Katherine's trial makes vivid the opposition between the law's requirements and private suffering; indeed, a pageant alone, without words, like the coronation procession of Anne, witnessed by all, may establish the national or public feeling towards an event, and the value of that event, directing the audience's feelings, too. Against this is opposed Katherine's vision, seen only by her, an inward triumph set against an outward triumph. Henry's appearance disguised as a shepherd in the masque of i. iv also represents an escape from the outside world: it is in his private capacity, as a person, that he falls in love with Anne—and this is the only occasion on which he appears informally, on which we see him otherwise than in his official role as King. But usually, as in the description of the Field of the Cloth of Gold in i. i, in the trial scene of Katherine, the coronation scene, and in the final scene with its procession from the christening, the pageantry reflects the public order and view of things.

This is emphasized in the other aspect of the play's structure, the numerous scenes of walking lords or gentlemen,[1] who discuss what has happened or is to happen, and, what is most important, continually direct or counterbalance the audience's reaction. These often unappreciated scenes are amongst the most deft, even brilliant, in the play, full of quick characterization, and conveying information or carrying forward the action with a remarkable economy of means—as may be seen for instance in ii. i. 137–69, where, in the space of thirty lines, the First and Second Gentlemen express sympathy for Buckingham and for Katherine, whose im-

---

1. The scenes of gossiping gentlemen may be compared with similar scenes in *Cymbeline* (i. i; i. ii; ii. i) and *The Winter's Tale* (i. i; v. ii).

pending fall and divorce they announce, impugn Wolsey as instigator of the divorce, and give news of the arrival of Campeius, and
all this so naturally and so much in character that the effect is
gained without the means being noticed. In addition to such func-
tions, these scenes provide a commentary at several levels upon the
main action. At one level are the figures who are involved or who
become involved from time to time in that main action, figures like
Buckingham and Abergavenny in the opening scene, who charac-
terize Wolsey, describe his influence with the King, and also set the
historical background, before going off under an arrest engineered
by the Cardinal. Buckingham, revealing all kinds of state secrets,
attacks Wolsey vehemently, shows him as acting without Henry's
knowledge, and presents a picture of intrigue and treachery, of a
king betrayed secretly by his most trusted servant. Wolsey appears
in this light to most of the lords, Suffolk, Norfolk, the Lord Chamberlain and, later, Surrey, who all complain against him, and put
the blame for the divorce of Katherine, and for most other evils, on
him. In Wolsey's reign of power we see the King spurn the nobles
to welcome him and Campeius; but it is they who announce the
Cardinal's fall and who are allowed to vent their spleens on him,
though even their hostility is modified by his dignity:

> Cham.   My heart weeps to see him
> So little of his great self.
> Sur.   I forgive him.   (III. ii. 335-6)

A different picture is provided in I. iii and iv, where Lovell, the
Chamberlain, and Sands reveal another aspect of the court, its
gaiety and splendour, and also another aspect of Wolsey, his courtesy and liberality.

At a second level the principal characters are sometimes made
to comment on one another, as Henry describes the virtues of
Katherine, and does something to counteract the united hostility
of the lords to Wolsey by his defence of him,

> You are not to be taught
> That you have many enemies that know not
> Why they are so, but like to village curs
> Bark when their fellows do.   (II. iv. 155-8)

The good and evil in Wolsey are later summed up in the two set
descriptions of him by Griffith and Katherine as a kind of chorus
after his ruin. Again in the last act one of the principal characters,
Gardiner, opens by speaking for the opposition against Cranmer.
In these and other scenes and instances characters involved in the
action as intermediaries, or, occasionally, as principals, comment

with a variety of bias on the King, Katherine, Anne, Wolsey, Cranmer, and their relationships. This commentary is personal, in the sense that the characters are all courtiers and speaking their own views, and it helps in particular to establish the private characters and actions of the main personages. The general hostility of the lords to Wolsey aids in fixing our attitude towards him, which is guided from the start by Buckingham's invective. It is important that in this commentary the influence Wolsey has over the King initially is condemned, but not Henry himself, who, like Katherine and Anne, is generally spoken of in terms of praise—here again affecting the sympathies of the audience.

At another level still are presented the unidentified gentlemen of II. i and IV. i, who indicate the popular view, the general opinion of men who follow the action of the play as a series of public events, and weigh these as they affect the nation, not the individual. These representatives of the 'public' are familiar with what is going on—one of them at least claims to have some influence at court, "Something I can command"—but they are not personally concerned in the action. They are introduced as knowledgeable commentators on two events in the play: one is the downfall of Buckingham, the other the coronation of Anne. The choice and placing of these is very important, for the first reflects the height of Wolsey's success and the greatest power of his influence over the King, while the second follows his fall; the first initiates the series of trials and falls in the play, the bitter side of the action, while the other is the first grand scene of jubilation, foreshadowing the triumphant ending. These two scenes are representative of the two poles of the action, as the First Gentleman indicates when he recalls at Anne's coronation the earlier scene, "that time offer'd sorrow, This general joy".

The Gentlemen continually refer to the national view, "This is noted, And generally", "As all think . . .", "All the land knows that . . .". They influence our response by reminding us of the national perspective. When, after his trial, Buckingham admits that the law "has done upon the premises but justice", they put his downfall in its general context, of the cardinal's malice, his skill at manufacturing "premises" and concealing his plotting from Henry.

> All the commons
> Hate him perniciously, and o' my conscience
> Wish him ten faddom deep: this duke as much
> They love and dote on; call him bounteous Buckingham,
> The mirror of all courtesy. . .   (II. i. 49–53)

Justice has been done according to the law, but also a wrong has been done through the malice of Wolsey, and we in the audience accept the law, but share the general sympathy. In this scene the Gentlemen express the national anger and sorrow at the fall of Buckingham and at the impending divorce of Katherine, also engineered by the Cardinal. When they return, at the coronation of Anne, they express the nation's joy and approval of the new Queen and of the "virtuous Cranmer", as well as sympathy for Katherine. As, earlier, anger at the fall of Buckingham was dominant, outweighing any sense of justice being done, so now joy is dominant, outweighing sympathy for the old, sick Katherine.[1] The contrasting moods of these two scenes reflect some of the major contrasts by means of which the play is organized, those between private sorrow and public joy, between justice and right, between the national wellbeing and the individual good. The variations of pace and style in *Henry VIII* emphasize these contrasts: in scenes of passion, or of strong oppositions between characters, the language is complex and compressed, the syntax often rugged, but in soliloquies, in the scenes of downfall or death, scenes of patient endurance and quietness of soul, the style becomes flowing and limpid, metaphor tends to give way to simile, and falling rhythms come into prominence.[2] The changes in style from tension to relaxation correspond to the movement of the play, and the transitions can be studied at many points, notably perhaps in III. ii, where between Wolsey's passive soliloquies, with their long, vivid, similes,

> I have ventur'd
> Like little wanton boys that swim on bladders,
> This many summers in a sea of glory,
> But far beyond my depth... (III. ii. 358–61)

comes the nobles' attack on him, expressed in a more involved, and active, style,

> If we live thus tamely,
> To be thus jaded by a piece of scarlet,
> Farewell nobility: let his grace go forward,
> And dare us with his cap, like larks. (III. ii. 279–82)

Yet a third style may be found in the speeches of the scenes of gaiety, or the scenes of walking gentlemen, a plain, friendly, jocular, manner, with little imagery, but muscular and active. The three styles

1. The national viewpoint is evoked again in v. iii, the scene where imaginary crowds almost overrun the Porter and his man in their eagerness to share the jubilation of the christening of Elizabeth.

2. G. Wilson Knight finds this effect deliberately sought in contrasts of style in all the late plays; for his analysis and evaluation of the transitions in *Henry VIII* see *The Crown of Life*, pp. 258 ff.

succeed one another in II. i and II. ii, where Buckingham's farewell, with its dropping rhythm, is followed by a short interchange between the two Gentlemen, imparting news, and sharing secrets, which in turn gives way to the weighty, serious dialogue of the lords discussing Wolsey and the divorce, which is tauter, more packed with imagery,

> this imperious man will work us all
> From princes into pages: all men's honours
> Lie like one lump before him, to be fashion'd
> Into what pitch he please.   (II. ii. 46–9)

These contrasts of style accompany and reveal the oppositions of values in *Henry VIII*, and like the ordered juxtapositions of contrasting moods, scenes, and characters, afford fine dramatic effects and conflicts. All of these are organized into a whole of visionary power, culminating in a mood of joy and reconciliation, and a prospect of lasting peace and wellbeing.

III

This careful organization goes to shape a play radically different from Shakespeare's earlier histories in dealing with peace, and in having for its general theme the promise of a golden future, after trials and sufferings terminating in the attainment of self-knowledge, forgiveness, and reconciliation. Except that the nation's interests are kept to the forefront, and that the promise for the future is more than a promise, having already been realized in the reign of Elizabeth long before the play was first produced, all its links in respect of themes are with the other late plays of Shakespeare, as was noted earlier. But it is worth emphasizing that, by the nature of the story of *Henry VIII*, two aspects are especially prominent. On one, the theme of justice and injustice, as embodied in the series of trials, with their contrast between heavenly and earthly justice, sufficient has been said. The other is the theme of patience in adversity.

Buckingham's initial anger and hotheadedness in rushing to attack Wolsey is, according to Norfolk, a yielding to passion, "let your reason with your choler question . . ." (I. i. 130); and his character is tempered through his trial and fall, so that when he has to face death he shows "a most noble patience" (II. i. 36). So it is with Katherine: she will not listen to the arguments at her trial, and sweeps from the court. "They vex me past my patience"; but patience is the lesson she has to learn, and learns so nobly, that she can boast of her "great patience" as exceptional in woman (III. i.

137). The patience Wolsey had prescribed for her during her trial is soon needed by him, and acquired through his downfall, which teaches him to overcome his pride,

> I am able now methinks
> (Out of a fortitude of soul I feel)
> To endure more miseries, and greater far
> Than my weak-hearted enemies dare offer.
>
> (III. ii. 387–90)

For Katherine's last scene, a new character, a notable addition to the sources, is introduced—her woman, Patience. There is a special meaning and poignancy in Katherine's cries, "Patience, be near me still", and "softly, gentle Patience", as she awaits her death, as though this quality above all is to be desired. Whereas all these characters have to learn to be long-suffering, to acquire the virtue of patience, Cranmer already possesses it, and the quality that goes with it, humility. He is prepared to "attend with patience" while the lords in council make him wait outside the door, and to bear whatever weight they lay upon his patience; and, unlike the other three, he passes successfully through his trial and is vindicated. But all exercise the active virtue displayed by Hermione in *The Winter's Tale*, and so sadly lacking in *King Lear*—a virtue important for Shakespeare when he wrote his later plays, and perhaps more significant for his audience than for a modern one.

For by the exercise of patience, Wolsey's "fortitude of soul", man was made able to control the tumultous passions which led to sin, and to overcome the vagaries and reverses of an often malicious fortune. Perhaps the nearest modern equivalent is steadfastness, the ability to maintain courage through a trust in ultimate goodness. This quality is prominent in Sir Philip Sidney's conception of epic and practice of romance in his *Arcadia*, which seems to have had considerable influence on the later work of Shakespeare. Often, as in *Henry VIII*, it has a Christian colouring as an active virtue, "a release of charity. It suffers long because it is kind, and its kindness remains. It loves its enemies who slay it."[1] Buckingham, Wolsey, Katherine, and Cranmer learn in their trials or falls to behave like the protagonists of the *Arcadia*, who, when imprisoned, "fortifying courage with the true rampire of patience, did so endure that they did rather appear governors of necessity, than servants of fortune";[2] and their behaviour may be compared with the reactions

1. J. F. Danby, *Poets on Fortune's Hill* (1952), p. 82. Chapters 2, 3, and 4 of this book contain a good account of Sidney's *Arcadia* and its relationship to *King Lear* and *Pericles* in particular among Shakespeare's plays.

2. Ed. E. A. Baker, pp. 592–3.

to adversity of other figures in the last plays, such as Hermione[1] in *The Winter's Tale*, who, when spurned by Leontes and sent to prison for no cause given, does not complain, but says,

> There's some ill planet reigns:
> I must be patient, till the heavens look
> With an aspect more favourable.   (II. i. 105–7)

The exercise of patience is, in fact, the way to self-knowledge, and it is again very important in *The Tempest*, where Gonzalo alone among the king's attendants displays it: so when Alonso bewails the loss of Ferdinand, Prospero has his retort ready,

> *Alonso.* Irreparable is the loss, and patience
>   Says it is past her cure.
> *Prospero.*   I rather think
>   You have not sought her help, of whose soft grace,
>   For the like loss I have her sovereign aid
>   And rest myself content.   (v. i. 140–4)

A recognition of the part this idea has in *Henry VIII* affords an important clue to the presentation of Buckingham, Wolsey, and Katherine, and to an understanding of these characters. What has been seen as an inconsistent sentimentalizing of them may also be considered a reflection of that enlarged humanity which gives Shakespeare's later plays their peculiar tone, and which could allow him in a protestant country, and after a great protestant celebration, to show in the fall of Wolsey patience and charity. In doing this he modified the violent hostility of the Tudor historians to Wolsey. In a similar way the death-scene of Katherine is given rich overtones, and the creation of a character Patience is wholly in accord with the atmosphere of the final plays. Through their falls these characters learn to know themselves; their worldly loss is their spiritual gain.

The delineation of these characters in the play is modified in two ways from their portrayal in the sources, so as to emphasize the poles of their nature. As is well known, the falls of each are made much more elaborate in the play than in the chronicles, and their acquisition of self-knowledge and exercise of patience are features quite lacking in Holinshed. It is less commonly realized that, particularly in the drawing of Buckingham and Katherine, but also in the portrayal of Wolsey, the initial fire or hotheadedness of these characters is heavily accentuated. For instance, Buckingham's

---

1. There is a remarkable similarity between the trials of Hermione and Katherine, who defend themselves in similar terms, and both appeal finally to an external religious authority, Hermione to Apollo, Katherine to the Pope.

rash outbursts in the opening scene, and the fieriness of Katherine throughout much of her interview with the cardinals, are additions to the sources. Wolsey's proud villainy is also marked in several touches, as when Campeius suggests his responsibility for the death of Pace, and the Cardinal dismisses the affair with his contemptuous

> Heav'n's peace be with him:
> That's Christian care enough . . .   (II. ii. 129–30)

Dr Pace's death is not mentioned in connection with Wolsey in the chronicles—in fact he outlived the Cardinal by several years.[1]

   The transition from their rashness, or pride in Wolsey's case, their inability to be patient, to their acquisition of "fortitude of soul", is deliberately and strikingly drawn, and is a variation of a theme constantly returning in Shakespeare's later work. The process is something like a conversion, and wins for them the sympathy of the audience—even for Wolsey, whose readiness to forgive and bless helps to bring us into a readiness to forgive him. Sympathy is necessary for the flow of the play, as a prelude to the triumphant ending; for, like *The Tempest*, it is a study in the ways in which men may be saved. Suffering is a mode of learning, and brings its own rewards, teaching virtue; and it is common to all humanity, for fortune or the machinations of evil men may bring it to anyone. But, in *Henry VIII* at any rate, God is above all, the heaven to which Buckingham and Katherine confidently aspire. The general progress is an optimistic one; forgiveness and reconciliation expiate past misdeeds, and the future, in the hands of the young and the good, offers a golden prospect.

   If God alone is stable, he has a kind of high-priest on earth, in the person of Henry, in some respects the most difficult character in the play. He is usually played as bluff King Hal, costumed and paunched as grossly as in the late portraits, with a full swagger, and a nervous eagerness to cry "Ha!". The playwright's conception surely embodies more than such a portrait, which enlarges incidentals, like the King's peremptoriness, into his whole character. All that can be said of his physical appearance is that he is lusty and vigorous, and the dramatic impression if anything is of youth. Much more important than his physical characteristics is his growth in spiritual stature during the play. Henry is shown as a strong, regal figure, the embodiment of authority; but initially this authority is subdued under the sway of Wolsey. Henry's progress in the play is to throw off the domination of Wolsey, fulfilling the confidence of the lords in him ("the king will know him [Wolsey] one

1. See II. ii. 121 and n.

day"). As long as Wolsey's sway persists, injustice is done, to Buckingham and then to Katherine, for whose downfall the Cardinal is presented as mainly responsible. At the fall of Wolsey, Henry emerges in the full panoply of kingship; from this point all goes well, and Cranmer is saved through his direct intervention in council. When he administers the law himself, justice as of heaven operates, and in his assumption of control Henry may be compared to Prospero, for he seems to stand above fate, and in all accidents of fortune which befall other characters is praised and blessed.

If his treatment of Katherine leaves a feeling of uneasiness in the modern mind, it is largely Henry's character as fixed by history, rather than by the play, to which this is due, as well as to the huge change that has been made in our historical perspective and religious attitude since Shakespeare wrote. In the play the divorce of Katherine is urged as necessary by conscience and takes place with the sanction of the entire Catholic Church, "all the clerks . . . in Christian kingdoms": and no blame attaches to Henry for her suffering. Once the power of Rome is quelled in England, the King assumes his rightful dominance, and Cranmer, symbolically kneeling to Henry, demonstrates the true idea of a protestant kingdom. This state of wellbeing is signalized in the appearance of an heir who was to become the great Queen Elizabeth. Now the religious opposition is not felt so strongly, and the promiscuous Henry of the popular conception is so dominant that in the play he may seem cruel and immoral. This is counteracted dramatically by the continual blessings showered on him, by the reflection of national feeling towards him afforded by the gentlemen and lords, by the blessing even of Katherine in distress. Perhaps more importantly it should be borne in mind that Katherine is in distress in her death scene, not in disgrace, and there is no question of a morally false equation between her downfall and Wolsey's. He is abandoned by God, she suffers only the loss of a husband.

At the same time there is an ambiguity in Henry, whose motives are not altogether of the best; even the courtiers are allowed one joke at his expense.[1]

> *Cham.* It seems the marriage with his brother's wife
> Has crept too near his conscience.
> *Suf.* [*Aside*]   No, his conscience
> Has crept too near another lady.   (II. ii. 16–18)

An audience familiar with Henry's history would be aware that he

1. With this passage should be compared Henry's noble praise of Katherine in the trial scene, II. iv. 132–40 and 221–8.

was capable of being misled again, and was to rid himself of several future wives, as well as Anne, in a very drastic fashion. He is shown as human and fallible, not an ideal ruler; and like all the last plays, *Henry VIII* leaves open the possibility of the repetition of a cycle of events such as it presents. Nevertheless, the most significant aspect of Henry's character, and the most neglected in performance, is his growth in stature. It does not come about through an inward change in him; it is an emergence into authority, the recognition and exercise of powers he has already possessed. In this he comes to have something of the nature of Prospero, in that his function is to control, to intervene in events involving others, to act as an agent or an organizer for most of the play, and this aspect of him, as high-priest, beneficent controller, should appear most strongly at the end of the play and after the fall of Wolsey. Like Prospero, he has a kind of vagueness, not a lack of solidity, but a lack of definition, as a representative of benevolent power acting upon others.

In this respect *Henry VIII* moves furthest away from the earlier histories, which display a growth of kingship with the strongest dramatic interest in the central figure, and shows a relationship with the other late plays of Shakespeare. It would be difficult to decide who is the leading character in any of the late plays, which are constructed from the point of view of themes and ideals rather than of an individual. Henry is the central figure as the controlling influence of the play, just as Prospero is of *The Tempest*, but the place of both of them in the action tends to be in the background, pulling the strings; they are central in as much as they are permanent, influencing others, and uniting a complex plot. And in both plays, as in *Cymbeline*, *The Winter's Tale*, and *Pericles*, the story is one of a satisfaction for old sins, not through tragic waste, or the perpetual suffering of vengeance, but in the joy and love of a new generation, bringing harmony to the old, and restitution too; the birth of Elizabeth in prophetic splendour corresponds to the weddings that round off these other plays. In all there is an increased use of symbolism, and an abstraction of character from individualization towards an ideal or quality.

All moreover suggest something of the cycle of suffering and joy which is found in *Henry VIII*. It is embodied in the masque of Ceres in *The Tempest* and in the allusions to the Ceres-Proserpine myth in *The Winter's Tale*, the legend of the daughter of the corn-goddess who is forced to spend six months of the year in the underworld, and is restored to earth for the other six; these correspond to the seasons, winter and summer, which reflect in their interchange her mother's endless alternation between grief and joy, and relate also to the sowing of the seed, placing it in the ground, and the rising of the crop to harvest. In *The Winter's Tale* the cycle relies on a break of sixteen years, in *The Tempest* it is compressed to a day, and in *Henry VIII* the action oscillates from pole to pole, joy gradually predominating through a historical sequence of events. Perhaps *Henry VIII* should be thought of as the last innovation of a mind forever exploring; and if the history of its supposed deficiencies can be forgotten, then the conception of the play may be allowed its full originality, as a felicitous new solution to problems posed by the nature of the material with which Shakespeare's last plays deal.

3. STAGE-HISTORY

The scanty records of performances of plays between 1613 and the closing of the theatres in 1642 reveal one performance of *Henry VIII*, "bespoken of purpose" by the great George Villiers Duke of Buckingham in July 1628, just before his own fall; he is reported to have "stayd till ye Duke of Buckingham was beheaded, & then departed".[1] After the restoration of Charles II, when the theatres were re-opened, the play seems for many years to have been one of a dozen or fewer of Shakespeare's plays which remained as stock plays in the repertory of Betterton, Booth, and Cibber;[2] Pepys saw it twice, in January 1663-4 and December 1668-9, Langbaine in 1691 said that *Henry VIII* "frequently appears on the present stage", and several references in letters and plays support Langbaine's testimony.[3]

The most interesting allusions throw some light on the acting and staging of the play during this period. In the burlesque play *The Rehearsal* (1672) by George Villiers, second Duke of Buckingham and others, a character is said to "dance worse than the Angels in *Harry* the Eight, or the fat spirits in *The Tempest*", and when Bayes promises a grand scene, he measures it by the "state, shew and magnificence" of "that great Scene in *Harry* the Eight . . . for, instead of two Bishops, I have brought in two other Cardinals".[4] Villiers remembers the pageantry and magnificence of, presumably, the trial scene, and the dance of spirits before Katherine. A reason why the "magnificence" of Betterton's *Henry VIII* should have been memorable is indicated in the remark of John Downes that the characters were all "new Cloath'd in proper Habits". This

1. Chambers, *W.S.*, II. 347-8.
2. G. C. D. Odell, *Shakespeare from Betterton to Irving*, 2 vols. (1921), I. 42, 224 ff.
3. *The Shakspere Allusion-Book, 1591-1700*, 2 vols. (1909), II. 91, 95, 187, 292, 321, 363, 418; Hazelton Spencer, *Shakespeare Improved* (1927), pp. 75-7, 105 n.
4. *The Shakspere Allusion-Book*, ii. 169.

means presumably that costumes of the Tudor period were reproduced, and it is probable that already in the Restoration period the tradition of historical realism, which has held sway ever since, was being established for this play.[1] One other valuable hint is given by Downes:

> The part of the King was so right and justly done by Mr. *Betterton*, he being instructed in it by Sir *William* Davenant who had it from old Mr. *Lowen*, that had his Instructions from Mr. *Shakespear* himself, that I dare and will aver, none can, or will come near him in this Age, in the performance of that part: Mr. *Harris's* performance of Cardinal *Wolsey*, was little Inferior to that . . .[2]

Whatever the truth of this story of the source of Betterton's instruction, it would seem that the part of Henry was regarded as the leading role in the play at this time.

A lavish production of *Henry VIII*, with Booth in the title role, was staged at Drury Lane in honour of the coronation of George II in 1727; it included a grand coronation scene, to which the ceremony of the Queen's champion making his general challenge on behalf of the new sovereign was added. This scene was so successful that it was used as a separate entertainment with other plays,[3] and encumbered many later productions of *Henry VIII*. As the years went by, processions and pageantry became more elaborate, being one of the main attractions of the play; the *Westminster Magazine* said of the 1773 production at Covent Garden, "It was selected from the numerous List of Shakespear's Plays, because it exhibited the most numerous Pageantry."[4] How "numerous" this could be the Drury Lane production of 1762 illustrates: over 130 figures were included in the procession of IV. i, among them "the Queen's herbwoman, strewing flowers", the Dukes of Aquitaine and Normandy, and six Beef-Eaters.[5]

By the end of the century Wolsey and Katherine seem to have become established as the leading roles. Kemble and Macready were notable as Wolsey, while Katherine was one of Mrs Siddons's great parts. As a result of the emphasis on these characters, the fifth

1. An engraving of Harris as Cardinal Wolsey in Betterton's production shows him in full robes; see Odell, *op. cit.*, I. 42–3. An attempt at historical accuracy so early was unusual, and many of Shakespeare's plays were performed in the dress then in fashion during the eighteenth century.

2. *Roscius Anglicanus* (1706), cited *Shakspere Allusion-Book*, II. 437.

3. Genest, *Some Account of the English Stage*, 10 vols. (1832), III. 199–203; C. Beecher Hogan chronicles 43 productions between 1701 and 1750 in his *Shakespeare in the Theatre 1701–1800. A Record of Performances in London 1701–1750* (1952), pp. 204–17.

4. Odell, *op. cit.*, I. 427.   5. *Ibid.*, I. 425.

act received little attention and was heavily cut, so that for his
elaborate production of 1855, Kean claimed to be restoring "The
fifth act ... of late years ... entirely omitted". Kean read the historians, Cavendish in particular, seeking for realistic detail, and
claimed that "information has been sought from every source" in
order to realize "the domestic habits of the English court, three
hundred years ago". This "most wonderful spectacle", as *The
Times* called it,[1] employed a moving panorama of London, and a
real barge in which Buckingham made his exit. It established a
vogue for realistic scenery and effects, and made necessary the use
of a drop-curtain for scene alterations.

In 1892 Sir Henry Irving had one of his greatest successes as
Wolsey in what was perhaps the most lavish spectacle ever staged,
improving on Kean's production by having a "genuine reproduction of old London" for the coronation, and an even more splendid
reproduction of the Church of Grey Friars at Greenwich for the
final scene. Although this production was immensely popular, it
lost money, so that succeeding producers have not sought to emu-
late its splendour. The attempt to reproduce faithfully costume and
historical detail of the Tudor period has, however, remained a
feature of nearly all twentieth-century performances.[2] A reviewer of
Sir Beerbohm Tree's production of 1910 said Arthur Bourchier as
Henry was "Holbein's picture reproduced in every detail", and
another observed that it was "a flagrantly sensual experience" to
see him with Anne, "a triumph of the flesh and the devil".[3] It seems
also to have been a triumph of history over Shakespeare's text.

More recently Tyrone Guthrie has produced the play three
times, in 1933 at Sadler's Wells (Charles Laughton as Henry,
Flora Robson as Katherine, Robert Farquharson as Wolsey), in
1949 at Stratford-upon-Avon (Anthony Quayle as Henry, Diana
Wynyard as Katherine, Harry Andrews as Wolsey), and in 1953 at
the Old Vic Theatre (in honour of the coronation of Queen Elizabeth II, with Paul Rogers as Henry, Gwen Ffrangçon-Davies as
Katherine, Alexander Knox as Wolsey). Each of these productions
was ingenious and at times unnecessarily, even disastrously, frivo-
lous, but all moved at great pace, with vitality and a sense of shape

1. Cited Odell, *op. cit.*, II. 289, 332.

2. The one exception seems to have been a highly stylized production by
Terence Gray at the Cambridge Festival Theatre in 1931; on a set of galvanized
steel the characters were costumed like playing-cards, and all entries were
danced. See Alistair Cooke, *Theatre Arts Monthly*, November 1931, 901–2.

3. *The Athenaeum*, 10 September 1910, p. 303, and *The Times*, 2 September
1910. *The Times* echoed its 1910 review on 24 December 1925, when it reported
of the production in which Dame Sybil Thorndike played Katherine, "this
Henry VIII is more a Holbein triumph than anybody else's."

and power, and it may well be that the dramatic potentialities of
many minor characters have rarely been so well realized. Some of
the major figures fared less well, and the Holbein portraiture was
retained, together with much traditional business, such as the
comic, staggering villainy of a drunken Gardiner in v. i. The success of the 1949 *Henry VIII*, probably the best, and least mannered,
of the three, may be gauged from the full description and review of
it by M. St Clare Byrne.[1]

While the tradition of the 'Holbein' Henry is firmly entrenched,
so that actors have not been able to make more than a conventional
portrait of the King,[2] the other tradition inherited by the present
century from a series of great actors and actresses ranging from
Kemble and Mrs Siddons to Irving and Ellen Terry, that of treat-
ing Wolsey and Katherine as the leading roles, has been modified.
The final act is now given in full, and something of the balance between Henry, Cranmer, and Wolsey has been restored. Although
the play is not popular now, and has long been subjected to a bar-
rage of hostile criticism, it will probably continue to tempt actors
by the fine parts it offers, and producers by its colour and pageantry.[3]

1. *Shakespeare Survey*, 3 (1950), 120–9. The 1953 production of *Henry VIII* has
also been reviewed at length, by Roy Walker in *The Twentieth Century*, cliii (June,
1953), 463–70.

2. Reviewers have found little to say about most Henrys, and have complained sometimes of the Holbein figure, as did *The Times* (25 April 1938) of B. Iden
Payne's production at Stratford-upon-Avon (with Gyles Isham as Henry), "The
Henry of the play is a puzzling character, and Mr. Isham can throw no fresh
light upon him."

3. It is worth noting that it was chosen by supporters of the new open-air
theatre in Regents' Park in 1936 for the first production there by Robert
Atkins; see the review in *The Times*, 23 June 1936.

KING HENRY VIII

KING HENRY VIII

DRAMATIS PERSONAE[1]

KING HENRY VIII.
CARDINAL WOLSEY.
CARDINAL CAMPEIUS.
CRANMER, *Archbishop of Canterbury.*
GARDINER, *Bishop of Winchester.*
Bishop of Lincoln.
DUKE OF BUCKINGHAM.
DUKE OF NORFOLK.
DUKE OF SUFFOLK.
EARL OF SURREY.
LORD ABERGAVENNY.
LORD SANDS (SIR WALTER SANDS).[2]
Lord Chancellor.
Lord Chamberlain.
SIR HENRY GUILFORD.
SIR THOMAS LOVELL.
SIR NICHOLAS VAUX.
SIR ANTHONY DENNY.
BRANDON.[3]
CROMWELL, *Wolsey's servant.*
DR. BUTTS.
GRIFFITH, *Gentleman-Usher to Queen Katherine.*[4]
CAPUCHIUS, *Ambassador from Emperor Charles V.*
1st, 2nd and 3rd Gentlemen.
Garter King-at-Arms.
Serjeant-at-Arms.
Porter and his Man.
Door-keeper of the Council-chamber.
Secretary to Wolsey. Page to Gardiner.
A Crier, a Messenger, and a Servant.

QUEEN KATHERINE,[5] *King Henry's wife, afterwards divorced.*
ANNE BULLEN, *her Maid of Honour, afterwards Queen.*
Old Lady, *Anne Bullen's friend.*
PATIENCE, *Queen Katherine's woman.*

Lords, Ladies, Bishops, Judges, Gentlemen and Priests;
Lord Mayor of London and Aldermen; Vergers, Scribes,
Guards, Attendants, Servants and Common People; Women
attending upon Queen Katherine; Spirits.

Scene: *London and Kimbolton.*

2

1. First given, imperfectly, by Rowe.

2. Lord Sands or Sandys appears as such in I. iii and iv, but in the entry at II. i. 54 as Sir Walter Sands. The discrepancy is due to the compression of chronology in the play. Buckingham's trial (1521), reported in II. i, preceded the meeting of Henry and Anne (I. iv) by several years. In the interval Sands was created Baron. See II. i. 54 S.D. and note.

3. "Brandon" enters to arrest Buckingham at I. i. 197; possibly he is to be identified with the Duke of Suffolk, whose name was Charles Brandon, and who appears in II. ii, etc. In V. i Suffolk is addressed as "Charles", so that Shakespeare was aware of his family name. See I. i. 197 S.D. and note.

4. Griffith is not named until IV. ii; in the stage directions and speech headings of II. iv there figures simply a "Gentleman Usher".

5. This is the spelling of F; most editors alter to "Katharine", following Pope.

KING HENRY THE EIGHTH

THE PROLOGUE

I come no more to make you laugh; things now *sombre opening*
That bear a weighty and a serious brow,
Sad, high, and working, full of state and woe;
Such noble scenes as draw the eye to flow
We now present. Those that can pity, here   5
May (if they think it well) let fall a tear,
The subject will deserve it. Such as give   *credible play*
Their money out of hope they may believe,
May here find truth too. Those that come to see
Only a show or two, and so agree   10
The play may pass, if they be still and willing,
I'll undertake may see away their shilling.

The Prologue

3. high, and] *F; and high- Staunton.*   full] *F; fall F2.*

Prologue.] Presumably this was written for the first or an early performance. Since Dr Johnson gave it to Ben Jonson, it has generally been assigned to an author other than Shakespeare, but there is no evidence. The function of the prologue is to prepare the audience for the mood of a history very different from the usual chronicle play, and it seems likely that a specific reference to Rowley's *When You See Me, You Know Me* is intended in ll. 14 ff.; see notes below.

3. *Sad . . . working*] serious, lofty, and moving. For "sad", cf. *Cæs.*, i. ii. 217 (a common usage), and for "working", cf. Marlowe, *1 Tamburlaine* (1590), ii. iii. 25, "You see, my lord, what working words he hath".

state] dignity, cf. *Ado*, ii. i. 80.

9. *truth*] The emphasis on the truth of the play here and at ll. 18, 21, and 25 ff. may refer to a sub-title *All is True*, as it is called by Wotton; see Appendix I, p. 180.

10. *show*] spectacle, cf. iv. i. 10; or perhaps 'scene', but there seems to be no parallel for this.

12. *shilling*] an allusion probably to the gallants who went to the theatre to display themselves by sitting in the more expensive rooms, and not to watch more than a "show or two" of the play; so Dekker advises his foolish gallant to "take up the twelve-penny rome next the stage; (because the Lords and you may seeme to be haile fellow wel-met) there draw forth this booke, read alowd, laugh alowd, and play the *Antickes . . .*" (*Gull's Horn Book*,

4

Richly in two short hours. Only they
That come to hear a merry bawdy play,
A noise of targets, or to see a fellow   15
In a long motley coat guarded with yellow,
Will be deceiv'd: for gentle hearers, know
To rank our chosen truth with such a show
As fool and fight is, beside forfeiting
Our own brains and the opinion that we bring   20
To make that only true we now intend,

19. beside] *F;* besides *Pope.*   21. To ... intend,] To ... true, ... intend, *F;*
(To ... true ... intend) *Malone.*

1609, cited Chambers, *E.S.,* II. 534,
where much information about theatre
admission prices is collected). The
price range at the Globe seems to have
extended from a penny or twopence
upwards, but its limits in 1613 are not
certainly known. The reference to a
"shilling" may be simply for the sake
of the rhyme.

13. *two ... hours*] The many references to the length of performance in
prologues etc. at this time seem to vary
indiscriminately between two and
three hours, and the figures may be
used merely as round numbers; the
prologue to *Rom.,* l. 12, speaks of "the
two hours' traffic of our stage", and for
other allusions see Chambers, *E.S.,* II.
543.

14–19. *merry ... fight is*] probably, as
Boswell noted, a slighting allusion to
Rowley's *When You See Me* (1605), reprinted and, it seems likely, revived on
the stage, in 1613; this play has two
fools and a sword and buckler fight between Henry and Black Will, a high-
wayman (see Introduction, p. xxvii),
and since its alternative title was "the
famous Chronicle Historie *of king
Henry the eight*", the present play may
have been liable to be confused with it.
Rowley's play belonged to the Prince's
(Elector's) Men at the Fortune
theatre.

15. *targets*] shields, cf. *Ant.,* I. iii.
82.

16. *long ... yellow*] A prominent part
in *When You See Me* is taken by Will

Summers, the famous clown of Henry
VIII, who seems to have worn the long
coat made of 'motley' a greenish-
yellow cloth, with strips of yellow cloth
or braid as trimmings on it ("guarded"), and the fool's cap; so the King
promises, "Ye shall have a new Coate
and a cap for this" (M.S.R., 1952,
l. 792, and see L. Hotson, *Shakespeare's
Motley,* 1952, pp. 77–9 and frontis-
piece). Hotson argues that the green
cloth 'motley', the undistinguished
wear of artisans, etc., was the normal
costume for fools on the stage, but it
was apparently more characteristic of
the 'natural' or idiot than of the pro-
fessional jester; 'motley' could also
mean "the motley-loome .. like a beggers cloake ... full of stolne patches,
and yet never a patch like one another" (Dekker, *Wonderful Year,* 1603;
Grosart, I. 80), and refer to the fool in
pied colours, and it is often difficult to
know which is meant.

17. *deceiv'd*] disappointed, cf. *All's
W.,* I. i. 243 (Pooler).

19–21. *beside ... intend*] besides
losing the labour of our brains, and
foregoing our intention to make what
we are about to present nothing but
the truth; for "opinion"='state of
mind', 'ready intention', cf. George
Wither, *Abuses Stript* (1613), I3^r–I3^v,
"to bring, / All men in the opinion to
confesse". Pooler, citing Case, interprets as 'the reputation that we bring',
for which sense cf. *Mer. V.,* I. i. 91, but
this hardly fits the syntax.

Will leave us never an understanding friend.
Therefore, for goodness' sake, and as you are known
The first and happiest hearers of the town,
Be sad, as we would make ye. Think ye see   25
The very persons of our noble story
As they were living: think you see them great,
And follow'd with the general throng, and sweat
Of thousand friends; then, in a moment, see
How soon this mightiness meets misery: 30
And if you can be merry then, I'll say
A man may weep upon his wedding day.

22. *understanding*] a quibble alluding to the 'groundlings' who stood round three sides of the platform stage in public theatres such as the Globe; cf. Jonson, *Bartholomew Fair* (1614-31), Induction, l. 49, "the understanding Gentlemen o' the ground here, ask'd my judgement", and for further citations, see Chambers, *E.S.*, II. 527.

23. *for . . . sake*] the first example of this phrase known to *O.E.D.*; it occurs again at III. i. 159.

24. *first . . . town*] first in importance and most favourable (to us, the players —so Steevens) audience in London. There may be some justification for this flattery, in that the King's Men, Shakespeare's company, maintained an unbroken existence longer, and seem to have been more prosperous, than any other group of actors; they

presented better plays on the whole than other companies, and the Globe probably attracted a better-class audience than the rest of the public theatres; see L. B. Wright, *Middle-Class Culture in Elizabethan England* (1935), pp. 610 ff.

25. *sad*] serious, cf. l. 3 above.

26. *story*] The rhyme falls here on an unaccented syllable, as is not uncommon; Pooler notes its frequency in Chapman's work, citing the rhyme "strings . . . doings", *The Shadow of Night* (1594), B2ʳ, etc.; cf. Epilogue, ll. 9-10.

27. *great*] i.e. in high position, cf. v. iv. 38.

28. *sweat*] cf. IV. i. 58 below.

29. *thousand*] for this use without an article, cf. *Per.*, I. ii. 97 and IV. ii. 89 below.

ACT I

SCENE I—[*London. A room in the court.*]

Enter the DUKE OF NORFOLK *at one door. At the other the*
DUKE OF BUCKINGHAM *and the* LORD ABERGAVENNY.

Buck. Good morrow, and well met. How have ye done
Since last we saw in France? *Directing audience to before play begins*

Nor.   I thank your grace,
Healthful, and ever since a fresh admirer
Of what I saw there.   *Expectation*

Buck.   An untimely ague
Stayed me a prisoner in my chamber, when   5
Those suns of glory, those two lights of men
Met in the vale of Andren.

Nor.   'Twixt Guynes and Arde,
I was then present, saw them salute on horseback,
Beheld them when they lighted, how they clung

ACT I
Scene I

Scene I] *Actus Primus. Scœna Prima. F.*   *London.] Var. 1785; A . . . court. This Ed.;
An ante-chamber in the palace. Theobald.*   2. *saw in*] *F; saw y'in F3.*   6. *suns*] *F*
(Sunnes); Sons F3.   7. *Andren . . . Arde] F; Ardres . . . Ardres Rowe.*
9. *lighted] F; 'lighted Staunton.*

Scene I] The material from Holinshed in this scene is considerably modified and re-arranged. Buckingham
was in fact present at the Field of the
Cloth of Gold, and his arrest (April
1521) did not follow directly upon that
celebration (May–June 1520). For excerpts from Holinshed relating to this
scene, see Appendix II, pp. 185–8, 192.

2. *saw*] sc. each other, cf. *Cym.*, I. i.
124, "when shall we see again?"; the
expression occurs in Halle, *Henry VIII*,
ii. 197, "the king and she never saw
together".

3. *fresh*] untired (Johnson); cf. IV. i.
99 and n.

5. *when*] 7 June 1520.

6. *suns*] The metaphor of a king as
the sun is very common in Shakespeare and is important later in the
scene, cf. ll. 33, 56; the reading "sons"
of F3 and Capell indicates what is
probably an intentional quibble.

7. *Guynes and Arde*] Guynes belonged
to the English, Arde to the French, and
the towns lay on either side the vale of
Andren. "Arde" is now spelled Ardres,
but Shakespeare follows Holinshed
and Halle (Reed).

9. *lighted*] alighted; a common form,
perhaps suggested here by "lights",
l. 6.

7

In their embracement as they grew together,   10
Which had they, what four thron'd ones could have
    weigh'd
Such a compounded one?

Buck.   All the whole time
I was my chamber's prisoner.

Nor.   Then you lost
The view of earthly glory: men might say   *happiness*
Till this time pomp was single, but now married   15
To one above itself. Each following day
Became the next day's master, till the last
Made former wonders, its. To-day the French,
All clinquant all in gold, like heathen gods
Shone down the English; and to-morrow they   20

11. Which . . . weigh'd] *so Rowe 3; two lines in* F, *ending* they, | . . . weigh'd.
17. next . . . last] F; last . . . next *Capell.*

10. *as*] as if; see Abbott 107.

grew together] Pooler notes this as a
frequent figure in B. and F. as in *Bonduca* (1613); *Works*, VI. 117), III. iii.
"How close they march, as if they grew
together?" and cf. *MND.*, III. ii. 208,
"So we grew together, | Like to a
double cherry".

11. *weigh'd*] counterbalanced, equalled in weight.

12–13. *All . . . prisoner*] the dramatist's invention, for Buckingham was
certainly present at some of the ceremonies connected with the meeting,
as Holinshed reports, p. 860, "The
lord cardinall . . . accompanied with
the duke of Buckingham, and other
great lords, conducted forward the
French king, and . . . met the king of
England and his companie right in the
vallie of Anderne . . .": Buckingham's
supposed illness here allows the
pageantry of the Field of the Cloth of
Gold to be described, setting the tone
for a play of pageantry; later on in this
scene he speaks familiarly of recent
events, cf. ll. 72 ff. and 168 ff.

15–16. *Till . . . itself*] the single
pomps (of each king) are now united
to (make) one greater pomp. Warburton interpreted as a marriage of Henry

to pomp; Mason as an expression of
rivalry between Henry and Francis,
but, as Johnson observed, "Pomp is
only married to pomp, but the new
pomp is greater than the old".

16–18. *Each . . . its*] each succeeding
day became the next day's teacher, i.e.
"Every day learnt something from the
preceding" (Johnson), until the last
day assembled all the earlier splen-
dours. For "master" meaning
'teacher', cf. *Shr.*, III. i. 54. Capell's
transposition of "next" and "last"
would make good sense, i.e. 'each succeeding day outdid the previous one,
till the next superseded that', but it is
not necessary.

19. *clinquant*] glittering, cf. Florio,
New Worlde of Words (1611), "*Aginina*,
a kind of networke worne over tinsell
or cloth of gold to make it shew clink-
ant" (cited by Halliwell). Steevens
quotes *A Memorable Masque* (1613),
performed at the wedding of Princess
Elizabeth and Frederick, "his buskins
clinquant as his other attire". The
noun Cotgrave (*Dictionary*, 1611) de-
fines as "Thinne plate-lace of Gold, or
Silver" (Clarendon Ed.).

heathen gods] possibly a biblical allusion, cf. Psalm cxv. 4.

Made Britain India: every man that stood
Show'd like a mine. Their dwarfish pages were
As cherubins, all gilt: the madams too,
Not us'd to toil, did almost sweat to bear
The pride upon them, that their very labour　　25
Was to them as a painting. Now this masque
Was cried incomparable; and th'ensuing night
Made it a fool and beggar. The two kings
Equal in lustre, were now best, now worst,
As presence did present them: him in eye　　30
Still him in praise, and being present both,
'Twas said they saw but one, and no discerner
Durst wag his tongue in censure. When these suns

23. cherubins] *F*; cherubims *Var. 1773.* 33. censure. When] *Rowe*; censure)
when *F*. when *F*.

21. *India*] cf. *1 H 4*, III. i. 169, "as bountiful / As mines of India"; India commonly represented a source of fabulous wealth, cf. IV. i. 45 and n.

23. *cherubins*] the earliest singular form was *cherubin*, not *cherub*, but the plural *-ins* was dying out in the sixteenth century, and does not appear in the Bishop's Bible or the Authorized Version. It does occur in the Coverdale Bible and in Sternhold and Hopkins' version of the Psalms, and is the usual spelling in Shakespeare, cf. *Cym.*, II. iv. 88; *Mer. V.*, v. i. 62. The idea here may be derived from Exodus, xxv. 18, "And thou shalt make two Cherubims of golde" (Bishop's Bible), glossed, "The Cherubims were wynged images, and . . . they had yᵉ shapes of boyes . . ."

madams] ladies of rank, cf. *Lr.*, I. ii. 9.

25. *pride*] splendid clothing and ornament, cf. *Oth.*, II. iii. 98.

that] so that; very common, cf. ll. 36, 38, Epilogue 7 (Clarendon Ed.); Abbott 283.

25–6. *their . . . painting*] their very exertion gave colour to their cheeks; cf. *Wint.*, IV. iv. 61.

26. *Was . . . painting*] made them flushed, as if with rouge (Pooler); gave them such a colour that the trouble of painting was saved (Warburton).

masque] The pageantry is described

at length by the chroniclers, Grafton, Halle, and Holinshed, for whose account see Appendix II, pp. 185, 187, but this may have been brought to mind for a 1613 audience the festivities at the wedding of Princess Elizabeth; John Chamberlain reported of them on 25 February, "Our revells . . . gave great contentment beeing both daintie and curious in device and sumptuous in shew: specially the ynnes of court whose two maskes stoode them in better [cost more] then 4000li besides the gallantrie and expence of private gentlemen. . ." (*Letters*, I. 430–1).

27. *cried*] proclaimed.

28. *Made . . . beggar*] showed it up as inferior and drab. For "fool" in this sense, cf. *Lr.*, II. ii. 132 and *Shr.*, III. ii. 159; for "beggar" see note on "masque", l. 26; costly display was a feature of court masques.

30–1. *him . . . praise*] The second "him" is ambiguous; probably to be interpreted as, 'the one on view was ever the one praised'. "Still", as commonly in Shakespeare, means "always".

32. *discerner*] beholder (Pooler). Not elsewhere in Shakespeare, though the verb is fairly common.

33. *wag . . . tongue*] cf. *Ham.*, III. iv. 39.
censure] judgement; "determination,

(For so they phrase 'em) by their heralds challeng'd
The noble spirits to arms, they did perform   35
Beyond thought's compass, that former fabulous story
Being now seen possible enough, got credit
That Bevis was believ'd.

Buck.   O you go far.

Nor. As I belong to worship, and affect
In honour honesty, the tract of ev'ry thing   40
Would by a good discourser lose some life
Which action's self was tongue to. All was royal;
To the disposing of it nought rebell'd,
Order gave each thing view: the office did
Distinctly his full function.

Buck.   Who did guide,   45
I mean who set the body and the limbs
Of this great sport together, as you guess?

Nor. One certes, that promises no element

42-7. All ... together,] *so Theobald; Buck.* All ... together? *F.*   47. as you guess?] *so F4; Nor.* As you guesse: *F.*

of which had the noblest appearance"
(Warburton).

34. *phrase*] describe; not elsewhere
in Shakespeare.

35. *perform*] discharged their function; cf. *Cor.*, I. i. 271.

38. *Bevis*] Bevis of Hampton (Southampton), a legendary hero, was renowned for feats of arms. His "at-
chievement great" was celebrated, as
Pooler notes, in Drayton's *Poly-Olbion*
(1613), Song II, l. 260 ff., and a medieval romance on his career was printed
in 1500. He lived on in tradition and
in ballads and popular literature, as
attested by H. Parrot's picture of a
farmer rejecting a play on a book-
stall, "It may be good (saith hee) for
those can use it. / Shewe mee King
Arthur, Bevis or Syr *Guye*" (*The Mastive*,
1615, I1r).

39-40. *affect ... honesty*] i.e. love
truth in accordance with my moral
duty; for "in honour", cf. *Wint.*, III. i.
64.

42-7. *All ... guess?*] This generally
accepted arrangement of these lines is

Theobald's: something must be wrong
with the division of them in F, which
gives to Buckingham the passage "All
... together" and to Norfolk the phrase
"As you guess", for even if ll. 42-5
could be an ironical comment of Buckingham's, "As you guess", as the editor of F4 realized, means nothing in
the mouth of Norfolk.

44-5. *Order ... function*] i.e. every-
thing was so well ordered as to be seen
easily, and the officials carried out
their tasks without confusion. For the
personification of "office" = an
official, or a body of officials, cf. *Ham.*,
III. i. 73.

47. *sport*] entertainment.

48. *certes*] surely; usually a disyllable
in Shakespeare, but cf. *Oth.*, I. i. 16,
"Nonsuits my mediators: for 'Certes',
says he" (Nichol Smith).

element] part, share (Onions); perhaps relating to the phrase "to be in
(out of) one's element" (Tilley, R 107-
8), or simply by metaphor from the
four elements, thought to be the con-
stituent parts of matter. Johnson (after

In such a business.

Buck.   I pray you who, my lord?

Nor. All this was order'd by the good discretion   50
    Of the right reverend Cardinal of York.

Buck. The devil speed him: no man's pie is freed
    From his ambitious finger. What had he   *Bucks anger*
    To do in these fierce vanities? I wonder
    That such a keech can with his very bulk   55
    Take up the rays o'th'beneficial sun,
    And keep it from the earth.

Nor.   Surely sir,
There's in him stuff that puts him to these ends;
For being not propp'd by ancestry, whose grace
Chalks successors their way, nor call'd upon   60
For high feats done to th'crown, neither allied
To eminent assistants, but spider-like,
Out of his self-drawing web, O, gives us note,

---

55. keech] *F;* Ketch *F4.*   63. of his] *F;* of's *Dyce.*   self-drawing web] *F;*
self-drawn web *Rowe 2;* himself drawing web *Theobald conj.;* his self drawing
web *Staunton.*   web, O, gives us note,] *This Ed.;* Web. O gives us note, *F;*
Web. O! gives us note, *F2;* web he gives us note, *Capell;* web—O! give us
note!— *Knight;* web, 'a gives us note *Kittredge (Kellner conj.).*

Pope) suggests "rudiments of knowledge", Halliwell "skill", but *O.E.D.*
has examples only of plural "elements"
in these senses.

    50. *order'd*] arranged.

    52. *speed*] prosper, reversing the
blessing 'God speed'.

    52–3. *pie . . . finger*] proverbial; see
Tilley, F 228.

    54. *fierce vanities*] extravagant, wild
follies (Onions): for "fierce" cf. *Cym.,*
v. v. 382, *Tim.,* IV. ii. 30, "the fierce
wretchedness that glory brings us".
Pooler, following Johnson, interprets
as "proud follies", citing a possible
parallel at *2 H 6,* IV. ix. 45.

    55. *keech*] the fat of a slaughtered
animal rolled up into a lump (*O.E.D.*).
Wolsey was said to be a butcher's son,
cf. l. 120 below, and Steevens compared the name "goodwife Keech, the
butcher's wife" in *2 H 4,* II. i. 101.
Shakespeare perhaps thought of Wolsey as a fat man.

    56. *sun*] an allusion to the King, as
at ll. 6, 33. "Take up" means 'occupy
entirely', as at *Cor.,* III. ii. 116.

    58. *stuff . . . ends*] qualities that set
him on to do these things; for "stuff",
cf. *Cym.,* I. i. 23.

    59. *grace*] virtue, or possibly for-
tune; cf. I. ii. 122.

    60. *Chalks . . . way*] i.e. marks out
their path; cf. *Tp.,* v. i. 203.

    61. *high feats*] exploits of great con-
sequence.

    allied] related; cf. *Meas.,* III. ii. 109,
"The vice is of a great kindred; it is
well allied".

    62. *assistants*] perhaps ministers of
state, cf. *Ham.,* II. ii. 166, "Let me be
no assistant for a state, / But keep a
farm and carters" (Pooler); or supporters, as in *R 3,* IV. iv. 526, "ask
those . . . If they were his assistants, yea
or no".

    63. *self-drawing*] "drawing" here
means 'spinning'; he has spun his web

The force of his own merit makes his way,
A gift that heaven gives for him, which buys   65
A place next to the king.
Aber.   I cannot tell
What heaven hath given him: let some graver
     eye
Pierce into that, but I can see his pride
Peep through each part of him: whence has he
     that?
If not from hell the devil is a niggard,   70
Or has given all before, and he begins
A new hell in himself.
Buck.   Why the devil,
Upon this French going-out, took he upon him

65. gives . . . buys] *F*; gives, which for him buys *Hanmer*; gives; which buys
for him *Warburton*; gives to him, which buys *Rann (Johnson conj.).*   69–70.
that? / . . . hell the] *Theobald*; that, / . . . Hell? *F*.   73. going-out] *Rann*;
going out *F*.

out of himself, cf. *Meas.*, III. ii. 289
"To draw with idle spiders' strings /
Most ponderous and substantial
things". The meaning is made clear by
the following line; Wolsey spins his
achievements out of his own qualities.
See next note.

web, O, gives] F has generally been
emended. Capell reduced the full stop
to a comma, and altered *O*, which he
took to be a misprint for *'a*, to *he*.
There is no difficulty about altering
punctuation, which is often erratic
(see ll. 69–70); *he* is indefensible as
an 18th-century regularization, and
though a case can be made out for *'a*,
it occurs nowhere else in the play.
Other emendations are ingenious
rather than helpful. I therefore keep
O, which provides good, if ungram-
matical sense, and reflects the speak-
ers' passion: Wolsey makes his own
dignities and high offices, and informs
everyone that the force of his merit
gains them for him. The image of the
spider is appropriate, for it was considered evil and poisonous, cf. *Cym.*,
IV. ii. 90, and *Edward III* (1596), C3ᵛ,

"a poison sucking envious spider".
For "gives us note" meaning 'informs', see *Troil.*, IV. i. 43, "give him
note of our approach", and for
"makes his way" meaning 'advances
him', see *Lr.*, V. iii. 29. The unfinished
construction here may be compared
with that at ll. 183 ff.

65. *A gift . . . him*] "Gifts of God"
was a common expression for natural
endowments, and Dogberry boasts of
his accomplishments as "Gifts that
God gives" (*Ado*, III. iv. 47). Emendation is unnecessary.

68–72. *pride . . . himself*] Abergavenny says he can see nothing in Wolsey that has come from heaven; all he
can see is his pride, which must have
come from hell—indeed he has so
much that the devil refused him any or
gave it away earlier, and he begins a
new hell, as Lucifer, falling through
pride, began the first: cf. III. ii. 371,
441 for further comparisons of Wolsey
and Lucifer.

73. *going-out*] expedition; Pooler
compares B. and F., *Wild-Goose Chase*
(c. 1621; *Works*, IV. 317), I. i, where

(Without the privity o'th'king) t'appoint
Who should attend on him? He makes up the file　　75
Of all the gentry; for the most part such
To whom as great a charge, as little honour
He meant to lay upon: and his own letter,
The honourable board of council, out
Must fetch him in he papers.

Aber.　　　　　　　　　　I do know　　80
Kinsmen of mine, three at the least, that have
By this so sicken'd their estates that never
They shall abound as formerly.

Buck.　　　　　　　　　　O many

76–7. such / To whom] *F;* such / On whom *Hanmer;* such / Too, whom *Capell;*
such too, / On whom *Keightley (Staunton conj.).*　　78–80. letter, . . . papers.]
This Ed.; Letter / . . . Councell, out / . . . him in, he Papers. *F;* letter / (The . . .
Council out) / . . . in him he papers. *Pope;* letter, / . . . Council out, / . . . in
him he papers. *Johnson.*　　80. papers] paupers *Staunton conj.*

"Upon my going out . . ." refers to
travel abroad.

74. *privity*] joint knowledge (Nichol
Smith); not elsewhere in Shakespeare,
but 'privy' is common in this sense, cf.
Wint., II. i. 94.

75. *file*] list, cf. *Mac.,* v. ii. 8, "I have
a file / Of all the gentry" (cited
Steevens).

76–8. *such To whom . . . upon*] a difficult construction, and Capell's reading of *to* as *too* is tempting; for the use of
a redundant preposition see *Cor.,* II. i.
18, "In what enormity is Marcius poor
in . . ." and for the general construction, *All's W.,* III. vi. 24 (Abbott
278).

78–80. *letter . . . papers*] i.e., as Pope
explained, Wolsey ignores the Council
and deals out office on his own authority. "The . . . board of council, out"
was suggested, as Malone noted, by a
passage in Holinshed, p. 855, "The
peers, receiving letters to prepare
themselves to attend the king in this
journie . . . seemed to grudge, that
such a costlie journie should be taken
in hand to their importunate charges
and expenses, without consent of the
whole boord of the councell. But name-

lie the duke of Buckingham . . . sore
repined that he should be at so great
charges". "Papers", I take it, means
'sends a note to', and follows on from
"letter". Johnson's punctuation, "letter, / . . . out," has been generally
accepted, but this is to make the passage mean either "council not then
sitting" (Johnson), or "all mention of
the . . . council being left out of the
letter" (Steevens). F has been ably
defended by A. P. Rossiter (*T.L.S.,*
15 July 1949), who, I think, is right in
equating "The honourable board of
council" with "letter", and in noting
the sarcasm of "honourable" and the
pun on "board" as 'boord', or mock-
ery; he agrees with Pope and *O.E.D.*
in explaining "papers" as 'notes down,
lists'. Interpret: his own letter, usurping the office of the honourable board
of council (and mocking it), once sent
out, compels the recipient to enter (or,
brings in the person whose name he
puts on paper).

82. *sicken'd*] impaired. No earlier
transitive use is known.

83. *abound*] be wealthy; *O.E.D.* cites
Philippians, iv. 18 (Authorized Version), "But I have all and abound".

Have broke their backs with laying manors on'em
For this great journey. What did this vanity   85
But minister communication of
A most poor issue?

Nor.   Grievingly I think,
The peace between the French and us not values
The cost that did conclude it.

Buck.   Every man,
After the hideous storm that follow'd, was   90
A thing inspir'd, and, not consulting, broke
Into a general prophecy; that this tempest
Dashing the garment of this peace, aboded
The sudden breach on't.

Nor.   Which is budded out,
For France hath flaw'd the league, and hath attach'd 95

---

87. issue?] *Pope;* issue. *F.*

84. *Have . . .'em*] a very common
idea; Malone cites *John*, II. i. 67–71
and Camden, *Remains* (1605), p. 221,
from a passage about Wolsey, "a
Nobleman . . . having lately sold a
Mannor . . . came ruffling into the
Court, in a new sute, saying: *Am not I
a mightie man, that beare an hundred
houses on my backe?*" (Tilley, L 452,
W 61).

85. *vanity*] waste, extravagant folly.

86–7. *But . . . issue*] an allusion to the
beggaring of their own children as well
as to the getting of more; also, literally,
'furnish talk (or occasion for talk) to
little purpose' ("issue" = outcome).
Shakespeare made use of Holinshed's
words (p. 855), which indicate the
literal sense, "he knew not for what
cause so much monie should be spent
and communication to be ministred of
things of no importance"; and compare an earlier passage in Holinshed,
p. 844, "the kings mercie ministred
abundant matter of communication,
everie one . . . sounding the benefit of
his roiall clemencie". "Poor issue"
alludes to the impoverishment of heirs
by selling manors, and perhaps contains a double pun with reference to

bastard children, if "communication"
is a quibble on sexual intercourse.
O.E.D. first records this sense for the
verb in 1624, but cf. *Err.*, II. ii. 178,
Troil., III. iii. 117; see also the notes on
I. iii. 19 and 27 below.

87. *Grievingly*] a coinage, cf. "guess-
ingly", *Lr.*, III. vii. 47.

88. *not values*] is not worth (Pooler).

91. *not consulting*] spontaneously
(Clarendon   Ed.);   independently
(Pooler). Holinshed says (pp. 860–1),
"the eighteenth of June, was such an
hideous storme of wind and weather,
that manie conjectured it did prognosticate trouble and hatred shortlie
after to follow betweene princes".

92. *general*] i.e. each one said the
same thing (Pooler).

93. *Dashing*] striking violently.

aboded] foreshadowed, quibbling on
"budded", l. 94 (Nichol Smith).

94. *sudden*] immediate; "on't" =
"of't", as commonly, see Abbott 182.

95. *flaw'd*] broken, cf. I. ii. 21 and
Lr., v. iii. 196, where "flaw'd heart"
means cracked or broken heart
(Pooler).

attach'd] seized by authority of law;
from Holinshed (p. 872), "the French

Our merchants' goods at Bordeaux.

Aber.   Is it therefore
Th'ambassador is silenc'd?

Nor.   Marry is't.

Aber. A proper title of a peace, and purchas'd
At a superfluous rate.

Buck.   Why, all this business
Our reverend Cardinal carried.

Nor.   Like it your grace,   100
The state takes notice of the private difference
Betwixt you and the Cardinal. I advise you
(And take it from a heart that wishes towards you
Honour and plenteous safety) that you read
The Cardinal's malice and his potency   105
Together; to consider further that,
What his high hatred would effect wants not
A minister in his power. You know his nature,
That he's revengeful, and I know his sword
Hath a sharp edge: it's long, and't may be said   110
It reaches far, and where 'twill not extend,

---

96. Bordeaux] Burdeux *F.*

king commanded all Englishmens
goods being in Burdeaux, to be attached, and put under arrest".

97. *silenc'd*] He was prevented from
fulfilling his office by being kept in
restraint, as is clear from Halle's words
(i. 243–4), "the Ambassador was commaunded to kepe his house in silence,
and not to come in presence, till he was
sent for": both Stow and Holinshed
merely say he was "commaunded to
kepe his house"; for another possible
reference to Halle's chronicle see v. ii.
44–9 and n.

98. *A proper ... peace*] "a fine thing to
call a peace" (Clarendon Ed.); "proper" is used ironically to mean 'excellent', cf. *Mac.*, III. iv. 60 (Steevens).
"Title" is both name, style, and also,
in its legal sense, title-deed, legal right
to something, so connecting with
"purchas'd" (Case, *apud* Pooler).
Pooler notes an ironical use of the

phrase "proper title" in B. and F.,
Beggar's Bush (1622?; *Works*, II. 211),
I. i, but without all the implications it
has here.

99. *superfluous rate*] excessive or extravagant cost, cf. *Lr.*, II. iv. 268, "our
basest beggars / Are in the poorest
things superfluous", and for "rate",
see *Wiv.*, II. ii. 213 (cited Pooler).

100. *carried*] managed, cf. I. ii. 134
(Nichol Smith).

Like ... grace] if it please your grace;
as Pooler notes, an apology for giving
unasked advice.

101. *difference*] quarrel, cf. *Lr.*, II. i.
125.

104. *read*] estimate.

105. *potency*] power, as at *Meas.*, II.
ii. 67.

107–8. *wants ... minister*] does not
lack an agent. This is the commonest
sense of "want" in Shakespeare, cf.
Tp., III. iii. 38 (Onions).

Thither he darts it. Bosom up my counsel,
You'll find it wholesome. Loe, where comes that rock
That I advise your shunning.

Enter CARDINAL WOLSEY, *the purse borne before him, certain of the
Guard, and two Secretaries with papers: the* CARDINAL *in his
passage fixeth his eye on* BUCKINGHAM, *and* BUCKINGHAM *on
him, both full of disdain.*

Wol. The Duke of Buckingham's surveyor, ha?   115
    Where's his examination?
First Sec.   Here so please you.
Wol. Is he in person ready?
First Sec.   Ay, please your grace.
Wol. Well, we shall then know more, and Buckingham
    Shall lessen this big look.
                    Exeunt Cardinal and his train.

Buck. This butcher's cur is venom-mouth'd, and I   120
    Have not the power to muzzle him, therefore best
    Not wake him in his slumber. A beggar's book

*bird
passing
appearance-
threatening*

115–18. S.H. *Wol.*] *Car. F.*   115. surveyor, ha?] Surveyor? Ha? *F.*   119.
this] *F;* his *F3.*   120. venom-mouth'd] *Pope (after Rowe);* venom'd-mouth'd
F.   122. book] *F;* brood *Collier 2;* look *Staunton conj.*

112. *Bosom up*] keep secret, hide in
the bosom; *O.E.D.* cites Day, *Isle of
Gulls* (1606), B4ᵛ, "Ile bosome what I
thinke", and cf. *Lr.*, IV. v. 26 for the
noun meaning 'secret confidence'.

113. *wholesome*] beneficial, as at
I. ii. 45.

114. S.D. the purse] the bag containing the great seal, carried before
the Chancellor as one of the insignia
of his office; see S.D.s at II. iv and
IV. i. 36.

115. *surveyor*] the overseer of his
estates, as is made clear at I. ii. 172.
This was Charles Knyvet, Buckingham's cousin.

116. *examination*] the paper containing the witness's deposition; see *Ado*,
III. v. 53, and below, II. i. 16.

120. *butcher's cur*] Wolsey's father is
said by many early writers to have
been a butcher; W. Roy in *Read me and
be not wroth* (1528) speaks of him as a

"Ragynge courre / wrapped in a
wolves skyne / O butcherly bisshop";
Halle notes how the common people
called him a "Bochers dogge", and
Skelton, as Steevens observed, also
refers to him as "the mastif cur ... the
butcher's dog" in *Why come ye not to
court?* (written *c.* 1522–3, in *Poems*, ed.
Henderson, 1931, p. 347). This name
has a double point as alluding to the
breed or kind of dog, listed among the
various kinds in *Return from Parnassus,
Part II* (1606; ed. Leishman, 1949,
p. 279), l. 845, which gave rise to the
proverb, "as surly as a butcher's dog"
(Tilley B764): so Dekker, *Work for
Armourers* (1609; Grosart, IV. 109),
has "better than curres ... baite the
Bull, or then Butchers Mastives when
they worry one another".

venom-] F has *venom'd*, doubtless a
misreading of *d* for *e*.

122. *Not ... slumber*] proverbial; see

Outworths a noble's blood.

Nor.   What, are you chaf'd?
Ask God for temp'rance, that's th'appliance only   *Necessity of patience*
Which your disease requires.

Buck.   I read in's looks   125
Matter against me, and his eye revil'd
Me as his abject object; at this instant
He bores me with some trick; he's gone to th' king:
I'll follow and out-stare him.

Nor.   Stay my lord,
And let your reason with your choler question   130
What 'tis you go about: to climb steep hills
Requires slow pace at first. Anger is like
A full hot horse, who being allow'd his way,
Self-mettle tires him: not a man in England
Can advise me like you; be to yourself   135
As you would to your friend.

---

123. chaf'd] chaff'd *F*.   133. full hot] *F;* full-hot *F4*.

Tilley, W 7, "It is evil waking of a
sleeping dog".

122–3. *A . . . blood*] a beggar's learning counts for more than a nobleman's
high descent. For "book" Pooler compares *Wiv.*, IV. i. 15, and cf. *Tp.*, III. i.
94, but as he notes, Buckingham is
learned himself, see I. ii. 111 ff. There
is possibly a pun on 'bouk' or 'bulk',
meaning mass or body, in opposition
to "blood", which would connect this
passage with l. 55 above. For 'bulk' in
this sense see *R 3*, I. iv. 40, "within my
panting bulk".

123. *chaf'd*] heated, hence angry
(Pooler); cf. *Cor.*, III. iii. 27 and below,
III. ii. 206.

124. *temp'rance*] forbearance, self-
control, as at *Cor.*, III. iii. 28 (Clarendon
Ed.).

appliance] remedy; not given in
O.E.D., but see *Ham.*, IV. iii. 10, "diseases desperate grown / By desperate
appliance are relieved . . ." and *Per.*,
III. ii. 86 (Pooler).

127. *abject object*] object of his contempt (Onions), but "abject" may
mean 'despicable' or 'rejected, spurn-

ed' (*O.E.D.*). "Object" is what is
seen by the eyes and the emotion
attached, cf. *Cym.*, V. iv. 55, *MND.*,
IV. i. 167, "The object and the pleasure
of mine eye, / Is only Helena", and
below, III. ii. 132. For a similar play on
these words see Jonson, *Poetaster*
(1602), I. iii. 58, "All other objects will
but abjects proove", and Marston,
Histriomastix (1610; Wood, III. 293),
"Once Objects, now all Abjects to the
world".

128. *bores*] cheats, deceives; the
word is identified with 'bourd', to
mock, cheat, jest; Steevens cites
Cromwell (1602; *Shakespeare Apocrypha*, 1918), III. ii. 167, "One that hath
gulled you, that hath bored you, sir".
As Pooler notes, "to bore one's nose"
meaning the same, or more especially,
'to cuckold', was a common phrase;
see Tilley, N 229.

133–4. *A full . . . him*] proverbial, see
Tilley H 642, "A free horse will soon
tire"; "full hot" is high-spirited, cf.
"horses hot at hand", *Cæs.*, IV. ii. 23
(Pooler). For "mettle" as the vigour of
a horse see *1 H 4*, IV. iii. 22.

Buck.   I'll to the king,
And from a mouth of honour quite cry down
This Ipswich fellow's insolence; or proclaim
There's difference in no persons.

Nor.   Be advis'd;
Heat not a furnace for your foe so hot   140
That it do singe yourself. We may outrun
By violent swiftness that which we run at,
And lose by over-running: know you not
The fire that mounts the liquor till't run o'er
In seeming to augment it wastes it? be advis'd;   145
I say again there is no English soul
More stronger to direct you than yourself,
If with the sap of reason you would quench,
Or but allay the fire of passion.

Buck.   Sir,
I am thankful to you, and I'll go along   150
By your prescription: but this top-proud fellow
(Whom from the flow of gall I name not, but

145. to] *F;* t' *Theobald.*   it?] *Theobald;* it: *F.*   150. I am] I'm *Pope.*
151-3. fellow / (Whom . . . motions)] fellow, / Whom . . . motions, *F.*

137. *mouth of honour*] Buckingham is emphasizing his nobility.

139. *difference*] distinction of rank or quality, as in *Lr.*, I. iv. 100, "Come, sir, arise, away! I'll teach you differences".

Be advis'd] be wary, take care; common in Shakespeare, cf. *Wint.*, IV. iv. 492.

140-1. *Heat . . . yourself*] based on proverbs, cf. Tilley F 230, 240, 249, 281. Norfolk's advice takes the form of a series of wise saws.

141-3. *We . . . over-running*] again based on proverbs, see Tilley F 518, "a fool's haste is no speed", and H 198.

144. *mounts*] causes to rise, as at I. ii. 205 and *Tp.*, II. ii. 11. "Liquor" is liquid of any kind.

147. *More stronger*] The double comparative is common in Shakespeare, See Abbott 11.

149. *allay*] moderate; strictly, 'allay', from O.E. *alecgan*, should mean

"to quell . . . any tumult of the passions" (*O.E.D.* 9), but here, as elsewhere in Shakespeare, there is confusion with 'allay', modern 'alloy', from the Latin *alligare*, meaning to temper or mix. See *Tp.*, I. ii. 392 and *Cor.*, v. iii. 85, "To allay my rages and revenges with / Your colder reasons".

151. *top-proud*] proud in the highest degree (Schmidt).

152-3. *flow . . . motions*] I speak not out of rancour, but from sincere motives. The gall-bladder was thought to control the flow of the humour 'choler', and hence to be the seat of anger, cf. *2 H 4*, I. ii. 199. "Motions" could mean motives, as at *Cor.*, II. i. 56, "hasty . . . upon too trivial motion", or, in its psychological sense, passions, cf. *Oth.*, I. iii. 335, "our raging motions, our carnal stings"; here are implied sincere feelings as opposed to the insincerity of sheer spite.

From sincere motions) by intelligence
And proofs as clear as founts in July when
We see each grain of gravel, I do know   155
To be corrupt and treasonous.

Nor.   Say not treasonous.

Buck. To th'king I'll say't, and make my vouch as strong
As shore of rock: attend. This holy fox,
Or wolf, or both (for he is equal rav'nous
As he is subtle, and as prone to mischief   160
As able to perform't), his mind and place
Infecting one another, yea reciprocally,
Only to show his pomp as well in France
As here at home, suggests the king our master
To this last costly treaty; th'interview   165
That swallowed so much treasure, and like a glass
Did break i' th' wrenching.

Nor.   Faith, and so it did.

Buck. Pray give me favour sir: this cunning cardinal
The articles o' th' combination drew

159–62. (for . . . perform't), . . . reciprocally,] F; —for . . . perform it, . . .
reciprocally— *Capell.*

153. *intelligence*] secret information, cf. *1 H 4*, IV. iii. 98, "sought to entrap me by intelligence".

157. *vouch*] allegation, evidence, as at *Meas.*, II. iv. 156 (Clarendon Ed.).

158–60. *This . . . subtle*] based on proverbs, cf. Tilley F 629 "as wily as a fox", and W 601 "as hungry as a wolf". See also the note on l. 120; such animal associations for Wolsey go back to Skelton and to Roy.

159. *equal*] equally; see Abbott 1 for this common adverbial usage.

160–2. *prone . . . reciprocally*] as Pooler notes, Buckingham echoes here what Norfolk has earlier said to him, cf. ll. 106–12, and note on ll. 12–13. By this means Wolsey's character is firmly established, although his one appearance has been so brief.

161–2. *mind . . . reciprocally*] his power and inclination work together, infect one another, in prompting and enabling him to do mischief. For "place"=

office or rank, cf. l. 66 above; "reciprocally" occurs nowhere else in Shakespeare.

164. *suggests*] prompts, tempts, in a bad sense, see *Oth.*, II. iii. 358, *H 5*, II. ii. 114, and *R 2*, III. iv. 75, where the word is used of the devil's temptations.

165. *interview*] ceremonial meeting of princes; Holinshed's word, and cf. *H 5*, V. ii. 27.

167. *wrenching*] a dialectal form of 'rinsing', to which it is usually emended here, following Pope; cf. *Two Noble Kinsmen*, I. i. 171, "Wrinching our holy begging in our eyes / To make petition cleere." I prefer the stronger reading, and keep F; besides its literal sense, "wrenching" signifies 'distortion of meaning' (*O.E.D.* 7, and cf. *2 H 4*, II. i. 120, "wrenching the true cause the false way"), which is very appropriate to what follows, cf. ll. 189–93.

169. *articles . . . drew*] arranged the

As himself pleas'd; and they were ratified   170
As he cried 'Thus let be', to as much end
As give a crutch to th' dead. But our court-cardinal
Has done this, and 'tis well; for worthy Wolsey
(Who cannot err) he did it. Now this follows
(Which as I take it, is a kind of puppy   175
To th' old dam treason), Charles the Emperor,
Under pretence to see the queen his aunt
(For 'twas indeed his colour, but he came
To whisper Wolsey), here makes visitation;
His fears were that the interview betwixt   180
England and France might through their amity
Breed him some prejudice, for from this league
Peep'd harms that menac'd him: privily
Deals with our cardinal, and as I trow
(Which I do well; for I am sure the emperor   185
Paid ere he promis'd, whereby his suit was granted
Ere it was ask'd) but when the way was made

---

172. court-cardinal] *Pope;* Count-Cardinall *F.*   183. him: privily] him.
Privily *F;* him. He privily *F2.*   184–7. trow / (Which . . . well; . . . sure . . . /
. . . ask'd)] *Cam. 1865 (after Var. 1778);* troa / Which . . . well; . . . sure
. . . / . . . ask'd. *F;* trow,— / Which . . . well, . . . sure,— . . . / . . . ask'd:
Staunton.

---

conditions, terms of the treaty; 'draw'
is the usual verb, cf. *3 H 6,* III. iii. 135;
we now say 'draw up'. For "combination" meaning 'league', see
Tw. N., v. i. 392. Holinshed says,
p. 858, "the king . . . had given unto
the said cardinall full authoritie . . . to
affirme and confirme, bind and un-
bind, whatsoever should be in question
betweene him and the French king:
and the like . . . did the French king . . .
grant".

172. *court-cardinal*] Pope's emendation of "count-" (F)—a probable misreading of a raised *r* as an abbreviation
for *n*—has been adopted; "court-
cardinal" makes sense, cf. "king-
cardinal" (II. ii. 19), and there is no
hint in the chronicles of Capell's ingenious solution, that Wolsey was
'Count-Palatine' by virtue of holding
the bishopric of Durham *in commendam.*

176. *dam*] bitch; female parent of
animals.

176–90. *Charles . . . peace*] These lines
are based on Holinshed's account,
p. 856, of the visit of Charles in May
1520: see Appendix II, p. 187.

178. *colour*] pretext; cf. *Wint.,* IV. iv.
566, "What colour for my visitation
shall I / Hold up before him?"
(Pooler).

179. *visitation*] Shakespeare's usual
word, cf. previous note; *visit* became
current only after 1620 (*O.E.D.*).

183. *privily*] secretly. As it stands this
line is a syllable short, and "he
privily" (F2) has generally been
adopted; it has no authority. For
similar short lines, see I. ii. 87 and III. ii
88 below.

184. *trow*] believe. The passion of the
speaker is too much for his grammar,
but the sense is clear, cf. above, ll. 59 ff.

And pav'd with gold, the emperor thus desir'd,
That he would please to alter the king's course
And break the foresaid peace. Let the king know   190
(As soon he shall by me) that thus the cardinal
Does buy and sell his honour as he pleases,
And for his own advantage.

Nor.   I am sorry
To hear this of him, and could wish he were
Something mistaken in't.

Buck.   No, not a syllable: 195
I do pronounce him in that very shape
He shall appear in proof.

Buck seems in a position of strength reversal

Enter BRANDON, *a Sergeant at Arms before him, and two or three of
the Guard.*

Bran. Your office Sergeant; execute it.
Serg.   Sir,   *Arrest of Buckingham*
My lord the Duke of Buckingham, and Earl
Of Hereford, Stafford and Northampton, I   200
Arrest thee of high treason, in the name
Of our most sovereign king.

---

194. he were] *F;* you were *F4.*   200. Hereford] *Capell;* Hertford *F.*

192. *buy and sell*] traffic in (Pooler),
cf. *Meas.,* III. ii. 2; the phrase is proverbial, meaning 'to betray for bribes',
see Tilley B 787, *R 3,* v. iii. 305
(Malone) and *Cor.,*III.ii. 10.

195. *Something mistaken*] misjudged
to some extent; cf. below, III. i. 101,
and *AYL.,* I. iii. 66, "mistake me not
so much / To think my poverty is
treacherous" for this common meaning. For "something"=somewhat, see
Tp., III.i. 58.

196. *pronounce*] announce, make
known.

197. *in proof*] in experience; cf.
*Ham.,*IV. vii. 155 (Pooler), and *Cym.,*I.
vi. 69, "who knows / By history, report, or his own proof, / What woman
is . . .?"

S.D. Brandon . . . Arms] The
sovereign has a body of Sergeants-at-
Arms of the rank of knights, whose

duties are to attend him or her and to
arrest traitors. Holinshed, p. 863, says
Buckingham was arrested by "Sir
Henrie Marneie, capteine of the
gard". Shakespeare may have been
thinking here of Charles Brandon,
Duke of Suffolk, who appears as Suffolk in II. ii; if so, this would make
sense perhaps of "my lords", l. 226
(F). Boswell-Stone suggests Sir
Thomas Brandon, master of the king's
horse, a pointless identification.

200. *Hereford*] Capell's correction
from Holinshed of "Hertford" (F), for
which there is no source; a possible
compositor's misreading, or perhaps
an expansion of MS 'Herford', cf. *R 2,*
I. iii. 1 ff. where 'Hereford' is spelled
'Herford' in Q1, and *R 3,* IV. v. 7,
where 'Haverford-west' appears as
"Herford-west" (Q2) and "Hertford-
west" (Q3).

Buck.   Loe you, my lord,
    The net has fall'n upon me; I shall perish
    Under device and practice.

Bran.   I am sorry
    To see you ta'en from liberty, to look on   205
    The business present. 'Tis his highness' pleasure
    You shall to th'Tower.

Buck.   It will help me nothing
    To plead mine innocence, for that dye is on me
    Which makes my whit'st part black. The will of heav'n
    Be done in this and all things: I obey.   210
    O my lord Aberga'nny, fare you well.

Bran. Nay, he must bear you company. [*To Abergavenny*]
        The king
    Is pleas'd you shall to th'Tower, till you know
    How he determines further.

Aber.   As the duke said,
    The will of Heaven be done, and the king's pleasure   215
    By me obey'd.

Bran.   Here is a warrant from
    The king t'attach Lord Montacute, and the bodies
    Of the duke's confessor, John de la Car,
    One Gilbert Perk, his chancellor—

---

205. liberty, to] *F*; liberty to *Keightley*.   208. dye] *F*; die *Var. 1821.*   211.
Aberga'nny] Aburgany *F*; Avergavenny *Rowe 1.*   212. S.D. *To Abergavenny*]
Johnson; not in F.   217. Montacute] Mountacute *F*; Montague *Rowe.*
218. Car] *F*; Court *Theobald 2.*   219. One] *F*; And *Pope 2 (from Theobald).*
Perk] *This Ed. (from Holinshed)*; Pecke *F.*   chancellor] *Pope 2, after Theobald;*
Councellour *F.*

202. *Loe you*] look you, behold,
as in *Wint.*, I. ii. 106, "Why, lo you
now, I have spoke to the purpose
twice".

203. *net*] probably an allusion to
catching birds, cf. below, III. ii. 282,
and *Mac.*, IV. ii. 34.

204. *device and practice*] trickery and
intrigue; cf. *Oth.*, II. iii. 394, and *Cor.*,
IV. i. 33.

205. *to look on*] i.e. and sorry to be a
witness of (Johnson).

207. *nothing*] not at all, cf. "something", l. 195.

211. *Aberga'nny*] F's spelling "Abur-

gany" indicates a common pronunciation of the time, not used in Holinshed's account, but see *Captain Thomas
Stukeley* (1605; T.F.T. 1911), A4ʳ,
where also "Aburgany" is found, and
Chamberlain, *Letters*, I. 415 (February
1613), where he refers to "Lady Aber-
geyney".

217. *attach*] arrest, cf. l. 95.

219. *Perk . . . chancellor*] Holinshed
has, p. 863, "sir Gilbert Perke priest,
the dukes chancellor". It is usual to
emend "councellor" in accordance
(cf. II. i. 20 below), but not "Pecke"
(F), which is much more likely to be a

Buck.   So, so;

   These are the limbs o'th'plot: no more I hope.   220

Bran. A monk o'th'Chartreux.

Buck.   O, Nicholas Hopkins?

Bran.   He.

Buck. My surveyor is false: the o'er-great cardinal

   Hath show'd him gold; my life is spann'd already:

   I am the shadow of poor Buckingham,

   Whose figure even this instant cloud puts on   225

   By dark'ning my clear <u>sun</u>. My lord, farewell.   *Exe[unt]*.

earlier used of monarchs

221. Nicholas] *Pope 2 (from Theobald, after Holinshed)*; Michaell *F.*   225.
figure . . . instant] *F;* figure, . . . instant, *Becket conj.*   226. By dark'ning] *F;*
Be-darkening *Steevens conj.*   lord] *Rowe;* Lords *F.*

misreading, as *c* and some forms of *r*
are easily confused in secretary hand.

  220. *limbs*] such imagery from the
body is especially frequent in this
play, cf. l. 46 above; for possible overtones of meaning, see v. iii. 63 and n.

  221. *Nicholas*] Theobald's correction, from Holinshed, of "Michaell"
(F), brings this passage into conform-
ity with i. ii. 147: *Mic.* could be an
easy misreading of *Nic.* in secretary
hand.

  222. *surveyor*] see above, l. 115.

  223. *spann'd*] measured out (*O.E.D.*
2c); limited (Onions); the verb occurs
nowhere else in Shakespeare. For *span*
= the duration of a life, cf. Psalm
xxxviii. 5 and *Tim.*, v. iii. 3, "Timon is
dead, who hath outstretch'd his span"
(cited Pooler).

  224–6. *I . . . sun*] a difficult passage;
"shadow" may mean 'semblance,
mere appearance' (often contrasted
with "substance", cf. *Ham.*, ii. ii. 265),
'departed spirit', as at *Cym.*, v. iv. 97,
or, Pooler suggests, 'picture', cf.
MND., v. i. 430. "Figure" has generally been interpreted as 'form, shape'

but may allude to a horoscope, a
figure of heaven, cf. Webster, *Duchess
of Malfi* (1614), ii. ii. 92, "I'll presently / Goe set a figure for's Nativitie".
"Instant" may be a noun, or an
adjective meaning 'now present'
(Onions), or 'impending', a sense not
elsewhere found in Shakespeare;
"cloud" may mean 'the heavens', or
'trouble', 'affliction', or 'gloom', or,
like "shadow", be a type of the fleeting
and unsubstantial; finally, "sun" may
refer to Buckingham or Henry. These
various double meanings enrich the
connections between the words, but
complicate the sense of the passage,
which may be interpreted, 'I am the
semblance of poor Buckingham, whose
form (and future) at this instant are
clothed in afflictions, in clouds, because I have darkened my bright self,
and made angry my king'. For "sun"
cf. ll. 6, 33, 56.

  226. *lord*] Rowe's correction of
"lords" (F), which may be right if
Buckingham is speaking to Norfolk
and Brandon; see note on l. 197
S.D

SCENE II—[*The same. A council-chamber.*]

Cornets. Enter KING HENRY, *leaning on the* CARDINAL's *shoulder, the Nobles, and* SIR THOMAS LOVELL: *the Cardinal places himself under the King's feet on his right side.* [*A Secretary of the Cardinal's is in attendance.*]

King. My life itself, and the best heart of it,
Thanks you for this great care: I stood i'th'level
Of a full-charg'd confederacy, and give thanks
To you that chok'd it. Let be call'd before us
That gentleman of Buckingham's; in person   5
I'll hear him his confessions justify,
And point by point the treasons of his master
He shall again relate.

A noise within crying room for the Queen, [*who is*] *usher'd by the Duke of Norfolk. Enter the* QUEEN, NORFOLK *and* SUFFOLK: *she kneels.* KING *riseth from his state, takes her up, kisses and placeth her by him.*

Scene II

Scene II] *Scena Secunda. F.   The same.*] *Staunton; A council-chamber. This Ed.; The council-chamber. Theobald.   Entry. A . . . attendance*] *This Ed., not in F.* 5. Buckingham's; in person] *Johnson; Buckinghams,* in person, *F;* Buckingham's in person, *Rowe.*   8. S.D. *who is*] *not in F; Enter the* Queen *usher'd by the Dukes of* Norfolk, *and* Suffolk. *Theobald.*

Scene II.] Katherine's championship of the people in their grievances seems to be the dramatist's invention: the commissions and the rebellion of the weavers belong to 1525, Knevet's betrayal of Buckingham to 1521; for Holinshed's accounts, see Appendix II, pp. 188–93.

Entry. under . . . feet] The 'state' or throne was raised, perhaps on a dais.

1. *best heart*] very essence, most precious part (Johnson).

2. *level*] literally, the line of fire or range of a weapon (*O.E.D.* sb. 9), cf. *Wint.*, II. iii. 6, "beyond mine arm, out of the blank / And level of my brain, plot-proof".

3. *full-charg'd*] fully loaded, cf. *John*, II. i. 382 (Pooler).

confederacy] conspiracy, cf. *1 H 4*, IV. iv. 38 (Clarendon Ed.).

4. *chok'd it*] suppressed it. Pooler, following the Clarendon Ed., sees here a continuation of the metaphor from cannon, citing B. and F. *Mad Lover* (*Works*, III. 5), "If he mount at me, / I may chance choak his Battery", but this is hardly appropriate to a "full-charg'd" cannon.

5. *gentleman*] man of gentle birth attached to his household, superior servant, cf. *Tw. N.*, V. i. 183.

6. *justify*] confirm, verify, cf. *Wint.*, I. ii. 278, and Pooler compares *Tp.*, V. i. 128, "I here could . . . justify you traitors".

8. S.D. state] canopied throne, chair of state, cf. *Cor.*, V. iv. 22.

Kath. Nay, we must longer kneel; I am a suitor.

King. Arise, and take place by us; half your suit   10
    Never name to us; you have half our power,
    The other moiety ere you ask is given;
    Repeat your will and take it.

Kath.   Thank your majesty;
    That you would love yourself, and in that love
    Not unconsider'd leave your honour nor   15
    The dignity of your office, is the point
    Of my petition.

King.   Lady mine, proceed.

Kath. I am solicited not by a few,
    And those of true condition, that your subjects
    Are in great grievance: there have been commissions   20
    Sent down among 'em, which hath flaw'd the heart
    Of all their loyalties; wherein, although
    My good lord cardinal they vent reproaches
    Most bitterly on you, as putter on
    Of these exactions, yet the king, our master   25
    Whose honour heaven shield from soil,—even he
        escapes not

9 ff. S.H. *Kath.*] *Queen. F.*   21. *hath*] *F; have F4.*   25-6. king, . . . master /
. . . soil,—] *This Ed.;* King, . . . Maister / . . . soile; *F;* king . . . master— /
. . . soil— *Capell.*

10. *take place*] sit, perhaps with the idea of sitting in state, cf. II. iv. Entry, v. ii. 167 and *All's W.*, I. i. 114, "these fix'd evils sit so fit in him, / That they take place": "place" is "the space which one person occupies by usage, allotment or right . . ." (*O.E.D.* sb. 13).

12. *moiety*] half.

13. *Repeat . . . will*] state your desire; for "repeat"=relate, see *Mac.*, IV. iii. 112 and below v. i. 96.

19. *true condition*] loyal nature or character, cf. *Cor.*, V. iv. 10, "Is't possible that so short a time can alter the condition of a man?", and *Tim.*, IV. iii. 139.

20. *grievance*] distress, cf. *Sonn.*, xxx. 9, "Then can I grieve at grievances foregone".

commissions] writs of authority (here for collecting taxes). See Holinshed, p. 891, ". . . by the cardinall there was devised strange commissions . . . that the sixt part of everie mans substance should be paid in monie or plate to the king without delaie. . . Hereof followed such cursing, weeping, and exclamations against both king & cardinall, that pitie it was to heare".

21. *flaw'd*] cracked, broken; i.e. has almost killed their loyalty, cf. above, I. i. 95.

24. *putter on*] instigator (Malone); elsewhere in Shakespeare only at *Wint.*, II. i. 141.

26. *soil*] moral stain, as at *Troil.*, II. ii. 148, "I would have the soil of her fair rape / Wiped off, in honourable keeping her".

Language unmannerly, yea, such which breaks
The sides of loyalty, and almost appears
In loud rebellion.

Nor.   Not almost appears,
It doth appear; for, upon these taxations,   30
The clothiers all not able to maintain
The many to them longing, have put off
The spinsters, carders, fullers, weavers, who,
Unfit for other life, compell'd by hunger
And lack of other means, in desperate manner   35
Daring th' event to th' teeth, are all in uproar,
And danger serves among them.

King.   Taxation?
Wherein? and what taxation? my lord cardinal,
You that are blam'd for it alike with us,
Know you of this taxation?

Wol.   Please you sir,   40

---

32. many] *F;* meiny *Johnson conj.*   longing] *F;* 'longing *F4.*   40 ff. S.H.
Wol.] Card. F.

27–9. *such . . . rebellion*] Holinshed
merely has, p. 891, "the commons were
in everie place so mooved, that it was
like to grow to rebellion", and Speed,
p. 861, "and almost grew to an open
rebellion".

27–8. *breaks | The sides*] a metaphor
from the body, common in Shakespeare, meaning bursts the bounds;
see *Cym.,* i. vi. 69, "Can my sides
hold . . . ?", and *Ant.,* iv. xiv. 39, "O,
cleave, my sides . . ."

30–7. *for . . . them*] For dramatic purposes Shakespeare makes a local stir in
Suffolk appear a general uprising; see
Holinshed's report, Appendix ii, p.
193.

32. *many . . . longing*] the large number of their servants or work-people:
"longing" is the simple verb from
which the compound *belong* derives, cf.
All's W., iv. ii. 42 and below, ii. iii. 48.
Johnson read "many" as "meiny",
train, household.

put off] dismissed from employment;
the first instance known to *O.E.D.* Cf.

below, ii. iv. 19 for a similar usage.

33. *spinsters*] spinners, usually female, as at *Tw. N.,* ii. iv. 45. Pooler
notes that "spinner" in Shakespeare
means spider, cf. *MND.,* ii. ii. 21;
Rom., i. iv. 59.

carders, fullers] to card is to comb
wool ready for spinning; to full cloth
is to beat it in order to clean or thicken
it.

36. *Daring . . . teeth*] challenging the
outcome with open defiance; cf. *Ham.,*
iv. vii. 57, "I shall live and tell him to
his teeth, 'Thus diddest thou'". The
idea was fairly commonplace, see
O.E.D., tooth, sb. 6b.

37. *danger*] probably mischief, as in
Cæs., ii. i. 16, "we put a sting in him, /
That at his will he may do danger
with". Pooler says, "the personification may have been suggested by the
rebels' answer to Norfolk", as recorded
in Holinshed, p. 891, "that Povertie
was their capteine, the which with his
cousin Necessitie, had brought them
to that dooing".

I know but of a single part in aught
Pertains to th' state, and front but in that file
Where others tell steps with me.

Kath.   No, my lord,
You know no more than others; but you frame   44
Things that are known alike, which are not wholesome
To those which would not know them, and yet must
Perforce be their acquaintance. These exactions
(Whereof my sovereign would have note) they are
Most pestilent to th'hearing, and to bear 'em
The back is sacrifice to th'load; they say   50
They are devis'd by you, or else you suffer
Too hard an exclamation.

King.   Still exaction:
The nature of it, in what kind let's know,
Is this exaction.

Kath.   I am much too venturous
In tempting of your patience, but am bolden'd   55
Under your promis'd pardon. The subjects' grief
Comes through commissions, which compels from each

43-4. lord, / . . . others;] *F4*; Lord? / . . . others? *F*; lord; / . . . others! *Kittredge.*
55. bolden'd] *Pope;* boldned *F.*   57. compels] *F*; compel *Pope.*

41-2. *I . . . state*] Wolsey says he knows of only one person's share (i.e. his own) in anything concerning the tate.

42. *front . . . file*] "I am first in order rather than in power, more conspicuous not more influential, just as the first of a file of soldiers is" (Pooler). *O.E.D.* cites as a unique use meaning 'march in the front rank'; *file* has many meanings, but never seems to be confused with *rank*. Cf. III. ii. 171 and n., and I. i. 75, v. iii. 55.

43. *tell steps*] count steps, i.e. march in step.

44-7. *you . . . acquaintance*] i.e. you originate measures that are known to all alike, measures which those men to whom they are not beneficial and who dislike or reject them yet must accept. Katherine is accusing Wolsey of controlling the Council.

48. *note*] knowledge, cf. I. i. 63.

50. *sacrifice*] a compositor's mis-reading of "sacrificd"?

52. *exclamation*] reproach; always so used in Shakespeare, and the apparent exception in *Ado*, III. v. 28, is a malapropism of Dogberry's (Pooler). It is Holinshed's word too, see citation above, l. 20 n.

53. *in . . . kind*] i.e. what form does it take? For "kind" meaning 'manner', 'form', see *Lr.*, IV. vi. 166, "Thou hotly lust'st to use her in that kind / For which thou whipp'st her", and *O.E.D.* kind, sb. 8.

55. *bolden'd*] made bold; it occurs once elsewhere in Shakespeare, at *AYL.*, II. vii. 91.

56. *grief*] grievance, as at *Cæs.*, I. iii. 118, "for redress of all these griefs" (Pooler).

57. *compels*] this form of third person plural is very common in Shakespeare; see Abbott 332-3.

The sixth part of his substance, to be levied
Without delay; and the pretence for this
Is nam'd your wars in France: this makes bold mouths,
Tongues spit their duties out, and cold hearts freeze   61
Allegiance in them; their curses now
Live where their prayers did; and it's come to pass
This tractable obedience is a slave
To each incensed will. I would your highness   65
Would give it quick consideration; for
There is no primer baseness.

King.   By my life,
This is against our pleasure.
Wol.   And for me,
I have no further gone in this than by
A single voice, and that not pass'd me but   70
By learned approbation of the judges: if I am
Traduc'd by ignorant tongues, which neither know
My faculties nor person, yet will be
The chronicles of my doing, let me say
'Tis but the fate of place, and the rough brake   75

58. sixth] sixt *F*.   64. This] *F;* That *Rowe;* Their *Collier 2*.   67. baseness] *F;*
business *Hanmer*.

58. *substance*] wealth; a common
biblical usage, see Psalm xvii. 4, and
also *2 H 4*, ii. i. 81.

62. *Allegiance*] here four syllables
(Clarendon Ed.).

64–5. *This . . . will*] i.e. the people's
readiness to obey has given way to
anger.

67. *primer baseness*] mischief more
urgently in need of redress; for
"primer", cf. *Tp.*, i. ii. 425, "my prime
request [= first in importance] /
Which I do last pronounce", cited by
O.E.D. as the first use in this sense.
"Baseness" has usually been emended
to "business" following Hanmer; the
latter occurs many times in the play,
cf. i. i. 206, ii. ii. 23, 56, 69, 71, etc., and
a misreading is plausible, but "baseness" is a Shakespearian word, makes
sense, and is much more expressive of
Katherine's feeling.

70. *single voice*] unanimous vote. For

"single" = undivided, cf. *Mac.*, i. iii.
140, "shakes so my single state of
man", and for "voice"= vote, cf. *Cor.*,
ii. iii. 112, "We . . . give you our voices
heartily". The sense is made clear by
the passage in Holinshed from which
this is taken, pp. 891–2, "The cardinall excused himselfe, and said . . .
the kings councell, and namelie the
judges, said, that he might lawfullie
demand anie summe by commission,
and that by consent of the whole
councell it was doone . . ."

72. *Traduc'd*] defamed.

73. *faculties*] personal qualities, as at
2 H 4, ii. iv. 273, or perhaps 'powers',
cf. *Mac.*, i. vii. 17 and K. Muir's note
ad loc. (Arden Ed.).

75. *place*] office, rank.

brake] literally a thicket or clump of
bushes, cf. *MND.*, iii. i. 110, "Through
bog, through bush, through brake,
through brier".

That virtue must go through: we must not stint
Our necessary actions in the fear
To cope malicious censurers, which ever
As rav'nous fishes, do a vessel follow
That is new trimm'd, but benefit no further　　　80
Than vainly longing. What we oft do best,
By sick interpreters (once weak ones) is
Not ours or not allow'd; what worst, as oft
Hitting a grosser quality, is cried up
For our best act. If we shall stand still,　　　85
In fear our motion will be mock'd or carp'd at,

18. censurers] *F;* censures *Pope 2.*　　82. sick] *F;* such *Keightley conj.*　　once] *F;*
or *Pope;* and *Becket conj.*　　83. oft] *F;* oft, *Capell.*　　85. act] *F;* action *Capell.*
86. motion] *F;* notion *Camb. 1892.*

76. *stint*] hold in check, discontinue, cf. *Tim.,* v. iv. 83, "make peace stint war".

78. *cope*] encounter, as at *AYL.,* ii. i. 67, "I love to cope him in these sullen fits" (Steevens). Originally, to join battle, to fight, and something of this sense may be preserved here, cf. *Troil.,* i. ii. 34.

80. *new trimm'd*] newly fitted out for sea. Pooler cites Holinshed, p. 872, "All the kings ships were put in a readinesse, so that . . . they were rigged and trimmed readie to make saile". Malicious critics are compared to sharks which follow a seaworthy and secure vessel to no purpose.

81–3. *What . . . allow'd*] what we often do best is attributed to others or condemned by interpreters who have formerly been wavering or foolish and are now envious or corrupt in judgement. For "sick", see below, ii. 82, ii. iv. 202, and *Troil.,* i. iii. 132, where "sick / Of his superior" means 'envious of' (Onions). "Weak ones" in the Biblical sense means people of unsound faith, cf. 1 Corinthians, viii. 11, "And through thy knowledge shall the weake brother perishe" (Bishop's Bible), and *O.E.D.* weak, 2b; Shakespeare uses this word to mean 'weak of mind' in *Tp.,* ii. ii. 149, "a very shallow monster! . . . A very weak monster! . . .

A most poor credulous monster!", but the former sense is preferable here. "Once" has been read as meaning 'once for all', 'in a word', for which there are one or two possible examples in Shakespeare, cf. *Cor.,* ii. iii. 1 and Abbott 57; so Pooler explains, "by persons incapable of a sound judgment, in fact of weak understanding", but one would then have expected "sick" to follow "weak" in the text' For "allowed" meaning 'approved', cf. *Troil.,* iii. ii. 98, "praise us as we are tasted, allow us as we prove" (Pooler), and below, ii. iv. 4.

83–4. *as . . . quality*] ambiguous; "quality" may refer to the action or to the response to it, so that the sense may be either 'falling in with, catching favour with, a coarser element of people', or 'achieving an inferior level of attainment'. For "quality" in the first sense, cf. *1 H 4,* iv. iii. 36, "Because you are not of our quality, / But stand against us like an enemy"; for the second sense, 'attainment', see *Tim.,* i. i. 125, "I have bred her at my dearest cost / In qualities of the best". The first meaning is preferable, as carrying on from "interpreters" in l. 82. Most edd., following Capell, add a comma after "oft", for which there is no authority.

86. *motion*] with the double sense

We should take root here, where we sit;
Or sit state-statues only.

King.   Things done well
And with a care exempt themselves from fear;
Things done without example, in their issue   90
Are to be fear'd. Have you a precedent
Of this commission? I believe, not any.
We must not rend our subjects from our laws
And stick them in our will. Sixth part of each?
A trembling contribution; why, we take   95
From every tree lop, bark and part o' th' timber,
And though we leave it with a root, thus hack'd,
The air will drink the sap. To every county
Where this is question'd, send our letters, with
Free pardon to each man that has denied   100
The force of this commission: pray look to 't;
I put it to your care.

Wol.   [*To the secretary*] A word with you.
Let there be letters writ to every shire,
Of the king's grace and pardon. The grieved commons
Hardly conceive of me: let it be nois'd   105

*Wolsey
gives himself
benefit of praise
for his act*

87–8. sit; / Or sit] *F*; sit: or sit / *Hanmer*.   91. precedent] President *F*.
94. Sixth] Sixt *F*.   95. trembling] *F*; trebling *Collier 2*.   97. root, thus]
Theobald; roote thus *F*.   102. S.D. *To . . . secretary*] *Rowe*; *not in F*.   104.
grieved] *F*; griev'd *Rowe*.

of movement and of proposition.

87. *We . . . sit*] the emphatic quality
of this line, and the dissyllabic force of
"here", compensate for its shortness;
cf. I. i. 183.

90. *example*] precedent, cf. *Ant.*, III.
x. 28.

issue] outcome.

94. *stick . . . will*] fasten in our will,
i.e. deal with them (possibly stab,
destroy them) according to our pleasure. For the latter sense, see *Troil.*,
III. ii. 202, "to stick the heart of false-
hood".

95. *trembling*] causing trepidation,
fearful; cf. "trembling winter", *Wint.*,
IV. iv. 81 (Pooler) and W. Parkes,
Curtaine-Drawer of the World (1612),
G2ʳ, "a very fearefull and trembling

sinne it is to be the author of anothers
destruction".

96. *lop*] "the smaller branches and
twigs of trees, such as are not measured
for timber" (*O.E.D.*, lop sb. 1).

98–108. *To . . . proceeding*] these lines
follow Holinshed closely; see Appendix II, p. 193.

101. *force*] validity, power, cf. *John*,
III. iii. 11, "Use our commission in his
utmost force". There is no parallel for
Pooler's interpretation, "rejected the
enforcement".

104. *grace*] mercy.

105. *Hardly conceive*] think harshly,
have a bad opinion; cf. *Cym.*, III. iii. 8,
"use thee not so hardly / As prouder
livers do".

nois'd] rumoured, as at *Tim.*, IV. iii.

That through our intercession this revokement
And pardon comes: I shall anon advise you
Further in the proceeding.   *Exit Secret[ary].*

Enter Surveyor.

Kath. I am sorry that the Duke of Buckingham
Is run in your displeasure.

King.   It grieves many: 110
The gentleman is learn'd, and a most rare speaker,
To nature none more bound; his training such
That he may furnish and instruct great teachers,
And never seek for aid out of himself: yet see,
When these so noble benefits shall prove   115
Not well dispos'd, the mind growing once corrupt,
They turn to vicious forms, ten times more ugly
Than ever they were fair. This man so complete,
Who was enroll'd 'mongst wonders (and when we,
Almost with ravish'd list'ning, could not find   120
His hour of speech a minute) he, my lady,
Hath into monstrous habits put the graces

Severe but right

---

109. I am] *F;* I'm *Pope.*   114. yet see] *F;* separate line *Capell.*   119-21. wonders (and . . . / . . . / . . . minute)] *This Ed.;* wonders; and . . . / . . . / . . . minute: *F.*   120. ravish'd list'ning] *F;* list'ning ravish'd *Pope.*

404, "It is noised he hath a mass of treasure".

106. *revokement*] a coinage, not earlier recorded in *O.E.D.*

109. *Is run in*] has incurred, cf. *All's W.,* II. v. 39 (Clarendon Ed.).

111. *learn'd*] as Pooler notes, Holinshed merely says, p. 865, "he was an eloquent man".

rare] excellent.

112. *bound*] indebted, i.e. for natural abilities.

114. *out of himself*] beyond his own mind; cf. below, III. ii. 13.

115. *benefits*] natural advantages, cf. *AYL.,* IV. i. 34, "disable all the benefits of your own country" (Onions).

116. *dispos'd*] directed, cf. above, I. i. 43 and *H 5,* IV. iii. 132, "And how thou pleasest, God, dispose the day!". Onions and Pooler interpret as 'be-

stowed', 'placed', as in *Troil.,* IV. v. 116, "His blows are well disposed", but this would suggest a mind already corrupt.

117. *vicious*] evil, cf. *Ham.,* I. iv. 24.

118. *complete*] accomplished. Accented on the first syllable, as is usual in Shakespeare when the word is used attributively; when used predicatively, as at III. ii. 49, it is accented on the second.

120. *ravish'd*] entranced.

122. *habits*] either 'appearance', 'shape', from *habit* = dress (so Pooler), or 'moral qualities', 'habits of mind', as in Burton, *Anatomy of Melancholy* (1621; ed. A. R. Shilleto, 1893, I. 192), "The principal *habits* are two in number, *virtue* and *vice* . . .". Perhaps both senses are intended.

That once were his, and is become as black
As if besmear'd in hell. Sit by us, you shall hear   125
(This was his gentleman in trust) of him
Things to strike honour sad. Bid him recount
The fore-recited practices, whereof
We cannot feel too little, hear too much.

Wol. Stand forth, and with bold spirit relate what you
Most like a careful subject have collected   130
Out of the Duke of Buckingham.

King.   Speak freely.

Surv. First, it was usual with him, every day
It would infect his speech, that if the king
Should without issue die, he'll carry it so
To make the sceptre his. These very words   135
I've heard him utter to his son-in-law,
Lord Aberga'nny, to whom by oath he menac'd
Revenge upon the cardinal.

Wol.   Please your highness note
This dangerous conception in this point,
Not friended by his wish to your high person;   140
His will is most malignant, and it stretches
Beyond you to your friends.

Kath.   My learn'd lord cardinal,
Deliver all with charity.

---

132. S.H. *Surv.*] *Sur. F.*   him, every day] *Pope;* him; every day *F;* him every day *F4;* him every day, *Rowe.*   134. he'll] *F;* he'd *Pope.*   137. Aberga'nny] *Aburgany F;* Abergavenny *Rowe 1.*   139. This dangerous] *F;* His dangerous *Pope.*   139–40. point, / . . . wish to . . . person;] *so F;* point: . . . wish to . . . person, *Pope;* point: / . . . wish, to . . . person / *Hanmer.*

125. *gentleman in trust*] confidential servant.

i.1 127. *practices*] intrigues, cf. above .204.

130. *collected*] sc. evidence.

132–8. *First . . . cardinal*] the surveyor's accusations are taken from Holinshed, p. 862, "the duke was accustomed by waie of talke, to saie, how he so meant to the use matter, that he would atteine to the crowne, if king Henrie chanced to die without issue". For the full account, see Appendix II, p. 188.

134. *carry it*] manage affairs.

140–2. *Not . . . friends*] not helped by, not successful in his wish that the king should die childless, his disposition is most evil, and goes beyond the king to affect his friends as well. Most editors, following Pope, have altered the punctuation to read "to your high person / His will is most malignant", but so far there has been no threat to the king, and the Folio pointing gives the better sense. For "friended" in its sense here, Pooler compares *Cym.,* II. iii. 52, "be friended / With aptness of the season".

143. *Deliver . . . charity*] tell without

King.   Speak on;
How grounded he his title to the crown
Upon our fail? to this point hast thou heard him   145
At any time speak aught?
Surv.   He was brought to this
By a vain prophecy of Nicholas Henton.
King. What was that Henton?
Surv.   Sir, a Chartreux friar,   *Anti clerical*
His confessor, who fed him every minute
With words of sovereignty.
King.   How know'st thou this?   150
Surv. Not long before your highness sped to France,
The duke being at the Rose, within the parish
Saint Lawrence Poultney, did of me demand
What was the speech among the Londoners
Concerning the French journey. I replied,   155
Men fear'd the French would prove perfidious,
To the king's danger: presently the duke
Said 'twas the fear indeed, and that he doubted
'Twould prove the verity of certain words
Spoke by a holy monk, that oft, says he,   160

145. fail?] *Rowe 3;* faile; *F.*   147, 148. Henton] *F;* Hopkins *Pope 2 (from Theobald).*   156. fear'd] *Pope;* feare *F.*

spite, charitably; for "deliver" in this sense, formerly common, see *Wint.,* v. ii. 4, "heard the old shepherd deliver the manner how he found it", and below, II. ii. 136, II. iii. 106.

145. *fail*] failure to have children, or more probably, death, as at l. 184, "had the king in his last sickness fail'd". For the first sense see II. iv. 196.

147. *Henton*] Theobald corrected to "Hopkins", in accordance with Holinshed and I. i. 221; Henton was the name of the priory, but as Pooler noted, the chronicler's words account for the error, "a vaine prophesie which one Nicholas Hopkins, a monke of an house of the Chartreux order beside Bristow, called Henton, sometime his confessor had opened unto him" (p. 863).

151–71. *Not . . . England*] This pas-

sage is an interesting dramatization of Holinshed, p. 864; see Appendix II, pp. 189–90.

152. *Rose*] Stow, *Survey of London* (1618), p. 437, speaks of "one notable Grammar Schoole, founded in the yeere 1561 by the . . . Marchant-Taylors, in the parish of Saint *Laurence Poultney.* Richard Hilles . . . having before given 500li. towards the purchase of an house, called the *Mannor of the Rose,* sometime belonging to the Duke of *Buckingham*".

154. *speech*] report, cf. *All's W.,* II. v. 57.

156. *fear'd*] *feare* in F; but *e* and *d* look alike in secretary hand, and this would be the easiest of misreadings.

157. *presently*] at once, promptly, the usual sense in Shakespeare; Pooler cites *Tp.,* IV. i. 42, "Presently?—Ay, with a twink".

Hath sent to me, wishing me to permit
John de la Car, my chaplain, a choice hour
To hear from him a matter of some moment:
Whom after under the confession's seal
He solemnly had sworn, that what he spoke   165
My chaplain to no creature living but
To me should utter, with demure confidence
This pausingly ensued: neither the king nor's heirs
(Tell you the duke) shall prosper; bid him strive
To [win] the love o'th'commonalty; the duke   170
Shall govern England.

Kath.   If I know you well,
You were the duke's surveyor, and lost your office
On the complaint o'th'tenants; take good heed
You charge not in your spleen a noble person
And spoil your nobler soul; I say, take heed;   175

---

162. Car] *F;* Court *Theobald 2 (from Holinshed).*   164. Whom] *F;* Who *Pope.*
confession's] *Theobald (from Holinshed);* Commissions *F.*   170. To [win] the
love] *Sisson (reading* To win the love*);* To the love *F;* To gain the love *F4.*
175. nobler] *F;* Noble *F2.*

162. *choice hour*] fitting time (Pooler).

163. *moment*] importance.

164. *confession's*] Theobald's correction of "Commissions" (F). Holinshed, p. 863, has, ". . . to bind his chapleine John de la Court, under the seale of confession, to keepe secret such matter". The mistake is perhaps due to the frequent occurrence of "commission" earlier, see ll. 20, 57, 92, 101. Theobald, in his 1740 edition, also altered "Car" to "Court" here and at I. i. 218, II. i. 20.

167. *demure confidence*] solemn assurance, so possibly, 'intimacy', 'trust'. For "demure", see *Tw. N.,* II. v. 59 (Pooler). The usual meaning of "confidence" in Shakespeare is boldness, certainty, but the two senses may merge, as at *Tp.,* I. ii. 97.

168. *pausingly*] with pauses in his speaking; apparently a coinage, cf. I. i. 87 and n.

170. *To . . . commonalty*] so Sisson; most editors read "gain the love" with F4. It seems certain that a word has been missed out. "Commonalty", Holinshed's word for the common people, occurs only here and in *Cor.,* I. i. 29 in Shakespeare.

172. *surveyor*] see above, I. i. 115. The rest of this scene is closely based on Holinshed, pp. 856, 864; see Appendix II, pp. 186–7, 189–90.

174. *spleen*] malice. The organ was regarded as the seat of mirth and of melancholy, and various meanings accrued in the 16th century, 'caprice', 'fit of passion', and hence 'anger'. Shakespeare uses it in a variety of senses.

175. *spoil*] ruin, destroy, cf. *Oth.,* v. i. 54, "O, I am spoil'd, undone by villains".

nobler soul] a play on the meanings of "noble" as relating to rank and moral qualities; perhaps an allusion to the Rational soul, held to distinguish man from animals (having a Sensible soul), and plants (having a Vegetable soul): see Burton, *Anatomy of Melancholy,* ed. Shilleto, I. 176 ff.

Yes, heartily beseech you.

King.   Let him on:
Go forward.

Surv.   On my <u>soul</u>, I'll speak but truth.
I told my lord the duke, by th'devil's illusions
The monk might be deceived, and that 'twas dangerous
For him to ruminate on this so far until   180
It forg'd him some design, which being believ'd
It was much like to do: he answer'd 'Tush,
It can do me no damage'; adding further,
That had the king in his last sickness fail'd,
The cardinal's and Sir Thomas Lovell's heads   185
Should have gone off.

King.   Ha? what, so rank? Ah, ha!
There's mischief in this man; canst thou say further?

Surv. I can my liege.

King.   Proceed.

Surv.   Being at Greenwich,
After your highness had reproved the duke
About Sir William Bulmer—   190

King. I remember of such a time, being my sworn servant,
The duke retain'd him his. But on; what hence?

Surv. 'If' (quoth he) 'I for this had been committed,

176–7. Let . . . forward] *so Pope; one line in F.*   179–80. dangerous / For him
to] *Rowe;* dangerous / For this to *F;* dangerous for him / To *Capell;* dangerous /
From this to *Collier 2.*   180. so far] *F; omitted Pope.*   190. Bulmer] *Clarendon
Ed. (from Holinshed);* Blumer *F.*   190–1. Bulmer . . . of] *so F, reading* Blumer;
Blumer. I remember / Of *Pope.*   191. time, being] *F;* time, he being *Pope;*
time. He being *Johnson;* time. Being *Var. 1773.*

---

178. *illusions*] tricks, deceptions;
Holinshed's word, p. 864, "The
moonke maie be deceived through the
divels illusion", and cf. *MND.*, III. ii.
98, "By some illusion see thou bring
her here".

180. *For him*] "For this" (F) makes
nonsense, and as the line stands, it is a
hexameter. It may be significant that
these words are redundant; perhaps
they were the beginning of a line the
rest of which was accidentally omitted.
Holinshed does not help, reading
(p. 864) "It was evill to meddle in such
matters".

181. *forg'd*] fashioned; for the construction, cf. *Wint.*, IV. iv. 17, "To me
the difference forges dread".

184. *fail'd*] died; cf. l. 145 above.
This sense seems to be a coinage of
Shakespeare.

186. *rank*] corrupt, cf. *Tp.*, v. i. 132,
"I do forgive / Thy rankest fault".

190. *Bulmer*] corrected from F's
"Blumer", doubtless a misprint, by
the Clarendon Ed. Both Halle and
Holinshed have "Bulmer".

191. *remember of*] have memory of;
the construction occurs nowhere else
in Shakespeare.

As to the Tower I thought, I would have play'd
The part my father meant to act upon   195
Th' usurper Richard, who being at Sal'sbury,
Made suit to come in his presence; which if granted,
As he made semblance of his duty, would
Have put his knife into him.'

King.   A giant traitor.

Wol. Now madam, may his highness live in freedom,   200
And this man out of prison?

Kath.   God mend all.

King. There's something more would out of thee; what say'st?

Surv. After 'the duke his father', with the 'knife',
He stretch'd him, and with one hand on his dagger,
Another spread on's breast, mounting his eyes   205
He did discharge a horrible oath, whose tenour
Was, were he evil us'd, he would outgo
His father by as much as a performance
Does an irresolute purpose.

King.   There's his period,
To sheath his knife in us: he is attach'd,   210
Call him to present trial; if he may
Find mercy in the law, 'tis his; if none,
Let him not seek't of us. By day and night,
He's traitor to th'height!   *Exeunt.*

---

196. Sal'sbury] Salsbury *F;* Salisbury *F2.*   203. 'the ... knife'] *quotation marks added by Capell.*

---

198. *semblance ... duty*] pretended to kneel, cf. Holinshed, p. 864, "having a knife secretlie about him, would have thrust it into the bodie of king Richard, as he had made semblance to kneele downe before him". The whole passage is close to Holinshed, see Appendix II, p. 189. Cf. also *R 3,* v. i. 1, which may reflect Shakespeare's earlier knowledge of this story.

200. *may*] can, as at *H 5,* II. ii. 100; see Abbott 309.

201. *mend all*] put all right, cf. *Cym.,* v. v. 68.

204. *stretch'd him*] straightened himself, rose to his full height. For "him" = himself, see Abbott 223.

205. *mounting*] raising, cf. I. i. 144.

207. *evil us'd*] badly treated.

outgo] surpass, as at *Cym.,* II. iv. 84.

208–9. *performance ... purpose*] for other allusions to this proverbial contrast, see III. ii. 154, IV. ii. 41–2 and n.

209. *period*] goal, cf. *Wiv.,* III. iii. 47, "this is the period of my ambition".

210. *attach'd*] arrested, cf. I. i. 95.

211. *present*] immediate, cf. *Wint.,* I. ii. 281, "without / My present vengeance taken".

213. *By ... night*] also in *Ham.,* I. v. 164; a common asseveration.

214. *to th'height*] in the highest degree; also in *Troil.,* v. i. 3.

SCENE III—[*A room in the court.*]

Enter LORD CHAMBERLAIN *and* LORD SANDS.

Cham. Is't possible the spells of France should juggle
  Men into such strange mysteries?
Sands.   New customs,
  Though they be never so ridiculous
  (Nay, let 'em be unmanly) yet are follow'd.
Cham. As far as I see, all the good our English   5
  Have got by the late voyage is but merely
  A fit or two o'th'face—but they are shrewd ones,

Scene III

Scene III] Scæna Tertia. F.   A . . . court.] This Ed.; An Apartment in the Palace.
Theobald.   Entry. Lord . . . Lord] L. . . . L. F.   Sands] Rowe; Sandys F.
2. mysteries] F; mimick'ries Hanmer; mockeries Warburton.   7. face—but . . .
ones,] This Ed.; face, (but . . . ones) F; face; but . . . ones, Collier.

Scene III] This and the following scene illustrate the dramatist's compression of events: Buckingham's trial was in 1521, but Henry and Anne did not meet until 1526, when Lord Sands, who had been created Baron in the interval, was himself Lord Chamberlain. See Holinshed's account, pp. 921–2; Appendix II, pp. 204–6.

1–2. *juggle . . . mysteries*] beguile men into such strange practices. 'Juggling' means 'trickery' or 'equivocation', cf. *Tom Tell-Troth* (c. 1620?), p. 6, "the *Count Gondamor* [Spanish ambassador, 1613–18 and 1619–22] have taught some of your active Ministers to juggle . . . by the penetrating faculty of a golden *Indian Demon*, he hath at his command"; spells and juggling are associated with the Witches in *Mac.*, v. viii. 19, and Lear swears by "the mysteries of Hecate" (I. i. 112), so that there seems to be a ready connection between the words. Johnson and the Clarendon Ed. take "mysteries" to be an allusion to mystery-plays, a term which, as Pooler noted, entered the language only in the 18th century; Douce as the Latin word meaning 'art' or 'craft', i.e. artificial fashions; and Capell explained as "mysterious

ones", by analogy with "vanities", l. 38.

4. *unmanly*] effeminate.

5–15. *As . . . Christendom*] This seems to be a reference to an event of 1520, when some Englishmen left at the French court after the handing-over of Tournai, in Holinshed's words, p. 850, "came againe into England, . . . all French in eating, drinking, and apparell, yea, and in French vices and brags . . . the ladies and gentlewomen were dispraised, so that nothing by them was praised, but if it were after the French turne, which after turned them to displeasure, as you shall heare" (see Appendix II, p. 184). But the more detailed criticism of the gallants in the play is no doubt topical, as reflecting a common complaint in James's reign, and one especially prevalent in and around 1613, as the following notes show.

7. *fit . . . face*] a grimace, a way of screwing up the face; "fit" literally means paroxysm, and for comparable usages, cf. *Cym.*, I. iii. 12, *Wint.*, III. ii. 175. So Overbury's character of a courtier, *A Wife Now the Widdow* (1614), D2ᵛ has, "Neither his motion nor his aspect are regular", and there

For when they hold 'em, you would swear directly
Their very noses had been counsellors
To Pepin or Clotharius, they keep state so.   10
Sands. They have all new legs, and lame ones; one would
    take it,
That never see 'em pace before, the spavin,
A springhalt reign'd among 'em.
Cham.   Death my lord,
    Their clothes are after such a pagan cut to't

11. They have] *F;* They've *Pope.*   They . . . it] *so Pope; two lines in F, ending*
legs, / . . . it,   12. see 'em] *F;* saw 'em *Pope.*   13. A] *F;* And *Pope;* Or *Dyce.*
reign'd] *F2;* rain'd *F.*   14. to't] too't *F;* too' *F3.*

are many attacks on their "nicenesse
. . . and their bought complections,
their borrowed fashions, & their fained
behaviours; their wanton gates, and
their endless delicacie" (Parkes, *Curtaine-Drawer of the World,* 1612, F3ʳ), so
that Dekker's remark in *Work for
Armourers* (1609; Grosart, IV. 131),
"Deceipt . . . studies *Machiavell,* and
hath a french face", becomes under-
standable.

8. *hold 'em*] i.e. maintain their
grimaces.

10. *Pepin or Clotharius*] kings of the
Franks in the 6th and 7th centuries.

11. *legs*] as Pooler noted, a quibble;
both new ways of walking and odd
ways of bowing or making a leg. For
"leg" in this sense, cf. *Cor.,* II. i. 77,
"You are ambitious for poor knaves'
caps and legs".

11–13. *lame . . . 'em*] for this attack on
affected gait, cf. Daniel Price, *Lamentations for the death of . . . Prince Henry*
(1613), C2ᵛ, "the quaint *Crane-paced*
Courtiers of this time . . ."; and
Thomas Adams, *The Gallants Burden*
(1612), H4ʳ, who scourges "the Proude
and gallant *Edomite* his gaye Cloathes,
and studyed carriage . . ."

12. *see*] so F; Pope's correction to
"saw" has been generally followed;
but as Pooler notes, *see* is a not uncommon form of the past tense, cf. B.
and F., *Bonduca* (1613; *Works,* VI. 150),
v. ii., "he swing'd us, / And swing'd us
soundly too: he fights by Witch-craft:/

yet for all that I see him lodg'd"; see
also *Cym.,* v. v. 126.

pace] walk, passing into the idea of
training a horse; cf. next note and
v. ii. 56, *Per.,* IV. vi. 68; the author may
have written "pac'd", for a confusion
between *e* and *d,* similar in secretary
hand, is frequent in printed texts.

12–13. *spavin . . . 'em*] diseases of
horses, the former a tumour on a
horse's leg, the latter "an unnaturall
binding of the sinewes" (Markham,
Cheape and Good Husbandry, 1614, F3ʳ),
causing a spasmodic contraction of the
leg-muscles. "A" (F) has generally
been emended to "And" (Pope), or
"Or" (Dyce), to both of which Pooler
objected that the diseases are different,
and that the terms are not inter-
changeable, although he retained the
reading "Or". But if "spavin" connects with "lame", l. 11, "springhalt"
extends the image further; they are
not merely lame, as with spavin,
(indeed) they jerk back their legs as if
they have springhalt. "Springhalt" is
a form of "stringhalt".

14–15. *Their . . . Christendom*] a frequent complaint in the sermons and
satirical writings of the time; cf.
Anthony Nixon, *A Straunge Foot-Post*
(1613), D1ᵛ, "the fantastical fellowes
of our time, which cannot keepe long
in one cut, but every foot have a fling
at a new fashion"; Parkes, *Curtaine-
Drawer* (1612), D1ᵛ, "Every moneths
quarter thou maist change thy sute /

That sure th'have worn out Christendom: how now? 15
What news Sir Thomas Lovell?

Enter SIR THOMAS LOVELL.

Lov.   Faith my lord,
    I hear of none but the new proclamation
    That's clapp'd upon the Court-gate.
Cham.   What is't for?
Lov. The reformation of our travell'd gallants,
    That fill the court with quarrels, talk and tailors.   20
Cham. I'm glad 'tis there; now I would pray our monsieurs
    To think an English courtier may be wise,
    And never see the Louvre.
Lov.   They must either

21. I'm ... monsieurs] *so Pope; two lines in F, ending* there; / ... Monsieurs.

Downe from thy head, as low as to thy foot, / Adorne thy selfe with all the strange disguise / Brought from all nations underneath the skyes ..."

14. *to't*] F "too't"; most editors read "too" with F4, for which there is no authority; for "to't"= in addition to it, cf. *Mac.*, III. i. 52 and Jonson, *Volpone* (1607), II. i. 87, "But he could read, and had your languages, / And to't, as sound a noddle" (Abbott 185). In addition to their absurd walk, says the Chamberlain, they affect outrageous fashions of clothes.

17–20. *proclamation ... tailors*] duelling ("quarrels") became so prevalent at this time (1613), that as G. Wither says, *Abuses Stript* (1613), P1r, those who would "brave gallant men be deem'd ... Quarrell, and fight with every one they meet". E. A. took the trouble to translate the French king's edicts against duels and excessive costliness in clothing of March and April 1613 (*The Kings Declarations*); in October came James's *Edict ... against Private Combats*, to abolish all "single Fights in the field after Challenge in cold blood", and to make it a capital offence for men "to speed their enemies upon private quarells" (C2v, B1v).

18. *clapp'd ... Court-gate*] cf. Chamberlain, letter of 25 March 1613 (I. 440), "Here is a flieng report ... that there is a Bull come from Rome against the King and clapt upon the court gate", and Samuel Rowlands, *Knave of Hearts* (1613), F3v, "Betweene the Court-gate hang'd, & Charing-Crosse". The Clarendon Ed. notes that on Agas's map of London, c. 1560, one of the gates of Whitehall is called the court-gate, probably that which "stood facing Charing Cross a little south of the banqueting house".

19. *travell'd gallants*] see above, ll. 5–15, and n. The long description that follows to l. 38 is much more elaborate than Holinshed's brief note, and is topical, reflecting a common complaint at this time, cf. William Walker, *A Sermon ... at the Funerals of ... Lord Russell* (1614, pp. 43–4, but delivered 16 September 1613), "travell did not infect him, nor strange fashions marre his manners ... O that our Gallants would imitate the example of this noble lord ... they should not rush headlong, as they now doe, into all vice and irreligion. Neyther should they returne from travell, as they doe too commonly ... two-fold more then they went out, the children of Hell".

(For so run the conditions) leave those remnants
Of fool and feather that they got in France,   25
With all their honourable points of ignorance
Pertaining thereunto, as fights and fireworks,
Abusing better men than they can be
Out of a foreign wisdom, renouncing clean
The faith they have in tennis and tall stockings,   30
Short blister'd breeches, and those types of travel,
And understand again like honest men,

27–9. as . . . wisdom] *in parentheses Var. 1773.*   31. blister'd] blistred *F;* bolstred *F4.*

25. *fool and feather*] cf. John Taylor, *The Praise and Vertue of a Jayle* (1623), B8ʳ, "There's many a Gallant, made of foole and feather", with a marginal note, "Thats an Asse". Feathers in hats provoked comment; see John Taylor, *The Sculler* (1612), E4ʳ, "what gallant Gull is that, / With the great Feather, and the Beaver Hat?", and Chamberlain, reporting on the marriage of Princess Elizabeth, 18 February 1613 (I. 424), "the King me thought was somwhat straungely attired in a cap and a feather, with a Spanish cape and a longe stocking".

26. *points*] i.e. of what they ignorantly regard as honourable conduct. The allusion to clothes may have suggested the word, which can mean "laces", cf. *2 H 4*, I. i. 53.

27. *fights and fireworks*] presumably an allusion to duelling, see ll. 17–20 and n., and to whoring or getting illegitimate children, cf. Henry Parrot *The Mastive* (1615), Gɪᵛ, where an epigram on a man who comes to see the sights of London, headed "Sine Flamma combustus", ends, "But mongst the rest that likewise did abound, / Nere thought on *Fyre-works*, which he first here found", and Webster, *White Devil* (1612), II. i. 346–8, "What should they do if hee were married / And should beget more, and those children / Make fier-workes like their father?" Possibly there is a reference also to the mock-battles and fireworks

staged on the Thames as part of the wedding celebrations of Princess Elizabeth; these were universally spoken of as fights and fireworks, cf. Chamberlain's letter of 4 February 1613 (I. 416), "Here is extraordinarie preparation for fireworkes and fights upon the water".

30. *tennis*] a game of which Henry VIII was fond (see Holinshed, p. 809), and which was very popular amongst courtiers in the reign of James I. See *Shakespeare's England*, II. 459–62.

30–1. *tall . . . breeches*] again probably topical: James attended his daughter's wedding in a "longe stocking" (see note on l. 25), and Overbury, *A Wife now the Widow* (1614), D2ᵛ, lists "a long stocking" as a mark of the courtier. The costume is perhaps represented in the engraving of Prince Henry prefixed to Drayton's *Poly-Olbion* (1613; reproduced in *Shakespeare's England*, II. 204), and in the elegant painting in the National Portrait Gallery of George Villiers, Duke of Buckingham (born 1592), as a young man. Short, puffed breeches seem to have been regarded as French; see next note.

31. *types of travel*] marks, badges of travel, cf. *R 3*, IV. iv. 244 (Onions); Wither, *Abuses Stript* (1613), listing the fashions borrowed from all nations by Englishmen, includes "*The spruce diminitive neat Frenchmans* hose" (M4ᵛ).

32. *understand*] a quibble on "stand under", be subject, cf. V. i. 112, and

Or pack to their old playfellows; there, I take it,
They may *cum privilegio* 'oui' away
The lag end of their lewdness, and be laugh'd at.   35
Sands. 'Tis time to give 'em physic, their diseases
Are grown so catching.
Cham.   What a loss our ladies
Will have of these trim vanities!
Lov.   Ay marry,
There will be woe indeed lords; the sly whoresons
Have got a speeding trick to lay down ladies.   40
A French song and a fiddle has no fellow.
Sands. The devil fiddle 'em, I am glad they are going,

34. 'oui'] *Collier 3;* wee *F;* weare *F2.*   42. The . . . going,] *so Pope; two lines in*
F, ending 'em, / . . . going,   I am . . . they are] *F;* I'm . . . they're *Pope.*

possibly a gesture to the audience standing round the platform stage, cf. *Prol.,* l. 22 and note. There are quibbles on the word in *Tw. N.,* III. i. 89 and *Gent.,* II. v. 28.

33. *pack*] go, clear off, cf. *Lr.,* II. iv. 81.

34. *cum privilegio*] i.e. with immunity; a phrase familiar from the licences of monopoly granted to print some books, e.g. the Bible, "Cum privilegio ad imprimendum solum", cited in *Shr.,* IV. iv. 93.

'*oui'*] F has "wee", but most editors have read "wear" with F2; there seems little doubt that Collier correctly altered to "oui" (Ed. 3), cf. Deloney, *The Gentle Craft* (1637; S.R. 19/10/1597, F4ʳ), "The good man askt him if hee lackt worke, *We par my foy,* quoth the *French-man*". This is appropriate to the text, and to the time, one when the English were notorious, according to the satirists, for aping the French in fashion, and wearing "the Frenchmans cast devises" (Rowlands, *Knave of Hearts* (1613), B1ʳ).

35. *lag end*] latter end, cf. *1 H 4,* v. i. 24, "To entertain the lag-end of my life / With quiet hours" (Clarendon Ed.).

lewdness] wickedness or lasciviousness, as always in Shakespeare; the

latter sense would connect with ll. 37 ff.

38. *trim vanities*] spruce follies, worthless things; cf. B. and F., *Wild-Goose Chase* (c. 1621; *Works,* IV. 343), II. iii, "Still troubled with these vanities? . . . Would ye vanities speak with any of my people?" (Pooler), and see *1 H 4,* II. iv. 500, where Falstaff is called "That vanity in years". For "trim" used ironically to mean 'fine', cf. *1 H 4,* v. i. 137; *Ado,* IV. i. 323.

40. *speeding*] effective (Pooler) quibbling on 'speedy', cf. Webster, *White Devil* (1612), v. i. 76, "There's no way / More speeding than this thought on". The word came into vogue about 1610, see *O.E.D.*

41. *French . . . fellow*] cf. the proverb, "the French neither pronounce as they write nor sing as they prick nor think as they speak" (Tilley, F 670); for "fiddle", cf. *Honest Man's Fortune* (c. 1613), v. i "*Lamira.* You two will make a pretty hansome Consort. *Montague.* Yes Madam, if my Fiddle faile me not. *Lam.* Your Fiddle? why your Fiddle? I warrant thou meanest madly"; and Heywood, *Fair Maid of the Exchange* (1607; Pearson, II. 21), "ne're a wench in all the towne but will scorne to dance after my fiddleee For "fellow" meaning 'equal', s". *MND.,* IV. i. 38.

> For sure there's no converting of 'em: now
> An honest country lord as I am, beaten
> A long time out of play, may bring his plain-song,   45
> And have an hour of hearing, and by'r lady
> Held current music too.

Cham.   Well said Lord Sands,
> Your colt's tooth is not cast yet?

Sands.   No my lord,
> Nor shall not while I have a stump.

Cham.   Sir Thomas,
> Whither were you a-going?

Lov.   To the cardinal's;   50
> Your lordship is a guest too.

Cham.   O, 'tis true;
> This night he makes a supper, and a great one,
> To many lords and ladies; there will be
> The beauty of this kingdom, I'll assure you.

Lov. That churchman bears a bounteous mind indeed,   55
> A hand as fruitful as the land that feeds us;
> His dews fall everywhere.

---

47. Held] *F*; Hold *Var. 1821.*   55. That ... indeed,] *so Pope; two lines in F,*
ending Churchman / ... indeed.   57. dews] dewes *F.*

43. *converting*] changing their character, cf. *Ado.*III.iv.91.

45. *play*] a quibble on "amorous dalliance" (*O.E.D.*, 6c); for similar puns see *Tp.*, v. i. 185, *Wint.*, I. ii. 187 and below I. iv. 46.

plain-song] simple melody without ornament, i.e. plain courtship, contrasting with the contrapuntal device of the "French song", l. 41, i.e. affectation, courtliness. Morley, *Plain and Easy Introduction to Practical Music* (1597, p. 86), has, "Your plainsong is as it were your theme, and your descant is as it were your declamation".

47. *current*] accepted, good, cf. *R 2*, I. iii. 231, "Thy word is current with him for my death".

48. *colt's tooth*] a proverbial expression for wantonness, especially in old

men, cf. Greene, *Perimedes* (1588) Grosart, VII. 91), "Hee hath beene a wag, but nowe age hath pluckt out all his Coltes teeth", cited by Tilley, C 525.

49. *stump*] continuing a series of bawdy quibbles.

52. *makes*] gives, cf. *Troil.*, I. iii. 191, "Ajax ... Makes factious feasts", and Halle, *Henry VIII*, i. 53, "made them a banket".

56. *fruitful*] generous, cf. *Oth.*, II. iii. 347, *Tim.*, v. i. 153,

57. *dews*] a common image of benediction, as at *Cym.*, v. v. 351, but a pun may well be intended on "dues", charges, impositions; the spelling "dewes" of F may represent either word, cf. v. i. 131, where "due" is spelt "dew".

Cham.   No doubt he's noble;
   He had a black mouth that said other of him.
Sands. He may my lord; 'has wherewithal: in him
          Sparing would show a worse sin than ill doctrine;   60
          Men of his way should be most liberal,
          They are set here for examples.
Cham.   True, they are so;
          But few now give so great ones. My barge stays;
          Your lordship shall along: come, good Sir Thomas,
          We shall be late else, which I would not be   65
          For I was spoke to, with Sir Henry Guilford,
          This night to be comptrollers.
Sands.   I am your lordship's.
                                      Exeunt.

59. He . . . him] *so Rowe 3; two lines in F, ending* Lord, | . . . him;   'has]
Dyce 2; Ha's *F.*   wherewithal: in him] *Theobald;* wherewithal in him; *F.*
61. way] *F;* sway *Collier 2.*   62. They are set] *F;* They're set *Pope.*
63. But . . . stays;] *so Rowe 3; two lines in F, ending* ones: | . . . stayes;   66.
Guilford] *F;* Guildford *Var. 1773.*   67. I am] *F;* I'm *Pope.*

58. *black mouth*] evil mouth, cf.
"black envy", II. i. 85; "blackest sins",
Oth., II. iii. 357.

other] anything else; for this usage
see *Oth.*, IV. ii. 13, "if you think other",
and Abbott 12.

59. *'has wherewithal*] he has the
means; F "ha's" is a less common
abbreviation of the period than "h'as",
and has been noted as a usage of the
scribe Ralph Crane (Middleton,
Witch, ed. Wilson and Greg, M.S.R.,
1949). There are examples in the
Folio at *All's W.*, IV. iii. 116, *Tim.*, III.

v. 63, etc., and elsewhere in Chettle's
Hoffman (1602, printed 1631; M.S.R.,
1950), l. 661, etc. Pooler notes that it
is very common in Fletcher.

61. *way*] i.e. of life, cf. *Ham.*, III. i. 41.

64. *shall along*] ellipsis of verbs,
especially of motion, is very common
in Shakespeare, cf. *Ham.*, III. iii. 4 and
Abbott 405.

66. *spoke to*] asked, cf. *Ant.*, I. ii. 188;
Tp., I. i. 3.

67. *comptrollers*] stewards; the spelling is still in use as applied to royal and
governmental officers.

SCENE IV—[*St. James's Palace (York Place).*]

Hautboys. A small table under a state for the CARDINAL, *a longer
table for the guests. Then enter* ANNE BULLEN, *and divers other
ladies and gentlemen, as guests at one door; at another door enter*
SIR HENRY GUILFORD.

Guil. Ladies, a general welcome from his grace
Salutes ye all; this night he dedicates
To fair content, and you: none here he hopes,
In all this noble bevy, has brought with her
One care abroad: he would have all as merry   5
As first, good company, good wine, good welcome
Can make good people.

Enter LORD CHAMBERLAIN, LORD SANDS *and* LOVELL.

                              O my lord, y'are tardy;
The very thought of this fair company
Clapp'd wings to me.
Cham.   You are young, Sir Harry Guilford.
Sands. Sir Thomas Lovell, had the cardinal   10
But half my lay-thoughts in him, some of these
Should find a running banquet ere they rested,

Scene IV

Scene IV] *Scena Quarta.* F.   *St. . . . Place.*] *This Ed.; York-house. Theobald; A Hall
in York-Place. Capell.*   Entry. *Guilford*] F; *Guildford Var.* 1793.   1. Ladies
. . . grace] *so Pope; two lines in* F, *ending* Ladyes, | . . . Grace   5. merry] merry:
F.   6. first, good] F; first-good *Theobald;* feast, good *Staunton.*   7. S.D.
Lord . . . Lord] L. . . . L. F.   S.D. *and Lovell*] F; *and Sir Thomas Lovell. Capell.*
9. You are] F; You're *Pope.*   12, 61. banquet] Banket F.

Scene IV] see note to Scene III, and
for Holinshed's account of the banquet
and masque, which took place in 1527,
see Appendix II, pp. 204–6.

Entry. under a state] The cardinal
has a chair of state, cf. l. 34 S.D., but
here the word includes the canopy
over it, cf. "cloth of state", II. iv.
Entry, l. 12.

4. *bevy*] company, especially of
ladies; so Heywood, *Marriage Triumphe
Solemniz'd* (1613), B2ʳ, "none so faire /

In all that Bevie", i.e. as the Princess
among her ladies.

6. *first*] Hanmer read "good company, then good wine", which indicates the sense.

11. *lay-*] secular, with perhaps a pun
on *lay* = throw down, cf. I. iii. 40, "to
lay down ladies".

12. *running banquet*] a slight or hur-
ried refreshment; here with a bawdy
quibble. It can also mean a whipping,
cf. v. iii. 64.

I think would better please 'em: by my life,
They are a sweet society of fair ones.

Lov. O that your lordship were but now confessor   15
To one or two of these.

Sands.   I would I were,
They should find easy penance.

Lov.   Faith, how easy?

Sands. As easy as a down-bed would afford it.

Cham. Sweet ladies, will it please you sit? Sir Harry
Place you that side, I'll take the charge of this: 20
His grace is ent'ring. Nay, you must not freeze,
Two women plac'd together makes cold weather:
My Lord Sands, you are one will keep 'em waking;
Pray sit between these ladies.

Sands.   By my faith,
And thank your lordship: by your leave sweet
   ladies,   25
If I chance to talk a little wild, forgive me;
I had it from my father.

Anne.   Was he mad sir?

Sands. O very mad, exceeding mad, in love too;
But he would bite none; just as I do now,
He would kiss you twenty with a breath.

Cham.   Well said my lord.   30
So now y'are fairly seated: gentlemen,
The penance lies on you if these fair ladies
Pass away frowning.

Sands.   For my little cure
Let me alone.

22. makes] *F;* make *Pope.*   25. ladies,] *F;* ladies; *Pope.*   28. mad, in] *F;*
mad; in *Collier.*   30. He would] *F;* He'd *Pope.*   33. cure] *F;* Cue *Rowe.*

14. *society*] party, assembly, cf. *Cym.,*
I. vi. 167, *Tim.,* IV. iii. 21, "be abhorr'd / All feasts, societies, and
throngs of men!".

20. *Place*] i.e. place the guests in
seats.

22. *Two . . . weather*] possibly a proverb, but I have not traced it.

23. *waking*] lively, cf. *Cor.,* IV. v. 238,
"war . . . it's spritely, waking, audible".

29. *bite*] Madmen were thought to

be liable to bite, cf. *Ant.,* II. v. 80, "Call
the slave again, / Though I am mad, I
will not bite him".

30. *Well said*] well done, as at *AYL.,*
II. vi. 14 (Clarendon Ed.).

33. *cure*] charge, duty; "I am quite
able to take care of my own parishioners; *cure* is cure of souls, an allusion
to Lovell's wish, l. 15" (Pooler). Perhaps it is also remedy, for frowning
and madness (Onions).

Hautboys. Enter CARDINAL WOLSEY *and takes his state.*

Wol. Y'are welcome my fair guests; that noble lady   35
　　Or gentleman that is not freely merry
　　Is not my friend. This to confirm my welcome,
　　And to you all, good health.   [*Drinks.*]

Sands.　　　　　　　　　　Your grace is noble;
　　Let me have such a bowl may hold my thanks,
　　And save me so much talking.

Wol.　　　　　　　　　　My Lord Sands,   40
　　I am beholding to you: cheer your neighbours:
　　Ladies, you are not merry; gentlemen,
　　Whose fault is this?

Sands.　　　　　　　The red wine first must rise
　　In their fair cheeks my lord, then we shall have 'em
　　Talk us to silence.

Anne.　　　　　　　You are a merry gamester   45
　　My Lord Sands.

Sands.　　　　Yes, if I make my play:

35 ff. S.H. *Wol.*] *Card. F.*　　38. S.D. *Drinks*] *Theobald; not in F.*　　41. behold-
ing] *F;* beholden *Pope.*　　neighbours] *F;* neighbour *F2.*　　45. You are] *F;*
You're *Pope.*　　gamester] Gamster *F.*

34. S.D. state] chair of state, cf.
above, I. ii. 8 S.D.

41. *beholding*] indebted. The word,
common in the 17th century, originated in a confusion of endings, and is the
same as "beholden", Pope's emendation.

cheer] enliven, entertain; cf. *Mer.*,
III. ii. 240, "cheer yon stranger; bid
her welcome" (Pooler), and *Mac.*, III.
iv. 33.

43–4. *red . . . cheeks*] It was thought
that red wine "engendreth very pure
bloud, it is very quickly converted into
nourishment" (La Primaudaye, *Third
Part of the French Academy*, 1601, p. 363),
and Marlowe refers in *2 Tamburlaine*,
III. ii. 107–8, to "aery wine, that being
concocted, turnes to crimson blood";
hence the idea of wine turning into
blood is a frequent image, as in
Dekker, *News from Hell* (1606; Grosart,
II. 105), "The bloud of the grape comming up into their cheeks . . ."

45. *gamester*] pleasant fellow; here
with a double sense. The spelling
"Gamster" (F) may represent pronunciation; it is common, as in Rowlands, *Knave of Hearts* (1613), A4^r,
"And come to Gamsters now a
while . . .".

46. *make my play*] cf. I. iii. 45 for the
sense 'amorous play'. To make play is
to win a trick at cards (*O.E.D.*, make
v^{1}30), so that Pooler is probably right
in glossing "when I'm winning".
There may be a pun on "plea", i.e. 'if
I put forward my plea', a legal use
which would connect with "laws of
war", l. 52: the sounds *ea* and *ay* were
much closer to each other than they
are now, cf. Skelton, *Why come ye not
to court?* (ed. Henderson, 1931, p. 348),
"In pleading of their case. / At the
Common *Place*, / Or at the King's
Bench . . .". See also below, III. i. 9–10,
and Kökeritz, *Shakespeare's Pronunciation*, p. 198.

Here's to your ladyship, and pledge it madam,
For 'tis to such a thing—
Anne.   You cannot show me.

Drum and trumpet; chambers discharg'd.

Sands. I told your grace they would talk anon.
Wol.   What's that?
Cham. Look out there, some of ye.   [*Exit a Servant.*]
Wol.   What warlike voice,   50
And to what end is this? Nay ladies, fear not;
By all the laws of war y'are privileg'd.

[*Re-]enter a Servant.*

Cham. How now, what is't?
Serv.   A noble troop of strangers,
For so they seem; th'have left their barge and
    landed,
And hither make, as great ambassadors   55
From foreign princes.
Wol.   Good lord chamberlain,
Go, give 'em welcome; you can speak the French
    tongue;
And pray receive 'em nobly and conduct 'em
Into our presence, where this heaven of beauty
Shall shine at full upon them. Some attend him.   60

[*Exit* CHAMBERLAIN *attended.*] *All rise, and tables remov'd.*

You have now a broken banquet, but we'll mend it.
A good digestion to you all; and once more
I shower a welcome on ye: welcome all.

50. S.D. *Exit a Servant*] Var. *1778; Exit an Att. Capell; not in F.*   52. S.D. *Re-
enter*] *Capell; Enter F.*   54. th'have] *F;* they've *Collier.*   60. S.D. *Exit . . .
attended*] *Capell; not in F.*   61. You have] *F;* You've *Pope.*

48. S.D. *chambers*] small cannon
used especially in salutes. It may have
been these that caused the burning
down of the Globe theatre in 1613, see
Introduction, p. xxvii.

54. *left their barge*] Holinshed says,
p. 921, "he [the King] came by water
to the water gate".

55. *make*] come.

59. *heaven*] punning on 'haven'?

61. *broken banquet*] probably with the
double sense of an interrupted feast
and the poor remains of a feast (cf.
"mend it"), as in the phrase "broken
meats"; see *Lr.*, II. ii. 15; "a rascal; an
eater of broken meats".

Hautboys. Enter KING *and others as masquers, habited like shepherds,
    usher'd by the* LORD CHAMBERLAIN. *They pass directly before
    the* CARDINAL, *and gracefully salute him.*

A noble company: what are their pleasures?
Cham. Because they speak no English, thus they pray'd   65
    To tell your grace: that having heard by fame
    Of this so noble and so fair assembly
    This night to meet here, they could do no less
    (Out of the great respect they bear to beauty)
    But leave their flocks, and under your fair conduct   70
    Crave leave to view these ladies, and entreat
    An hour of revels with 'em.
Wol.   Say, Lord Chamberlain,
    They have done my poor house grace; for which I pay
        'em
    A thousand thanks and pray 'em take their pleasures.

        Choose ladies; KING *and* AN[NE] BULLEN.

King. The fairest hand I ever touch'd: O beauty,   75
    Till now I never knew thee.   *Music; dance.*
Wol. My lord.
Cham.   Your grace?
Wol.   Pray tell 'em thus much from me:
    There should be one amongst 'em, by his person,
    More worthy this place than myself; to whom
    (If I but knew him) with my love and duty   80
    I would surrender it.
Cham.   I will, my lord.   *Whisper.*
Wol. What say they?
Cham.   Such a one they all confess
    There is indeed, which they would have your grace

73-4. They . . . pleasures] *so Pope; three lines in F, ending* grace: | . . . thankes, |
. . . pleasures.   73. They have] *F;* they've *Pope.*   74. S.D. *Choose . . . Bullen.
so F, reading* An *for* Anne; *The King chooses Anne Bullen. Var. 1793.*   81. S.D.
Whisper] *after* surrender it *in F.*

63. S.D. like shepherds] from Holinshed, pp. 921–2; see Appendix II,
p. 204.
66. *fame*] report, as at *Ant.,* II. ii.
166, "Cæs. . . . by sea | He is an ab-
solute master. *Ant.* So is the fame"]
70. *conduct*] allowance. The accent
may be on the second syllable; cf. *Lr.,*
III.vi. 104.
79. *place*] i.e. the chair of state.

Find out, and he will take it.

Wol.   Let me see then,
By all your good leaves, gentlemen; here I'll make   85
My royal choice.

King. [*Unmasking*]   Ye have found him Cardinal;
You hold a fair assembly; you do well lord:
You are a churchman, or I'll tell you cardinal,
I should judge now unhappily.

Wol.   I am glad
Your grace is grown so pleasant.

King.   My Lord Chamberlain,
Prithee come hither; what fair lady's that?   91

Cham. An't please your grace, Sir Thomas Bullen's daughter,
The Viscount Rochford, one of her highness' women.

King. By heaven she is a dainty one. Sweet heart,
I were unmannerly to take you out   95
And not to kiss you. A health gentlemen,
Let it go round.

Wol. Sir Thomas Lovell, is the banquet ready
I'th'privy chamber?

Lov.   Yes my lord.

Wol.   Your grace,
I fear, with dancing is a little heated.   100

King. I fear too much.

Wol.   There's fresher air, my lord,
In the next chamber.

86. S.D. *Unmasking*] *Capell; not in F.*   Ye have] *F;* Ye've *Dyce 2.*   89. I am]
F; I'm *Pope.*   92–3. An't . . . women] *so Pope; three lines in F, ending* Grace, /
. . . Rochford, / . . . women.   93. highness'] *Rowe 3;* Highness *F.*   94. she is]
F; she's *Rowe.*   98. banquet] banket *F.*

84. *take it*] take the chair of
state.

85–6. *here . . . him*] In point of fact,
"the person to whom he offered the
chaire was sir Edward Nevill, a comelie knight, that much more resembled
the kings person in that maske than
anie other" (Holinshed, p. 922); history is again altered for dramatic
effect.

89. *unhappily*] unfavourably, cf.
Ham., IV. v. 12, "there might be
thought, / Though nothing sure, yet
much unhappily" (Clarendon Ed.).

90. *pleasant*] merry, cf. *Cym.,*I. vi. 59.

91. *fair lady*] It is the dramatist's
invention to make Henry meet Anne
at this masque, which she did not
attend.

93. *highness'*] i.e. Queen Katherine's.

95. *take . . . out*] into the dance; "the
maskers 'took out' the principal spectators of the opposite sex to dance"
(Chambers, *E.S.,*I. 197) at the end of a
masque.

96. *kiss*] a custom in a dance; cf.
Tp., I. ii. 378, "Courtsied when you
have and kiss'd" (Clarendon Ed.).

King. Lead in your ladies ev'ry one: sweet partner,
  I must not yet forsake you. Let's be merry,
  Good my lord cardinal: I have half a dozen healths   105
  To drink to these fair ladies, and a measure
  To lead 'em once again, and then let's dream
  Who's best in favour. Let the music knock it.

  Exeunt with trumpets.

104–5. merry, / ... cardinal:] *so F;* merry. / ... Cardinal, *Theobald 2.*   105. I
have] *F;* I've *Dyce 2.*

106. *measure*] dance, especially a
stately dance, cf. *Ado,* II. i. 79, "as a
measure, full of state and ancientry".

108. *favour*] Pooler interprets "i.e.
who was the prettiest girl to-night",
taking "favour" to mean 'appearance'; more simply, 'in favour with the
ladies'.

knock it] strike up; cf. Marston,
Antonio and Mellida (1602; Wood, 1.

22), "the song will seeme to come off
hardly . . . Pert *Catzo,* knock it lustily
then" (Steevens); Halliwell cites T.
Ravenscroft's hunting song (1614;
Fellowes, *English Madrigal Verse,* p.
184), "The hounds do knock it lustily"; and in the MS Percy Play *Arabia
Sitiens* (1601?) the S.D. "Here they
knockt up the consort" occurs between
all the acts.

ACT II

SCENE I—[*A street.*]

Enter two Gentlemen at several doors.

1 Gent. Whither away so fast?

2 Gent.   O, God save ye:
Ev'n to the hall, to hear what shall become
Of the great Duke of Buckingham.

1 Gent.   I'll save you
That labour sir. All's now done but the ceremony
Of bringing back the prisoner.

2 Gent.   Were you there?   5

1 Gent. Yes indeed was I.

2 Gent.   Pray speak what has happen'd.

1 Gent. You may guess quickly what.

2 Gent.   Is he found guilty?

1 Gent. Yes truly is he, and condemn'd upon't.

2 Gent. I am sorry for't.

1 Gent.   So are a number more.

2 Gent. But pray, how pass'd it?   10

1 Gent. I'll tell you in a little. The great duke
Came to the bar; where to his accusations
He pleaded still not guilty, and alleg'd

Scene 1

Act II Scene I] *Actus Secundus. Scena Prima. F.*   *A Street.*] *Theobald.*   Entry. *at . . . doors*] *F; meeting. Capell.*   1 ff. S.H. *1 Gent. . . . . 2 Gent.*] *1. . . . 2. F.* 8. Yes . . . upon't] *so Pope; two lines in F, ending* he, / . . . upon't.   9. I am] *F;* I'm *Pope.*

Scene I] For Holinshed's account of the trial, which took place in 1521, see Appendix II, pp. 190–2.

Entry. several] different.

2. hall] cf. Holinshed, p. 865, "the duke . . . was arreigned in Westminster hall".

10. *pass'd it*] i.e. how did the trial proceed?

11. *in a little*] in a few words, briefly (Onions).

13–14. *alleg'd . . . reasons*] put forward many strong arguments; the words are Holinshed's, p. 865, "the

51

Many sharp reasons to defeat the law.
The king's attorney on the contrary   15
Urg'd on the examinations, proofs, confessions
Of divers witnesses, which the duke desir'd
To have brought *viva voce* to his face;
At which appear'd against him his surveyor,
Sir Gilbert Perk his chancellor, and John Car,   20
Confessor to him, with that devil monk,
Hopkins, that made this mischief.

2 Gent.   That was he
That fed him with his prophecies.

1 Gent.   The same;
All these accus'd him strongly, which he fain
Would have flung from him; but indeed he could not, 25
And so his peers upon this evidence
Have found him guilty of high treason. Much
He spoke, and learnedly for life; but all
Was either pitied in him or forgotten.

2 Gent. After all this, how did he bear himself?   30

1 Gent. When he was brought again to th'bar, to hear
His knell rung out, his judgment, he was stirr'd
With such an agony, he sweat extremely,

---

18. have] *F4;* him *F.*   20. Perk] *This Ed.* (*from Holinshed*)*;* Pecke *F.*   Car] *F;*
Court *Theobald 2.*   23. prophecies.] *F;* prophecies? *Capell.*   24–5. strongly
... him;] *so F;* strongly; ... him, *Var. 1778.*

duke ... alledged reasons to falsifie the
indictment", but for "reasons" in this
sense see II. iv. 223 and v. i. 50 below.

14. *defeat*] frustrate, as in *H 5,* IV. i.
175, "these men have defeated the law
and outrun native punishment"; in
law the phrase means to annul, make
void.

16. *Urg'd ... proofs*] pressed as evidence the depositions and statements.
For "examinations" see I. i. 116 above,
and for "proofs" meaning written
statements or evidence, cf. *Wint.,*III.ii.
113, *Oth.,*III.iii. 324. Again the words
are Holinshed's, p. 865, "against the
dukes reasons alledged the examinations, confessions, and proofes of witnesses".

20. *Perk*] F has *Pecke* here, as at I. i.

219; perhaps an indication that the
same author or scribe wrote these passages, which different compositors set
in type.

Car] Holinshed has, p. 863, "maister
John de la Car *alias* de la Court,
the dukes confessor, and sir Gilbert
Perke priest, the dukes chancellor".
"Sir" was a common courtesy title for
a priest, as at *Tw.N.,*IV. ii. 25.

24. *which*] sc. accusations; or perhaps = whom, as commonly, cf. *Tp.,*
III.i. 6 and Abbott 265.

29. *Was ... forgotten*] either produced no effect or produced only in-
effectual pity (Malone).

32. *judgment*] sentence.

33. *agony*] a paroxysm, here of anger
or grief (*O.E.D.,* sb. 1), cf. Dekker.

And something spoke in choler, ill and hasty:
But he fell to himself again, and sweetly   35
In all the rest show'd a most noble patience.
2 Gent. I do not think he fears death.
1 Gent.   Sure he does not,
He never was so womanish; the cause
He may a little grieve at.
2 Gent.   Certainly
The cardinal is the end of this.
1 Gent.   'Tis likely   40
By all conjectures: first Kildare's attendure,
Then deputy of Ireland, who remov'd,
Earl Surrey was sent thither, and in haste too,
Lest he should help his father.
2 Gent.   That trick of state
Was a deep envious one.
1 Gent.   At his return   45
No doubt he will requite it; this is noted
(And generally) whoever the king favours,
The card'nal instantly will find employment,

---

41. attendure] *F;* attainder *Rowe.*   48. employment,] *F;* employment for *F4.*

Westward Hoe! (1607; Pearson 1873, II. 347), "shees sicke and taken with an Agony", and *R 3*, I. iv. 42.

sweat extremely] from Holinshed, p. 865, who has "The duke . . . swet marvellouslie".

34. *ill*] offensive, malicious, cf. *Ado*, III. i. 86, "How much an ill word may empoison liking".

35. *fell to himself*] regained self-control; cited in *O.E.D.* (fall v. 36) as the first use of this expression.

37. *Sure*] surely.

40. *end*] responsible for; an unusual usage.

41. *Kildare's attendure*] this unusual form of "attainder" may have been taken from Holinshed, p. 928, "The king having purchased from the Cardinall after his attendure . . . his house", though it does not occur in the passages relevant to this scene. For the story of the Earl of Kildare's loss of office, arranged by Wolsey according

to Holinshed, see Appendix II, p. 186.

42. *deputy*] i.e. of the king; Holinshed calls him "the kings lieutenant", and later refers to Surrey as the "kings deputie".

44. *Lest . . . father*] cf. III. ii. 260–4; Surrey, Buckingham's son-in-law, was sent to Ireland, Holinshed says, p. 855, "to remaine rather as an exile, than as lieutenant to the king, even at the cardinalls pleasure". "Father" is often used for father-in-law, cf. *Tp.*, IV. i. 123.

45. *envious*] malicious, the usual Shakespearian sense, cf. *Cæs.*, II. i. 178, *AYL.*, I. ii. 253.

47. *generally*] by everyone.

47–8. *whoever . . . employment*] i.e. for whomever; for other instances of the omission of prepositions see Abbott 201. The Clarendon Ed. compares *H 5*, II. ii. 158, "God be thanked for prevention; / Which I in sufferance heartily will rejoice".

And far enough from court too.

2 Gent.   All the commons
        Hate him perniciously, and o' my conscience   50
        Wish him ten faddom deep: this duke as much
        They love and dote on; call him bounteous Buckingham,
        The mirror of all courtesy—

Enter BUCKINGHAM *from his arraignment, tipstaves before him, the*
        axe with the edge towards him, halberds on each side, accom-
        panied with SIR THOMAS LOVELL, SIR NICHOLAS VAUX,
        SIR WALTER SANDS, *and common people, &c.*

1 Gent.   Stay there sir,
        And see the noble ruin'd man you speak of.
2 Gent. Let's stand close and behold him.
Buck.   All good people,   55
        You that thus far have come to pity me,
        Hear what I say, and then go home and lose me.
        I have this day receiv'd a traitor's judgment,
        And by that name must die; yet heaven bear witness,
        And if I have a conscience, let it sink me,   60

53. S.D. *Enter . . . &c.*] so F; *after* speak of, *l. 54, Capell.   Sir Walter*] F;
Sir William Theobald (after Holinshed).

50. *perniciously*] so as to desire his death (Clarendon Ed.), or ruin; the original meaning of "pernicious" was fatal, destructive.

53. *The . . . courtesy*] model, paragon. The phrase is Holinshed's, p. 870, "He is tearmed . . . the floure & mirror of all courtesie".

S.D. 1 tipstaves] officers who take into custody persons committed by the court, so called because they carried staves tipped with metal (Onions, citing Bailey). Holinshed simply has, "Then was the edge of the axe turned towards him, and he led into a barge" (p. 865).

S.D. 2 halberds] a weapon consisting of a sharp-edged blade and spearpoint mounted on a shaft 5 to 7 feet long (*O.E.D.*).

S.D. 4 Sir Walter Sands] At this time (1521) Sands was a knight, but was elevated to the peerage before the banquet and meeting of Henry and Anne of I. iii and IV; the compression of time in the play thus accounts for the confusion between this entry and the "Lord Sands" of the earlier scenes. In Holinshed his name is Sir William Sands; the change to Walter may be due to a confusion between abbreviations. He has no speaking part in this scene.

55. *close*] seems to carry several senses, 'close together', 'silent', perhaps 'secret', cf. IV. i. 36 and *Ant.*, IV. ix. 6, "What man is this? Stand close and list him".

57. *lose*] forget, as at *MND.*, I. i. 114 and *AYL.*, II. vii. 112.

58. *judgment*] sentence, cf. l. 32 above; it was that he be hanged, drawn and quartered, but it was commuted to beheading.

60. *sink*] destroy; as Pooler notes, citing examples from *Philaster* (1609?)

Even as the axe falls, if I be not faithful.
The law I bear no malice for my death,
'T has done upon the premises but justice:
But those that sought it I could wish more Christians:
Be what they will, I heartily forgive 'em;   65
Yet let 'em look they glory not in mischief,
Nor build their evils on the graves of great men,
For then my guiltless blood must cry against 'em.
For further life in this world I ne'er hope,
Nor will I sue, although the king have mercies   70
More than I dare make faults. You few that lov'd me,
And dare be bold to weep for Buckingham,
His noble friends and fellows, whom to leave
Is only bitter to him, only dying;
Go with me like good angels to my end,   75
And as the long divorce of steel falls on me,
Make of your prayers one sweet sacrifice
And lift my soul to heaven. Lead on a' God's name.

62. The law] *F;* To th' law *F3.*   71. More . . . me] *so Rowe 3; two lines in F,*
ending faults. / . . . me,   78. And . . . name] *so Pope; two lines in F, ending*
Heaven. / . . . name.   a'] a *F;* o' *Theobald.*

and other plays, this usage is common
in B. and F.; see *Works,* I. 113, 335; II.
216, 273, 335, and cf. also *All's W.,* v.
iii. 181, and *O.E.D.,* sink v. 21.

63. *upon the premises*] in the circumstances (Onions and Pooler); more
probably upon the evidence, proceedings.

65. *Be . . . will*] whoever they may
be; similar phrases are common in B.
and F., as Pooler notes, cf. *Chances*
(1625?; *Works,* IV. 191), "Be what he
will and let his foes be devils", but not
infrequent elsewhere, cf. "Let 'em be
what they will", Webster and Rowley
(?), *Thracian Wonder* (printed 1661),
D4ᵛ, and *Mer. V.,* II.ii. 56.

66. *look*] take care.

67. *evils*] *O.E.D.* lists this as a separate word of uncertain meaning, citing
only this passage and *Meas.,* II.ii. 172,
"Having waste ground enough / Shall
we desire to raze the sanctuary / And
pitch our evils there?", and suggests
the meaning 'hovels' instead of the

commentators' 'privies, jakes', for
which cf. 2 Kings, x. 27 (Dyce). The
word had some obscene sense, cf.
Middleton and Rowley, *Fair Quarrel*
(1617; Bullen, IV. 264), v. i. 176, "I
could have had a whore at Plymouth
. . . or under the Mount . . . Or as you
came, at Euill . . . or at the Hanging-
stones . . . Or at Maidenhead . . .",
where "Euill" ("Ivel" in Bullen's
text,= Yeovil) seems to be punning on
a meaning like 'brothel'; perhaps
there is a quibble involving the usual
senses of the word.

great men] noblemen, cf. *Wint.,* IV. iv.
779.

71. *make faults*] commit offences; cf.
Wint., III. ii. 218, "You have made
fault / I'the boldness of your speech".

74. *only dying*] i.e. dying alone.

76. *divorce*] a common idea, cf.
Tw. N., III. iv. 260, "souls and bodies
hath he divorced three" and *Ven.,* 932.

77. *sacrifice*] offering, as at *Troil.,*
I. ii. 308.

Lov. I do beseech your grace, for charity,
  If ever any malice in your heart   80
  Were hid against me, now to forgive me frankly.
Buck. Sir Thomas Lovell, I as free forgive you
  As I would be forgiven: I forgive all.
  There cannot be those numberless offences
  'Gainst me that I cannot take peace with: no black envy
  Shall make my grave. Commend me to his grace,   86
  And if he speaks of Buckingham, pray tell him
  You met him half in heaven: my vows and prayers
  Yet are the king's, and till my soul forsake
  Shall cry for blessings on him. May he live   90
  Longer than I have time to tell his years;
  Ever belov'd and loving may his rule be;
  And when old time shall lead him to his end,
  Goodness and he fill up one monument!
Lov. To th'water-side I must conduct your grace,   95
  Then give my charge up to Sir Nicholas Vaux,

85-6. 'Gainst . . . grace] *so Pope; three lines in F, ending with:* / . . . Grave. / . . .
Grace: 85. that I cannot] *F;* I can't *Pope;* that I can't *Var. 1773;* I cannot
Dyce 2.   86. make] *F;* mark *Hanmer.*   89. forsake] *F;* forsake me *F4.*

79–81. *I . . . frankly*] Lovell's remark
refers back to I. ii. 185–6 (Nichol
Smith).

85. *take peace with*] make peace with;
an old expression, cf. "take truce
with", *Rom.*, III. i. 162 (Pooler), and
Sonn., XLVII. 1, "Betwixt mine eye and
heart a league is took".

envy] malice, cf. *Tp.*, I. ii. 258; envy
is black because it is evil, cf. "black
mouth" at I. iii. 58 and "black villany"
in *Per.*, IV. iv. 44; as the colour of
mourning, black is also associated with
"grave".

86. *make*] i.e. I will not go to my
death leaving any ill-will against me.
Most editors have emended to "mark"
following Hanmer, and a similar
generally accepted emendation at *H 5,*
II. ii. 139, has been cited in support
(Malone, Clarendon Ed.); but in both
cases the Folio reading can be defended, and in the present instance either
reading gives the same general sense.
Steevens interpreted, "No action expressive of malice shall conclude my
life", but Buckingham is talking of the
sins of others against him. His suggestion that "make" may mean
"close" is possible, cf. II. iv. 163
and n.

89. *forsake*] leave, sc. the body. A
possible parallel for this absolute use
may be found in *Sonn.*, XII. 11, "Since
sweets and beauties do themselves forsake / And die as fast as they see other
grow". F4 reads "forsake me";
Pooler suggests "soul's forsake", but
forsake as a noun is unrecorded.

91. *tell*] count.

93. *old time*] perhaps a personification, as at *John*, III. i. 324; or old age
(Onions), as at *LLL.*, I. ii. 18, where
"thy young days" of Moth are contrasted with "your old time" of
Armado.

94. *monument*] tomb, as frequently in
Shakespeare, cf. *Ant.*, IV. xiii. 3, *Rom.*,
III. v. 203, "In that dim monument
where Tybalt lies".

 Who undertakes you to your end.

Vaux.   Prepare there,
 The duke is coming: see the barge be ready,
 And fit it with such furniture as suits
 The greatness of his person.

Buck.   Nay, Sir Nicholas,   100
 Let it alone; my state now will but mock me.
 When I came hither I was Lord High Constable
 And Duke of Buckingham: now poor Edward Bohun;
 Yet I am richer than my base accusers,
 That never knew what truth meant: I now seal it,   105
 And with that blood will make 'em one day groan for't.
 My noble father Henry of Buckingham,
 Who first rais'd head against usurping Richard,
 Flying for succour to his servant Banister,
 Being distress'd, was by that wretch betray'd,   110
 And without trial fell; God's peace be with him.
 Henry the Seventh succeeding, truly pitying
 My father's loss, like a most royal prince
 Restor'd me to my honours; and out of ruins
 Made my name once more noble. Now his son,   115
 Henry the Eighth, life, honour, name and all
 That made me happy, at one stroke has taken
 For ever from the world. I had my trial,
 And must needs say a noble one; which makes me
 A little happier than my wretched father: 120
 Yet thus far we are one in fortunes; both

---

116. Eighth] Eight *F.*   121. fortunes] *F;* fortune *Rowe.*

97. *undertakes*] takes in charge; not in this sense elsewhere in Shakespeare, but an old usage.

99. *furniture*] equipment, cf. II. ii. 3.

103. *Bohun*] so Holinshed, p. 865, "when I went to Westminster I was duke of Buckingham, now I am but Edward Bohune the most caitife in the world". His real family name was Stafford, as Holinshed has later (p. 870), and though he was descended from the Bohuns, Earls of Hereford, from whom he derived the hereditary office of Lord High Constable, it was

through the female line (Clar. Ed.).

105–6. *truth . . . for't*] "truth" is loyalty, and "seal" means 'attest'; interpret, 'I now attest it, and with that blood (which) will make them one day suffer for it'.

108. *rais'd head*] gathered a force, rebelled, cf. *1 H 4,* I. iii. 284, "to save our heads by raising of a head", and *Cym.*, III. v. 25.

109–15. *Flying . . . noble*] based on Holinshed, pp. 869–70; see Appendix II, p. 192.

117. *stroke*] perhaps a punning allusion to his execution, cf. II. ii. 35.

As Wolsey is bad servant of King

Fell by our servants, by those men we lov'd most:
A most unnatural and faithless service.
Heaven has an end in all; yet you that hear me,
This from a dying man receive as certain: 125
Where you are liberal of your loves and counsels,
Be sure you be not loose; for those you make friends
And give your hearts to, when they once perceive
The least rub in your fortunes, fall away
Like water from ye, never found again   130
But where they mean to sink ye. All good people
Pray for me; I must now forsake ye; the last hour
Of my long weary life is come upon me:
Farewell;
And when you would say something that is sad,   135
Speak how I fell. I have done, and God forgive me.

Exeunt Duke and train.

tragedy

1 Gent. O, this is full of pity; sir, it calls
          I fear, too many curses on their heads
          That were the authors.
2 Gent.   If the duke be guiltless,
          'Tis full of woe: yet I can give you inkling   140
          Of an ensuing evil, if it fall,
          Greater than this.

134-5. Farewell . . . sad] *so Capell; one line in F.*   136. Speak . . . me] *so Pope, reading* I've *for* I have; *two lines in F, ending* fell. / . . . me.

124. *end*] purpose (Pooler).

125. *dying . . . certain*] accept as truth. It was thought that people on the point of death were bound to speak truth, cf. *Cym.*, v. v. 41, "And but she spoke it dying, I would not / Believe her lips in opening it".

127. *loose*] wanting in restraint, cf. *Oth.*, iii. iii. 416, "There are a kind of men so loose of soul, / That in their sleep will mutter their affairs" (Steevens).

129. *rub*] check; in the game of bowls a rub is the touch of any obstacle which diverts a wood from its course, either towards or away from the jack, and in this last sense, of disastrous hindrance, the word passed into common usage in the 16th–17th centuries. See *Cor.*, iii. i. 60 and *Ham.*, iii. i. 65.

131. *sink*] ruin; cf. l. 60 above.

133. *long weary life*] Buckingham was forty-three when he died in 1521 (Clarendon Ed.); see iii. i. 120 and n.

137. *calls*] summons; the idea of curses falling on men's heads is common, cf. *R 3*, iii. iv. 94, and Tilley C 924.

139. *authors*] originators, cf. *Cor.*, v. iii. 36, "As if a man were author of himself".

140. *inkling*] hint; it occurs once elsewhere in Shakespeare, in *Cor.*, i. i. 59.

1 Gent.   Good angels keep it from us:
What may it be? you do not doubt my faith sir?
2 Gent. This secret is so weighty, 'twill require
A strong faith to conceal it.
1 Gent.   Let me have it;   145
I do not talk much.
2 Gent.   I am confident;
You shall sir: did you not of late days hear
A buzzing of a separation   *leads onto next*
Between the king and Katherine?   *incident   subplot*
1 Gent.   Yes, but it held not;
For when the king once heard it, out of anger   150
He sent command to the lord mayor straight
To stop the rumour, and allay those tongues
That durst disperse it.
2 Gent.   But that slander, sir,
Is found a truth now; for it grows again
Fresher than e'er it was, and held for certain   155
The king will venture at it. Either the cardinal,
Or some about him near, have, out of malice
To the good queen, possess'd him with a scruple
That will undo her: to confirm this too,
Cardinal Campeius is arriv'd, and lately,   160
As all think, for this business.

---

151. mayor straight] *F;* Mayor strait *Pope;* mayor, straight *Capell.*   154. Is
found a] *F;* Is a sound *F3.*   160. lately,] *F;* lately; *Var. 1778.*

143. *faith*] trustworthiness.

146. *I am confident*] I am assured.
"You shall" goes ambiguously with
"have it" and "not talk much".

148. *buzzing*] rumour; cf. *Ham.,* IV.
v. 90, "And wants not buzzers to infect
his ear / With pestilent speeches", and
3 H 6, v. vi. 86.

148–64. *buzzing . . . purpos'd*] these
lines are based on widely separated
passages in Holinshed, pp. 897 and
906; see Appendix II, pp. 193–4).

149. *held not*] ceased (Pooler).

151. *straight*] straightway, at once,
cf. *Wint.,* II. iii. 135.

152. *allay*] control, cf. I. i. 149 and n.

155. *held for certain*] i.e. it is thought

certain; cf. "hold for true", *Tim.,* v. i.
4, and for the elliptical construction,
Abbott 382.

157. *about him near*] intimate with
him; cf. II. ii. 134.

158. *possess'd . . . scruple*] imbued him
with a doubt; for "possess" in this
common sense, cf. *Tp.,* I. ii. 471.

159. *undo*] ruin; a common usage, cf.
Cor., I. i. 65.

160. *Campeius*] Laurence Campeggio
or Campeius came to London in
October 1528 (Holinshed, p. 906),
seven years after Buckingham's death:
this is another instance of the dramatist's compression of events, cf. I. iii
and n.

1 Gent.   'Tis the cardinal;
    And merely to revenge him on the emperor,
    For not bestowing on him at his asking
    The archbishopric of Toledo, this is purpos'd.
2 Gent. I think you have hit the mark; but is't not cruel   165
    That she should feel the smart of this? The cardinal
    Will have his will, and she must fall.
1 Gent.   'Tis woeful.
    We are too open here to argue this;
    Let's think in private more.   *Exeunt.*

SCENE II—[*A room at court.*]

Enter LORD CHAMBERLAIN, *reading this letter.*

Cham. 'My lord, the horses your lordship sent for, with
    all the care I had, I saw well chosen, ridden and fur-
    nish'd. They were young and handsome, and of the
    best breed in the north. When they were ready to set
    out for London, a man of my lord cardinal's, by com-   5

---

165. I . . . cruel] *so Pope, reading* you've *for* you have; *two lines in F, ending* thinke /
. . . cruell,

Scene II

Scene II] *Scena Secunda. F.   A . . . court.*] *This Ed.; An Ante-chamber in the Palace.*
Theobald.   *Entry. Enter Lord . . . this*] *F; Enter the Lord . . . a | Rowe.*   1. S.H.
Cham.] *not in F.*

162. *emperor*] Charles V, Holy
Roman Emperor and King of Spain,
was Queen Katherine's nephew; cf.
II. ii. 25.

165. *hit the mark*] guessed right; a
common phrase, cf. Tilley, M 667–9.

168. *open*] exposed to view, public;
cf. III. ii. 404 below and *Wint.*, II. iii.
205. Pooler explains as 'indiscreet' and
says "here" goes with "argue", but
this is needlessly subtle, and there is no
parallel for it.

Scene II

Scene II] This scene seems to be
largely original, and is indebted to
Holinshed only for a few ideas and

points of information; see Appendix
II, pp. 192–4. One notable distortion of history is the assigning of Dr
Pace's death to persecution by Wolsey,
cf. l. 121 n.

1–9. *My . . . sir*] This letter seems to
be the dramatist's invention.

2–3. *ridden and furnish'd*] broken in,
trained and equipped with trappings;
"ride" often means control, cf. *Tw. N.*,
III. iv. 318, "I'll ride your horse as well
as I ride you".

5–6. *by . . . power*] by warrant and
superior force; "main", formerly a
common epithet with force, strength,
power, is still used in the phrase "by
main force".

mission and main power took 'em from me, with this
reason: his master would be serv'd before a subject,
if not before the king, which stopp'd our mouths
sir.'
I fear he will indeed; well, let him have them;   10
He will have all I think.

Enter to the LORD CHAMBERLAIN, *the* DUKES OF NORFOLK *and*
SUFFOLK.

Nor. Well met my lord chamberlain.
Cham. Good day to both your graces.
Suf. How is the king employ'd?
Cham.   I left him private,
Full of sad thoughts and troubles.
Nor.   What's the cause?   15
Cham. It seems the marriage with his brother's wife
Has crept too near his conscience.
Suf. [*Aside*]   No, his conscience
Has crept too near another lady.
Nor.   'Tis so;
This is the cardinal's doing: the king-cardinal,
That blind priest, like the eldest son of fortune,   20
Turns what he list. The king will know him one day.
Suf. Pray God he do, he'll never know himself else.

10–11. I fear . . . think] *so Theobald; as prose in F.*   12. my lord] *F;* my good /
Lord *Hanmer.*   17. S.D. *Aside*] *Neilson and Hill; not in F.*   19. doing: . . .
king-cardinal,] *F;* doing; . . . King-Cardinal: *Rowe;* doing, . . . king-cardinal
Var. 1785.   22. Pray . . . else] *so Pope; two lines in F, ending* doe, / . . . else.

14. *private*] alone; a rare usage, as
in *Rom.,* I. i. 144, "And private in
his chamber pens himself" (cited
Pooler).
    15. *sad*] serious, as at ll. 57, 62.
    17–18. *No . . . lady*] an aside, as
Vaughan thought; Norfolk's "'Tis so"
must refer to the Chamberlain's words,
ll. 16–17. Is Suffolk's aside the first
allusion to Anne's being with child?
    20–1. *That . . . list*] cf. *H 5,* III. vi. 33,
"Fortune is painted blind, with a
muffler afore her eyes . . . and she is
painted also with a wheel, to signify
. . . that she is turning and incon-

stant"; Wolsey, as the eldest son, in-
herits these proverbial attributes, and
"turns what he list" (i.e. what he
wishes) is an allusion to the wheel. As
Pooler notes, Wolsey controls the fates
of other men, "not distinguishing
merit", just as Fortune serves "fooles
with riches which they know not how
to use, & wise men are sent away like
beggers" (Dekker, *Work for Armourers,*
1609; Grosart, IV. 165).
    21–2. *know him . . . know himself*]
learn to understand him. Otherwise
he will never learn to understand himself. Cf. III. ii. 378 and n.

Nor. How holily he works in all his business,
      And with what zeal! for now he has crack'd the league
      Between us and the emperor (the queen's great nephew),
      He dives into the king's soul, and there scatters   26
      Dangers, doubts, wringing of the conscience,
      Fears and despairs, and all these for his marriage:
      And out of all these, to restore the king,
      He counsels a divorce, a loss of her   30
      That like a jewel has hung twenty years
      About his neck, yet never lost her lustre;
      Of her that loves him with that excellence
      That angels love good men with; even of her
      That when the greatest stroke of fortune falls   35
      Will bless the king: and is not this course pious?
Cham. Heaven keep me from such counsel: 'tis most true
      These news are everywhere, every tongue speaks 'em,
      And every true heart weeps for't. All that dare
      Look into these affairs see this main end,   40
      The French king's sister. Heaven will one day open
      The king's eyes, that so long have slept upon
      This bold bad man.
Suf.   And free us from his slavery.

23. his] *F;* this *Capell.*   40. this] *F;* his *F4.*

25. *nephew*] Charles V was the son of
Katherine's sister Joanna (Clarendon
Ed.). At the suit of the emperor Wolsey
had agreed to break the peace with
France (I. i. 177–90), and now he
breaks the league with Charles, cf. II. i.
162.

27. *wringing . . . conscience*] remorse;
literally, affliction, as at *H 5,* IV. i. 252,
"fool, whose sense no more can feel /
But his own wringing".

31. *jewel*] the chain, or ornament on
the gold chain usually worn by
gentlemen (see *Shakespeare's England,*
II. 115): "jewel" signified any costly
ornament, and was not limited to precious stones; cf. *Tw. N.,* III. iv. 228,
"wear this jewel for me, 'tis my picture". The idea in this passage is not
uncommon, cf. *Wint.,* I. ii. 308.

33. *excellence*] surpassing virtue.

35. *stroke*] perhaps a punning allusion to execution, cf. II. i. 117.

36. *bless the king*] as she does at IV. ii.
163 (Nichol Smith).

36. *course*] course of action, proceeding.

38. *These news*] The plural was common, as "news" is properly the plural
of "new", meaning new things; cf.
Oth., I. iii. 1.

40. *main end*] chief object (Pooler).

41. *French . . . sister*] the Duchess of
Alençon; so Holinshed reports, p. 906.
See III. ii. 85–6 and n.

42. *slept upon*] been blind to; cf. *Tim.,*
III. v. 43 (Onions).

43. *bold bad man*] This phrase occurs
in Spenser's *Faerie Queene* (1590), I. i.
37 (Nichol Smith), and elsewhere in
the dramatists, and was perhaps
already a commonplace.

Nor. We had need pray,
        And heartily, for our deliverance,   45
        Or this imperious man will work us all
        From princes into pages: all men's honours
        Lie like one lump before him, to be fashion'd
        Into what pitch he please.
Suf.   For me, my lords,
        I love him not, nor fear him, there's my creed: 50
        As I am made without him, so I'll stand,
        If the king please; his curses and his blessings
        Touch me alike, th'are breath I not believe in.
        I knew him, and I know him: so I leave him
        To him that made him proud, the Pope.
Nor.   Let's in,   55
        And with some other business put the king
        From these sad thoughts that work too much upon
            him:
        My lord, you'll bear us company?
Cham.   Excuse me,
        The king has sent me otherwhere: besides,
        You'll find a most unfit time to disturb him: 60
        Health to your lordships.

48. Lie like] *F; Lie in Var. 1793.*   49. pitch] *F; pinch Hanmer.*

47–9. *all . . . please*] a difficult passage, suggested probably by Romans,
ix. 21, "Hath not the potter power of
the clay to make of the same lumpe
one vessell to honour, and another
unto dishonour?" (Geneva). If this is
right, "pitch" means status, level, as in
T. Morton, *Treatise of the Nature of God*
(1599), A6ʳ, "I am bolde to send unto
you with a little treatise of repentance
. . . another of the same pitch and
stature . . .", and T. Floyd, *Picture of a
perfect Commonwealth* (1600), A7ᵛ,
"caused mee rashly to reach above my
pitch, and to adventure the more".
The word is connected with the sea in
Tw. N., I. i. 12, and may have been
suggested by "vessell" in the passage
in Romans; it might also be that which
defiles, i.e. here an evil shape ("dishonour"). I suggest, 'all men's dig

nities, titles, lie before him, like a lump
of clay, to be fashioned to what level
(of high or low rank, honour or dishonour) he please'. This links with the
previous line, with which cf. Holinshed, p. 847, "when he [Wolsey] said
masse . . . he made dukes and earles to
serve him of wine", and 873, "Before
masse, two barons gave him water, and
after the gospell two earles; and at the
last lavatorie, two dukes: which pride
the Spaniards sore disdained". Pooler
compares III.ii. 281 below.

50. *creed*] not elsewhere in Shakespeare; *O.E.D.* cites as the first use in a
non-religious sense.

51. *stand*] stand firm, remain, cf.
Cor., IV. ii. 7.

53. *not . . . in*] a common construction; see *Tp.*, II. i. 121 and Abbott
305.

Nor.   Thanks, my good lord chamberlain.
*Exit Lord Chamberlain, and the King draws
the curtain and sits reading pensively.*

Suf. How sad he looks; sure he is much afflicted.
King. Who's there? Ha?
Nor.   Pray God he be not angry.
King. Who's there I say? How dare you thrust yourselves
Into my private meditations?   65
Who am I? Ha?

Nor. A gracious king that pardons all offences,
Malice ne'er meant: our breach of duty this way
Is business of estate, in which we come
To know your royal pleasure.

King.   Ye are too bold: 70
Go to; I'll make ye know your times of business:
Is this an hour for temporal affairs? Ha?

Enter WOLSEY *and* CAMPEIUS *with a commission.*

Who's there? my good lord cardinal? O my Wolsey,
The quiet of my wounded conscience;
Thou art a cure fit for a king; [*To Camp.*] you're welcome
Most learned reverend sir, into our kingdom;   76
Use us and it: [*To Wol.*] my good lord, have great care
I be not found a talker.

70. Ye are] *F;* ye're *Dyce 2 (after Capell).*   75. a king] *F;* the King *F2.*   S.D.
To Camp.] *Theobald; not in F.*   77. S.D. *To Wol.*] *Johnson; not in F.*

61. S.D. King . . . curtain] The king
is thus discovered sitting within the
inner stage; presumably the action
moves back on to the platform when
the Cardinals enter and the lords
leave. For other allusions to the curtains covering the inner stage, see
Chambers, *E.S.*,III. 80 ff.

62. *sad*] serious, as at l. 57; "afflicted" means troubled in mind.

68. *this way*] in this respect, cf. *Cym.*,
I. iv. 101.

69. *business of estate*] state affairs; for
estate = state, cf. *Ham.*, III. iii. 5
(Clarendon Ed.).

72. S.D. commission] Holinshed
says, p. 906, "the college of Rome sent

thither Laurence Campeius, a preest
cardinall . . . and with him was joined
in commission the cardinall of Yorke".
See Appendix II, p. 194.

74. *quiet*] ease, repose, cf.II. iv. 61.

75. *cure*] cf. I. iv. 33; perhaps the
sense "spiritual charge" adds overtones of meaning.

78. *I . . . talker*] "that my professions
of welcome be not found empty talk"
(Johnson); it will be Wolsey's care to
entertain Campeius. The phrase
derives from the proverbial opposition
between words and deeds; see Tilley,
T 64, W 820, and *R 3*, I. iii. 352,
"Talkers are no good doers" (cited
Steevens).

Wol.   Sir, you cannot;
I would your grace would give us but an hour
Of private conference.
King. [*To Nor. and Suf.*]   We are busy; go.   80
Nor. [*Aside to Suf.*] This priest has no pride in him?
Suf. [*Aside to Nor.*]   Not to speak of:
I would not be so sick though for his place;
But this cannot continue.
Nor. [*Aside to Suf.*]   If it do,
I'll venture one; have at him!
Suf. [*Aside to Nor.*]   I another.
                               Exeunt Norfolk and Suffolk.
Wol. Your grace has given a precedent of wisdom   85
Above all princes, in committing freely
Your scruple to the voice of Christendom:
Who can be angry now? what envy reach you?
The Spaniard tied by blood and favour to her,
Must now confess, if they have any goodness,   90
The trial just and noble. All the clerks
(I mean the learned ones in Christian kingdoms)

[margin note: flattery]

---

80. S.D. *To . . . Suf.*] *Theobald; not in* F.   81–4. S.D. *Aside . . . Aside . . .*] *Var.
1778 (after Capell); not in* F.   82. sick though] F; sick, though F4.   83–4. If
. . . him!] *so Pope; one line in* F.   84. one; have at him!] one; have at him. F;
one heave at him F2; one have-at-him *Dyce and Staunton (after Var. 1821).*
85. precedent] President F.   92. ones in] F; ones, in *Theobald.*

82. *sick . . . place*] sick with pride even
though I had his position (Clarendon
Ed.); with which Pooler compares
Troil., II. iii. 92, "sick of proud heart".
"Sick" could mean corrupt, for which
see II. iv. 202, or envious, cf. I. ii. 82 and
n., and the lack of pointing leaves
an ambiguity. The conversation presumably relates to Wolsey, and Norfolk's remark is a sneer rather than a
question; he spoke of Wolsey's pride
at l. 46.

84. *one . . . him*] The words are uttered as a threat; Norfolk says, "I'll be
one to venture", and looking towards
Wolsey, speaks his challenge "have at
him"; cf. *2 H 4*, I. ii. 217, "let him lend
me the money, and have at him!".
Dyce, following Steevens, emended to
"one have-at-him", coining a noun

out of the challenge "Have at you"
(cf. III. ii. 309), to mean "attack"; in
this he was perhaps fortified by "one
heave at him" (F2), which has no
authority, or by "give her the avaunt",
II. iii. 10, where a verb is turned into a
noun.

87. *voice*] vote; Henry sent to the
universities of France and Italy, "and
to the great clearkes of all christendome, to know their opinions" (Holinshed, p. 906; see Appendix II,
p. 194).

88. *envy*] malice, cf. II. i. 85.

89. *favour*] goodwill.

91. *clerks*] clerics, men in holy
orders; cf. *Sonn.*, LXXXV. 6, "And like
unletter'd clerk still cry 'Amen' / To
every hymn . . .". Holinshed's word,
cf. note on l. 87.

Have their free voices: Rome, the nurse of judgment,
Invited by your noble self, hath sent
One general tongue unto us; this good man,   95
This just and learned priest, Cardinal Campeius,
Whom once more I present unto your highness.

King. And once more in mine arms I bid him welcome,
And thank the holy conclave for their loves;   99
They have sent me such a man I would have wish'd for.

Cam. Your grace must needs deserve all strangers' loves,
You are so noble: to your highness' hand
I tender my commission; by whose virtue,
The court of Rome commanding, you my lord
Cardinal of York, are join'd with me their servant   105
In the unpartial judging of this business.

King. Two equal men: the queen shall be acquainted
Forthwith for what you come. Where's Gardiner?

Wol. I know your majesty has always lov'd her
So dear in heart, not to deny her that   110
A woman of less place might ask by law,
Scholars allow'd freely to argue for her.

King. Ay, and the best she shall have; and my favour
To him that does best, God forbid else: Cardinal,
Prithee call Gardiner to me, my new secretary.   115

---

93. Have] *F;* Gave *R. G. White 1.*   100. They have] *F;* they've *Pope.*
104. commanding, you] *F4;* commanding. You *F.*   106. unpartial] *F;*
impartiall *F3.*

---

93. *free voices*] may vote freely; cf.
"free speech", *Oth.,* III. iv. 129.

judgment] perhaps good judgment,
wisdom; or in the Biblical sense of justice, cf. Isaiah, lxi. 18, "For I the Lord
love Judgment, I hate robbery . . .".

95. *general tongue*] one to speak for all
(Pooler).

99. *conclave*] the body of cardinals;
cited by *O.E.D.* as the first use in this
sense.

101. *strangers*] foreigners, cf. II. iii.
17 and n

106. *unpartial*] impartial; common
from 1590 to 1660, but not used elsewhere in Shakespeare.

107. *equal*] fair, impartial, cf. *2 H 4,*

IV. i. 67, "I have in equal balance
justly weigh'd . . .", and below, II. iv.
16.

acquainted] informed; an obsolete
use, cf. *Err.,* III. ii. 15.

111. *less place*] lower rank.

113. *best*] cf. Holinshed, p. 907, "the
king . . . bad hir choose the best clearks
of his realme to be of hir counsell, and
licenced them to doo the best on hir
part that they could"; see Appendix
II, p. 194.

115. *Gardiner*] Stephen Gardiner
was appointed Secretary, 28 July 1529,
replacing Dr Pace (see below, l. 121),
and became Bishop of Winchester in
1531, cf. v. ii. 92.

I find him a fit fellow.

Enter GARDINER.

Wol. [*Aside to Gard.*] Give me your hand: much joy and
    favour to you;
    You are the king's now.   *King as Wol's fool*
Gard. [*Aside to Wol.*]   But to be commanded
    For ever by your grace, whose hand has rais'd me.
King. Come hither Gardiner.   *Walks and whispers.* 120
Cam. My lord of York, was not one Doctor Pace
    In this man's place before him?
Wol.   Yes, he was.
Cam. Was he not held a learned man?
Wol.   Yes surely.
Cam. Believe me, there's an ill opinion spread then,
    Even of yourself, lord cardinal.
Wol.   How? of me?   125
Cam. They will not stick to say you envied him,
    And fearing he would rise (he was so virtuous)
    Kept him a foreign man still, which so griev'd him
    That he ran mad and died.
Wol.   Heav'n's peace be with him:
    That's Christian care enough; for living murmurers 130
    There's places of rebuke. He was a fool,
    For he would needs be virtuous. That good fellow,
    If I command him follows my appointment,

---

116. S.D. *Enter Gardiner*] F; *Exit Wolsey. Re-enter . . . with Gardner. Capell.*
117. S.D. *Aside . . .*] *Dyce (after Capell); not in F.*   118. S.D. *Aside . . .*] *Var. 1773
(after Capell); not in F.*

116. *fit*] suitable.
121. *Pace*] according to Holinshed,
p. 907, "being continuallie abroad in
ambassages, and the same oftentimes
not much necessarie, by the cardinals
appointment, at length he tooke such
greefe therewith, that he fell out of his
wits"; see Appendix 1, p. 194. Pooler
notes that the exactions and imprisonment he suffered while abroad on
Wolsey's missions may have caused
insanity, but he did not die until 1536,
six years after Wolsey.

126. *stick*] hesitate, cf. *Cor.*, ɪɪ. iii. 17,
"he himself stuck not to call us the
many-headed multitude".
128. *foreign . . . still*] continually employed abroad, cf. note on l. 121. The
sense may be 'away from court', i.e.
from the chance of promotion, a pecu-
liarly Shakespearian usage, for which
see *Oth.*, ɪv. iii. 89 and *Per.*, ɪv. i. 34.
130. *murmurers*] grumblers; cf. *John*,
ɪv. ii. 53, "the murmuring lips of dis-
content".
133. *appointment*] direction; i.e.

I will have none so near else. Learn this brother,
We live not to be grip'd by meaner persons.   135
King. Deliver this with modesty to th' queen.   *Exit Gardiner.*
The most convenient place that I can think of
For such receipt of learning is Black-Friars:
There ye shall meet about this weighty business.
My Wolsey, see it furnish'd; O my lord,   140
Would it not grieve an able man to leave
So sweet a bedfellow? But conscience, conscience;
O 'tis a tender place, and I must leave her.   *Exeunt.*

*Shks scenes
do not run on
in straight forward
narrative line. Building up*

SCENE III—[*A room in the queen's apartments.*]

Enter ANNE BULLEN *and an* OLD LADY.

Anne. Not for that neither; here's the pang that pinches:
His highness having liv'd so long with her, and she
So good a lady that no tongue could ever
Pronounce dishonour of her (by my life,

140. furnish'd; O] *F2 (reading* furnish'd. O) *;* furnish'd, O *F.*

Scene III

Scene III] *Scena Tertia. F.   A . . . apartments.*] *This Ed. (after Theobald).*   4–5
her (by . . . / . . . harm-doing)—] *This Ed.;* her; by . . . / . . . harm-doing: *F*

'does as I bid him'; cf. the phrase "by
the cardinals appointment" in Holinshed (l. 121 n.).

134. *near*] familiar, cf. *2 H 4*, v. i. 81,
"I would humour his men with the
imputation of being near their
master", and *Cæs.*, II. ii. 124.

135. *grip'd*] grasped by the hand, as a
mark of familiarity or equality, or perhaps, grappled with; cf. *Cym.*, I. vi. 106,
III. i. 40, "We have yet many among us
can gripe as hard as Cassibelan;
I do not say I am one; but I have a
hand".

136. *Deliver*] make known, cf. I. ii.
143.

modesty] i.e. with mildness, without
exaggerating, cf. *Ham.*, III. ii. 21,
"o'erstep not the modesty of nature",
and below, IV. ii. 74, V. ii. 103.

138. *receipt*] reception, accommoda-
tion; for the probable transposition
(reception of such learning), cf. III. i.
134 and Abbott 419a–421.

Black-Friars] from Holinshed, p.
907; see Appendix II, p. 194.

Scene III

Scene III] The character of the Old
Lady and her interview with Anne
seem to be the dramatist's invention:
the scene foreshadows the fall of
Katherine, and establishes Anne, for
the Lord Chamberlain at least, as a
worthy successor.

1. *pinches*] torments, cf. *2 H 4*, I. ii.
258, "the gout galls the one, and the
pox pinches the other".

4. *Pronounce*] make known, cf. I. i.
196.

She never knew harm-doing)—O, now after   5
So many courses of the sun enthroned,
Still growing in a majesty and pomp, the which
To leave a thousand-fold more bitter than
'Tis sweet at first t'acquire: after this process,
To give her the avaunt, it is a pity   10
Would move a monster!

Old L.   Hearts of most hard temper
Melt and lament for her.

Anne.   O God's will, much better
She ne'er had known pomp; though 't be temporal,
Yet if that quarrel, fortune, do divorce

7–9. pomp, the which / . . . bitter than / 'Tis sweet] *F;* pomp, / The which . . . bitter / Than sweet *Pope.*   8. leave] *F;* leave's *Theobald.*   14. quarrel, fortune, do] *F2;* quarrell. Fortune, do *F;* quarr'lous Fortune do *Theobald (after Warburton);* quarr'ler Fortune do *Hanmer;* quarrel fortune to *Steevens conj.;* cruel fortune do *Collier 2;* squirrel, fortune, do *Staunton conj.;* fortune's quarrel do *Hudson (Lettsom conj.).*

6. *courses . . . sun*] years, as at *Oth.,*III. iv. 71 (Deighton); in the Ptolemaic system, the sun was thought to revolve round the earth as the centre of the universe.

7–8. *the . . . leave*] Various transpositions have been suggested, always involving the deletion of a word, to turn l. 7 into a pentameter: but it is one as it stands, unless a needless stress is laid on the word "in".

9. *process*] course of time or events, cf. II. iv. 36, and *All's W.,*I. i. 18.

10. *avaunt*] the order to go; to reject her (Pooler); not otherwise used as a noun by Shakespeare, but *O.E.D.* cites Barlow, *Three Sermons* (1596), III. 132, "the divell tempted him, but he gave him the avaunt".

pity] cause for pity.

11. *temper*] disposition, cf. III. i. 165.

12. *God's will*] a common ejaculation used several times by Shakespeare, as at *Oth.,*II. iii. 162.

13. *temporal*] worldly, i.e. not eternal (Pooler).

14. *quarrel . . . divorce*] unexplained: "quarell. Fortune do divorce" (F) may be the compositor's reading of a hurriedly written ampersand or abbre-

viation mark which would give "quarrel and fortune do divorce", or "quarreller, fortune, do divorce" (Hanmer's suggestion), neither of which is very satisfactory. Either of these is, however, preferable to the emendation of "do" to "to", making "fortune" a verb, or the alteration of "quarrel" to "churl", "carle" or "cruel"; though it is just possible that Staunton made a nearer guess than he knew when he suggested "squirrel", which was a term for a strumpet, a common epithet for Fortune. More radical alterations are more easily proposed than defended, and the usual reading, "quarrel, fortune, do" has been skilfully defended by Johnson and the Clarendon Ed. as a use of the abstract noun for the agent, "quarrel" for *quarreller,* cf. "reports" for *reporters* and "charm" for *charmer, Ant.,*II. ii. 47, IV. xii. 16. "quarrel and fortune" seems the best reading, but it presumes that Anne thinks first of the quarrel between Henry and Katherine, and then generalizes her thought into "bearer" in l. 15. The additional ambiguity in "that", which may be demonstrative ("that quarrel"), or

It from the bearer, 'tis a sufferance panging   15
As soul and body's severing.

Old L.   Alas poor lady,
She's a stranger now again.

Anne.   So much the more
Must pity drop upon her: verily
I swear, 'tis better to be lowly born,
And range with humble livers in content,   20
Than to be perk'd up in a glist'ring grief
And wear a golden sorrow.

Old L.   Our content
Is our best having.

Anne.   By my troth and maidenhead,
I would not be a queen.

Old L.   Beshrew me, I would,
And venture maidenhead for't, and so would you,   25
For all this spice of your hypocrisy:
You that have so fair parts of woman on you,
Have too a woman's heart, which ever yet
Affected eminence, wealth, sovereignty;
Which, to say sooth, are blessings; and which gifts   30

28. too] (too) *F*.

relate to the whole clause, does not seriously affect the major difficulty.

15. *sufferance panging*] suffering painful. For *sufferance* see *Meas.*, II. iv. 167, "shall his death draw out / To lingering sufferance", and below, v. i. 68; for *panging* cf. *Cym.*, III. iv. 98. Malone compares the thought in this and the next line with *Ant.*, IV. xiii. 6.

17. *stranger*] foreigner, cf. II. iv. 13, and Dekker, *Magnificent Entertainment* (1604; Pearson I. 267), "As well by the English as by the Strangers . . ."

20. *range . . . livers*] rank with humble people; cf. *Ado*, II. ii. 7, "whatsoever comes athwart his affection ranges evenly with mine" (Pooler), and *1 H 4*, I. iii. 169. For "livers" see *Cym.*, III. iv. 143.

21. *perk'd up*] pranked out, made fine, linking with "wear" in the next line (Pooler); or just possibly, 'perched up', 'elevated' (Clarendon Ed.), for

which sense *O.E.D.* cites (*perk* v²), Greene's *Pandosto* (1588; Grosart, IV. 231), "*Caesars* Crowe . . . when she was pearked on the Capitoll".

24. *Beshrew me*] evil befall me!; a common expression, cf. *Oth.*, III. iv. 150.

26. *For . . . spice*] in spite of this touch, sample, of hypocrisy on your part; cf. *Wint.*, III. ii. 185, "Thy by-gone fooleries were but spices of it", and *Cor.*, IV. vii. 46.

27. *fair parts*] beauty, and fine personal qualities, cf. *Cym.*, III. v. 71, *Ado*, v. ii 60, "for which of my bad parts didst thou first fall in love with me?" and *A Warning for Fair Women* (1599), A4ᵛ, "a man of your faire parts".

29. *Affected*] loved or aspired to, cf. *Cym.*, v. v. 38, "she never loved you, only / Affected greatness got by you".

30. *to . . . sooth*] to speak truth, cf. *Mac.*, I. ii. 36.

(Saving your mincing) the capacity
Of your soft cheveril conscience would receive,
If you might please to stretch it.

Anne.   Nay, good troth.

Old L. Yes troth and troth; you would not be a queen?

Anne. No, not for all the riches under heaven.   35

Old L. 'Tis strange; a threepence bow'd would hire me
          Old as I am, to queen it: but I pray you,
          What think you of a duchess? Have you limbs
          To bear that load of title?

Anne.   No in truth.

Old L. Then you are weakly made; pluck off a little,   40
          I would not be a young count in your way
          For more than blushing comes to: if your back
          Cannot vouchsafe this burthen, 'tis too weak

---

32. cheveril] Chiverell *F*.   36. bow'd would] *F*; bow'd now would *F2*.

31. *Saving your mincing*] with all respect to your affectation; cf. *Lr.*, IV. vi. 122, "yond simpering dame . . . that minces virtue", and E.A., *Strange Foot-post* (1613), F2^v–F3^r, "your peart *Juvenals*, that mince it, as if they were citizens wives". Pooler interprets "mincing" as prudery, and notes that the phrase is formed by analogy with *salva reverentia*, saving your reverence.

32. *cheveril*] kid-leather, proverbial for its stretching capacity, especially as applied to the conscience; cf. Tilley, C 608, who cites Marston, *Histriomastix* (1610; Wood, III. 284), "the cheverell conscience of corrupted law", and Jonson, *Poetaster* (1602), I. ii. 131, "in the power of thy chev'ril conscience".

33. *troth*] faith, possibly punning on "trot", a contemptuous term for an old lady, cf. *Meas.*, III. ii. 52.

36–7. *three-pence bow'd . . . it*] a bent or worthless coin (or bawd) would hire me to be a queen (or quean, strumpet); the pun on "queen" runs throughout this scene. For "bow'd" cf. Heywood *Proverbs* "No sylver, bowde, broken, clypt, crakt, nor cut" (cited Clarendon Ed.), and Kemp, *Nine Daies Wonder* (1600), A3^v, "many good old people

. . . of meere kindnes, gave me bowd sixpences and grotes"; and for the sense, cf. *Bonduca* (1613; Works, VI. 100), "I would have given my life for a bent two-pence", and Jonson, *Every Man In His Humour* (1616), II. i. 70, "he values me, at a crackt three-farthings, for ought I see". No threepenny pieces were coined until 1552, so that this reference is an anachronism, as various editors have noticed.

40. *pluck off*] come down to a lower rank; literally, disrobe, as in *Lust's Dominion* (printed 1657), C7^v, "Prithee good *Cardinal* pluck off".

41. *count . . . way*] A count is equivalent to an earl in rank, i.e. a step down from a duke, but there are puns involved in both words: the Old Lady says that if Anne cannot bear the load of Duchess, she will get no further than blushing with an earl, and implies that she would not be in Anne's condition (i.e. a virgin; "way" has the double sense of path and condition) for more than blushing comes to—she would give up her virginity with no more than a blush. Cf. the pun in l. 36.

43. *vouchsafe*] deign to accept, cf. *Tim.*, I. i. 152, "Vouchsafe my labour" (Onions).

Ever to get a boy.

Anne.   How you do talk!
I swear again, I would not be a queen   45
For all the world.

Old L.   In faith, for little England
You'ld venture an emballing: I myself
Would for Carnarvonshire, although there long'd
No more to th'crown but that: lo, who comes here?

Enter LORD CHAMBERLAIN.

Cham. Good morrow ladies; what were't worth to know   50
The secret of your conference?

Anne.   My good lord,
Not your demand; it values not your asking:

---

47. emballing] *F;* empalling *Malone conj.;* embalming *Whalley conj.;* empaling
Collier conj. (*edition 2*)*;* embailing *Kellner conj.*   48. long'd] *F;* 'long'd
Capell.

---

46. *little England*] "Little England
beyond Wales" was a common name
for Pembrokeshire, so described in
John Speed, *Theatre of the Empire of
Great Britain* (1611), Cc1, and see
Tilley, E 151; there may be an allusion
to Anne's becoming Marchioness of
Pembroke, cf. l. 63 below. "Little
England" had a variety of other meanings, which could apply here; (*a*) to
describe England as compared with
larger countries; Pooler cites Greene,
Spanish Masquerado (1589; Grosart, v.
263), where the Spanish clergy are
"sorie that litle *England* should sup-
presse their graund Patronesse [i.e.
Rome]", and Fletcher, *Woman's Prize*
(1616?; *Works*, VIII. 89), v. iv, "Well,
little England, when I see a husband
of any other nation . . ."; (*b*) with
special reference to James's assumption of the title 'King of Great Britain'
in 1604, as in the attack on him in *Tom
Tell-Troth* (*c.* 1620?), p. 4, "They
make a mock of your word, Great
Brittaine, and offer to prove, that it is a
great deal lesse, than Little England
was wont to be"; (*c*) perhaps as an-

other name for Westminster Hall
where Anne's wedding feast was to be
held, in Shakespeare's time the centre
of legal transactions, cf. Wilson, *Art of
Rhetoric* (1560), D3^r, "And where is al
this adoe? Even in little England, or in
Westminster hall, where never yet
wanted businesse".

47. *emballing*] investing with the ball
as the emblem of royalty (Johnson),
with a quibble carrying on from the
puns in ll. 37, 41, 45. Emendation is
unnecessary; the word is recorded in
O.E.D. as early as 1580.

48. *Carnarvonshire*] The point may be
that this county was noted for being
poor, mountainous and barren; or
possibly, as the Old Lady's speeches
are full of quibbles, there may be an
allusion to its shape, "The forme
thereof is much like a wedge, long and
narrow towards the south" (Speed,
Theatre of the Empire, 1611), Hh1^r.

long'd] belonged, cf. I. ii. 32.

51. *conference*] conversation, cf.
Wint., II. ii. 17.

52. *values not*] is not worth, cf. I. i.
88.

Our mistress' sorrows we were pitying.

Cham. It was a gentle business, and becoming
    The action of good women; there is hope   55
    All will be well.

Anne.   Now I pray God, amen.

Cham. You bear a gentle mind, and heav'nly blessings
    Follow such creatures. That you may, fair lady,
    Perceive I speak sincerely, and high note's
    Ta'en of your many virtues, the king's majesty   60
    Commends his good opinion of you, and
    Does purpose honour to you no less flowing
    Than Marchioness of Pembroke; to which title
    A thousand pound a year, annual support,
    Out of his grace he adds.

Anne.   I do not know   65
    What kind of my obedience I should tender;
    More than my all is nothing: nor my prayers
    Are not words duly hallow'd, nor my wishes
    More worth than empty vanities; yet prayers and
        wishes
    Are all I can return. Beseech your lordship,   70
    Vouchsafe to speak my thanks and my obedience,
    As from a blushing handmaid, to his highness,
    Whose health and royalty I pray for.

Cham.   Lady,
    I shall not fail t'approve the fair conceit

59–60. and . . . virtues,] *F;* an . . . virtues; *Johnson.*   59. note's] *Theobald;*
notes F.   61. of you, and] *Capell;* of you, to you; and *F;* to you, and *Pope.*
64. pound] *F;* pounds *Theobald.*   67. nor] *F;* for *Pope.*   74. t'approve] *F;*
to improve *Knight.*

61. *Commends . . . you*] i.e. presents his
compliments (Pooler); Capell's correction of "of you, to you; and" (F),
gives a better reading: it looks as
though the compositor (or scribe)
caught up the phrase "to you" from
the next line.

63. *Marchioness of Pembroke*] Holinshed records, p. 928, that on 1 September 1532, "the K. being come to
Windsor, created the ladie Anne

Bullongne marchionesse of Penbroke,
and gave to hir one thousand pounds
land by the yeare".

67–8. *nor . . . not*] The double nega-
tive is for emphasis, cf. *Mer. V.*, v. i. 35
(Clarendon Ed.); Abbott 406.

71. *Vouchsafe*] be so kind as.

74. *approve . . . conceit*] confirm the
good opinion; cf. *Lr.*, i. i. 187, "And
your large speeches may your deeds
approve", and Dekker, *Wonder of a*

The king hath of you. [*Aside*] I have perus'd her well; 75
Beauty and honour in her are so mingled
That they have caught the king: and who knows yet
But from this lady may proceed a gem
To lighten all this isle.—I'll to the king,
And say I spoke with you.   *Exit Lord Chamberlain.*

Anne.   My honour'd lord.   80

Old L. Why this it is: see, see,
    I have been begging sixteen years in court
    (Am yet a courtier beggarly) nor could
    Come pat betwixt too early and too late
    For any suit of pounds: and you (O fate!)   85
    A very fresh fish here (fie, fie, fie upon
    This compell'd fortune) have your mouth fill'd up
    Before you open it.

Anne.   This is strange to me.

Old L. How tastes it? Is it bitter? Forty pence, no:

---

75. S.D. *Aside*] *Pope; not in F.*   I have] *F;* I've *Pope.*   78. gem] Iemme *F.*
80. S.D. *Exit . . . Chamberlain*] *so F; after* lord *Capell.*   86–7. here (fie . . . / . . .
fortune)] here; fie . . . / . . . fortune: *F.*   86. fie, fie, fie] *F;* fie, fie *Pope.*

Kingdom (printed 1636; Pearson, IV.
242), "this attempt your loyalty shall
approve". A quibble on *conceit = conception* may be intended.

75. *perus'd*] examined, cf. *Cym.*, I. iv.
7, "I to peruse him by items".

79. *lighten*] give light to; gems and
jewels were thought to emit light, cf.
A Warning for Fair Women (1599), B2ᵛ,
"to light this obscure streete, / Like a
bright diamond worne in some dark
place"; Dekker, *Magnificent Entertainment* (1604; Pearson, I. 291), "So did
they shine afarre off, like Chrysolites,
and sparkled like Carbuncles"; see
also II. ii. 32 above. It is notable that
this reference to Elizabeth, foreshadowing V. iv, appears in a scene
generally allowed to Shakespeare.

81. *this it is*] thus it is!, i.e. 'such is
life!'; cf. *Ant.*, II. vii. 12.

83. *beggarly*] still begging and very
poor.

85. *suit of pounds*] petition that would
bring in money; possibly also an allu-

sion to cast-off clothing, for *panes* or
pauns (cf. "Powle's"= Paul's, v.iii. 16)
were furs or strips of cloth of different
colours, and Halle, I. 179, speaks of
"large garmentes of Blewe saten
pauned with Sipres [cypress, a valuable cloth]": "pounds" are also ponds,
confined waters, and the word may
have suggested "fresh fish" in the next
line.

86. *fie, fie, fie*] metrically there is one
"fie" too many, and there may be an
unintended duplication, a common
error.

87. *compell'd fortune*] i.e. one that is
forced on her, cf. "compell'd valour",
Ham., IV. vi. 17. The modern accentu-
ation is usual in Shakespeare, but the
word is accented on the first syllable in
Meas., II. iv. 57 (Clarendon Ed.).

89. *Forty pence*] a common expression, and a usual amount for a small
bet or fee, equivalent to ten groats, the
fee of an attorney (cf. *All's W.*, II. ii.
22), and the fee given to a company of

There was a lady once ('tis an old story)   90
That would not be a queen, that would she not
For all the mud in Egypt; have you heard it?

Anne. Come, you are pleasant.

Old L.   With your theme I could
O'ermount the lark: the Marchioness of Pembroke?
A thousand pounds a year, for pure respect?   95
No other obligation? by my life,
That promises moe thousands: honour's train
Is longer than his foreskirt; by this time
I know your back will bear a duchess. Say,
Are you not stronger than you were?

Anne.   Good lady,   100
Make yourself mirth with your particular fancy,
And leave me out on't. Would I had no being
If this salute my blood a jot; it faints me
To think what follows.
The queen is comfortless, and we forgetful   105
In our long absence: pray do not deliver
What here y'have heard to her.

Old L.   What do you think me?—
                                              Exeunt.

---

95. year, ... respect?] *so F;* year, ... respect! *Pope;* year! ... respect; *Var. 1773.*
97. moe] mo *F;* more *Rowe.*   103. salute] *F;* elate *Collier conj. (edition 2).*
107. y'have] *F;* you have *Capell;* you've *Collier.*

players in Marston's *Histriomastix*
(1610; Wood, III. 266); also half a
noble (6s. 8d.), which gave rise to a
proverb of contemptuous dismissal,
"Farewell, forty pence, Jack Noble is
dead" (Tilley, F 618). Cf. III. ii. 253
and n.

92. *mud in Egypt*] i.e. its wealth, cf.
"the riches under heaven", l. 35
(Pooler).

93. *pleasant*] merry, cf. I. iv. 90.

97. *moe*] more in number; common
in Shakespeare.

98. *foreskirt*] not earlier recorded in
O.E.D.

101. *particular*] private, cf. *Cor.*, IV. v.
92, "Thine own particular wrongs".

103. *salute ... a jot*] gives pleasure to
me, exhilarates me at all (Pooler);
Walker, *apud* Deighton, compares
Sonn., CXXXI. 6, "others' eyes / Give
salutation to my sportive blood".

faints me] makes me faint; no earlier
impersonal use is recorded in *O.E.D.*

106. *deliver*] make known, cf. I. ii.
143.

SCENE IV—[*Black-Friars*]

Trumpets, sennet and cornets.

*Enter two Vergers with short silver wands; next them two scribes in the
     habit of doctors; after them the* ARCHBISHOP OF CANTERBURY
     alone; after him the BISHOPS OF LINCOLN, ELY, ROCHESTER
     and ST. ASAPH: *next them, with some small distance, follows a
     Gentleman bearing the purse, with the great seal and a Cardinal's
     hat: then two Priests, bearing each a silver cross: then a* GENTLE-
     MAN USHER *bare-headed, accompanied with a Sergeant-at-
     Arms bearing a silver mace: then two Gentlemen bearing two
     great silver pillars: after them, side by side, the two* CARDINALS,
     two Noblemen, with the sword and mace. The KING *takes place
     under the cloth of state. The two Cardinals sit under him as
     Judges. The* QUEEN *takes place some distance from the King.
     The Bishops place themselves on each side the court in manner of
     a consistory: below them the scribes. The Lords sit next the
     Bishops. The rest of the attendants stand in convenient order about
     the stage.*

Wol. Whilst our commission from Rome is read,

appears above King   Scene IV

Scene IV] *Scena Quarta. F.* *Black-Friars.*] *Theobald.*   Entry 3. *habit*] habite.
F; habits F3.   *Archbishop*] *Johnson; Bishop F.*   Entry 5. *St.*] *S. F.*   1, 5. S.H.
Wol.] *Car. F.*

Scene IV] This scene is very closely
derived from Holinshed, see Appendix
II, pp. 194 ff. The trial of Katherine
began in June 1528.

S.D. I. sennet] a frequent direction
for ceremonial entrances; a fanfare or
prelude played on trumpets or cornets,
perhaps on both in this instance. The
exact meaning and derivation are not
known; cf. *Lr.*, I. i. 33 and Muir's note
ad loc. (Arden Ed.).

S.D. 3. habit of doctors] i.e. in the
long furred black gowns and flat caps
of Doctors of Law, cf. *Meas.*, III. ii.
8.

S.D. 7–10. cross . . . pillars] Wolsey
"had . . . his two great crosses of silver,
the one of his archbishoprike, the
other of his legacie, borne before him

whither soever he went" (Stow,
Annals, 1592, p. 838); the silver pillars,
substituted by Wolsey for the mace to
which a cardinal had a right, were
noted as a mark of his pride in his own
lifetime; cf. Roy, *Read me and be not
wroth* (1528), d1ᵣ, "After theym fol-
owe two laye men secular / And each
of theym holdynge a pillar / In their
hondes steade of a mace"; but Holinshed says he had a mace carried before
him as well, see Appendix II, p. 204.

S.D. 11, 13. takes place] sits in
state, cf. I. ii. 10 and n.

S.D. 12–15. cloth of state . . . con-
sistory] the terminology derives from
Holinshed, p. 907; see Appendix II,
p. 194.

1. *commission*] see II. ii. 103 ff.

Let silence be commanded.

King.   What's the need?
    It hath already publicly been read,   *appeal*
    And on all sides th'authority allow'd;
    You may then spare that time.

Wol.   Be't so; proceed.   5

Scribe. Say, Henry King of England, come into the court.

Crier. Henry King of England, &c.

Scribe. Say, Katherine Queen of England, come into the
        court.

Crier. Katherine Queen of England, &c.   10

*The Queen makes no answer, rises out of her chair, goes about the
court, comes to the King, and kneels at his feet: then speaks.*

Kath. Sir, I desire you do me right and justice,
    And to bestow your pity on me; for
    I am a most poor woman, and a stranger,
    Born out of your dominions: having here
    No judge indifferent, nor no more assurance   15
    Of equal friendship and proceeding. Alas sir,
    In what have I offended you? What cause
    Hath my behaviour given to your displeasure,
    That thus you should proceed to put me off,

6. King] *Rowe;* K. F.   8–9. Say . . . court] *as prose Capell; two lines in F, ending*
England, / . . . Court.   11. S.H. *Kath.*] *not in F.*   you do] *F;* you, do
Theobald.

6–10. *Say . . . &c.*] taken directly
from Holinshed, see Appendix II,
p. 195; even the etceteras were probably suggested by his use of them.

    10. S.D. goes . . . court] another S.D.
taken from Holinshed, p. 907, who
explains her procedure; "bicause she
could not come to the king directlie,
for the distance severed betweene
them, shee went about by the court,
and came to the king, kneeling downe
at his feet".

    11–55. *Sir . . . fulfill'd*] This speech is
Holinshed versified, but with some
significant changes, cf. Appendix II,
pp. 195–6: ll. 29–32, "what friend . . .
discharg'd?", is an addition of the
author's, and the passion of ll. 39–42,

"in God's name / Turn me away, and
let the foul'st contempt / Shut door
upon me . . ." is entirely lacking in the
historian's tame "I am content to
depart to my shame and rebuke". It is
such changes that make Katherine's
character.

    13. *stranger*] foreigner, cf. II. iii. 17.

    15. *indifferent*] impartial; so the *Book
of Common Prayer* has "that they may
truly and indifferently minister justice" (Pooler).

    16. *equal . . . proceeding*] fair friend-
ship and just legal process; for "equal"
cf. II. ii. 107.

    19. *put me off*] discard me (Clarendon
Ed.); cf. I. ii. 32. Holinshed has "to put
you from me".

And take your good grace from me? Heaven witness, 20
I have been to you a true and humble wife,
At all times to your will conformable,
Ever in fear to kindle your dislike,
Yea, subject to your countenance, glad or sorry
As I saw it inclin'd. When was the hour   25
I ever contradicted your desire
Or made it not mine too? Or which of your friends
Have I not strove to love, although I knew
He were mine enemy? What friend of mine,
That had to him deriv'd your anger, did I   30
Continue in my liking? nay, gave notice
He was from thence discharg'd? Sir, call to mind
That I have been your wife in this obedience
Upward of twenty years, and have been blest
With many children by you. If in the course   35
And process of this time you can report,
And prove it too, against mine honour aught,
My bond to wedlock, or my love and duty
Against your sacred person; in God's name
Turn me away, and let the foul'st contempt   40
Shut door upon me, and so give me up
To the sharp'st kind of justice. Please you, sir,
The king your father was reputed for
A prince most prudent, of an excellent
And unmatch'd wit and judgment: Ferdinand   45

21. I have] _F;_ I've _Pope._   25. inclin'd.] _Rowe 3;_ inclin'd? _F._   27. Or
which] _F;_ Which _Pope._   31. gave notice] _F;_ gave not notice _Hanmer._   37-9.
aught, ... person;] aught; ... person; _F;_ aught, ... person, _Rowe._   38. duty]
_F;_ duty, _Theobald 2._

20. _your ... grace_] in the double sense
of 'your favour' and 'your person'; for
"your good grace" as a complimentary phrase = you, cf. _Oth._, I. iii.
287.

28. _strove_] a form common in Shakespeare, cf. _Cym._, III. v. 21, "Lucius hath
wrote already"; Abbott 343 explains
as a use of the past tense for a participle in the case of verbs like _strive_,
where a dropping of the _-en_ inflection
of the participle _striven_ might have led
to confusion with the infinitive.

30. _deriv'd ... anger_] drawn your
anger upon him; cf. _All's W._, v. iii.
265, "things which would derive me
ill will to speak of" (Deighton).

38-9. _duty | Against_] so F; "against"
means 'towards', for which _O.E.D._
cites an apprenticeship indenture of
1557, "He shall behave himself gently
ageynst his seyde Master". The usual
addition of a comma after "duty"
wrecks the sense and stops the flow of
rhythm.

45. _wit_] intelligence, wisdom.

My father, King of Spain, was reckon'd one
The wisest prince that there had reign'd by many
A year before. It is not to be question'd
That they had gather'd a wise council to them
Of every realm, that did debate this business,　50
Who deem'd our marriage lawful: wherefore I humbly
Beseech you sir, to spare me till I may
Be by my friends in Spain advis'd, whose counsel
I will implore. If not, i'th'name of God
Your pleasure be fulfill'd.

Wol.　　　　　　　　　You have here lady　55
(And of your choice) these reverend fathers, men
Of singular integrity and learning,
Yea, the elect o'th'land, who are assembled
To plead your cause. It shall be therefore bootless
That longer you desire the court, as well　60
For your own quiet as to rectify
What is unsettled in the king.

Cam.　　　　　　　　　　His grace
Hath spoken well and justly: therefore madam,
It's fit this royal session do proceed,
And that without delay their arguments　65

---

60. desire] *F;* defer *F4.*

46–7. *one / The*] an old usage to emphasize superlatives, cf. "one / The truest manner'd", *Cym.*, I. vi. 165–6, and Abbott 18. Holinshed has "one of the finest princes".

56. *choice*] so Holinshed, p. 907, "he [Henry] bad hir choose the best clearks of his realme to be of hir counsell".

reverend fathers] bishops and archbishops, whose formal titles are respectively Right Reverend and Most Reverend Father in God. The Bishops of Ely, Rochester, and St Asaph were the Queen's counsellors.

59. *bootless*] profitless.

60. *longer . . . court*] "desire" probably means entreat; i.e. it is useless to plead longer with the court (for postponement, cf. l. 52). Malone may be

right in explaining "That you desire to *protract* the business of the court; that you solicit a more distant session and trial. 'To pray for a *longer* day', i.e. a more distant one . . . is yet the language of the bar"; as it was of the hard-driven debtor, cf. Massinger, *City Madam* (1632; Gifford, IV. 22), "you must give me longer day". Pooler noted a possible quibble on *court*=short, in opposition to "longer", and suggested corruption from *delay*; if an emendation is desired, "defer" of F4 is the best, but elsewhere in Shakespeare only occurs in *1* and *2 H 6*, whereas "desire" meaning 'entreat' is fairly common, cf. *Troil.*, IV. v. 157, *Cor.*, II. iii. 61. Holinshed offers no parallel.

61. *quiet*] peace of mind.

Be now produc'd and heard.
Kath.   Lord Cardinal,
To you I speak.
Wol.   Your pleasure, madam.
Kath.   Sir,
I am about to weep; but thinking that
We are a queen (or long have dream'd so) certain
The daughter of a king, my drops of tears   70
I'll turn to sparks of fire.
Wol.   Be patient yet.
Kath. I will, when you are humble; nay before,
Or God will punish me. I do believe
(Induc'd by potent circumstances) that
You are mine enemy, and make my challenge   75
You shall not be my judge. For it is you
Have blown this coal betwixt my lord and me
(Which God's dew quench), therefore I say again
I utterly abhor; yea, from my soul
Refuse you for my judge, whom yet once more   80
I hold my most malicious foe, and think not

66, 67, 72. S.H. *Kath.*] *Qu. F.*   66-7. Lord . . . speak] *so Pope; one line in F.*
67. madam.] *F; Madam? Theobald.*   67-8. Sir . . . that] *so Pope; one line in F.*
75. challenge] *Dyce;* Challenge, *F;* Challenge. *F2.*   79-80. abhor; . . . judge,]
F; abhor, . . . judge, *F4;* abhor, . . . judge; *Capell.*

66. *produc'd*] brought forward; the
common legal sense.
68. *weep*] cf. *Wint.*, II. i. 108
(Steevens); this and the next three
lines are not suggested by Holinshed.
Here, as elsewhere in the scene, there
is a striking similarity between the
demeanour of Katherine and that of
Hermione in *Wint.*, II. i and III. ii.
69. *certain*] certainly, cf. *Wint.*, I. ii.
362.
71. *patient*] see Introduction, pp.
lvii ff.
72. *before*] i.e. before you are humble, for you will never be so (Pooler).
74. *Induc'd by potent*] persuaded, pre-
vailed upon by cogent circumstances;
cf. *Cym.*, II. iv. 125, and for "potent",
Troil., III. iii. 192, "The reasons are
more potent and heroical".
75. *challenge*] objection; a law term

with the special meaning of refusal to
accept a juryman (Johnson): not
used elsewhere in this sense by Shakespeare.
77. *blown . . . coal*] an old expression
meaning 'stirred up strife', see Tilley,
C 465.
78. *dew*] cf. *Cym.*, v. v. 351, "The
benediction of these covering heavens /
Fall on their heads like dew".
79. *abhor*] cf. *Err.*, III. ii. 164, "She
. . . my soul / Doth for a wife abhor",
where also the meaning seems to be
'loathe and reject'; as Malone noted,
the phrase is from Holinshed, p. 908,
"the queene . . . openlie protested,
that she did utterlie abhorre, refuse,
and forsake such a judge, as was not
onlie a most malicious enimie to hir,
but also a manifest adversarie to all
right and justice".

    At all a friend to truth.

Wol.   I do profess

    You speak not like yourself; who ever yet

    Have stood to charity and display'd th'effects

    Of disposition gentle, and of wisdom   85

    O'ertopping woman's power. Madam, you do me

        wrong:

    I have no spleen against you, nor injustice

    For you or any: how far I have proceeded,

    Or how far further shall, is warranted

    By a commission from the consistory,   90

    Yea, the whole consistory of Rome. You charge me

    That I have blown this coal: I do deny it;

    The king is present; if it be known to him

    That I gainsay my deed, how may he wound,

    And worthily, my falsehood, yea, as much   95

    As you have done my truth. If he know

    That I am free of your report, he knows

    I am not of your wrong. Therefore in him

    It lies to cure me, and the cure is to

    Remove these thoughts from you: the which before   100

    His highness shall speak in, I do beseech

---

88. I have] *F;* I've *Pope.*   96. If he] *F;* But if he *Pope;* If he then *Keightley.*

82. *profess*] affirm, cf. *Cor.,* I. iii. 24, and below, III. ii. 44.

84. *stood to*] upheld, cf. *Cor.,* III. i. 208, "let us stand to our authority" (cited Deighton). "Charity" is used in the sense of Christian love for fellow-men, as at III. ii. 298.

87. *spleen*] malice, cf. I. ii. 174 and n. This speech of Wolsey's may have been suggested by a passage in Halle, II. 148, describing an interview between him and Katherine, where she says, "of malice you have kindled thys fyre, and set thys matter a broche, and in especial for the great malice that you beare to my nephew the Emperour... The cardinal... excused himself, say-ing, that he was not the begynner, nor the mover of the doubte, & that it was sore agaynst hys wyl, that ever the mariage should come in question, but

he sayd that by his superior the Bishop of Rome, he was deputed as a Judge to heare the cause, which he sware on his professyon to heare indifferently".

94. *gainsay*] have done as you say and now deny it, cf. *Wint.,* III. ii. 57 (Pooler).

95. *worthily*] rightly, cf. *H 5,* IV. vii. 9.

97–8. *report . . . wrong*] "report" is a milder word than accusation; see *1 H 4,* I. iii. 67, "let not his report / Come current for an accusation" (Pooler) and l. 36 above. The sense is, 'if he know that I am guiltless of your accusations, he knows I am not [free of] the wrong you have done me in accusing me'.

99. *cure*] cf. II. ii. 75, where Wolsey is "a cure fit for a king".

101. *in*] in reference to; cf. *All's W.,* I. i. 147, "There's little can be said

You, gracious madam, to unthink your speaking
And to say so no more.

Kath.   My lord, my lord,
I am a simple woman, much too weak
T'oppose your cunning. Y'are meek and humble-
    mouth'd,   105
You sign your place and calling, in full seeming,
With meekness and humility: but your heart
Is cramm'd with arrogancy, spleen and pride.
You have by fortune, and his highness' favours,
Gone slightly o'er low steps, and now are mounted   110
Where powers are your retainers, and your words
(Domestics to you) serve your will as't please
Yourself pronounce their office. I must tell you,
You tender more your person's honour than
Your high profession spiritual; that again   115
I do refuse you for my judge, and here
Before you all, appeal unto the Pope,
To bring my whole cause 'fore his holiness

---

103. S.H. *Kath.*] *Queen. F.*   110. slightly] *F;* lightly *S. Walker conj.*   111.
words] *F;* wards *Singer (Tyrwhitt conj.).*

in't" (Clarendon Ed.), and *Oth.*, I. iii.
74.

103 ff. *My lord . . .*] The remainder
of this scene follows Holinshed fairly
closely, see Appendix II, pp. 196–8; the
most significant additions, as earlier,
cf. ll. 11–55 and n., relate to Katherine,
especially in this speech (ll. 103–19),
which develops with great fire the
mere hints given by the historian.

106. *sign your place*] mark your high
office, give an outward show in it of
humility (Onions); perhaps there is a
quibble on "sign"='mark with the
sign of the cross, consecrate' (*O.E.D.*,
v[1]).

108. *arrogancy*] Holinshed's word,
from his marginal note, "Example of /
pride and ar- / rogancie"; but cf.
"extravagancy", also unique in Shakespeare, *Tw. N.*, II. i. 12.

110. *slightly*] lightly, easily (Pooler);
O.E.D. cites as the first use in this
sense, but cf. Holinshed, p. 834, "ran

cleane with it a long course and
slightlie avoided it". Wolsey's first
important appointment was to the
Deanship of Lincoln in 1509, and by
1515 he had risen to be Cardinal,
Archbishop of York, and Lord
Chancellor.

111. *powers . . . retainers*] men in
authority serve him, cf. II. ii. 47–9 and
n.; possibly suggesting spirits, deities,
as in *Tp.*, III. iii. 73, *Wint.*, III. ii. 29,
Cym., v. iv. 26.

111–13. *words . . . office*] The sense is,
Wolsey has only to speak and his words
are acted upon, become deeds; cf. the
play on words and deeds at III. ii. 154.
O.E.D. cites as the first use of "domestic" meaning servant. Singer's emendation of "words" to "wards" is ingenious but unnecessary.

114. *tender*] cherish, cf. *Ham.*, IV. iii.
43, "thine especial safety, / Which we
do tender, as we dearly grieve / For
that which thou hast done".

And to be judg'd by him.

She curtsies to the King, and offers to depart.

Cam.　　　　　　　The queen is obstinate,
Stubborn to justice, apt to accuse it, and　　　　120
Disdainful to be tried by't; 'tis not well.
She's going away.

King. Call her again.

Crier. Katherine Queen of England, come into the court.

Gent. Ush. Madam, you are call'd back.　　　　125

Kath. What need you note it? pray you keep your way,
When you are call'd return. Now the Lord help,
They vex me past my patience. Pray you pass on;
I will not tarry; no, nor ever more
Upon this business my appearance make　　　　130
In any of their courts.

Exit Queen, and her attendants.

King.　　　　　　Go thy ways Kate;
That man i'th'world who shall report he has
A better wife, let him in nought be trusted,
For speaking false in that; thou art alone
(If thy rare qualities, sweet gentleness,　　　　135
Thy meekness saintlike, wife-like government,
Obeying in commanding, and thy parts
Sovereign and pious else, could speak thee out)

---

124. Queen] *Rowe;* Q. *F.*　　125. S.H. *Gent. Ush.*] *F; Griff. Var. 1793.*　　126.
S.H. *Kath.*] *Que. F.*　　131. S.D. *Exit*] *F; Exeunt Rowe.*

---

119. S.D. She . . . depart] from
Holinshed, p. 907, "she arose up,
making a lowe curtesie to the king, and
departed from thence".

120. *Stubborn . . . it*] unyielding to
justice and inclined to find fault with
it. For "accuse", cf. *R 2*, I. i. 47, "Let
not my cold words here accuse my
zeal".

125. S.H. Gent. Ush.] i.e. Griffith,
as the entry to IV. ii makes clear; Holinshed, p. 907, has "With that (quoth
maister Griffith) Madame, you be
called againe".

126. *keep your way*] keep going.

135. *rare*] fine, excelling; Halle's
version, II. 151, "for I dare saye that

for her womanhode, wysdom, nobilitie, and gentlenes, never Prince had
suche another", is perhaps closest to
this catalogue of virtues, which is expanded beyond anything in the historians; see Appendix II, p. 196 for
Holinshed's account.

136. *government*] self-control, cf.
1 H 4, I. ii. 32, *Oth.*, III. iii. 256, "*Iago*:
And hold her free, I do beseech your
honour. *Othello*: Fear not my government".

137. *parts*] qualities, cf. II. iii. 27.
"Sovereign" means 'excellent'.

138. *speak . . . out*] describe you, cf.
Mac., IV. iii. 159; see also l. 164 and
IV. ii. 32 below.

The queen of earthly queens: she's noble born,
And like her true nobility she has   140
Carried herself towards me.

Wol.   Most gracious sir,
In humblest manner I require your highness,
That it shall please you to declare in hearing
Of all these ears (for where I am robb'd and bound,
There must I be unloos'd, although not there   145
At once and fully satisfied) whether ever I
Did broach this business to your highness, or
Laid any scruple in your way which might
Induce you to the question on't; or ever
Have to you, but with thanks to God for such   150
A royal lady, spake one the least word that might
Be to the prejudice of her present state
Or touch of her good person?

King.   My lord cardinal
I do excuse you; yea, upon mine honour
I free you from't: you are not to be taught   155
That you have many enemies that know not
Why they are so, but like to village curs
Bark when their fellows do. By some of these
The queen is put in anger; y'are excus'd:
But will you be more justified? you ever   160
Have wish'd the sleeping of this business, never
    desir'd
It to be stirr'd, but oft have hinder'd, oft

144. I am] *F;* I'm *Pope.*   146. At once] *F;* Atton'd *Hanmer* (*Warburton*).
162. hinder'd, oft] *F;* hinder'd, oft, *F4.*

141. *Carried herself*] behaved.
142. *require*] beg, make request of, cf. *Cor.*, II. ii. 160, "He will require them, as if he did contemn what he requested". It is Holinshed's word.
146. *satisfied*] compensated.
148. *scruple*] doubt, cf.II.i. 158.
149. *on't*] of it; very common, cf. Abbott 182.
150–1. *Have . . . spake*] see note on "strove", l. 28 above; Abbott 344 lists as an irregular participial form, for which there is no close parallel in

Shakespeare, but it may well be an *a–o* confusion, a misreading of "spoke".
151. *one*] see above, l. 46 and n.
152. *prejudice*] detriment, cf. I. i. 182 and n.
153. *touch*] reproach, taint (Onions), cf. *AYL.*, III. ii. 366, "to be touched with so many giddy offences"; or 'injury' (Pooler), from *touch* meaning a wound or hit in fencing, as in *Ham.*, v. ii. 297.
159. *excus'd*] i.e. freed from imputation, as in l. 154.

The passages made toward it; on my honour,
I speak my good lord card'nal to this point,
And thus far clear him. Now what mov'd me to't,   165
I will be bold with time and your attention:
Then mark th'inducement: thus it came; give heed to't:
My conscience first receiv'd a tenderness,
Scruple and prick, on certain speeches utter'd
By th'Bishop of Bayonne, then French ambassador,   170
Who had been hither sent on the debating
A marriage 'twixt the Duke of Orleans and
Our daughter Mary: i'th'progress of this business,
Ere a determinate resolution, he
(I mean the Bishop) did require a respite,   175
Wherein he might the king his lord advertise
Whether our daughter were legitimate
Respecting this our marriage with the dowager,
Sometimes our brother's wife. This respite shook

163-4. honour, / . . . point,] *Capell;* Honour, / I speake my . . . Cardnall, to . . . point; *F;* Honour, / I speake my . . . Cardinal to . . . point; *F2;* Honour / I speak, my . . . Cardinal, to . . . point; *Rowe 3.*   165. And . . . to't] *so Rowe 3;* two lines in F, ending him. / . . . too't.   172. A] *Rowe 3;* And *F.*   179. Sometimes] *F;* sometime *Rowe 2.*

---

163. *passages*] proceedings, cf. *1 H 4,* III. ii. 8, "in thy passages of life". Steevens's interpretation of "made" as closed (cf. II. i. 86 and n.), is also possible if a stop is placed after "hinder'd". The meaning then becomes, 'oft have hindered it (the business); oft blocked the way toward it'.

163-5. *on . . . him*] As Theobald noted, the king here breaks off from speaking directly to Wolsey and addresses the whole court: 'on my honour I bear witness for the cardinal to this extent, and so far, clear him'. For "speak", cf. IV. ii. 32, "thus far . . . speak him". Alternatively, "my . . . cardinal" may be taken as a parenthesis, a direct address to Wolsey, and the sense becomes, 'I treat (my lord, bowing to Wolsey) of this point, this accusation, and clear him of it'; *O.E.D.* cites J. Dove, *Advertisement to the English Seminaries* (1610), p. 42, "to

speake to these four points", and cf. v. ii. 35 below.

167. *inducement*] cf. l. 74 and n.

168. *tenderness*] sensitivity, cf. II. ii. 143. Holinshed, p. 907, has "a certeine scrupulositie that pricked my conscience, upon certeine words spoken . . . by the bishop of Baion the French ambassador".

172. *Duke of Orleans*] second son of Francis I, and later Henry II of France.

174. *determinate resolution*] final settlement; a compression of Holinshed's "Upon the resolution and determination wherof..."

175. *require*] desire (Holinshed's word), as at l. 142.

176. *advertise*] inform. Accented on the second syllable, as always in Shakespeare (Clarendon Ed.).

179. *Sometimes*] formerly, cf. *R 2,* I. ii. 54, Dekker, *News from Hell* (1606;

The bosom of my conscience, enter'd me,   180
Yea, with a spitting power, and made to tremble
The region of my breast, which forc'd such way
That many maz'd considerings did throng
And press'd in with this caution. First, methought
I stood not in the smile of heaven, who had   185
Commanded nature, that my lady's womb,
If it conceiv'd a male-child by me, should
Do no more offices of life to't than
The grave does to th' dead: for her male issue
Or died where they were made, or shortly after   190
This world had air'd them. Hence I took a thought
This was a judgment on me, that my kingdom
(Well worthy the best heir o'th'world) should not
Be gladded in't by me. Then follows that
I weigh'd the danger which my realms stood in   195
By this my issue's fail, and that gave to me
Many a groaning throe: thus hulling in

---

180. bosom] *F;* bottom *Theobald 2 (from Holinshed).*   181. spitting] *F;*
splitting *F4.*   194. gladded] *F;* glad *F2.*   197. throe] *Pope;* throw F.

Grosart, ii. 103), "thou sometimes
Secretary to *Pierce Pennylesse* . . . T.
Nash". Holinshed has the more usual
"sometime".

180. *bosom*] Theobald, Ed. 2, read
"bottom", a correction from Holinshed's "the secret bottom of my conscience", as the chronicle is followed
fairly closely here, cf. Appendix ii,
p. 197. But the bosom, the heart, was
regarded as the seat not only of the
passions, but of the conscience, and is
so referred to several times by Shakespeare, cf. *Cym.*, v. ii. 1, *Tp.*, ii. i. 278,
"conscience . . . I feel not / This deity
in my bosom".

181. *spitting*] transfixing; literally,
to put on a spit, to transfix on something sharp, cf. *H 5*, iii.iii. 38, "infants
spitted upon pikes". The word may
have been suggested as a quibble on
"respite", l. 179. "Splitting" (F2) has
been accepted by most editors, but the
image is of piercing ("forc'd such
way"), not of dividing.

183. *maz'd*] perplexed; perhaps the

idea of a maze was suggested by
"region".

185. *smile . . . who*] the favour of God;
"heaven" may be one of the erratic
substitutions in F for "God" due to
the Act of Abuses of 1606, restraining
profanity in stage plays; see Chambers,
W.S., i. 238 ff.

188. *offices*] services, with a quibble
perhaps on the special sense of obsequies, rites due to the dead.

191. *air'd*] first used by Shakespeare
in *Cym.*, i. i. 110.

194. *gladded*] made happy; cf. v. i.
71, *Per.*, ii. iii. 21.

196. *fail*] probably 'death', cf. i. ii.
145. The same phrase, "fail of issue",
meaning failure to have a son, occurs
in *Wint.*, v. i. 27.

197. *throe*] pang, especially birth-
pangs; an ironic quibble following on
"issue's fail".

hulling] of sailing ships, "to drift
to the wind with the sails furled"
(*O.E.D.*, hull v²1). The word occurs
also in *Tw. N.*, i. v. 217 and *R 3*, iv. iv.

The wild sea of my conscience, I did steer
Toward this remedy whereupon we are
Now present here together: that's to say,   200
I meant to rectify my conscience, which
I then did feel full sick, and yet not well,
By all the reverend fathers of the land
And doctors learn'd. First I began in private
With you my Lord of Lincoln; you remember   205
How under my oppression I did reek
When I first mov'd you.

Linc.   Very well my liege.

King. I have spoke long, be pleas'd yourself to say
How far you satisfied me.

Linc.   So please your highness,
The question did at first so stagger me,   210
Bearing a state of mighty moment in't
And consequence of dread, that I committed
The daring'st counsel which I had to doubt,
And did entreat your highness to this course
Which you are running here.

King.   I then mov'd you,   215
My Lord of Canterbury, and got your leave
To make this present summons: unsolicited

---

206. reek] *F;* reel *Rowe.*   217. summons: unsolicited] *Theobald;* Summons
unsolicited. *F.*

438. The idea was no doubt suggested
by Holinshed, p. 907, "Thus my conscience being tossed in the waves of a
scrupulous mind..."

198. *steer*] as Pooler noted, a vessel
hulling could not be steered.

201. *rectify*] set right, cf. l. 61 above;
elsewhere in Shakespeare only at *Tp.,*
v. i. 245.

204. *doctors*] the pun on law and
medicine carries on the metaphor; for
"doctor" meaning learned lawyer, cf.
Mer. V., IV. i. 144.

206. *oppression . . . reek*] sweated
under, was tormented by the weight of
my distress. For "oppression" cf. *Ham.,*
II. ii. 606, and for "reek", *Lr.,* II. iv. 30,
"came there a reeking post, / Stew'd in
his haste".

207. *mov'd*] Holinshed's word, p.
908, "I mooved it in confession to you
my lord of Lincolne", and cf. l. 165
above.

211–12. *Bearing . . . dread*] concerning a state of things of great importance and fearful outcome. For "state"
cf. *Cæs.,* I. iii. 71, "instruments of fear
and warning / Unto some monstrous
state".

212–13. *committed . . . doubt*] i.e. dis-
trusted the boldest advice which I had
to give (Case, *apud* Pooler). This
speech is the dramatist's amplification
of Holinshed's bare "as then you your
selfe were in some doubt".

217. *summons*] i.e. the citation of the
Queen to appear in court; Holinshed
has, "to put this matter in question"

I left no reverend person in this court,
But by particular consent proceeded
Under your hands and seals; therefore go on,   220
For no dislike i'th'world against the person
Of the good Queen, but the sharp thorny points
Of my alleged reasons drives this forward:
Prove but our marriage lawful, by my life
And kingly dignity, we are contented   225
To wear our mortal state to come with her
(Katherine our Queen) before the primest creature
That's paragon'd o'th'world.

Cam.   So please your highness,
The queen being absent, 'tis a needful fitness
That we adjourn this court till further day;   230
Meanwhile must be an earnest motion
Made to the queen to call back her appeal
She intends unto his holiness.

King. [*Aside*]   I may perceive
These cardinals trifle with me: I abhor
This dilatory sloth and tricks of Rome.   235

---

223. drives] *F;* drive *Pope.*   228. paragon'd o'th'] *F;* paragon'd i'th' *Pope;*
paragon o'th' *Hanmer.*   233. holiness.] *F;* holiness. | [S.D.] *They rise to
depart. The King speaks to Cranmer.* | *Johnson.*   S.D. *Aside*] *Var. 1793 (after
Capell).*

220. *Under . . . seals*] with your written consent, signed and sealed.
    222–3. *sharp . . . reasons*] cf. II. i. 13–14
and n.
    223. *drives*] The plural ending in -*s*
is very common, cf. *Ham.*, III. ii. 214,
"his favourites flies" (emended in the
Globe text to "favourite"), and
Abbott 333.
    226. *state*] pomp, and condition of
existence, cf. III. ii. 352.
    227. *primest*] first in excellence, cf.
I. ii. 67.
    228. *paragon'd*] put forward as most
perfect; the verb occurs also in *Oth.*,
II. i. 62 and *Ant.*, I. v. 71, as Steevens
noted, but not in this sense, which may
be unique.
    230. *further day*] a future day, cf.
Lr., v. iii. 53, "To-morrow, or at fur-

ther space", and above, l. 60 and n.
    231. *motion*] appeal, cf. "mov'd
you", l. 215.
    233–8. *I . . . along*] often interpre-
ted as a direct remark to Cranmer,
who is introduced into this scene in
many stage performances (as in the
production in 1949 at Stratford, cf.
M. St Clare Byrne, *Shakespeare Survey*, 3
(1950), 125–6); but as the next scenes
make clear, cf. III. ii. 63, 400, Cranmer
cannot be present here, and his
dramatic function is to reveal the
king's power and mercy in the last act,
not to replace Wolsey. See Introduction, pp. li ff. The Archbishop of
Canterbury called for in the Entry to
this scene is only one of a group of
silent bishops, and is named in
Holinshed as Warham.

My learn'd and well-beloved servant Cranmer,
Prithee return; with thy approach, I know
My comfort comes along.—Break up the court;
I say set on.   *Exeunt, in manner as they enter'd.*

239. *set on*] advance, cf. *Cym.*, v. v. 484.

ACT III

SCENE I—[*A room in the Queen's apartments.*]

Enter QUEEN *and her women as at work.*

Kath. Take thy lute wench, my soul grows sad with troubles
Sing, and disperse 'em if thou canst: leave working.

SONG

Orpheus with his lute made trees,
And the mountain tops that freeze,
   Bow themselves when he did sing: 5
To his music plants and flowers
Ever sprung, as sun and showers
   There had made a lasting spring.

Every thing that heard him play,
Even the billows of the sea,   10

ACT III

Scene I

Act III Scene I] *Actus Tertius. Scena Prima. F.*   *A . . . apartments.*] *Capell.*   1–102.
S.H. *Kath.*] *Queen. F.*   1. Take . . . troubles] *so Pope; two lines in F, ending*
wench, / . . . troubles,   3. Song.] *printed as consecutive lines in F; indented for rhyme*
by Pope; split into stanzas by Warburton.   7. sprung] *F*; spring *F2;* rose *Pope.*

Scene I] For Holinshed's report of
the interview between Katherine and
the Cardinals, see Appendix II, pp.
198–9; the scene is considerably expanded from his account, notable
additions being the song and the
queen's outbursts, ll. 30 ff and ll. 68 ff.
The latter may be compared with the
additions to Katherine's speeches in
II. iv; see note on ll. 11–55 of this scene.

Entry. as at work] from Holinshed;
see Appendix II, p. 199, and l. 74 and
n. below.

2. *leave*] cease, as in *Wint.,* IV. iv. 349,
"Leave your prating".

3. Song.] cf. *Mer. V.,* v. i. 79–80,
"the poet / Did feign that Orpheus
drew trees, stones and floods", i.e., by
"the sweet power of music". The poet
was probably Ovid, *Metamorphoses,*
Bks. x and xi (so Clarendon Ed.), but
see also Apollonius Rhodius, *Argo-
nautica,* I. 23–31. Pooler cites B. and F.,
Captain (?1612; *Works,* v. 263), III. i.

7. *as*] as if; cf. I. i. 10 and Abbott 107.

9–10. *play . . . sea*] cf. I. iv. 46 and n.:
the sounds were close enough to afford
a good rhyme; see Kökeritz, *Shakespeare's Pronunciation,* pp. 197–9, and
1 H 4, II. iv. 263, "Give you a reason on

    Hung their heads and then lay by:
    In sweet music is such art,
    Killing care and grief of heart
    Fall asleep, or hearing die.

Enter a Gentleman.

Kath. How now?   15
Gent. And't please your grace, the two great cardinals
    Wait in the presence.
Kath.   Would they speak with me?
Gent. They will'd me say so madam.
Kath.   Pray their graces
    To come near: [*Exit Gent.*] what can be their business
    With me, a poor weak woman, fall'n from favour?   20
    I do not like their coming; now I think on't,
    They should be good men, their affairs as righteous:
    But all hoods make not monks.

Enter the two Cardinals, WOLSEY *and* CAMPEIUS.

Wol.   Peace to your highness.
Kath. Your graces find me here part of a housewife;

13. heart] *Theobald;* heart, F.   16. And't] *F;* An't *Theobald 2.*   19. S.D. *Exit Gent.*] *Capell; not in* F.   21. coming; . . . on't,] *F;* coming, . . . on't. *Capell.* 23. S.D. *Campeius*] *F4; Campian* F.

compulsion! if reasons were as plenti-ful as blackberries, I would give no man a reason . . .", where *reason* puns on *raisin.*

  11. *lay by*] rested; *O.E.D.* (lay, 20d) first records in 1709 (Pooler).

  13. *Killing*] cf. "killing tongue", *H 5*, III. ii. 36, "killing lust", *Tit.*, II. iii. 175; Fletcher uses the word several times, cf. "killing griefs", "killing anger", *Bonduca* (1613; *Works*, VI. 89, 112), I. ii, III. i.

  17. *presence*] i.e. "the queenes cham-ber of presence" (Holinshed, p. 908); Speed has, p. 768, "staied in presence for the Queene"; a common usage, cf. *R 2*, I. iii. 289.

  18. *will'd*] desired (Clarendon Ed.).

  20–3.] The change here from the Katherine of II. iv. 72 ff. is often criti-cized as a sentimentalizing by Flet-cher; but in II. iv her trial has just be-gun, whereas here she has already been sentenced, in effect, if not in law. The transition is clear, acceptable, and moving on the stage, and is based on Holinshed: it is significant that most of the additions in this scene add strength and force to the historian's portrait of her sweetness and meek-ness, cf. note above.

  22. *affairs*] business, cf. v. i. 53.

  23. *all . . . monks*] an old proverb, Tilley, H 586. The latin form, "cucul-lus non facit monachum" appears in *Tw. N.* and *Meas.* The implication is that clothing alone does not prove a man to be religious or righteous.

  24–5. *part . . . all*] i.e. she is now something of a housewife, at work

I would be all, against the worst may happen: 25
What are your pleasures with me, reverent lords?
Wol. May it please you noble madam, to withdraw
Into your private chamber; we shall give you
The full cause of our coming.
Kath.   Speak it here.
There's nothing I have done yet o' my conscience   30
Deserves a corner; would all other women
Could speak this with as free a soul as I do.
My lords, I care not (so much I am happy
Above a number) if my actions
Were tried by ev'ry tongue, ev'ry eye saw 'em,   35
Envy and base opinion set against 'em,
I know my life so even. If your business
Seek me out, and that way I am wife in,
Out with it boldly: truth loves open dealing.
Wol. Tanta est erga te mentis integritas Regina serenis-   40
    sima—
Kath. O good my lord, no latin;
I am not such a truant since my coming

25. I . . . all,] *Var. 1773;* (I . . . all) *F.*   26. reverent] *F;* reverend *F2.*
38. wife] *F;* wise *Rowe.*   40, 50. S.H. *Wol.*] *Card. F.*

among her women, and would learn to
be a complete one, in case nothing else
is left to her.

26. *reverent*] a common spelling, cf.
Leigh, *Queen Elizabeth Paraleld* (1612),
H2ʳ, "you reverent fathers of the
Church".

31. *corner*] secrecy. Perhaps an echo
of the proverb 'Truth seeks no corners'
(Tilley, T 587), which emerges at l. 39
in the form "truth loves open dealing".
As Pooler notes, the meaning survives
in the phrase 'hole and corner'.

32. *free*] innocent; cf. II. iv. 97.

34. *a number*] i.e. many others; cf.
Cæs., III. i. 68.

36. *Envy . . . opinion*] malice and low
gossip (Pooler); for "opinion", cf. II. ii.
124 above.

37. *even*] just, true, as at *Cæs.*, II. i.
133, "stain / The even virtue of our
enterprise"; or possibly, 'untroubled',
as at l. 166 below.

37–9. *If . . . boldly*] if your business
concerns me and my condition as a
wife, speak it boldly. Many have objected to the passage as obscure and
unrhythmical, mainly because of the
repetition of "out": it is just possible
that "Seeke me out" should read
"Seek me on't", or that "wife" is a
misprint for "wise" (cf. *Tp.*, IV. i. 123,
where "So rare a wonder'd father and
a wise" is often emended to "wife");
but "wife" here has a richer meaning,
as relating not merely to Katherine's
present occupation, but to her conduct
as Henry's wife.

39. *truth . . . dealing*] see note on
l. 31.

40–1. *Tanta . . . serenissima*] I have
found no source for this; Holinshed,
following Cavendish, merely has, p.
908, "Then began the cardinall to
speake to hir in Latine".

43. *truant*] idler; cf. *1 H 4*, III. i. 207,

As not to know the language I have liv'd in;
A strange tongue makes my cause more strange,
   suspicious: 45
Pray speak in English; here are some will thank you,
If you speak truth, for their poor mistress' sake;
Believe me she has had much wrong. Lord cardinal,
The willing'st sin I ever yet committed
May be absolv'd in English.

Wol.   Noble lady,   50
I am sorry my integrity should breed
(And service to his majesty and you)
So deep suspicion where all faith was meant;
We come not by the way of accusation,
To taint that honour every good tongue blesses,   55
Nor to betray you any way to sorrow—
You have too much, good lady: but to know
How you stand minded in the weighty difference
Between the king and you, and to deliver
(Like free and honest men) our just opinions   60
And comforts to your cause.

Cam.   Most honour'd madam,
My lord of York, out of his noble nature,
Zeal and obedience he still bore your grace,
Forgetting (like a good man) your late censure
Both of his truth and him (which was too far)   65

51. I am] *F*; I'm *Pope.*   52, 53.] *transposed by Singer 2, following Edwards.*
61. your] *F2*; our *F*.

"I will never be a truant, love, / Till I have learn'd thy language".

  45. *strange, suspicious*] more strange (or foreign), even suspicious (Clarendon Ed.). The queen's cause is that of a foreigner, cf. II. iv. 13, 53, and to speak of it in a foreign tongue makes it sound more strange to English ears.

  49. *willing'st*] most deliberate (Pooler); cf. *Tim.*, IV. iii. 242.

  52, 53.] The phrasing suggests a dramatic intention; Wolsey thinks first of his self-importance, his own worth, then mentions, as an afterthought, his service to others. Cyrus Hoy, *Studies in Bibliography*, XV (1962),

82–3, shows that the construction is "distinctly Fletcherian".

  53. *faith*] loyalty, cf. II. i. 143.

  54. *by . . . accusation*] in order to accuse; cf. II. ii. 68.

  56. *any way*] in any respect; cf. *Err.*, III. ii. 153 (Onions).

  58. *minded . . . difference*] what attitude you take in the dispute; for "minded", cf. *Tp.*, V. i. 126, and for "difference" see above, I. i. 101.

  59. *deliver*] declare; cf. I. ii. 143.

  60. *free*] honourable, guiltless, cf. *Oth.*, III. iii. 199, "your free and noble nature", and l. 32 above.

  65. *far*] extreme, severe; cf. I. i. 38.

Offers, as I do, in a sign of peace
His service and his counsel.
Kath. [*Aside*]   To betray me.——
My lords, I thank you both for your good wills,
Ye speak like honest men (pray God ye prove so)
But how to make ye suddenly an answer   70
In such a point of weight, so near mine honour
(More near my life I fear) with my weak wit,
And to such men of gravity and learning,
In truth I know not. I was set at work
Among my maids, full little (God knows) looking   75
Either for such men or such business;
For her sake that I have been (for I feel
The last fit of my greatness)—good your graces
Let me have time and counsel for my cause:
Alas, I am a woman friendless, hopeless.   80
Wol. Madam, you wrong the king's love with these fears,
Your hopes and friends are infinite.
Kath.   In England
But little for my profit; can you think lords,
That any Englishman dare give me counsel?
Or be a known friend 'gainst his highness' pleasure   85
(Though he be grown so desperate to be honest)
And live a subject? Nay forsooth, my friends,
They that must weigh out my afflictions,

67. S.D. *Aside*] *Var. 1773, following Capell; not in F.*   77–8. been (for . . . | . . .
greatness)—] *This Ed.;* been, for . . . | . . . greatness; *F.*   81. Madam] *so Pope;*
a separate line in F.   82. England] *Johnson;* England, *F;* England! *Capell.*
83. profit; can] *F2;* profit can *F.*

66. *in a sign*] as a token; a usual
phrase, as in *3 H 6*, IV. ii. 9.

70. *suddenly*] extempore; cf. V. ii.
156. Holinshed's word.

71, 72. *near*] intimately affecting; cf.
Tim., III. vi. 11.

72. *wit*] understanding, as at II. iv.
45.

74. *set*] seated; a common usage, cf.
Cor., IV. v. 204, "Set at upper end o'
the table". Holinshed has, p. 908, "I
was set among my maids at worke,
thinking full little of aoie such
matter".

78. *fit*] spell; the period during
which a fit lasts.

83. *But . . . profit*] little indeed for my
good; Holinshed has, p. 908, "for anie
counsell or freendship that I can find
in England, they are not for my profit".

86. *so . . . honest*] so mad, reckless, as
to say what he thinks; cf. *Wint.*, IV. iv.
496, "*Flo.* . . . my senses, better pleased
with madness, / Do bid it welcome.
Cam. This is desperate, sir".

88. *weigh out*] counterbalance (Johnson); compensate for (Onions); see

They that my trust must grow to, live not here;
They are (as all my other comforts) far hence   90
    In mine own country, lords.
Cam.   I would your grace
Would leave your griefs, and take my counsel.
Kath.   How sir?
Cam. Put your main cause into the king's protection,
    He's loving and most gracious. 'Twill be much
    Both for your honour better and your cause,   95
    For if the trial of the law o'ertake ye,
    You'll part away disgrac'd.
Wol.   He tells you rightly.
Kath. Ye tell me what ye wish for both, my ruin:
    Is this your Christian counsel? Out upon ye.
    Heaven is above all yet; there sits a judge   100
    That no king can corrupt.
Cam.   Your rage mistakes us.
Kath. The more shame for ye; holy men I thought ye,
    Upon my soul two reverend cardinal virtues;
    But cardinal sins and hollow hearts I fear ye:
    Mend 'em for shame my lords. Is this your comfort? 105
    The cordial that ye bring a wretched lady,
    A woman lost among ye, laugh'd at, scorn'd?
    I will not wish ye half my miseries,
    I have more charity. But say I warn'd ye;
    Take heed, for heaven's sake take heed, lest at once   110
    The burthen of my sorrows fall upon ye.

above, I. i. II. Steevens explained as "out-weigh", and Pooler compares "last out" for "outlast", *Meas.*, II. i. 139, etc., but this interpretation seems forced.

93. *main*] cf. II. ii. 40.

97. *part away*] depart, go away.

101. *mistakes*] misjudges; cf. I. i. 195.

103-4. *cardinal . . . sins*] The four cardinal virtues were justice, prudence, temperance, and fortitude; which, with the three theological virtues, faith, hope, and charity, made up seven virtues to match the seven deadly sins, the 'cardinal sins' of the next line. Katherine is punning on 'car-

d'nal' and 'carnal', as Johnson observed; see Kökeritz, *Shakespeare's Pronunciation*, pp. 97, 299. Personification of the virtues and vices was frequent, as in Dekker's pageant, *The Magnificent Entertainment* (1604; Pearson, 1873, I. 318), "on severall Greeces [chairs] sate the foure cardinall vertues".

105. *Mend*] reform; cf. *Lr.*, II. iv. 232, "Mend when thou canst; be better at thy leisure".

107. *lost*] brought to ruin; cf. *Wint.* v. iii. 135 and *All's W.*, I. iii. 236, "languishings whereof / The king is render'd [said to be] lost".

110. *at once*] at some time, one day.

Wol. Madam, this is a mere distraction;
     You turn the good we offer into envy.
Kath. Ye turn me into nothing. Woe upon ye,
     And all such false professors. Would you have me   115
     (If you have any justice, any pity,
     If ye be anything but churchmen's habits)
     Put my sick cause into his hands that hates me?
     Alas, 'has banish'd me his bed already,
     His love, too long ago. I am old my lords,   120
     And all the fellowship I hold now with him
     Is only my obedience. What can happen
     To me, above this wretchedness? All your studies
     Make me a curse like this.
Cam.   Your fears are worse.
Kath. Have I liv'd thus long (let me speak myself,   125
     Since virtue finds no friends) a wife, a true one?
     A woman (I dare say without vainglory)
     Never yet branded with suspicion?
     Have I with all my full affections
     Still met the king? lov'd him next heav'n? obey'd him?

112, 138, 142, 153. S.H. *Wol.*] *Car. F.*   114. S.H. *Kath.*] *Quee. F.*   119. 'has]
Dyce; ha's *F;* he has *Capell;* he's *R. G. White.*   120. love, too] *F;* love too,
Rowe.   I am] *F;* I'm *Pope.*   124. curse like this.] Curse, like this. *F;* curse,
like this! *Theobald;* curse, like this? *Hanmer.*   125 ff. S.H. *Kath.*] *Qu. F.*

---

112. *mere distraction*] sheer frenzy, or
distortion, as at *Wint.*, v. ii. 52, "with
countenances of such distraction that
were to be known by garment, not by
favour".

113. *envy*] malice.

115. *professors*] i.e. of Christianity;
cf. *Wint.*, v. i. 108, "a sect, might
quench the zeal/Of all professors else".

117. *habits*] robes; cf. l. 23 and n.

119. *'has*] F "ha's"; see note on
I. iii. 59 above.

120. *old*] At the time of this interview (1529), Katherine was forty-
three, having been born late in 1485.
She might fairly describe herself as
old, i.e. middle-aged, for Shakespeare
speaks of a man as "old" at forty years
in *Sonn.*, II, "When forty winters shall
besiege thy brow...".

121. *fellowship*] intercourse; cf.
MND., I. i. 85.

123. *above*] beyond.

124. *a curse*] so F; Pooler takes
"make" as an imperative, comparing
"Bring me...", l. 134, and interprets
'do your worst and I shall be no more
miserable'. Possibly *e* has been mis-
read for *d* or *t*, as is possible in secretary
hand, giving "ac(c)ursd(t)", in which
case the meaning would be, 'whatever
you do brings me misery like this'.

worse] i.e. than "this wretchedness"
(Pooler).

125. *speak myself*] describe, bear witness for myself; cf. IV. ii. 32.

129. *affections*] love or desires; the
plural is common in Shakespeare's
later plays, cf. *Tp.*, I. ii. 481.

130. *Still*] ever.

Been (out of fondness) superstitious to him?   131
Almost forgot my prayers to content him?
And am I thus rewarded? 'tis not well, lords.
Bring me a constant woman to her husband,
One that ne'er dream'd a joy beyond his pleasure,   135
And to that woman (when she has done most)
Yet will I add an honour, a great patience.

Wol. Madam, you wander from the good we aim at.

Kath. My lord, I dare not make myself so guilty
To give up willingly that noble title   140
Your master wed me to: nothing but death
Shall e'er divorce my dignities.

Wol.   Pray hear me.

Kath. Would I had never trod this English earth,
Or felt the flatteries that grow upon it:
Ye have angels' faces, but heaven knows your hearts. 145
What will become of me now, wretched lady?
I am the most unhappy woman living.
Alas poor wenches, where are now your fortunes?
Shipwrack'd upon a kingdom where no pity,
No friends, no hope, no kindred weep for me,   150

138-9. Madam . . . guilty] *so Rowe 3; four lines in F, ending* good / . . . aim at.
. . . Lord, / . . . guilty,   145. Ye have] *F;* Ye've *Pope.*   150. hope,] *F;* hope;
Capell.   150-1. me, / . . . me:] *Capell;* me? / . . . me? *F.*

131. *superstitious*] extravagantly devoted; cf. Lyly's letter to Thomas Watson (1582; *Works,* ed. R. W. Bond, 1902, I. 27), "were not men more supersticious in their praises, thē womē are constant in their passions: Love would . . . be worne out of use" (*O.E.D.* 2b.). Pooler cites B. and F., *Queen of Corinth* (c. 1617; *Works,* VI. 47), III. ii, "Poor superstitious innocent that I am, / Give leave that I may . . . love".

134. *constant woman*] i.e. a woman constant to her husband; such transpositions are not uncommon, as in *Wint.,* IV. iv. 65, "bid / These unknown friends to's welcome". See Abbott 419a.

135. *pleasure*] i.e. what he willed (cf. I. i. 215), and his enjoyment.

145. *Ye . . . hearts*] an allusion to the proverb, 'Fair face, foul heart', Tilley, F 3; also, as Pooler noted, a reference to a well-known tale concerning St Gregory, who, hearing that some beautiful boys about to be sold in the market at Rome were 'Angles' (English), remarked that they had 'angels' faces', and said, "Alas for pittie . . . that the foul fiend should be Lord of such faire folkes, and they which carrie such grace in their countenances, should be voide of grace in their hearts" (Camden, *Remains,* 1605, C1ʳ-C1ᵛ).

149. *Shipwrack'd*] the usual spelling and pronunciation, cf. *Per.,* IV, Chorus, 11-12, where "wrack" rhymes with "alack" and III. ii. 437 below, where Wolsey likens his fall to a "wrack".

Almost no grave allow'd me: like the lily
That once was mistress of the field and flourish'd,
I'll hang my head and perish.

Wol.   If your grace
Could but be brought to know our ends are honest,
You'ld feel more comfort. Why should we, good lady,
Upon what cause wrong you? alas, our places,   156
The way of our profession is against it;
We are to cure such sorrows, not to sow 'em.
For goodness' sake consider what you do,
How you may hurt yourself, ay, utterly   160
Grow from the king's acquaintance by this carriage.
The hearts of princes kiss obedience,
So much they love it; but to stubborn spirits
They swell and grow as terrible as storms.
I know you have a gentle, noble temper,   165
A soul as even as a calm; pray think us
Those we profess, peace-makers, friends and servants.

Cam. Madam you'll find it so: you wrong your virtues
With these weak women's fears. A noble spirit,
As yours was put into you, ever casts   170
Such doubts as false coin from it. The king loves you,
Beware you lose it not: for us (if you please
To trust us in your business) we are ready
To use our utmost studies in your service.

Kath. Do what ye will, my lords; and pray forgive me;   175
If I have us'd myself unmannerly,
You know I am a woman, lacking wit

168. Madam . . . virtues] *so Pope; two lines in F, ending so:* | . . . Vertues.
170. was] *Pope;* was, F.   175. Do . . . me] *so Rowe 3; two lines in F, ending*
Lords: | . . . me;   175–6. me; | . . . unmannerly,] *F;* me, | . . . unmannerly;
F4 and edd.

151–2. *lily . . . field*] Singer compares Spenser, *Faerie Queene* (1590), II. vi. 16, "The lily, Ladie of the flowring field".

154. *ends . . . honest*] our purposes are honourable.

156. *places*] offices.

159. *goodness' sake*] see Prologue, l. 23 and n.

160. *hurt*] harm, bring disgrace on.

161. *Grow . . . acquaintance*] become estranged; "grow to" meaning "to

become united with, cling to" is frequent in Shakespeare, cf. l. 89 above.
carriage] conduct.

165. *temper*] disposition, cf. *Cym.*, II. iii. 6, "patient after the noble temper of your lordship".

174. *studies*] endeavours, cf. l. 123 above.

176. *us'd myself*] behaved.

177. *wit*] understanding; a return to Holinshed's words, p. 908, "I am a

To make a seemly answer to such persons.
Pray do my service to his majesty;
He has my heart yet, and shall have my prayers   180
While I shall have my life. Come reverend fathers,
Bestow your counsels on me; she now begs
That little thought when she set footing here
She should have bought her dignities so dear.   *Exeunt.*

SCENE II—[*A room at court.*]

Enter the DUKE OF NORFOLK, DUKE OF SUFFOLK, LORD SURREY,
and LORD CHAMBERLAIN.

Nor. If you will now unite in your complaints
    And force them with a constancy, the cardinal
    Cannot stand under them. If you omit
    The offer of this time, I cannot promise
    But that you shall sustain moe new disgraces   5
    With these you bear already.
Sur.   I am joyful
    To meet the least occasion that may give me
    Remembrance of my father-in-law, the duke,

Scene II

Scene II.] *Scena Secunda. F.   A. . . . court*] *This Ed.; Antechamber to the King's
Apartments. Theobald.   5. moe] F; more Rowe.*

poore woman, lacking wit, to answer
anie such noble persons of wisdome as
you be", and an echo of l. 72.

179. *do my service*] pay my respects,
assure him of my obedience.

Scene II

Scene II] For Holinshed's account of
the fall of Wolsey, see Appendix II,
pp. 200 ff. The opening conversation
of the lords is partly invention, partly
an amalgam of information taken from
the historian; the motive of Wolsey's
fall, the incident of the inventory
(ll. 124 ff.) is transferred from the
account in Holinshed of a mistake
made by Thomas Ruthall, Bishop of

Durham during the reign of Henry
VII; the taunting of the cardinal by
Norfolk, Suffolk, and Surrey (ll. 228
ff.) is based on material in Holinshed,
who, however, provided only a bare
hint for the long farewell between
Wolsey and the faithful Cromwell.
There are parallels for parts of Wolsey's great speeches in Speed's *History
of Great Britain* (1611).

2. *force . . . constancy*] press them with
determination; cf. *Troil.*, I. iii. 21.

3. *omit*] neglect; cf. *Tp.*, II. i. 194,
"Do not omit the heavy offer of it".

5. *moe*] more, as at II. iii. 97.

8. *duke*] i.e. of Buckingham; cf. II. i.
43 ff.

To be reveng'd on him.
Suf.   Which of the peers
Have uncontemn'd gone by him, or at least   10
Strangely neglected? When did he regard
The stamp of nobleness in any person
Out of himself?
Cham.   My lords, you speak your pleasures:
What he deserves of you and me I know;
What we can do to him (though now the time   15
Gives way to us) I much fear. If you cannot
Bar his access to th'king, never attempt
Any thing on him; for he hath a witchcraft
Over the king in's tongue.
Nor.   O fear him not,
His spell in that is out: the king hath found   20
Matter against him that for ever mars
The honey of his language. No, he's settled
(Not to come off) in his displeasure.
Sur.   Sir,
I should be glad to hear such news as this
Once every hour.
Nor.   Believe it, this is true.   25
In the divorce his contrary proceedings
Are all unfolded; wherein he appears
As I would wish mine enemy.

10. *uncontemn'd*] cited in *O.E.D.* as the first use of this word.

11. *neglected*] disregarded.

13. *Out of*] except.

speak your pleasures] say freely what you will; cf. *Troil.*, III. i. 51 (Onions).

16. *Gives way*] gives scope, favours us; cf. *Per.*, v. i. 232, "it is not good to cross him; give him way", and below, v. i. 143.

17–18. *attempt . . . him*] make any kind of attack on him. Cited in *O.E.D.* (*attempt* v. 8b) as the earliest use of the phrase; for the sense "attack", cf. *Mac.*, III. vi. 39, *Cor.*, v. iii. 146.

20. *spell . . . out*] influence is at an end. For "out", cf. *Tp.*, III. ii. 1, "when the butt is out, we will drink water".

23. *come off*] escape; usually of fighting, as at *Cor.*, I. vi. 1: "he's settled" could refer to the king, in which case "come off" would mean 'desist', but the first sense seems better (Pooler).

26. *contrary proceedings*] best taken as meaning 'opposed to each other', 'contradictory', as explained in ll. 30–5, "While Wolsey was apparently favouring the divorce, he was secretly urging the Pope to stay his judgment" (Clarendon Ed.). "Contrary" could mean 'hostile', but this is not likely, in the context, which seems to refer to what Holinshed calls Wolsey's "cloked dissimulation".

27. *unfolded*] disclosed; cf. *Lr.*, I. i. 283, "Time shall unfold what plaited cunning hides".

Sur.   How came
    His practices to light?
Suf.   Most strangely.
Sur.   O how? how?
Suf. The cardinal's letters to the Pope miscarried,   30
    And came to th'eye o'th'king, wherein was read
    How that the cardinal did entreat his holiness
    To stay the judgement o'th'divorce; for if
    It did take place, 'I do' (quoth he) 'perceive
    My king is tangled in affection to   35
    A creature of the queen's, Lady Anne Bullen'.
Sur. Has the king this?
Suf.   Believe it.
Sur.   Will this work?
Cham. The king in this perceives him, how he coasts
    And hedges his own way. But in this point
    All his tricks founder, and he brings his physic   40
    After his patient's death; the king already
    Hath married the fair lady.
Sur.   Would he had.
Suf. May you be happy in your wish my lord,
    For I profess you have it.
Sur.   Now all my joy
    Trace the conjunction.
Suf.   My amen to't.
Nor.   All men's.   45

---

30. letters] *F*; letter *Var. 1778.*   44. have it] *F*; have't *Dyce 2.*

29. *practices*] intrigues, cf. I. i. 204.

30. *miscarried*] went astray; this passage is from Holinshed, pp. 908–9, cited in Appendix II, p. 200.

35. *tangled*] Holinshed has merely "set his affection upon".

36. *creature*] instrument, agent.

38–9. *coasts . . . way*] goes indirectly and secretly towards his own ends. "Coasts" here is cited in *O.E.D.* as a sole example of a figurative use; the metaphor is carried on in "founder", l. 40. For "hedges" cf. *Troil.*, III. iii. 158, "hedge aside from the direct forthright" (Pooler).

42. *married*] According to Holinshed,

p. 929, the marriage took place 14 November 1532, but "was kept so secret, that verie few knew it till Easter next insuing": in the play it is brought forward before the fall of Wolsey, who was in disgrace by 1529, and died in 1530.

44. *profess*] declare, as at II. iv. 82.

45. *Trace the conjunction*] follow the marriage; cf. *H 5*, v. ii. 480, and Nixon, *Great Brittaines Generall Joyes* (1613), B1ʳ, "Our hopes are happy in thy [Prince Frederick's] conjunction". For possible astrological overtones, see *2 H 4*, II. iv. 286.

Suf. There's order given for her coronation:
   Marry this is yet but young, and may be left
   To some ears unrecounted. But my lords
   She is a gallant creature, and complete
   In mind and feature. I persuade me, from her   50
   Will fall some blessing to this land, which shall
   In it be memoriz'd.

Sur.   But will the king
   Digest this letter of the cardinal's?
   The Lord forbid!

Nor.   Marry amen.

Suf.   No, no;
   There be moe wasps that buzz about his nose   55
   Will make this sting the sooner. Cardinal Campeius
   Is stolen away to Rome, hath ta'en no leave,
   Has left the cause o'th'king unhandled, and
   Is posted as the agent of our cardinal,
   To second all his plot. I do assure you,   60
   The king cried 'Ha' at this.

---

55. moe] *F;* more *Rowe.*   57. Rome, . . . leave,] *F;* Rome; . . . leave; *Capell.*
58. Has] Ha's *F;* He's *R. G. White.*

47. *Marry*] in origin the name of the Virgin Mary; here, as commonly, an ejaculation of emphasis, surprise, etc.

   young] new, recent, cf. *Troil.*, I. iii. 312.

48. *unrecounted*] the only example cited in *O.E.D.*

49. *gallant*] fine, cf. *Wint.*, I. i. 42, "a gallant child".

   complete] perfect; cf. I. ii. 118 and n.

50-2. *I . . . memoriz'd*] Suffolk here echoes the hope expressed by the Lord Chamberlain, II. iii. 77–9, and provides a second hint foreshadowing v. iv; see especially v. iv. 17 ff.

51. *fall*] a quibble on the sense 'give birth', cf. *John*, III. i. 90.

52. *memoriz'd*] made memorable, as at *Mac.*, I. ii. 40, "Or memorize another Golgotha", the only other instance in Shakespeare (cited Steevens).

53. *Digest*] 'stomach', fail to resent (Pooler), cf. *H 5*, III. iv. 136, "the disgrace we have digested".

55. *moe*] more, as at II. iii. 97.

56-60. *Cardinal . . . plot*] Holinshed says Campeius "tooke his leave of the king", and the dramatist went to Foxe, p. 906, for this passage (he records that the cardinal "craftily shifted hym self out of the realme"), or more probably, to Halle, II. 155, "Thus departed out of England in high displeasure the crafty Cardinall Campeius . . . which after their [i.e. his and Wolsey's] departinge from the kynge at Grafton, never saw the kynge, nor came in his presence".

58. *unhandled*] not dealt with; the primary meaning was 'untamed', 'not broken in', as at *Mer. V.*, v. i. 72, and its use here may have been suggested by "posted" in the next line.

59. *posted*] to "post" was to travel by relays of horses, hence to hasten.

61. *'Ha'*] the king's cry of indignation, as at II. ii. 63, 66; it is his favourite ejaculation also in Rowley's

Cham.   Now God incense him
    And let him cry 'Ha' louder.
Nor.   But my lord,
    When returns Cranmer?
Suf. He is return'd in his opinions, which
    Have satisfied the king for his divorce,   65
    Together with all famous colleges
    Almost in Christendom: shortly (I believe)
    His second marriage shall be publish'd, and
    Her coronation. Katherine no more
    Shall be call'd queen, but princess dowager,   70
    And widow to Prince Arthur.
Nor.   This same Cranmer's
    A worthy fellow, and hath ta'en much pain
    In the king's business.
Suf.   He has, and we shall see him
    For it an archbishop.
Nor.   So I hear.
Suf.   'Tis so.

64. in his] *F;* with his *Rowe.*   66. Together with all] *F;* Gather'd from all
Rowe.   colleges] *F;* colleges' *Neilson and Hill (Vaughan conj.).*

When You See Me, You Know Me; see
Introduction, p. xxxvii.
    64–7. *return'd . . . Christendom*] re-
turned with opinions (i.e. collected
abroad) which have satisfied the king
and the colleges; or, returned with the
judgments of the colleges, which support his own and together have satisfied the king. The first interpretation is
preferable, and was accepted by Tyrwhitt, Steevens, who interpreted "in
his opinions" as 'with opinions un-
changed', and Pooler; the second,
that of Rowe and Vaughan, forces the
grammar, but is not to be rejected, as
Pooler says it may, because it is not in
accordance with history. Holinshed,
p. 923, says Henry sent the Bishop of
London, Edmund Bonner, abroad,
but Shakespeare perhaps based this
passage on the mistaken report in
Foxe, p. 1471 (1563 edn), that Cranmer "was . . . sent into France . . . and
with him . . . Stokisley Byshop of Lon-

don. Moreover three Doctors of the
lawe . . . whiche with the divines should
debate this matter in Paris & other
Universities . . . Cranmer takynge his
journey through Germanie, drewe
manye into his opinion". This account
was modified in later editions of Foxe,
which, however, still speak of Cranmer being sent abroad (pp. 1689, 1690
in edn 1597). "Return'd" may carry
overtones of another normal meaning,
"reported in answer to an official
demand" (*O.E.D.*, v. 16), cf. *Per.*, II.
ii. 4.
    68. *publish'd*] proclaimed; cf. *Cym.*,
v. v. 478, "Publish we this peace . . ."
    70. *dowager*] so Holinshed, p. 929;
she has a title "as the widow of prince
Arthur", not as Henry's ex-wife.
    72. *pain*] pains, as at *Lr.*, III. i. 53.
    74. *archbishop*] Holinshed, p. 929,
says Cranmer became Archbishop in
1533, succeeding Warham, who died
in the summer of 1532.

Enter WOLSEY *and* CROMWELL.

The cardinal.

Nor.   Observe, observe, he's moody.   75

Wol. The packet Cromwell, gave't you the king?

Crom. To his own hand, in's bedchamber.

Wol.   Look'd he

O' th' inside of the paper?

Crom.   Presently

He did unseal them, and the first he view'd,

He did it with a serious mind; a heed   80

Was in his countenance. You he bade

Attend him here this morning.

Wol.   Is he ready

To come abroad?

Crom.   I think by this he is.

Wol. Leave me awhile.   *Exit Cromwell.*

[*Aside*] It shall be to the Duchess of Alençon,   85

The French king's sister; he shall marry her.

Anne Bullen? no; I'll no Anne Bullens for him,

There's more in't than fair visage. Bullen?

No, we'll no Bullens: speedily I wish

To hear from Rome. The Marchioness of Pembroke? 90

Nor. He's discontented.

Suf.   May be he hears the king

Does whet his anger to him.

Sur.   Sharp enough

Lord for thy justice.

---

74. S.D. Enter . . . Cromwell] *so F; after* cardinal! *Var. 1773 and edd.*   76–
252. S.H. *Wol.*] Car(d). *F.*   76–8. The . . . Presently] *This Ed.; five lines in F,
ending* Cromwell, / . . . King? / . . . Bed-chamber. / . . . Paper? / . . . Presently.
78. paper] *F;* papers *Keightley.*   82–3. Attend . . . is] *so Hanmer; three lines in F,
ending* Morning. / abroad? / . . . is.   85. S.D. Aside] *Rowe; not in F.*   Alen-
çon] Alanson *F.*   88. There's . . . in't] *F;* There is . . . in it *Var. 1793.*
90. Pembroke] Penbroke *F.*

76. *packet*] i.e. of letters; applied
especially "to the State parcel or 'mail'
of dispatches to and from foreign
countries" (*O.E.D.* sb. 1).

78. *paper*] wrapper; often including
contents also; cf. *All's W.*, v. iii. 94.

Presently] at once, cf. i. ii. 157.

85. *Duchess of Alençon*] a scheme
Wolsey had, so Holinshed reports, in
1528; see Appendix II, pp. 193–4.

90. *Pembroke*] Anne attained this
dignity only in 1532; cf. II. iii. 63.

Wol. [*Aside*] The late queen's gentlewoman? a knight's
    daughter
    To be her mistress' mistress? the queen's queen?   95
    This candle burns not clear, 'tis I must snuff it,
    Then out it goes. What though I know her virtuous
    And well-deserving? yet I know her for
    A spleeny Lutheran, and not wholesome to
    Our cause, that she should lie i'th'bosom of   100
    Our hard-rul'd king. Again, there is sprung up
    An heretic, an arch-one, Cranmer, one
    Hath crawl'd into the favour of the king
    And is his oracle.
Nor.   He is vex'd at something.

    Enter KING, *reading of a schedule* [*, and* LOVELL].

Sur. I would 'twere something that would fret the string,   105
    The master-cord on's heart.
Suf.   The king, the king!

94. S.D. *Aside*] *Rowe; not in* F.   The . . . daughter] *so Pope; two lines in* F,
ending Gentlewoman? / . . . Daughter.   100–1. cause, that . . . king.] F;
Cause!—that . . . king! *Rowe.*   102. arch-one] F; arch one *Rowe.*   104. He
is] He's F4.   S.D. *and Lovell*] *Theobald; not in* F.

96. *This . . . it*] "clear" means
'bright', cf. I. i. 226; the expression
'To go out like a candle in snuff' was
proverbial (Tilley, C 49); possibly, as
Staunton thought, there is a play on
"bullen" meaning 'hemp-stalks peel-
ed' (*O.E.D.* first records in 1674), and
hence the wick of a candle.

99. *spleeny Lutheran*] passionate; not
elsewhere in Shakespeare, but cf. I. ii.
174 above, and *Ham.*, v. i. 284,
"splenetive and rash". This passage,
like several others in the scene (cf. ll.
56–60, 64–7, 212–13) seems to be
based on Foxe, who says, p. 959, "the
cardinall of Yorke perceived the kyng
to cast favour to the Lady Anne,
whome hee knew to be a Lutheran".
    wholesome] cf. I. ii. 45.
100. *lie . . . bosom*] with the double
sense of 'marry' and 'share the secrets
of', cf. *Cæs.*, v. i. 7, "I am in their

bosoms, and I know / Wherefore they
do it".

101. *hard-rul'd*] managed or advised
with difficulty, cf. *Lr.*, ii. iv. 150, "You
should be ruled and led / By some discretion".

102. *arch-one*] chief, cf. v. i. 45.

102–3. *one / Hath*] the omission of the
relative pronoun is common, cf. iii. i.
55, Abbott 244.

104. *oracle*] i.e. trusted adviser.

105–6. *fret . . . heart*] torment, or
perhaps "gnaw through the chie
sinew" (Pooler). Heart-strings were
real to the Elizabethans, cf. *John*, v.
vii. 55 and *Lr.*, v. iii. 216, "the strings
of life / Began to crack". There is perhaps a quibble on the musical terms,
fret (a bar to regulate fingering on
stringed instruments)—*string*—*chord*.

106. *on's*] of his; common, see
Abbott 182.

King. What piles of wealth hath he accumulated
        To his own portion! and what expense by th'hour
        Seems to flow from him! How i'th'name of thrift
        Does he rake this together? Now my lords,   110
        Saw you the cardinal?

Nor.   My lord, we have
        Stood here observing him. Some strange commotion
        Is in his brain; he bites his lip, and starts,
        Stops on a sudden, looks upon the ground,
        Then lays his finger on his temple; straight   115
        Springs out into fast gait, then stops again,
        Strikes his breast hard, and anon he casts
        His eye against the moon: in most strange postures
        We have seen him set himself.

King.   It may well be,
        There is a mutiny in's mind. This morning   120
        Papers of state he sent me, to peruse
        As I required: and wot you what I found
        There (on my conscience put unwittingly)
        Forsooth an inventory, thus importing

108–9. portion!...him!] *Rowe;* portion?...him? *F.*   119. We have] We've
Pope.   be,] *F;* be; *Capell;* be *Hudson* (*W. S. Walker conj.*).   123. There (on
...unwittingly)] *so F;* There, on...unwittingly, *Rowe;* There, on...un-
wittingly? *Pope;* There; on...unwittingly? *Capell;* There?—on...unwitting-
ly;— *Staunton.*   124. importing] *F;* importing; *Theobald;* importing, *Johnson*

108. *portion*] allotted share; a biblical
word, see 1 Samuel, i. 4, 5.

expense] Holinshed, pp. 920–1 describes at length Wolsey's lavish manner of living, and his house, "like a
princes court for all kind of braverie &
sumptuousnesse".

112. *commotion*] mutiny, linking with
l. 120; cf. v. ii. 62, and *Troil.*, II. iii.
185, "Kingdom'd Achilles in commotion rages / And batters down himself".

113–19.] an interesting speech for
the actor playing Wolsey, being a
direct description of his movements
and gestures during the preceding
forty lines.

120. *mutiny in's mind*] as Pooler notes,
a common metaphor; see note on l.
112, and *Cæs.*,II.i. 63–9.

122. *wot*] know.

124. *inventory*] The mistake attributed here to Wolsey is transferred
from the account in Holinshed, p. 796,
of an inventory sent unintentionally
by Thomas Ruthall, Bishop of Durham, to Wolsey, as a result of which,
Ruthall was brought into disgrace;
see Introduction, p. xxxiv, and Appendix II, pp. 183–4. This event is recorded
by Holinshed in 1508, in the reign of
Henry VII, and indicates the width of
Shakespeare's reading. Possibly a hint
was taken also from a story told in
Foxe, p. 901, of some letters of Wolsey's falling into the king's hands,
after which Henry never trusted him
again.

importing] signifying, cf. *Wint.*, I. ii.
57.

The several parcels of his plate, his treasure,   125
Rich stuffs and ornaments of household, which
I find at such proud rate, that it out-speaks
Possession of a subject.

Nor.   It's heaven's will;
Some spirit put this paper in the packet
To bless your eye withal.

King.   If we did think   130
His contemplation were above the earth
And fix'd on spiritual object, he should still
Dwell in his musings, but I am afraid
His thinkings are below the moon, not worth
His serious considering.

King takes his seat, whispers Lovell, who goes to the Cardinal.

Wol.   Heaven forgive me.   135
Ever God bless your highness.

King.   Good my lord,
You are full of heavenly stuff, and bear the inventory
Of your best graces in your mind, the which
You were now running o'er: you have scarce time
To steal from spiritual leisure a brief span   140
To keep your earthly audit; sure in that

---

131. contemplation] *F;* contemplations *F2.*   132. object] *F;* objects *F4.*
140. leisure] *F;* labour *Collier 3.*

125. *several parcels*] various items; for
"several", cf. II. i. Entry, and for
"parcels", *2 H 4,* IV. ii. 36, "The parcels and particulars of our grief".

plate] Household plate of gold and
silver was a common form in which to
display and store wealth; costly presents were often made in plate, as
Prince Frederick gave the Archbishop
of Canterbury "plate to the value o.
1000 li." before he left England
(Chamberlain, I. 449, in a letter of
6 May 1613). Cf. *Cym.,*I. vi. 189.

126. *ornaments*] i.e. furniture, household-stuff.

127. *rate*] value, as at *Ham.,* I. iii.
122; or quantity, as at *2 H 4,* IV. i. 22.

127–8. *out-speaks . . . subject*] "describes what is too great for a subject to
possess" (Clarendon Ed.); "out-
speak" does not occur elsewhere in
Shakespeare.

130. *withal*] therewith.

132. *object*] see I. i. 127 and n.

134. *below the moon*] i.e. worldly,
material, cf. *Lr.,*IV. vi. 26.

137. *stuff*] qualities,cf. I. i. 58, with a
quibble on household-stuff, listed in
the inventory, l. 126.

140. *spiritual leisure*] Onions explains
as the "time withdrawn from earthly
business and devoted to religious
duties", for which sense cf. *Meas.,*III.ii.
261, *All's W.,*I. i. 227; perhaps there is
a quibble implying also that Wolsey
treats as leisure the time he should
devote to spiritual affairs, cf.l. 134.

141. *earthly audit*] as opposed to the

I deem you an ill husband, and am glad
To have you therein my companion.

Wol.   Sir,
For holy offices I have a time; a time
To think upon the part of business which   145
I bear i'th'state; and nature does require
Her times of preservation, which perforce
I her frail son, amongst my brethren mortal,
Must give my tendance to.

King.   You have said well.

Wol. And ever may your highness yoke together   150
(As I will lend you cause) my doing well
With my well saying.

King.   'Tis well said again,
And 'tis a kind of good deed to say well,
And yet words are no deeds. My father lov'd you,
He said he did, and with his deed did crown   155
His word upon you. Since I had my office
I have kept you next my heart, have not alone
Employ'd you where high profits might come home,
But par'd my present havings to bestow
My bounties upon you.

Wol. [*Aside*]   What should this mean?   160
Sur. [*Aside*] The Lord increase this business.
King.   Have I not made you

---

142. glad] *F2;* gald *F.*   157. I have] *F;* I've *Pope.*   160, 161. S.D. *Aside*]
so *Rowe; not in F.*

heavenly audit, the day of judgement;
see *O.E.D.*, audit, sb. 3, and *Ham.*,III.
iii.82, "how his audit stands who knows
save heaven".

142. *ill husband*] bad economist or
manager, cf. *Meas.*,III.ii. 73, "you will
turn good husband now, Pompey; you
will keep the house" (Pooler). Wolsey
is mocked for amassing riches, and in
the next line, for judging Henry to be a
bad husband to Katherine and opposing the marriage with Anne. Thus a
double pun on both words is exploited.

149. *tendance*] attention, care, cf.
Cym.,v.v. 53 (Clarendon Ed.).

151-6. *doing ... upon you*] a play upon

various common proverbs, 'Saying is
one thing, doing another', 'From
words to deeds is a great space', etc.;
see Tilley, S 121, 123, W 802. The contrast between words and deeds is
common in Shakespeare, cf. *Mac.*,II.i.
61, *Ham.*,III.i. 53, and is prominent in
this play, see above, I. ii. 208, and below, IV. ii. 42, v. ii. 106.

155. *crown*] complete, cf. *Tp.*, III. i.
69, "And crown what I profess with
kind event" (Pooler). Is there a hint
here of Wolsey as "king-cardinal" (II.
ii. 19)?—cf. *Wint.*,IV. iv. 145.

159. *havings*] possessions, cf. II. iii.
23.

The prime man of the state? I pray you tell me,
If what I now pronounce you have found true:
And if you may confess it, say withal
If you are bound to us, or no. What say you?   165
Wol. My sovereign, I confess your royal graces
Shower'd on me daily, have been more than could
My studied purposes requite, which went
Beyond all man's endeavours. My endeavours
Have ever come too short of my desires,   170
Yet fil'd with my abilities: mine own ends
Have been mine so, that ever more they pointed
To th'good of your most sacred person, and
The profit of the state. For your great graces
Heap'd upon me (poor undeserver) I   175
Can nothing render but allegiant thanks,
My prayers to heaven for you, my loyalty
Which ever has and ever shall be growing,
Till death, that winter, kill it.
King.   Fairly answer'd:
A loyal, and obedient subject is   180
Therein illustrated; the honour of it
Does pay the act of it, as i'th'contrary

---

171. fil'd] *Hanmer;* fill'd *F.*   172. so, that] *F;* so that *Camb. 1865.*

162. *prime*] principal; cf. *Tp.*, I. ii.
72, "Prospero the prime duke", which
O.E.D. cites as the earliest use in this
sense.

163. *pronounce*] declare, cf. II. iii. 4.

168–70. *which . . . desires*] i.e. my
efforts ("studied purposes") went beyond all men's endeavours, and my
attempts to fulfil them have always
fallen far short of my desires. Malone
referred "which" to "royal graces".

171. *fil'd*] have matched with, kept
pace with my abilities. Ff. "fill'd" was
altered to "fil'd" by Hanmer, an
emendation so generally accepted as to
appear in *O.E.D.* as a first use of the
verb to mean "To march in line, keep
pace *with*" (file, v³, 4b), for which one
possible parallel is cited from B. and
F., *Monsieur Thomas* (1615?, *Works*, IV.
101), I. ii, "To file with her affections".

The idea of keeping pace is present in
the use of *file* at I. ii. 42, "that file /
Where others tell steps with me."
Fill'd and *fil'd* are liable to be confused
in early texts, as is shown in *Wint.*, IV.
iv. 624, "I could have filed keys off",
where Ff. 1 and 2 read "fill'd"; "fil'd"
for "fill'd" seems to be more common,
as at II. iii. 87 above. Sisson interprets
this passage as meaning "fulfilled to
the best of my abilities", but I can find
no parallel for this.

ends] aims.

172. *so*] in this way, to this extent.

176. *render . . . thanks*] pay back only
loyal thanks; cited in *O.E.D.* as the
first use of "allegiant".

181–2. *honour . . . act of it*] the honour
of being loyal is the reward of loyalty;
cf. the proverb, 'Honour is the reward
of virtue', Tilley H 571.

The foulness is the punishment. I presume
That as my hand has open'd bounty to you,
My heart dropp'd love, my power rain'd honour, more
On you than any; so your hand and heart,   186
Your brain and every function of your power,
Should, notwithstanding that your bond of duty,
As 'twere in love's particular, be more
To me your friend, than any.

Wol.   I do profess   190
That for your highness' good I ever labour'd
More than mine own: that am, have, and will be
(Though all the world should crack their duty to you
And throw it from their soul, though perils did
Abound as thick as thought could make 'em, and   195
Appear in forms more horrid) yet my duty,
As doth a rock against the chiding flood,
Should the approach of this wild river break,
And stand unshaken yours.

King.   'Tis nobly spoken:
Take notice lords, he has a loyal breast,   200
For you have seen him open't. [*Giving him papers*]

---

192. that . . . be] *F*; that am I, have been, will be: *Pope*; that aim I have, and
will. *Collier 2 (Knight conj.)*; that I am true, and will be *Singer 2*; that am true,
and will be *R. G. White 1*.   201. S.D. *Giving . . . papers*] *Pope; not in F.*

---

183. *foulness*] stain of guilt, as at *Lr.*,
I. i. 230, "It is no vicious blot, murder,
or foulness".

184. *open'd*] given generously; perhaps from the sense 'to give free access
to', cf. *Ham.*, I. iii. 31, or from the
adjective "open" meaning 'generous',
as at *Tim.*, v. i. 61, "often of your open
bounty tasted".

188. *notwithstanding . . . duty*] in spite
of your bond of duty, i.e. to the Holy
See. Johnson, Schmidt, and Pooler
interpret 'over and above, besides
your bond of duty to me', but there is
no parallel for this sense of "notwithstanding".

189. *particular*] intimate regard, cf.
Cor., v. i. 3, "his general; who loved
him / In a most dear particular".

192. *have*] have been, cf. "has",

l. 178. The many suggested emendations destroy the passion for the sake of
the grammar, as Pooler noted. For the
unfinished construction, compare I. i.
63, 183 ff.

193. *crack*] cf. "crack'd the league",
II. ii. 24.

197. *chiding*] wild and noisy; frequently used by Shakespeare of water
and wind, cf. *1 H 4*, III. i. 45, *Per.*, III. i.
32 etc.

198. *break*] stem, as in 'breakwater'.

201. *open't*] disclose his feelings, cf.
Wint., IV. iv. 764; just possibly there is
an allusion also to some action of Wolsey's during his speech, for the phrase
could mean, literally, to uncover the
breast, cf. *Cæs.*, I. iii. 51, "lightning
seem'd to open / The breast of
heaven".

> Read o'er this,
> And after, this, and then to breakfast with
> What appetite you have.
>
> *Exit King, frowning upon the Cardinal; the nobles
> throng after him, smiling and whispering.*

Wol.　　　　　　　　　What should this mean?
What sudden anger's this? How have I reap'd it?
He parted frowning from me, as if ruin　　　　　205
Leap'd from his eyes. So looks the chafed lion
Upon the daring huntsman that has gall'd him;
Then makes him nothing. I must read this paper;
I fear, the story of his anger. 'Tis so;
This paper has undone me: 'tis th'accompt　　　210
Of all that world of wealth I have drawn together
For mine own ends (indeed to gain the popedom
And fee my friends in Rome). O negligence!
Fit for a fool to fall by: what cross devil
Made me put this main secret in the packet　　215
I sent the king? Is there no way to cure this?
No new device to beat this from his brains?
I know 'twill stir him strongly; yet I know
A way, if it take right, in spite of fortune
Will bring me off again. What's this? 'To th'Pope'?　220

202. after, this] *Theobald;* after this F.　　204. reap'd] F; rous'd *Keightley.*
209. fear, the] *Rowe;* fear the F.　　211, 223. I have] F; I've *Pope.*

203. S.D. frowning] as again at v. ii. 147.

206. *chafed*] angry, cf. i. i. 123.

207. *gall'd*] wounded, cf. *Ham.*, IV. vii. 148, "I'll touch my point / With this contagion, that if I gall him slightly, / It may be death".

208. *makes him nothing*] annihilates him, cf. IV. ii. 42, *MND.*, V. i. 315.

210. *undone*] ruined.

211. *world*] huge quantity; so Florio called his dictionary (1598), *A World of Words.*

212. *mine own ends*] thus expressly denying what he said earlier, l. 171, where this phrase is also used.

212–13. *gain . . . Rome*] Wolsey hoped to be elected when a false report of the Pope's death reached him in 1529, and sent to Gardiner, then in Rome, "willing hym to sticke for no coste" (Foxe, p. 963).

214. *cross*] thwarting, cf. *Rom.*, IV. iii. 5.

215. *main*] very important; cf. *All's W.*, III. vi. 17, "He might . . . in a main danger fail you". Pooler cites several examples from B. and F., e.g. *False One* (1620?; *Works*, III. 344), IV. i, "Your Sister he ne're gaz'd on: that's a main note".

219. *take right*] succeed, take effect, cf. *Cor.*, II. ii. 112.

220. *bring me off*] enable me to escape; cf. l. 23 above (Clarendon Ed.).

220–2. *What's . . . holiness*] This seems to conflict with the idea expressed in

The letter, as I live, with all the business
I writ to's holiness. Nay then, farewell:
I have touch'd the highest point of all my greatness,
And from that full meridian of my glory
I haste now to my setting. I shall fall   225
Like a bright exhalation in the evening,
And no man see me more.

[Re-]enter to WOLSEY the DUKES OF NORFOLK and SUFFOLK, the
     EARL OF SURREY, and the LORD CHAMBERLAIN.

Nor. Hear the king's pleasure Cardinal, who commands you
      To render up the great seal presently
      Into our hands, and to confine yourself   230
      To Asher-house, my Lord of Winchester's,

---

227. S.D. *Re-enter*] *Capell; Enter F.*   228. Hear . . . you] *so Pope; two lines in F. ending* Cardinall, / . . . you.

---

ll. 211–13 above, possibly because it stems from Holinshed, cf. l. 326 ff., whereas ll. 211–13 seem to be based on Foxe.

222. *writ*] the usual form in Shakespeare; "wrote" is rare.

222–7. *Nay . . . more*] These lines are based probably on a passage in Speed's *History of Great Britain* (1611), p. 769, "Cardinall *Wolsey*, fell likewise in great displeasure of the King . . . but now his Sunne having passed the Meridian of his greatnesse, began by degrees againe to decline, till lastly it set under the cloud of his fatall eclipse". Cf. Buckingham's lines, I. i. 224–6.

224. *meridian*] the point of highest altitude of a star.

226. *exhalation*] falling star, cf. *1 H 4*, II. iv. 352, "do you see these meteors? do you behold these exhalations?", and *Cæs.*, II. i. 44. The word could be used of any kind of brightness in the air, and is associated with the idea that lightning, meteors, etc. originated from vapours drawn from the earth or kindled in the heavens, and exhaled by the sun or the stars; cf. *Rom.*, III. v. 13, "Yon light is not daylight . . . It is some meteor that the sun exhales".

227. S.D.] Holinshed, p. 909, mentions only Norfolk and Suffolk as present at this interview. Reed noted that at this time (1529), Thomas Howard, Earl of Surrey, was also Duke of Norfolk.

228–349.] This altercation between Wolsey and the lords is developed from material in Holinshed, see Appendix II, pp. 200 ff.; the main quarrel, ll. 253 ff., is enlarged from the mere statement in the chronicle that "This matter was greatlie debated betweene them with manie great words" (p. 909), and the "articles" against Wolsey, ll. 293 ff., are listed in a different context by the historian (p. 912).

229. *presently*] immediately.

231. *Asher-house . . . Winchester's*] Holinshed has "Asher . . . belonging to the bishoprike of Winchester"; Esher was at this time Wolsey's own house, as he held this bishopric. The deviation from Holinshed here may have been deliberately made to suggest Gardiner, "my good lord of Winchester" in v. ii. 92, 107, 204, who succeeded Wolsey as Bishop; see IV. i. 101 ff.

Till you hear further from his highness.

Wol.   Stay:
Where's your commission lords? words cannot carry
Authority so weighty.

Suf.   Who dare cross 'em,
Bearing the king's will from his mouth expressly?   235

Wol. Till I find more than will or words to do it
(I mean your malice) know, officious lords,
I dare, and must deny it. Now I feel
Of what coarse metal ye are moulded, envy,
How eagerly ye follow my disgraces   240
As if it fed ye, and how sleek and wanton
Ye appear in every thing may bring my ruin!
Follow your envious courses, men of malice;
You have Christian warrant for 'em, and no doubt
In time will find their fit rewards. That seal   245
You ask with such a violence, the king
(Mine and your master) with his own hand gave me;
Bade me enjoy it, with the place and honours
During my life; and to confirm his goodness,
Tied it by letters patents. Now, who'll take it?   250

Sur. The king that gave it.

---

233. commission lords?] *Rowe;* Commission? Lords, *F.*   239. coarse metal]
course Mettle *F.*   moulded, envy,] *F;* moulded—Envy: *Rowe.*   242. Ye] *F;*
Y' *Pope.*   244. You have] *F;* You've *Warburton.*

233. *commission*] written warrant, cf.
II. ii. 72 S.D.

234. *cross*] oppose, cf. *Cym.*, v. iv.
101.

236. *do it*] i.e. carry authority
(Johnson).

239. *metal*] *mettle* (F) is in origin the
same word as "metal", which doubtless suggested "moulded". "Envy", as
is usual, means 'malice'.

240–1. *follow . . . fed ye*] perhaps an
echo of the "ravenous fishes" (I. ii. 79)
from which Wolsey had earlier felt
himself immune.

241. *wanton*] unrestrained, reckless
of justice and humanity, cf. *Troil.*, III.
iii. 137, *Ham.*, II. i. 22, and *O.E.D.*,
wanton, a. 5.

244–5. *You . . . rewards*] ironical; cf.

the proverb 'Wrong has no warrant',
(Tilley, W 947), which is what Wolsey
is really saying; by "rewards" he
means punishment, cf. l. 348; for
"find" meaning 'meet with', cf. l.
267.

246. *violence*] vehemence.

248. *enjoy it*] i.e. have the use and
benefits of it.

place and honours] office (i.e. of Lord
Chancellor), with its marks of distinction.

250. *letters patents*] an open docu-
ment conveying some right or power
(Pooler). The form is common from
the 15th to the 18th centuries, as a
literal translation of French *lettres
patentes* (*O.E.D.* patent, a. 1); cf. *R 2*,
II.i.202.

Wol.   It must be himself then.

Sur. Thou art a proud traitor, priest.

Wol.   Proud lord, thou liest:

    Within these forty hours Surrey durst better

    Have burnt that tongue than said so.

Sur.   Thy ambition,

    Thou scarlet sin, robb'd this bewailing land   255

    Of noble Buckingham, my father-in-law;

    The heads of all thy brother-cardinals

    (With thee and all thy best parts bound together)

    Weigh'd not a hair of his. Plague of your policy;

    You sent me deputy for Ireland,   260

    Far from his succour, from the king, from all

    That might have mercy on the fault thou gav'st him;

    Whilst your great goodness, out of holy pity,

    Absolv'd him with an axe.

Wol.   This, and all else

    This talking lord can lay upon my credit,   265

    I answer, is most false. The duke by law

    Found his deserts. How innocent I was

    From any private malice in his end,

    His noble jury, and foul cause can witness.

    If I lov'd many words, lord, I should tell you   270

    You have as little honesty as honour,

---

252. Thou art] *F;* Thou'rt *Pope.*   271–2. honour, / That] *F; line omitted,*
W. S. Walker conj.

253. *forty*] in common use as a round number, and not to be taken precisely; cf. *Cor.,* III. i. 243, "On fair ground / I could beat forty of them", and Day, *Law Tricks* (1608; M.S.R. 1949), l. 1432, "ile spend after fortie pound a day". See also II. iii. 89 and v. iii. 50 below.

255. *scarlet sin*] a double allusion, to the cardinal's robes, and to Isaiah i. 18, "though your sins were as crimson, they shall bee made white as snow: though they were redde like scarlet, they shall be as wool" (Geneva). "Scarlet" is the name of a cloth, as well as the colour, cf. l. 280 below.

258. *parts*] qualities, cf. II. iii. 27 and n.

259. *Weigh'd*] equalled in weight, hence in value, cf. I. i. 11 and v. i. 124.

Plague of] i.e. on; common in Shakespeare, and the same phrase occurs in e.g. *1 H 4,* II. iv. 147, *Troil.,* III. iii. 265; Abbott 175.

260. *deputy*] this refers back to a much earlier passage in Holinshed, p. 855, "the earle of Surrie was sent into Ireland as the kings deputie"; see II. i. 40 ff.

262. *fault*] the offence you put upon him; cf. II. i. 71.

265. *credit*] good name; or perhaps, charge.

267. *Found*] cf. ll. 244–5.

268. *From*] i.e. of; cf. *2 H 6,* III. i. 70 (Pooler).

That in the way of loyalty and truth
Toward the king, my ever royal master,
Dare mate a sounder man than Surrey can be,
And all that love his follies.

Sur.   By my soul,   275
Your long coat, priest, protects you, thou should'st
    feel
My sword i'th'life blood of thee else. My lords,
Can ye endure to hear this arrogance?
And from this fellow? If we live thus tamely,
To be thus jaded by a piece of scarlet,   280
Farewell nobility: let his grace go forward,
And dare us with his cap, like larks.

Wol.   All goodness
Is poison to thy stomach.

Sur.   Yes, that goodness
Of gleaming all the land's wealth into one,
Into your own hands, cardinal, by extortion;   285
The goodness of your intercepted packets
You writ to th'Pope against the king: your goodness,
Since you provoke me, shall be most notorious.
My Lord of Norfolk, as you are truly noble,
As you respect the common good, the state   290
Of our despis'd nobility, our issues
(Who if he live, will scarce be gentlemen)

---

272. That in the] That I, i'th' *Theobald.*   276. Your . . . feel] *so Rowe 3; two lines in F, ending* you, / . . . feele.   282, 297. S.H. *Wol.*] *Car(d). F.*   289. you are] *F*; you're *Pope.*   292. Who] *F2*; Whom *F.*

272. *in the way of*] in respect of, cf. II. ii. 68.

274. *mate*] match, rival (*O.E.D.*, mate v. 2b); not elsewhere in Shakespeare in this sense, but common.

276. *coat*] i.e. the mark of his profession; see Prologue, l. 16 and n.

279. *fellow*] a gross insult to apply this customary title for a servant, as at IV. ii. 100, to Wolsey; cf. *Cym.*, I. ii. 27.

280. *jaded*] cowed, treated with contempt, cf. the "jaded groom" of *2 H 6*, IV. i. 52, and *Ant.*, III. i. 34, "The ne'er-yet-beaten horse of Parthia / We have jaded out o'the field" (Case, *apud*

Pooler). *O.E.D.* cites as meaning 'befooled', as in *Tw. N.*, II. v. 179, "I do not now fool myself, to let imagination jade me", but the first sense is better.

282. *dare . . . larks*] dazzle, make helpless; an allusion to the method of catching larks by using a mirror, a piece of red cloth, or a hobby (a small hawk), "that the larks' eyes being ever upon the hoby, should not see the net that is laid on their heads" (*O.E.D.*, citing Cranmer, *Works*, I. 107). For "dare" in this sense, cf. *H 5*, IV. ii. 36.

287. *writ*] see l. 222 and n.

291. *issues*] sons (Pooler).

Produce the grand sum of his sins, the articles
Collected from his life. I'll startle you
Worse than the sacring bell, when the brown
    wench   295
Lay kissing in your arms, lord cardinal.

Wol. How much methinks, I could despise this man,
But that I am bound in charity against it.

Nor. Those articles, my lord, are in the king's hand:
But thus much, they are foul ones.

Wol.   So much fairer   300
And spotless shall mine innocence arise,
When the king knows my truth.

Sur.   This cannot save you:
I thank my memory, I yet remember
Some of these articles, and out they shall.
Now, if you can blush, and cry 'guilty' cardinal,   305
You'll show a little honesty.

Wol.   Speak on sir,
I dare your worst objections: if I blush,
It is to see a nobleman want manners.

---

298. I am] *F;* I'm *Pope.*   300. But thus] *F;* But, thus *Capell.*   305. can
blush] *F;* can, blush *Pope.*

293. *articles*] charges, counts of indictment; Holinshed's word, and cf. *R 2*, IV. i. 233, "one heinous article, / Containing the deposing of a king".

295. *sacring bell*] consecrating bell; originally the "small bell rung at the elevation of the host" (*O.E.D.*), but here used anachronistically in the post-reformation sense of a bell rung to summon parishioners to morning prayers.

brown wench] probably implying a slut, or an ill-favoured girl, cf. E. Guilpin, *Skialethia* (1598), B3ʳ "(*Lydia*) so mote I thee thou art not faire, / A plaine brownetta when thou art at best". Wolsey was frequently accused of lechery, as Skelton said, "He froynes and he frigs, / Spareth neither maid nor wife" (*Why come ye not to court?* ed. Henderson, p. 345). He had children, and one became Dean of Lincoln.

300. *But . . . ones*] i.e. the king has them, but I can say this much, that they are evil ones. Vaughan took "hand" to mean 'handwriting', but l. 293 shows this to be incorrect.

302. *truth*] loyalty.

305. *Now . . . cardinal*] rhythmically not very satisfactory; perhaps "cardinal" should begin the next line, leaving "Speak on sir" as an extra-metrical phrase, a common device in Shakespeare, cf. Abbott 511 and l. 449 below. Pope's addition of a comma after "can" is needless, for the sense is good; if Wolsey is able to blush and admit guilt, it will show that he has at least a little honesty.

307. *objections*] accusations; cf. *2 H 6*, I. iii. 158, "your spiteful false objections, / Prove them, and I lie open to the law" (cited Pooler).

308–9. *want*] lack.

Sur. I had rather want those than my head; have at you.
    First, that without the king's assent or knowledge   310
    You wrought to be a legate, by which power
    You maim'd the jurisdiction of all bishops.

Nor. Then, that in all you writ to Rome, or else
    To foreign princes, *Ego et Rex meus*
    Was still inscrib'd; in which you brought the king   315
    To be your servant.

Suf.   Then, that without the knowledge
    Either of king or council, when you went
    Ambassador to the emperor, you made bold
    To carry into Flanders the great seal.

Sur. Item, you sent a large commission   320
    To Gregory de Cassado, to conclude
    Without the king's will or the state's allowance,
    A league between his highness and Ferrara.

Suf. That out of mere ambition, you have caus'd

---

309. I . . . you] *so Rowe 3; two lines in F, ending* head; / . . . you.   I had] *F;*
I'd *Pope.*   310, 313, 316. First, that . . . Then, that . . . Then, that] *F;* First
that, . . . Then that, . . . Then that, *Camb. 1865.*   318. the] *F;* th' *Pope.*

309. *have at you*] announcing his on-slaught, cf. II. ii. 84 and n.

310–32.] These accusations are listed as nos. 1, 2, 4, 5, 7, and 9 of the nine articles of indictment against Wolsey; see Appendix II, p. 202. The three omitted relate to more petty or particular offences, that Wolsey had slandered the Church of England, that, having the pox, he had breathed on Henry, and that he had prevented the king's clerk of the market from sitting in St Albans. The same three are left out from the articles as cited in Rowley's *When You See Me, You Know Me* (1605), but there is no need to see a connection here between the plays, for in both it is dramatically appropriate that only the more general and serious crimes of Wolsey should be mentioned.

311. *legate*] i.e. deputed to represent the Pope.

312. *maim'd . . . jurisdiction*] Holinshed has merely "tooke awaie the right".

314–16. *Ego . . . servant*] Douce points out that the original article says Wolsey "had joyned himself with your Grace, as in saying and writing, *The king and I would ye should do thus* . . .", i.e. that Wolsey had placed himself on a level of equality with the king. The mistaken idea that he had brought the king to be his "servant" seems to be due to the chronicles; as Pooler notes, *Ego et rex meus* is the normal form in Latin, equivalent to 'My king and I'.

315. *still inscrib'd*] always written conspicuously. The verb does not occur elsewhere in Shakespeare, and in origin was a 16th-century geometrical term, meaning to trace a figure inside and touching the periphery of an encircling figure.

318. *emperor*] i.e. Charles V; cf. I. i. 176 ff.

322. *allowance*] permission; first recorded by *O.E.D.* in 1628, but cf. *Lr.* I. iv. 228 and *Oth.*, I. i. 128.

Your holy hat to be stampt on the king's coin.   325

Sur. Then, that you have sent innumerable substance
(By what means got, I leave to your own conscience)
To furnish Rome and to prepare the ways
You have for dignities, to the mere undoing
Of all the kingdom. Many more there are,   330
Which since they are of you, and odious,
I will not taint my mouth with.

Cham.   O my lord,
Press not a falling man too far; 'tis virtue:
His faults lie open to the laws, let them,
Not you, correct him. My heart weeps to see him   335
So little of his great self.

Sur.   I forgive him.

Suf. Lord cardinal, the king's further pleasure is,
Because all those things you have done of late
By your power legative within this kingdom
Fall into th'compass of a præmunire;   340
That therefore such a writ be sued against you,

---

326. you have] *F*; you've *Dyce 2.*   339. legative] *F*; Legantive *F2*; Legantine
F4; Legatine *Rowe 2.*

---

325. *hat . . . coin*] Wolsey had the
right to coin half-groats and half-
pennies at York, as did Archbishop
Warham at Canterbury, but by issuing
a groat, a silver coin, with his initials
and cardinal's hat upon it, he "usurp-
ed the king's prerogative" (G. C.
Brooke, *English Coins*, 3rd edn, 1950,
p. 177).

326. *innumerable substance*] countless
wealth; Holinshed's phrase, and cf.
I. ii. 58.

328. *furnish*] supply.

329. *mere undoing*] utter ruin; cf.
Cym., IV. ii. 92, "to thy mere confusion". This passes easily into the
modern sense of "mere", as at l. 324.

333. *Press*] oppress, afflict, cf. *Lr.*,
IV. iii. 128.

'*tis virtue*] i.e. not to do so.

334. *open to*] exposed to, cf. *2 H 6*, I.
iii. 159; *2 H 4*, v. ii. 8, "Hath left me
open to all injuries".

339. *legative*] so *F*; a perfectly good

word, meaning "as a legate" (cf. l. 311
above), but most editors from Rowe on
alter to "legatine". Holinshed's usual
form is "power legantine" (p. 848,
etc.); "legative" is found in the
chronicles, e.g. in Speed, p. 757.

340. *præmunire*] a writ, so called because the phrase *praemunire facias* appears in it, by which a person may be
summoned on a charge of asserting
papal jurisdiction in England, of
appealing "to *Rome* from any of the
King's Courts" (Jacob, *Law-Dictionary*), and other similar offences. In the
wording of the writ, the phrase means
'give warning', *munire* being confused
apparently with *monere*. Forfeiture of
goods and outlawry were the punishment assigned by statute. For the
wording of the text cf. Day, *Law
Tricks* (1608; M.S.R. 1949), l. 1895,
"I stand in compass of a praemon-
ire".

341. *sued*] put in action.

To forfeit all your goods, lands, tenements,
Chattels and whatsoever, and to be
Out of the king's protection. This is my charge.

Nor. And so we'll leave you to your meditations　　345
How to live better. For your stubborn answer
About the giving back the great seal to us,
The king shall know it, and (no doubt) shall thank you.
So fare you well, my little good lord cardinal.

　　　　　　　　　　　　　　　Exeunt all but Wolsey.

Wol. So farewell, to the little good you bear me.　　350
Farewell? a long farewell to all my greatness.
This is the state of man; to-day he puts forth
The tender leaves of hopes, to-morrow blossoms,
And bears his blushing honours thick upon him:
The third day comes a frost, a killing frost,　　355
And when he thinks, good easy man, full surely
His greatness is a-ripening, nips his root,

---

343. Chattels] *Theobald;* Castles *F.*　　350. farewell, to] *F;* farewel to *F4.*
little good] *F;* little-good *Keightley.*　　351. Farewell? a] *F;* Farewell, a *Rowe;*
Farewell! A *Staunton.*　　farewell to] *F;* farewell, to *Capell.*　　353. hopes] *F;*
hope *Var. 1773.*

342–3. *goods . . . | Chattels*] Theobald's emendation of "Castles" (F) has been generally accepted, and is very plausible as a corruption of the form "cattels" which occurs in Holinshed, p. 909, "to forfeit all his lands, tenements, goods, and cattels, and to be out of the kings protection". It seems odd that the legal formula, as given here, should be broken in the text, and "Castles" may be defended as a climax to "goods, lands, tenements . . .", and as an allusion to the notoriety Wolsey suffered for his building palaces such as Hampton Court and York Place; cf. IV. i. 94–7.

344. *Out . . . protection*] i.e. "excluded the Benefit of the laws" (Jacob, *Law-Dictionary*).

349. *little good*] presumably = little-good; as Pooler notes, Norfolk modifies the usual phrase, 'my good lord'.

351. *Farewell?*] so F; most editors, following Rowe and Staunton, replace the query mark by a comma or an

exclamation mark, turning this line into the beginning of a set speech, as though it were unconnected with the previous line. The reading of F, kept by Sisson, suggests that Wolsey catches up the "farewell" of l. 350, suddenly realizes its more general application, and follows this up in the next lines.

a long farewell] Pooler notes that this phrase occurs several times in B. and F. but only once elsewhere in Shakespeare (*Ant.*, v. ii. 295). These two writers have no monopoly of it; it appears, for instance, in Marston's *Sophonisba* (1606; Wood, II. 18).

354. *blushing*] glowing, cf. *R 2*, III. iii. 63, "the blushing discontented sun".

356. *easy*] ready to believe; cf. *Wint.*, IV. iv. 516, "I would your spirit were easier for advice".

357. *nips his root*] a common idea; Steevens cites A.W. in G. Gascoigne, *Whole Works* (1587), ¶¶¶ 2r, "And frosts of frūps so nip the roots, of vertuous mening minds", and cf. the

And then he falls as I do. I have ventur'd
Like little wanton boys that swim on bladders,
This many summers in a sea of glory,   360
But far beyond my depth: my high-blown pride
At length broke under me, and now has left me,
Weary and old with service, to the mercy
Of a rude stream that must for ever hide me.
Vain pomp and glory of this world, I hate ye;   365
I feel my heart new open'd. O how wretched
Is that poor man that hangs on princes' favours!
There is betwixt that smile we would aspire to,
That sweet aspect of princes, and their ruin,
More pangs and fears than wars or women have;   370
And when he falls, he falls like Lucifer,
Never to hope again.

Small image reflects greatness

ambivalence of tragic fall

360. This] *F*; These *Pope*.   362–3. me, / Weary] *so Warburton*; me / Weary, *F*.
369. their] *F*; our *Pope*; his *Hanmer*.

phrase 'to nip (something) in the bud',
which goes back to 1606.

358–64. *I . . . hide me*] probably, like
an earlier passage (ll. 222–7), suggested by Speed's *History* (1611), p. 769,
"Formerly wee have spoken of the
rising of this man [Wolsey], who now
being swolne so bigge by the blasts of
promotion, as the bladder not able to
conteine more greatnesse, suddenly
burst, and vented foorth the winde of
all former favours. Vaine glorious he
was . . .". The idea is not uncommon,
and in a very early passage relating to
Wolsey in the reign of Henry VIII,
Holinshed says, III. 837, he was "led
with the like spirit of swelling ambition, wherwith the rable of popes have
beene bladder like puffed and blowne
up: a divelish and luciferian vice . . ."
It was usual to learn to swim by using
bladders, cf. Middleton and Rowley,
Fair Quarrel (1617; Bullen IV. 248),
IV. iv. 51, "Did'st thou bargain for the
bladders with the butcher, Trim?
Trim. Ay, sir . . . I'll practise to swim
too, sir".

359. *wanton*] frolicsome, cf. *Lr.*, IV. i.
38, "As flies to wanton boys are we to
the gods, / They kill us for their sport".

360. *This many*] Numerals are often
taken collectively as one, especially
where the reference is to a space of
time, cf. *1 H 4*, II. ii. 17, "this two and
twenty years" (cited Pooler), and
Abbott 87.

364. *rude stream*] rough current; cf.
"rude imperious surge", *2 H 4*, III. i.
20.

365. *Vain . . . world*] cf. *Book of Common Prayer*, "Dost thou forsake the vain
pomp, and glory of the world . . . ?"
(Baptism service). No doubt the allusion is intended, for Wolsey learns in
his fall to be a Christian, cf. l. 440 ff.

368. *aspire to*] mount up to, cf. *Wiv.*,
v. v. 101, "whose flames aspire / . . .
higher and higher".

369. *ruin*] the ruin they inflict, cf.
l. 205 above (Malone).

371. *Lucifer*] see note on ll. 358–64
above; as Malone noted, Churchyard
in *The Mirror for Magistrates* (1587)
makes Wolsey say "so great as was my
pryde, / For which offence, fell *Lucifer*
from skyes" (ed. L. B. Campbell, 1938,
p. 507). The original reference is to
Isaiah, xiv. 12, "How art thou fallen
from heaven, O Lucifer, son of the
morning" (Douce).

Enter CROMWELL, *standing amazed.*

Why how now, Cromwell?
Crom. I have no power to speak, sir.
Wol.   What, amaz'd   *grand calmness*
  At my misfortunes? Can thy spirit wonder
  A great man should decline? Nay, and you weep   375
  I am fall'n indeed.
Crom.   How does your grace?
Wol.   Why well;
  Never so truly happy, my good Cromwell;
  I know myself now, and I feel within me
  A peace above all earthly dignities,
  A still and quiet conscience. The king has cur'd me,   380
  I humbly thank his grace; and from these shoulders,
  These ruin'd pillars, out of pity taken
  A load would sink a navy, too much honour.
  O 'tis a burden Cromwell, 'tis a burden
  Too heavy for a man that hopes for heaven.   385
Crom. I am glad your grace has made that right use of it.
Wol. I hope I have: I am able now, methinks,

373 ff. S.H. *Wol.*] *Car(d). F.*   375. and] *F; if Pope; an Capell.*   376, 386,
387. I am] *I'm Pope.*   396–7. I am . . . methinks,] *so Pope; four lines in F,
ending* Grace, / . . . it. / . . . have: / . . . (me thinks).

372. S.D. Cromwell] Cromwell's
faithful attentions here are expanded
from the mere hint in Holinshed, who
notes, p. 913, "diverse of his [Wolsey's]
servants departed from him to the
kings service, and in especiall Thomas
Crumwell one of his chief counsell".

375. *decline*] fall from prosperity, cf.
Cor., I. i. 197, "who's like to rise, / Who
thrives and who declines".

and] if; the same as "an" (I. iv. 92,
etc.). See Abbott 101.

378. *know myself*] i.e. I recognize my
limitations and my sins and am able to
transcend them. The phrase 'know
thyself' was a catchword to Shakespeare's age, for only through self-
knowledge could the passions be controlled and sin avoided; as Davies said
in *Nosce Teipsum* (1599; in ed. Bullett,
Silver Poets of the Sixteenth Century, p.

347), "how may we to others' things
attain / When none of us his own soul
understands?". "The knowledge of a
mans selfe" was for Sidney "the highest end of the mistres Knowledge . . .
with the end of well dooing and not of
well knowing onely" (*Apologie for
Poetry*, 1595, D1ʳ). The idea is important in the later plays of Shakespeare,
cf. Introduction, pp. xliii ff.

382. *pillars*] Perhaps the author has
in mind the pillars Wolsey had carried
before him, cf. II. iv. Entry.

384–5. *burden . . . heavy*] The image of
a burden or weight runs all through
the play, and is especially marked
here, cf. ll. 391, 407; although Wolsey
is pulled down by one weight, it is to
sustain another, for "his overthrow
heap'd happiness upon him" (IV. ii.
64).

(Out of a fortitude of soul I feel)
To endure more miseries, and greater far
Than my weak-hearted enemies dare offer.   390
What news abroad?

Crom.   The heaviest and the worst
Is your displeasure with the king.

Wol.   God bless him.

Crom. The next is, that Sir Thomas More is chosen
Lord Chancellor in your place.

Wol.   That's somewhat sudden,
But he's a learned man. May he continue   395
Long in his highness' favour, and do justice
For truth's sake, and his conscience; that his bones,
When he has run his course and sleeps in blessings,
May have a tomb of orphans' tears wept on him.
What more?

Crom.   That Cranmer is return'd with welcome;
Install'd Lord Archbishop of Canterbury.   401

Wol. That's news indeed.

Crom.   Last, that the Lady Anne,
Whom the king hath in secrecy long married,
This day was view'd in open as his queen,
Going to chapel; and the voice is now   405
Only about her coronation.

---

389. To endure] *F;* T'endure *Theobald.*   399. orphans'] *Theobald 2;* Orphants
F.   him] *F;* 'em *Capell and Edd.*

388. *fortitude of soul*] These lines
might stand for a definition of the
"patience" shown by Buckingham (ii.
i. 36), Katherine (iii. i. 137, etc.), and
Cranmer (v. i. 105); cf. also l. 458
below, and Introduction, pp. lvii ff.

392. *displeasure*] the disgrace you are
in, cf. *Oth.*, iii. i. 45, "I am sorry / For
your displeasure".

393–402. *More ... Anne*] Chronology
is severely compressed here; Sir
Thomas More was made Chancellor
in 1529, Cranmer was named to the
archbishopric of Canterbury in 1532,
and Anne crowned in 1533, three
years after Wolsey's death in 1530.
The references are to Holinshed, pp.

910, 929 ff., for which see Appendix ii,
pp. 201, 207 ff.

399. *tomb ... him*] The point of this
allusion is that the Chancellor is the
general guardian of infants, i.e. persons under the age of twenty-one,
"whose Acts are in many Cases either
void, or voidable" in law (Jacob, *Law-
Dictionary*). For the image, Steevens
compares W. Drummond, *Tears on the
Death of Moeliades*, an elegy for Prince
Henry (3rd edn, 1614), B2r, "The
Muses ... have raised of their teares /
A Crystal Tomb to Him, where
through his worth appears".

406. *coronation*] pronounced as five
syllables, cf. iv. ii. 121 and n.

Wol. There was the weight that pull'd me down. O
        Cromwell,
    The king has gone beyond me: all my glories
    In that one woman I have lost for ever.
    No <u>sun</u> shall ever usher forth mine honours,   410
    Or gild again the noble troops that waited
    Upon my smiles. Go get thee from me Cromwell,
    I am a poor fall'n man, unworthy now
    To be thy lord and master. Seek the king
    (That <u>sun</u> I pray may never set) I have told him   415
    What, and how true thou art; he will advance thee:
    Some little memory of me will stir him
    (I know his noble nature) not to let
    Thy hopeful service perish too. Good Cromwell
    Neglect him not; make use now, and provide   420
    For thine own future safety.

Crom.   O my lord,
    Must I then leave you? must I needs forgo
    So good, so noble and so true a master?
    Bear witness, all that have not hearts of iron,
    With what a sorrow Cromwell leaves his lord.   425
    The king shall have my service; but my prayers
    For ever and for ever shall be yours.

Wol. Cromwell, I did not think to shed a tear
    In all my miseries; but thou hast forc'd me,
    Out of thy honest truth, to play the woman.   430

---

407. There ... Cromwell] *so Pope; two lines in F, ending* downe. / ... Cromwell.
down. O Cromwell] *F;* down, O Cromwell! *Halliwell.*   415. I have] *F;*
I've *Pope.*

408. *gone beyond*] overreached; cf.
I Thess., iv. 6, "That no man go beyond and defraud his brother in any
matter" (Authorized Version, cited
Clarendon Ed.).

411. *noble troops*] The number of
Wolsey's retainers grew to be legendary, and in *The Mirror for Magistrates*
they were said to have stretched two
by two "much more then half a mile"
(ed. Campbell, p. 500). Holinshed
says, p. 920, "He had ... a great number dailie attending upon him, both of
noblemen & worthie gentlemen, with

no small number of the tallest yeomen ...". The "sun" here may contain an allusion to the king, cf. l. 415,
and I. i. 6 ff.

420. *make use*] take advantage, cf.
Wint., IV. iv. 616, "what I saw, to my
good use I remembered". "Use" is the
legal term for profit derived from pro-
perty (*O.E.D.*, sb. 18).

422. *forgo*] renounce.

424. *hearts of iron*] a common idea,
cf. II. iii. 11 and *Tim.*, III. iv. 84, "show
me an iron heart".

430. *honest truth*] Cavendish says that

Let's dry our eyes; and thus far hear me Cromwell,
And when I am forgotten, as I shall be,
And sleep in dull cold marble, where no mention
Of me more must be heard of, say I taught thee;
Say Wolsey, that once trod the ways of glory,   435
And sounded all the depths and shoals of honour,
Found thee a way (out of his wrack) to rise in,
A sure and safe one, though thy master miss'd it.
Mark but my fall, and that that ruin'd me:
Cromwell, I charge thee, fling away ambition,   440
By that sin fell the angels; how can man then,
The image of his maker, hope to win by it?
Love thyself last, cherish those hearts that hate thee;
Corruption wins not more than honesty.
Still in thy right hand carry gentle peace   445
To silence envious tongues. Be just, and fear not;
Let all the ends thou aim'st at be thy country's,
Thy God's and truth's: then if thou fall'st, O Cromwell,
Thou fall'st a blessed martyr.
Serve the king: and prithee lead me in: 450

434. heard of] *F;* heard *Rowe.*   435. trod the ways] *F;* rode the waves
Warburton conj.   442. by it] *F;* by't *Hanmer.*   449–50. Thou . . . in] *so F;*
two lines, ending king: / . . . in *Rowe 3 and Edd.*   450. and prithee] *F;* And—
Pr'ythee, *Johnson.*

Cromwell "was esteemed the most
faithfullest servant to his maister of all
other" (p. 160), but this passage was
not taken over into the chronicles
(Clarendon Ed.); probably the author
is merely elaborating on Holinshed's
material, cf. note on l. 372 S.D.

play the woman] a common expression
for shedding tears (Pooler); cf. *Mac.,*
IV. iii. 230, "O, I could play the
woman with mine eyes".

433. *dull*] inanimate (*O.E.D.,*
Onions); but also 'gloomy, cheerless',
cf. "dull woe" (*Rom.,* I. iv. 21), "So
dull . . . so woe-begone (*2 H 4,* I. i. 71).

436. *sounded*] fathomed. This is the
culmination of a series of sea-images
relating to Wolsey, who has been
likened to a rock (I. i. 113, III. II. 197),
and a boat (III. ii. 38, and cf. ll. 360,
383), and now, like Katherine (III. i.

149), is "shipwrack'd" in his fall.
441. *sin . . . angels*] cf. l. 371 above
(Pooler).
442. *image*] see Genesis, i. 27.
win] profit.
443. *Love . . . hate thee*] a paraphrase
of Matthew, v. 44, "Love your enemies . . . doe good to them that hate
you" (Geneva).
445. *Still*] ever.
446–9. *Be . . . martyr*] Cromwell rose
to be Earl of Essex and Lord Great
Chamberlain, but fell from power
even more suddenly than Wolsey and
was beheaded; his career is depicted in
the play *Thomas Lord Cromwell* (1602,
reprinted 1613), in which he is shown
as something of a martyr.
450. *Serve . . . in*] so F; most editors,
following Rowe, have transferred
"Serve the king" to the previous line,

There take an inventory of all I have,
To the last penny, 'tis the king's. My robe,
And my integrity to heaven, is all
I dare now call mine own. O Cromwell, Cromwell,
Had I but serv'd my God with half the zeal   455
I serv'd my king, he would not in mine age
Have left me naked to mine enemies.

Crom.   Good sir, have patience.   *Patience recommended not just as a quality, but as a word each since*

Wol.   So I have. Farewell
The hopes of court, my hopes in heaven do dwell. *Exeunt.*

---

as if it were yet another injunction from Wolsey: the phrase is more fitly taken as a dismissal of Cromwell, and as beginning the train of thought continued in ll. 450 ff. A dramatic pause after "martyr" is appropriate.

451. *inventory*] as reported by Holinshed, p. 909; see Appendix II, p. 201.

455-7. *Had . . . enemies*] Holinshed records that Wolsey spoke to this effect on his deathbed, p. 917; see Appendix II, p. 203. Many other examples have been found in literature of similar expressions put into the mouths of fallen men; the idea derives here from Cavendish, who reports Wolsey as saying, "if I had served God as diligently as I have done the king, he would not have given me over in my grey hairs" (p. 250).

457. *naked*] defenceless; cf. *Oth.*, v. ii. 258, "naked as I am, I will assault thee", where the word means 'unarmed'.

458. *patience*] see Introduction, p. lvii.

ACT IV

SCENE I—[*A street*]

Enter two gentlemen, meeting one another.

1 Gent. Y'are well met once again.

2 Gent.   So are you.

1 Gent. You come to take your stand here, and behold
    The Lady Anne pass from her coronation?

2 Gent. 'Tis all my business. At our last encounter
    The Duke of Buckingham came from his trial.   5

1 Gent. 'Tis very true. But that time offer'd sorrow,
    This general joy.

2 Gent.   'Tis well: the citizens
    I am sure have shown at full their royal minds
    (As let 'em have their rights, they are ever forward)
    In celebration of this day with shows,   10

ACT IV

Scene 1

Scene I] *Actus Quartus. Scena Prima. F.*   *A street.*] *Capell.*   1 ff. S.H. *1 Gent.* . . . *2 Gent.* . . . *3 Gent.*] *Var. 1793 after Rowe; 1* . . . . *2.* . . . *3. F.*   3. coronation?] *Capell;* Corronation. *F.*   8. I am] *F;* I'm *Pope.*   8–9. minds / (As . . . forward)] minds, / As . . . forward *F.*   8. royal] *F;* loyal *Pope.*   9. they are] *F;* they're *Pope.*

Scene 1] For Holinshed's account of the coronation of Anne and divorce of Katherine, pp. 929 ff., see Appendix II, pp. 207–9. These are events of 1533, three years after Wolsey's death.

  1. *again*] For their previous meeting, see II. i.

  6. *offer'd*] cf. III. ii. 4 above.

  8. *royal minds*] devotion to the king, cf. "our royal faiths", *2 H 4*, IV. i. 193 (Malone).

  9. *let . . . rights*] give them their due; Pooler notes that such parentheses are common in Fletcher and Massinger; but they are found elsewhere, as in

Dekker, *News from Hell* (1606; Grosart, II. 107), "let's doe them right, 'tis not their fault".

  forward] eager; cf. *Cym.*, III. v. 29.

  10–11. *shows . . . honour*] Holinshed, p. 932, describes the pageants made for the wedding in some detail; perhaps for a contemporary audience these lines would have recalled the much more elaborate shows of the early 17th century, e.g. at the installation of a new Lord Mayor, or the pageantry of the marriage of Princess Elizabeth, which included "fowre floting castles with fire workes, and the

Pageants and sights of honour.

1 Gent.   Never greater,
    Nor I'll assure you, better taken sir.

2 Gent. May I be bold to ask what that contains,
    That paper in your hand?

1 Gent.   Yes, 'tis the list
    Of those that claim their offices this day,   15
    By custom of the coronation.
    The Duke of Suffolk is the first, and claims
    To be high steward; next the Duke of Norfolk,
    He to be earl marshal: you may read the rest.

2 Gent. I thank you sir: had I not known those customs,   20
    I should have been beholding to your paper:
    But I beseech you, what's become of Katherine
    The princess dowager? how goes her business?

1 Gent. That I can tell you too. The Archbishop
    Of Canterbury, accompanied with other   25
    Learned and reverend fathers of his order,
    Held a late court at Dunstable, six miles off
    From Ampthill where the princess lay, to which
    She was often cited by them, but appear'd not:
    And to be short, for not-appearance, and   30
    The king's late scruple, by the main assent
    Of all these learned men, she was divorc'd

---

20. S.H. *2 Gent.*] so *F4; 1. F.*   21. beholding] *F;* beholden *Pope.*   30. not-
appearance] not Appearance *F;* non-appearance *Steevens conj.*

---

representation of the towne, fort and
haven of Argier upon the land", as
well as Chapman's Inns of Court
masque, which "is generally held for
the best shew that hath ben seen many
a day" (Chamberlain, I. 421, 425).

    12. *taken*] received; cf. *Lr.*, II. ii. 166,
"The duke's to blame in this; 'twill be
ill taken".

    15–19. *claim . . . marshal*] from Holin-
shed, p. 930; see Appendix II, p. 208.

    21. *beholding*] indebted; cf. I. iv. 41
and n.

    26. *reverend . . . order*] Holinshed, pp.
929–30, lists "the bishops of London,
Winchester, Bath, Lincolne, and
divers others learned men"; "order"

presumably means 'status' (i.e.
bishops), though this duplicates the
sense of "reverend fathers", cf. II. iv.
56.

    27. *late*] recent, as in l. 31.

    28. *lay*] lodged, cf. *Cor.*, I. ix. 82.

    29. *cited*] summoned to appear.

    30. *not-appearance*] an unusual com-
bination, but cf. "he professes not-
answering", *Troil.*, III. iii. 270.

    31. *main assent*] general agreement,
cf. *Ham.*, I. iii. 28, "the main voice of
Denmark" and *H 5*, I. ii. 144; Pooler
explains as "firm assent", citing "a
main note = strong evidence in B. and
F., *False One* (1620?; *Works*, III. 344),
IV. i; see III. ii. 215 and n. above.

And the late marriage made of none effect:
Since which she was remov'd to Kimmalton,
Where she remains now sick.

2 *Gent.*   Alas good lady.   35
The trumpets sound: stand close, the queen is coming.
Hautboys.

The Order of the Coronation.

1. *A lively flourish of trumpets.*
2. *Then, two judges.*
3. LORD CHANCELLOR, *with purse and mace before him.*
4. *Choristers singing. Music.*
5. MAYOR OF LONDON, *bearing the mace. Then* GARTER, *in his coat of arms, and on his head he wore a gilt copper crown.*

34. Kimmalton] Kymmalton *F;* Kimbolton *F3.*   35. lady.] *F;* lady. S.D. *Trumpets. Capell.*   36. The . . . coming] *so Pope; two lines in F, ending* close, | . . . comming.   S.D. 4. *Choristers*] Quirristers *F.*   Music] *F;* Musicians. Camb. *1865.*   5. he wore] *F; omitted* Rowe; he wears *Camb. 1865.*

33. *of none effect*] null; Holinshed's phrase.

34. *Kimmalton*] "Kymmalton" (F) has usually been emended to "Kimbolton", following F3 and Holinshed's "Kimbalton", but doubtless represents a common pronunciation of the time. The spellings "Kimoltoun" and "Guimolton" are recorded in *The Victoria County History of Huntingdonshire*, vol. III (1936), p. 75, as 16th-century spellings.

36. *close*] silent, concealed, or aside; cf. II. i. 55 and n.

The Order . . . Coronation] This is carefully abstracted, with several alterations, from Holinshed's account, for which see Appendix II, pp. 208–9. The dramatist omits various earls, dukes, and gentlemen, including the Earl of Oxford, Lord High Chamberlain (who carried the crown), probably to keep the number of characters down. Doubtless for the same reason, the historian's "Arundel" becomes "Surrey", and "William Howard" is changed to "the Duke of Norfolk", who like Surrey has already figured in the play. Holinshed's "the kings chapell and the moonks solemnlie

singing" becomes Item 4, "Choristers . . .". The direction for "Collars of Esses" (i.e. ornamental chains made of a series of letters 'S' joined; originally a Lancastrian badge in the Wars of the Roses, and still worn by some officials) may have been suggested by Holinshed's "everie knight of the garter had on his collar of the order". The indications of costume are borrowed from a passage a little below the description of the procession, "Now in the meane season everie duches had put on their bonets a coronall of gold wrought with flowers, and everie marquesse a demie coronall of gold, everie countesse a plaine circlet of gold without flowers, and everie king of armes put on a crowne of coper and guilt, all which were worne till night".

Item 5. Garter] one of the three Kings-at-Arms (Garter, Clarenceux, and Norroy) who serve under the Earl Marshal; his duties include proclaiming the accession and greeting the coronation of a new sovereign; cf. v. iv. Entry.

he wore . . . crown] see quotation above, and Introduction, p. xv. Although this phrase was taken direct-

6. MARQUESS DORSET, *bearing a scepter of gold, on his head a demi-coronal of gold. With him, the* EARL OF SURREY, *bearing the rod of silver with the dove, crowned with an earl's coronet. Collars of Esses.*

7. DUKE OF SUFFOLK, *in his robe of Estate, his coronet on his head, bearing a long white wand, as High Steward. With him, the* DUKE OF NORFOLK, *with the rod of marshalship, a coronet on his head. Collars of Esses.*

8. *A canopy, born by four of the Cinque-ports, under it the* QUEEN, *in her robe; in her hair, richly adorned with pearl, crowned. On each side her, the* BISHOPS OF LONDON *and* WINCHESTER.

9. *The old* DUCHESS OF NORFOLK, *in a coronal of gold, wrought with flowers, bearing the queen's train.*

10. *Certain ladies or countesses, with plain circlets of gold without flowers.*

> *Exeunt, first passing over the stage in order and state, and then, a great flourish of trumpets.*

2 Gent. A royal train, believe me: these I know;
Who's that that bears the sceptre?

1 Gent.   Marquess Dorset,
And that the Earl of Surrey with the rod.

2 Gent. A bold brave gentleman. That should be   40

6, 7. *Esses*] SS. Rowe.   8. *in her hair,*] F; *in her hair* Pope; *her hair* Dyce 2 (W. S. Walker conj.).   *Exeunt . . . trumpets.*] F; *They pass over the stage in order and state.* Var. 1778.

ly from Holinshed, as the past tense shows, stage practice may have been to use gilt copper crowns, cf. *Troil.*, IV. iv. 107, "Whilst some with cunning gild their copper crowns, / With truth and plainness do I wear mine bare" (Troilus is speaking of his honesty).

Item 6. demi-coronal] presumably a smaller or less ornate form of the "coronal" (circlet) indicated in Item 9.

Item 7. Estate] state, as at II. ii. 69.

Item 8. Cinque-ports] It was the "ancient right" of the barons of the Cinque-ports, i.e. Hastings, Sandwich, Dover, Romney, Hythe, and others added later, to carry the canopy over the sovereign (Selden, *Titles of Honor*, 1614, p. 216, cited in *O.E.D.*).

in her hair] i.e. with her hair loosely hanging, as was the custom for brides: Princess Elizabeth was married in February 1613 "in her haire that hung downe long, with an exceeding rich coronet on her head" (Chamberlain, I. 424), "with a Coronet on her head of Pearle, and her haire disheveled, and hanging downe over her shoulders" (Peacham, *Period of Mourning*, 1613, H2r–H2v, cited Pooler). An allusion to this wedding may well be intended, as Holinshed says Anne wore "a coife with a circlet about it full of rich stones", and does not mention pearls: see Introduction, pp. xxx ff.

side her] for the omission of 'of', cf. *Ant.*, II. ii. 206 (Deighton).

37. *train*] retinue.

The Duke of Suffolk.

1 Gent.   'Tis the same: high steward.

2 Gent. And that my Lord of Norfolk?

1 Gent.   Yes.

2 Gent. [*Looking on the Queen.*]   Heaven bless thee!
Thou hast the sweetest face I ever look'd on.
Sir, as I have a soul, she is an angel;
Our king has all the Indies in his arms,   45
And more, and richer, when he strains that lady;
I cannot blame his conscience.

1 Gent.   They that bear
The cloth of honour over her, are four barons
Of the Cinque-ports.

2 Gent. Those men are happy, and so are all are near her. 50
I take it, she that carries up the train
Is that old noble lady, Duchess of Norfolk.

1 Gent. It is, and all the rest are countesses.

2 Gent. Their coronets say so. These are stars indeed—

1 Gent. And sometimes falling ones.

2 Gent.   No more of that. 55
[*The end of the procession leaves; the trumpets sound.*]

41. Suffolk.] *F; Suffolk? Dyce.*   42. S.D. *Looking . . . Queen*] *Johnson; not in F.*   48. over] *F;* o'er *Hudson.*   50. Those . . . her] *so Pope; two lines in F, ending* happy, / . . . her.   54–6. S.H. *2 Gent.* Their . . . / *1 Gent.* And . . . *2 Gent.* No . . . / *1 Gent.* God] *Hudson, following W. S. Walker;* 2. Their . . . / And . . . 2. No . . . / *1.* God *F;* 2. Their . . . / And . . . *1.* No . . . / God *F3 and Edd.*   55. S.D. *The . . . sound.*] *This Ed.; not in F; Exit Procession. A great Flourish of Trumpets. Capell.*

45. *Indies*] presumably the East Indies (which included India), and the West Indies (which included America), both regarded as sources of fabulous wealth; cf. i. i. 21 above.

46. *strains*] embraces; formerly common, cf. *O.E.D.*, v¹ 2, though not elsewhere in Shakespeare.

48. *cloth of honour*] canopy; cf. "cloth of state", ii. iv. Entry.

53. *countesses*] i.e. at least of the rank of Earl, or the wives or widows of earls; the word is from Holinshed, who says "everie countesse [wore] a plaine circlet of gold" (p. 933), cf. The Order of the Coronation, note, and Item 10.

54. *stars*] a frequent image for nobles, cf. *Per.*, ii. iii. 39.

55–6.] The speech-headings in F do not make sense; earlier, at l. 20, F has *1.* for *2.*, and here it looks as though a *1.* has slipped out. Hudson's emendation, adding a S.H. for *1 Gent.* at l. 55, seems more appropriate than that of F3, which involves removing the S.H. for l. 56, given in F.

55. *falling*] the common quibble meaning to surrender chastity; cf. E. A., *Strange Foot-Post* (1613), B2ʳ, "*Cadentes*, that is, falling Starres, whereunto wantons may bee compared, which fall from the Heaven of Honesty".

Enter a third Gentleman.

1 Gent. God save you sir. Where have you been broiling?

3 Gent. Among the crowd i'th'abbey, where a finger
　　　Could not be wedg'd in more: I am stifled
　　　With the mere rankness of their joy.

2 Gent. 　　　　　　　　　　　　　You saw
　　　The ceremony?

3 Gent. 　　　　　That I did.

1 Gent. 　　　　　　　　　How was it?　　　　　　　60

3 Gent. Well worth the seeing.

2 Gent. 　　　　　　　　Good sir, speak it to us.

3 Gent. As well as I am able. The rich stream
　　　Of lords and ladies, having brought the queen
　　　To a prepar'd place in the choir, fell off
　　　A distance from her; while her grace sat down　　65
　　　To rest a while, some half an hour or so,
　　　In a rich chair of state, opposing freely
　　　The beauty of her person to the people.
　　　Believe me sir, she is the goodliest woman
　　　That ever lay by man: which when the people　　70
　　　Had the full view of, such a noise arose
　　　As the shrouds make at sea in a stiff tempest,
　　　As loud, and to as many tunes. Hats, cloaks
　　　(Doublets, I think) flew up, and had their faces
　　　Been loose, this day they had been lost. Such joy　　75
　　　I never saw before. Great-bellied women,
　　　That had not half a week to go, like rams
　　　In the old time of war, would shake the press
　　　And make 'em reel before 'em. No man living

59–60. You . . . ceremony] *so Hanmer; one line in F.*　　64, 90. choir] Quire *F.*
68–70. people. / . . . man:] *F;* people,— / . . . man;— *Neilson.*　　78. press] *F4;*
prease *F.*

---

59. *rankness*] cf. *Cor.*, III. i. 66, "The mutable rank-scented many".

61. *speak it*] describe it; cf. IV. ii. 32.

64. *fell off*] withdrew; the earliest example known to *O.E.D.*

67. *opposing*] exposing, placing opposite, cf. *2 H 6*, IV. x. 48, "Oppose thy . . . eyes to mine", and *Lr.*, IV. vii. 32.

69. *goodliest*] fairest.

72. *shrouds*] the sail-ropes or ropes running from the mast-head; part of a ship's standing rigging, cf. *John*, v. vii. 53.

77. *rams*] battering-rams.

78. *press*] crowd, cf. *Cæs.*, I. ii. 15, "Who is it in the press that calls on me?". The spelling "prease" of F was common.

Could say 'This is my wife' there, all were woven   80
So strangely in one piece.

2 Gent.   But what follow'd?

3 Gent. At length her grace rose, and with modest paces
Came to the altar, where she kneel'd, and saintlike
Cast her fair eyes to heaven and pray'd devoutly:
Then rose again and bow'd her to the people;   85
When by the Archbishop of Canterbury
She had all the royal makings of a queen,
As holy oil, Edward Confessor's crown,
The rod, and bird of peace and all such emblems
Laid nobly on her: which perform'd, the choir   90
With all the choicest music of the kingdom
Together sung *Te Deum*. So she parted,
And with the same full state pac'd back again
To York-place, where the feast is held.

1 Gent.   Sir,
You must no more call it York-place, that's past;   95
For since the cardinal fell, that title's lost,
'Tis now the king's, and call'd Whitehall.

3 Gent.   I know it;
But 'tis so lately alter'd that the old name
Is fresh about me.

87. She had] *F;* Sh' had *Pope.*   94–5. Sir / You must] *F;* Sir, you / Must
Var. 1793.   95. that's] *F;* that is *Var. 1793.*   98. the] *F;* th' *Dyce 2.*

81. *piece*] length of cloth, cf. III. ii.
280 above.

82. *modest*] moderate, decorous, cf.
Tw. N., I. iii. 9, "the modest limits of
order", and below, v. ii. 103.

85. *bow'd her*] for this common use of
now intransitive verbs as reflexive, see
Abbott 296.

87. *makings*] attributes that go to
make; apparently a coinage. "To have
the makings of" in the modern sense of
'potentialities' is first recorded in
O.E.D. in 1837. This description of the
ceremony is from Holinshed, cf.
Appendix II, p. 209.

91. *music*] musicians (Pooler); the
word often means a band of players,
cf. *Cym.*, II. iii. 12, and above, Order of
the Coronation, Item 4.

92. *parted*] departed.

93. *state*] pomp, as at II. i. 101.

94. *York-place*] The feast was actually held in Westminster Hall, as
Holinshed says, p. 932, though he adds
that Anne later retired to Whitehall;
see Appendix II, p. 209: the change
here to York-place is a device to enable the dramatist to refer to Wolsey.
His mansion was taken over at his fall
by Henry and enlarged into Whitehall Palace (which no longer exists),
as reported earlier by Holinshed, p.
928.

96. *lost*] perished, cf. III. i. 107 above.

99. *fresh*] i.e. persists as if it were still
in use; cf. v. ii. 65 below, and *H 5*, IV.
iii. 55, "then shall our names . . . Be in
their flowing cups freshly remem-

2 Gent.   What two reverend bishops
    Were those that went on each side of the queen?   100
3 Gent. Stokesley and Gardiner, the one of Winchester,
    Newly preferr'd from the king's secretary;
    The other, London.
2 Gent.   He of Winchester
    Is held no great good lover of the archbishop's,
    The virtuous Cranmer.
3 Gent.   All the land knows that: 105
    However, yet there is no great breach; when it comes
    Cranmer will find a friend will not shrink from him.
2 Gent. Who may that be, I pray you?
3 Gent.   Thomas Cromwell,
    A man in much esteem with th'king, and truly
    A worthy friend. The king has made him master   110
    O'th'jewel-house,
    And one already of the privy council.
2 Gent. He will deserve more.
3 Gent.   Yes, without all doubt.
    Come gentlemen, ye shall go my way,
    Which is to th'court, and there ye shall be my guests:
    Something I can command. As I walk thither   116
    I'll tell ye more.
Both.   You may command us, sir.   *Exeunt.*

---

101. Stokesley] *F4;* Stokeley *F.*   104. the] *F;* th' *Pope.*   106. there is] *F;*
there's *Pope.*   when it] *F;* when 't *Pope.*   110–11. king . . . / O'th'] *so
Collier 2;* King . . . him / . . . o' th' *F;* king / . . . him . . . of the *Var. 1793.*
114–15. way, / Which] *F;* way, which / *Capell.*

ber'd", where "freshly" means 'with
undiminished force'. The change of
name was in fact very stale news by the
time of Anne's coronation, cf. l. 94 and
note.

102. *Newly . . . secretary*] as indicated
at II. ii. 115 above.

105. *Cranmer*] foreshadowing the
events of v. i and ii; our sympathetic attitude to Cranmer is pre-

pared by this and earlier references to
him, cf. II. iv. 236, III. ii. 63, 102,
401.

110–12. *master . . . council*] as reported
in Holinshed, p. 929. The master of
the Jewel House had charge of all the
plate used at the king's table, as well as
the crown jewels, etc.

116. *Something*] to some extent, cf.
I. i. 195.

SCENE II—[*Kimbolton.*]

Enter KATHERINE DOWAGER, *sick, led between* GRIFFITH, *her Gentleman Usher, and* PATIENCE, *her woman.*

Grif. How does your grace?

Kath.   O Griffith, sick to death:
My legs like loaden branches bow to th'earth,
Willing to leave their burthen: reach a chair;
So now, methinks, I feel a little ease.
Didst thou not tell me Griffith, as thou ledst me,   5
That the great child of honour, Cardinal Wolsey,
Was dead?

Grif.   Yes madam; but I think your grace,
Out of the pain you suffer'd, gave no ear to't.

Kath. Prithee good Griffith, tell me how he died.
If well, he stepp'd before me happily   10
For my example.

Grif.   Well, the voice goes, madam,
For after the stout Earl Northumberland
Arrested him at York, and brought him forward

Scene II

Scene II] *Scena Secunda. F.*   *Kimbolton.*] *Theobald.*   2. loaden] loaded *F2.*
4. So now] *F;* So—now *Rowe.*   7. think] *F2;* thanke *F.*   10. me happily]
so F; me happily, *Rowe;* me, happily, *Capell.*

Scene II] The faithful ministrations of Griffith and Patience to Katherine in this scene, like those of Cromwell to Wolsey in III. ii, seem to be the dramatist's invention, enlarged from mere hints in the chronicles. Griffith's name is not mentioned in connection with her death in Holinshed, but he is named in relation to her trial (II. iv. 125 and n.); Katherine's maid Patience is wholly an invention, and for the significance of the name, see Introduction, p. lviii. For Holinshed's account of the queen's death, of the visit of Capuchius, her letter, and his description of Wolsey's death, see Appendix II, pp. 202-4, 210-11.

3. *burthen*] cf. III. ii. 384 and n.

6. *child of honour*] the title applied to Hotspur (*1 H 4*, III. ii. 139), and carrying overtones of chivalry and romance, from the use of "child" to designate a noble youth, cf. *Lr.*, III. iv. 186, "Child Rowland to the dark tower came".

7. *dead*] Wolsey died in 1530, more than five years before Katherine.

10. *happily*] appropriately, cf. *Mer. V.*, II. ii. 191, "Parts that become thee happily enough", and below, v. i. 85. Most editors, following Capell, have placed the word between commas, and interpreted it as 'haply, perhaps'.

11. *voice*] common talk, cf. III. ii. 405 (Clarendon Ed.); the story of Wolsey's death is from Holinshed, p. 917; see Appendix II, pp. 202 ff.

As a man sorely tainted, to his answer,
He fell sick suddenly, and grew so ill   15
He could not sit his mule.

Kath.   Alas poor man.

Grif. At last, with easy roads, he came to Leicester,
Lodg'd in the abbey, where the reverend abbot
With all his covent honourably receiv'd him;
To whom he gave these words: 'O father abbot,   20
An old man, broken with the storms of state,
Is come to lay his weary bones among ye:
Give him a little earth for charity'.
So went to bed, where eagerly his sickness
Pursued him still, and three nights after this,   25
About the hour of eight, which he himself
Foretold should be his last, full of repentance,
Continual meditations, tears and sorrows,
He gave his honours to the world again,
His blessed part to heaven, and slept in peace.   30

Kath. So may he rest, his faults lie gently on him:
Yet thus far, Griffith, give me leave to speak him,
And yet with charity. He was a man
Of an unbounded stomach, ever ranking

---

17. roads] Rodes *F.*   19. covent] *F;* convent *Rowe.*   31. So . . . him] *so Pope; two lines in F, ending* rest, / . . . him.

14. *sorely tainted*] severely disgraced, or, guilty in the extreme.

answer] i.e. to charges, cf. v. i. 104.

17. *roads*] stages (Steevens); originally the act of riding, cf. to "make road", to make an attack, *Cor.*, III. i. 5. The phrase is not in Holinshed, but Cavendish's "by easy journies" was copied into Foxe, p. 909.

19. *covent*] an old form of 'convent', originally a company of people, then a company of either sex living under religious discipline; cf. *Meas.*, IV. iii. 133; Holinshed has "convent", Stow, *Annals* (1592), p. 940, "covent".

21-2. *old . . . weary*] Wolsey was between fifty-five and sixty years old at his death; cf. the similar descriptions of Buckingham (II. i. 133), and Katherine (III. i. 120), which increase

the pathos of their deaths, and our readiness to accept their downfalls.

28. *sorrows*] laments, cf. *Ant.*, IV. xiv. 136.

30. *blessed part*] soul, cf. "the immortal part", *2 H 4*, II. ii. 114 (Onions).

32. *thus . . . him*] to this extent let me describe him; cf. I. i. 38 and II. iv. 165 above.

33-68.] These accounts of Wolsey's character are based on two passages in Holinshed, pp. 917 and 922, for which see Appendix II, pp. 203-4, 206.

34. *stomach*] ambition; Holinshed's word, and cf. La Primaudaye, *French Academy* (1586), p. 223, "It is natural in man, the greater his stomach is, the more to labor to excel others". In Shakespeare the word usually means 'courage', 'anger', etc.

Himself with princes; one that by suggestion   35
Tied all the kingdom; simony was fair play;
His own opinion was his law: i'th'presence
He would say untruths, and be ever double
Both in his words and meaning. He was never
(But where he meant to ruin) pitiful: 40
His promises were as he then was, mighty,
But his performance, as he is now, nothing:
Of his own body he was ill, and gave
The clergy ill example.

Grif.   Noble madam,
Men's evil manners live in brass, their virtues   45
We write in water. May it please your highness
To hear me speak his good now?

36. Tied] Ty'de *F;* Tyth'd *Hanmer.*

35-6. *by ... kingdom*] by underhand dealing brought the kingdom into bondage. Holinshed has "by craftie suggestion gat into his hands innumerable treasure", and for this sense of "suggestion" cf. also *R 3,* III. ii. 103 (Clarendon Ed.); the more usual meaning in Shakespeare is 'incitement to evil', as at *Tp.,* IV. i. 26. For "tied", cf. Kyd, *Cornelia* (1595; *Works,* ed. Boas, 1901), Act I, l. 68, "thou ty'dst / The former world to thee in vassalage" (cited *O.E.D.,* tie 5c), and *Wint.,* v. i. 213, "Where you were tied in duty". There is also a quibble on 'tith'd', i.e. plundered by tithes, cf. *John,* III. i. 154 (Hanmer's emendation), which connects the word with "simony", and with the "treasure" of Holinshed's account; cf. III. ii. 284 above.

36. *simony*] trafficking in ecclesiastical preferments. "Fair-play" seems to be a coinage of Shakespeare's, cf. *John,* v. i. 67, *Tp.,* v. i. 175.

37. *presence*] presence-chamber, cf. I. i. 30.

38-9. *double ... meaning*] ambiguous in his manner and in his meaning; for "double", cf. *Mac.,* v. viii. 20. "Words", the ornaments of style and rhetoric, are frequently opposed to "matter" or meaning, cf. *Rom.,* II. vi.

30, "Conceit, more rich in matter than in words, / Brags of his substance, not of ornament", and for further examples and comment, see T. W. Baldwin, *Shakspere's Small Latin,* II. 182-4. To Bacon it was "the first distemper of learning, when men study words and not matter" (*Adv. of Learning,* I. iv. 3).

41-2. *promises ... nothing*] cf. III. ii. 151-6 and n. for the common contrast between words and deeds, and Dekker, *News from Hell* (1606; Grosart, II. 116), "their Promises are Eeves, their performances hollidayes, for they work hard upon the one, and are idle on the other". For "nothing", cf. III. ii. 208 above.

43. *ill*] depraved; cf. III. ii. 295 above.

45-6. *Men's ... water*] a combination of proverbial phrases, see Tilley, I 71, W 114. Brass (stone or other metals) is a symbol of permanence, whereas water (dust or sand) retains no lasting impression. "To live in brass" occurs in *H 5,* IV. iii. 97, and cf. Marston, *Malcontent* (1604; Wood, I. 166), "Favours are writ in dust, but stripes we feele, / Depraved nature stamps in lasting steele".

47. *speak ... good*] describe his good qualities.

2 Sides of Wolsey

Kath.   Yes good Griffith,
   I were malicious else.
Grif.   This cardinal,
   Though from an humble stock, undoubtedly
   Was fashion'd to much honour. From his cradle   50
   He was a scholar, and a ripe and good one,
   Exceeding wise, fair-spoken and persuading:
   Lofty and sour to them that lov'd him not,
   But to those men that sought him, sweet as summer.
   And though he were unsatisfied in getting   55
   (Which was a sin) yet in bestowing, madam,
   He was most princely: ever witness for him
   Those twins of learning that he rais'd in you,
   Ipswich and Oxford; one of which fell with him,
   Unwilling to outlive the good that did it,   60
   The other (though unfinish'd) yet so famous,
   So excellent in art, and still so rising,
   That Christendom shall ever speak his virtue.
   His overthrow heap'd happiness upon him,
   For then, and not till then, he felt himself,   65

50. honour. From . . . cradle] *F;* honour, from . . . cradle; *Theobald;* honour from . . . cradle: *Hanmer and Edd.*   60. good . . . it] *F;* good he did it *Pope;* good man did it *Collier 3.*

50. *honour. From*] so F, but often emended, following Theobald, to "honour from his cradle". The thought transition from "cradle" to "and became a ripe and good one" is not difficult, and was doubtless suggested by Wolsey's fabulous reputation, cf. Holinshed, p. 917, "being but a child, verie apt to be learned . . . he was made bachellor of art, when he passed not fifteene yeares of age, and was called . . . the boie bachellor"; this seems to have been combined in the dramatist's mind with the passage (also p. 917) which is otherwise closely followed here, and which has merely, "This cardinall . . . was a man undoubtedly borne to honor . . .".

53. *Lofty*] haughty.

54. *sought him*] i.e., as Holinshed has, "sought his freendship".

58. *rais'd*] built. Wolsey founded

colleges at Ipswich, his birthplace, and at Oxford; the latter still exists as Christ Church.

60. *good . . . it*] the goodness that built it (did raise it), or, perhaps, that made it. For the latter sense of "did", Pooler cites *Tw. N.,* I. v. 253, "is't not well done? *Viola.* Excellently done, if God did all.", where the reference is to Olivia's face: he suggests that "good" may mean 'wealth' or 'prosperity', but it is more naturally taken as equivalent to "virtue", l. 63.

62. *art*] learning, as in *Sonn.,* LXVI. 9, "And art made tongue-tied by authority".

rising] in fame, influence, and in structure.

63. *speak*] cf. l. 47 above.

64–5. *happiness . . . himself*] cf. III. ii. 377 ff.; "felt" means 'recognized', 'knew'.

And found the blessedness of being little;
And to add greater honours to his age
Than man could give him, he died fearing God.

Kath. After my death I wish no other herald,
No other speaker of my living actions   70
To keep mine honour from corruption,
But such an honest chronicler as Griffith.
Whom I most hated living, thou hast made me,
With thy religious truth and modesty,
Now in his ashes honour: peace be with him.   75
Patience, be near me still, and set me lower;
I have not long to trouble thee. Good Griffith,
Cause the musicians play me that sad note
I nam'd my knell, whilst I sit meditating
On that celestial harmony I go to.   80

Sad and solemn music.

Grif. She is asleep: good wench, let's sit down quiet,
For fear we wake her. Softly, gentle Patience.

THE VISION

*Enter solemnly tripping one after another, six personages, clad in white
robes, wearing on their heads garlands of bays, and golden vizards
on their faces, branches of bays or palm in their hands. They first
congee unto her, then dance: and at certain changes, the first two*

80. celestial] Cœlestiall *F.*   82. *The Vision.* 4. *congee*] *Conge F.*

70. *living*] while alive; cf. *R 2*, v. i. 39.

74. *religious*] scrupulous, strict; cf. *All's W.*, II. iii. 190, "Thy love's to me religious; else does err".

modesty] moderation, cf. II. ii. 136.

78. *note*] melody, cf. *Cym.*, IV. ii. 237, "sing him to the ground . . . use like note and words".

80. *harmony*] It was thought that the liberated soul could hear the music made by the spheres in their revolution round the earth, a sound too rarefied for mortal ears; so Pericles thinks he hears this harmony when Marina is restored to him, *Per.*, v. i. 231 ff. The idea is a poetic commonplace.

82. The Vision.] There is no source for this in the chronicles.

l. 2. bays] in token of joy.

golden vizards] probably to indicate spirits; so in Dekker's *Old Fortunatus* (1600; Pearson, I. 104), Vice and other spirits enter "wearing golded vizards, and attirde like devils". In a similar way, the "white robes" indicate virtue and purity, and in the same entry in Dekker's play, Virtue and her nymphs enter "all in white".

l. 4. congee] the equivalent of "make reverend curtsies" below; cf. Heywood, *Fair Maid of the Exchange* (1607; Pearson, II. 27–8), "Bowdler. . . . I am yours for a congee. *Fiddle.* After the French salutation".

hold a spare garland over her head, at which the other four make reverend curtsies. Then the two that held the garland deliver the same to the other next two, who observe the same order in their changes, and holding the garland over her head. Which done, they deliver the same garland to the last two, who likewise observe the same order. At which (as it were by inspiration) she makes (in her sleep) signs of rejoicing, and holdeth up her hands to heaven. And so in their dancing vanish, carrying the garland with them. The music continues.

Kath. Spirits of peace, where are ye? are ye all gone?
And leave me here in wretchedness behind ye?
Grif. Madam, we are here.
Kath.　　　　　　　　It is not you I call for;　　85
Saw ye none enter since I slept?
Grif.　　　　　　　　None, madam.
Kath. No? Saw you not even now a blessed troop
Invite me to a banquet, whose bright faces
Cast thousand beams upon me, like the sun?
They promis'd me eternal happiness,　　90
And brought me garlands, Griffith, which I feel
I am not worthy yet to wear; I shall assuredly.
Grif. I am most joyful, madam, such good dreams
Possess your fancy.
Kath.　　　　　　　Bid the music leave,
They are harsh and heavy to me.　　*Music ceases.*
Pat.　　　　　　　　Do you note　　95
How much her grace is alter'd on the sudden?

6. *reverend*] *F*; *reverent Warburton.*　　85. we are] *F*; we're *Pope.*　　92. I am] *F*;
I'm *Keightley.*　　assuredly] *so F*; *separate line in Capell.*　　95. They are] *F*;
They're *Hudson.*

changes] figures or movements in the dance; cf. *LLL.*, v. ii. 209, "in our measure do but vouchsafe one change" (Pooler), and Marston, *Insatiate Countess* (1613; Wood, III. 21), S.D., "They take the women, and dance the first change".

89. *thousand*] cf. Prologue, l. 29.

92. *I . . . assuredly*] an odd line metrically, requiring the slurring of "I am" to "I'm" and the elision of *e* in "assuredly" in order to be read as an irregular pentameter; perhaps it should be read as a hexameter. There are several lines of a similar kind in the play, cf. I. ii. 71, 114; III. ii. 137, etc.

94. *Possess*] occupy.

Bid . . . leave] bid the musicians cease playing; cf. *Ham.*, II. i. 51, "I was about to say something: where did I leave?"

95. *heavy*] tedious, cf. *Cym.*, III. vi. 91, "Discourse is heavy, fasting".

How long her face is drawn! how pale she looks,
And of an earthy cold! Mark her eyes!
Grif. She is going wench; pray, pray.
Pat.   Heaven comfort her.

Enter a Messenger.

Mess. And't like your grace—
Kath.   You are a saucy fellow,   100
Deserve we no more reverence?
Grif.   You are to blame,
Knowing she will not lose her wonted greatness
To use so rude behaviour. Go to, kneel.
Mess. I humbly do entreat your highness' pardon,
My haste made me unmannerly. There is staying   105
A gentleman, sent from the king, to see you.
Kath. Admit him entrance Griffith. But this fellow
Let me ne'er see again.   *Exit Messeng[er].*

Enter LORD CAPUCHIUS.

97–8. drawn! . . . cold! . . . eyes!] *Camb. 1891;* drawne? . . . cold? . . . eyes? *F.*
98. cold] *F;* coldness *Collier 2;* colour *Dyce 2 (W. S. Walker conj.).*   Mark] *F;*
Mark you *Capell.*   99. She is] *F;* She's *Hanmer.*   100. And't] *F;* An't
Hanmer and Edd.   105. There is] *F;* There's *Dyce 2.*   108. S.D. *Exit . . .*
Capuchius.] so *F (reading Messeng.); Exit . . . Capucius. Rowe; Exeunt Griffith and
Messenger. Re-enter Griffith, with Capucius. Capell.*

98. *earthy cold*] i.e. coldness. This was
a sign of death; the body was thought
to be composed of the four elements,
and earth, the cold and dry element,
being heavy, was left behind at death,
while air and fire, the lighter ones,
ascended to heaven, cf. *Ant.*, v. ii. 292,
"I am fire and air; my other elements
[i.e. earth and water] I give to baser
life", and *1 H 4*, v. iv. 84, "the earthy
and cold hand of death". Emendation
to "colour" is pointless as regards the
sense, and the omission of a syllable,
as elsewhere in Shakespeare, may indicate a dramatic pause; see 1. i. 183
and n., and Abbott 508.

99–108.] A slight hint for this epi-
sode, Katherine's last show of strength,
was perhaps afforded in Holinshed's
report, p. 936, that the king sent the

Duke of Suffolk to her, who discharged
"a great sort of hir houshold servants,
and yet left a convenient number . . .
which were sworne to serve hir not as
queene, but as princesse Dowager.
Such as tooke that oth she utterlie
refused, and would none of their
service. . ."

102. *lose*] forgo.

105. *staying*] waiting, cf. *Troil.*, III. ii.
11 (Pooler).

107. *Admit*] allow; cf. *Tp.*, II. i. 149,
"no kind of traffic / Would I admit",
and *O.E.D.*, admit 2 a.

108. S.D. Exit . . . Capuchius] Most
editors, following Capell, alter the
directions to make Griffith go out and
return with Capuchius; but there is no
need for him to leave the stage in order
to fetch or beckon for the waiting am-

                        If my sight fail not,
You should be lord ambassador from the emperor,
My royal nephew, and your name Capuchius.   110

Cap. Madam, the same: your servant.

Kath.   O my lord,
The times and titles now are alter'd strangely
With me, since first you knew me. But I pray you,
What is your pleasure with me?

Cap.   Noble lady,
First mine own service to your grace, the next   115
The king's request that I would visit you,
Who grieves much for your weakness, and by me
Sends you his princely commendations,
And heartily entreats you take good comfort.

Kath. O my good lord, that comfort comes too late, 120
'Tis like a pardon after execution;
That gentle physic, given in time, had cur'd me;
But now I am past all comforts here but prayers.
How does his highness?

Cap.   Madam, in good health.

Kath. So may he ever do, and ever flourish,   125
When I shall dwell with worms, and my poor name
Banish'd the kingdom. Patience, is that letter
I caus'd you write yet sent away?

Pat.   No madam.

Kath. Sir, I most humbly pray you to deliver
This to my lord the king.

Cap.   ;   Most willing, madam.   130

Kath. In which I have commended to his goodness
The model of our chaste loves, his young daughter

---

110. Capuchius] *F;* Capucius *Rowe.*   113. But . . . you] *so Rowe 3; separate
line in F.*   123. I am] *F;* I'm *Pope.*   129. most] *F;* must *Rowe.*   130. will-
ing] *F;* willingly *F2.*   132-3. daughter / (The . . . her)] daughter, / The . . .
her, *F.*

---

bassador. For Holinshed's account of
Capuchius and Katherine's letter, see
Appendix II, p. 211.

112. *strangely*] greatly, extremely, cf.
Mac., IV. iii. 150, "strangely-visited
people / . . . The mere despair of sur-
gery, he cures".

118. *commendations*] compliments.

121. *execution*] "-tion" must be pronounced as two syllables to make a full
verse, as commonly, cf. Abbott 479.

130. *willing*] willingly, cf. *Tim.,* III.
vi. 32 and Abbott 1.

132. *model*] image, epitome; cf. *R 2,*
I. ii. 28, "thou seest thy wretched
brother die, / Who was the model of

(The dews of heaven fall thick in blessings on her)
Beseeching him to give her virtuous breeding
(She is young and of a noble modest nature,   135
I hope she will deserve well) and a little
To love her for her mother's sake, that lov'd him,
Heaven knows how dearly. My next poor petition
Is that his noble grace would have some pity
Upon my wretched women, that so long   140
Have follow'd both my fortunes faithfully,
Of which there is not one, I dare avow
(And now I should not lie) but will deserve
For virtue and true beauty of the soul,
For honesty and decent carriage,   145
A right good husband (let him be a noble),
And sure those men are happy that shall have 'em.
The last is for my men, they are the poorest
(But poverty could never draw 'em from me),
That they may have their wages duly paid 'em,   150
And something over to remember me by.
If heaven had pleas'd to have given me longer life
And able means, we had not parted thus.
These are the whole contents, and good my lord,
By that you love the dearest in this world,   155
As you wish Christian peace to souls departed,

134–6. breeding / (She . . . / . . . well)] breeding. / She . . . / . . . well; *F*.
135. She is] *F;* She's *Pope*.   138. Heaven . . . petition] *so Rowe 3; two lines in F*,
ending dearly. / . . . petition.   143. will] *F;* well *F3*.   146. husband (. . .
noble),] *so F;* husband, . . . noble: *Pope;* husband; . . . noble; *Capell*.   152. to
have] *F;* to've *Pope*.   153. able] *F;* abler *Hudson (W. S. Walker conj.)*.

thy father's life" (Clarendon Ed.), and
Haughton, *Englishmen for my Money*
(1598–1616; M.S.R., 1912, l. 2495,
"this is but Deaths modell in mans
shape". The daughter was Mary, who
succeeded to the throne in 1553.

133. *dews . . . blessings*] cf. II. iv. 78
above, and for a close parallel in idea,
Cym., v. v. 350–1.

134. *virtuous breeding*] a good up-
bringing.

141. *both*] i.e. her prosperity as
Queen and her present misery.

143. *now . . . lie*] It was generally be-

lieved that people spoke truth when
on the point of death, cf. II. i. 125
and n.

145. *honesty . . . carriage*] chastity (the
probable meaning, cf. *Ham.*, III. i. 108)
and propriety of conduct. For "carriage", cf. III. i. 161 above. "Decent"
occurs nowhere else in Shakespeare.

146. *noble*] The queen's gentlewomen would normally marry into
rank, being themselves ladies of rank;
Katherine hopes her fall will not spoil
their prospects (Nichol Smith).

153. *able*] sufficient, cf. *Meas.*, I. i. 9.

Stand these poor people's friend, and urge the king
To do me this last right.

Cap.   By heaven I will,
Or let me lose the fashion of a man.

Kath. I thank you honest lord. Remember me   160
In all humility unto his highness:
Say his long trouble now is passing
Out of this world. Tell him in death I bless'd him,
For so I will; mine eyes grow dim. Farewell
My lord. Griffith farewell. Nay Patience,   165
You must not leave me yet. I must to bed,
Call in more women. When I am dead, good wench,
Let me be us'd with honour; strew me over
With maiden flowers, that all the world may know
I was a chaste wife to my grave: embalm me,   170
Then lay me forth; although unqueen'd, yet like
A queen, and daughter to a king inter me.
I can no more.   *Exeunt leading Katherine.*

167. I am] *F;* I'm *Pope.*   171. forth; . . . unqueen'd,] *Pope;* forth (although unqueen'd) *F.*

159. *fashion*] nature, characteristics, cf. *Ham.*, iii. i. 183, "This something-settled matter in his heart, / . . . puts him thus / From fashion of himself" (Nichol Smith).

160. *honest*] a vague epithet here, meaning 'worthy', 'kind', etc., cf. *Cor.*, i. i. 63, "mine honest neighbours".

163. *bless'd him*] as did Buckingham, cf. ii. i. 90.

169. *maiden flowers*] i.e. befitting chastity; it was customary to strew flowers on the dead, as Ophelia has her "maiden strewments" (*Ham.*, v. i. 256); for lists of appropriate flowers, see *Wint.*, iv. iv. 113–29 and *Cym.*, iv. ii. 218–24.

171. *lay me forth*] i.e. lay me out for burial (Onions).

173. *can no more*] i.e. can say or do no more, cf. *Ham.*, v. ii. 331, *Ant.*, iv. xv. 59.

ACT V

SCENE I—[*A gallery in the court.*]

Enter GARDINER BISHOP OF WINCHESTER, *a Page with a torch*
before him, met by SIR THOMAS LOVELL.

Gar. It's one a'clock boy, is't not?
Boy.   It hath struck.
Gar. These should be hours for necessities,
Not for delights; times to repair our nature
With comforting repose, and not for us
To waste these times. Good hour of night Sir Thomas: 5
Whither so late?
Lov.   Came you from the king, my lord?
Gar. I did Sir Thomas, and left him at primero
With the Duke of Suffolk.
Lov.   I must to him too
Before he go to bed. I'll take my leave.

ACT V

Scene 1

Scene I] *Actus Quintus. Scena Prima. F.*   *A . . . court.*] *This Ed.; Gallery in the*
Palace. Capell.   1. a'clock] *F;* o'clock *Theobald* 2.

Scene I] For Foxe's account of the
attack on Cranmer and his interview
with the king, see Appendix II, pp. 211
ff. Foxe says that Gardiner provoked
the attack, but it is Shakespeare's invention to show him actually inciting
Lovell, and to associate this in time
with the birth of Elizabeth (1534), the
description of which is owed to Holinshed.

3. *repair*] restore, cf. *Cym.*, II. ii. 12,
"man's o'er-labour'd sense / Repairs
itself by rest".

5. *times*] The repetition of this word
seems odd, and possibly it was caught

up accidentally from l. 3; if so, the
correct reading here is lost.

7. *primero*] a card game which was
popular at court and played for high
stakes; the game was played with a
limited number of cards, the seven, six,
five, and ace having special values;
"each player had four cards dealt to
him, and then he had to show them.
He whose cards were of different suits
won the prime; if they were all of one
colour he won the flush, which was the
best hand . . ." (Sieveking, *Shake-*
speare's England, II. 473).

8. *must*] must go; see Abbott 405.

Gar. Not yet Sir Thomas Lovell: what's the matter?　　10
　　It seems you are in haste; and if there be
　　No great offence belongs to't, give your friend
　　Some touch of your late business: affairs that walk
　　(As they say spirits do) at midnight, have
　　In them a wilder nature than the business　　15
　　That seeks dispatch by day.

Lov.　　　　　　　　My lord, I love you,
　　And durst commend a secret to your ear
　　Much weightier than this work. The queen's in labour,
　　They say in great extremity, and fear'd
　　She'll with the labour end.

Gar.　　　　　　　　The fruit she goes with　　20
　　I pray for heartily, that it may find
　　Good time, and live: but for the stock, Sir Thomas,
　　I wish it grubb'd up now.

Lov.　　　　　　　　Methinks I could
　　Cry the amen, and yet my conscience says
　　She's a good creature, and sweet lady, does　　25
　　Deserve our better wishes.

Gar.　　　　　　　　But sir, sir,

---

11. and] *F;* an *Capell and Edd.*　　18. work] *F;* Word *Rowe 2.*　　26–7. sir, /
. . . Thomas,] *F;* Sir. / . . . Thomas, *F2;* Sir— / . . . Thomas,— *Rowe;* sir,— /
. . . Thomas: *Capell.*

---

11. *and if*] if indeed; cf. III. ii. 375
and Abbott 105.

12. *offence*] breach of propriety.

13. *touch*] hint, cf. Chamberlain,
I. 423, "I will give you a little touch or
taste of that" (i.e. of what "passed at
this wedding" of Princess Elizabeth).

late] recent, and perhaps, late at
night.

walk] the usual word applied to
ghosts, cf. *Ham.,* I. iv. 6 and Dekker,
Seven Deadly Sins (1606; Grosart, II.
45), "about the houre when Spirits
walke"; spirits were thought to be free
to range abroad from midnight to
cockcrow. There is also a quibble (cf.
"wilder", l. 15) on the idea of 'night-
walkers', a name for rogues, cf. S.
Rowlands, *Knave of Hearts* (1613), A2ᵛ,
"he . . . / Is kept from sleepe by knaves
a nights. / Night-walkers, such as

sleepe by day: / And in the night hunt
out for pray".

17. *commend*] entrust.

18. *work*] the matter I have been
engaged in.

19. *fear'd*] i.e. it is feared that; or,
possibly, 'feared for' (Pooler), cf.
1 H 4, IV. i. 24, "He was much fear'd
by his physicians".

22. *Good time*] i.e. to be born; a
happy issue, cf. *Wint.,* II. i. 20, "She is
spread of late / Into a goodly bulk:
good time encounter her".

22–3. *stock . . . grubb'd up*] the stem
dug up by the roots; the play on the
family tree and the natural tree is
common in Shakespeare, cf. *Wint.,* IV.
iv. 93. "Grubb'd up" occurs nowhere
else in Shakespeare.

24. *Cry the amen*] give assent, cf. *H 5,*
v. ii. 21.

Hear me Sir Thomas, y'are a gentleman
Of mine own way: I know you wise, religious,
And let me tell you, it will ne'er be well,
'Twill not Sir Thomas Lovell, take't of me,   30
Till Cranmer, Cromwell, her two hands, and she
Sleep in their graves.

Lov.   Now sir, you speak of two
The most remark'd i'th'kingdom: as for Cromwell,
Beside that of the jewel-house, is made master
O'th'rolls, and the king's secretary; further sir,   35
Stands in the gap and trade of moe preferments,
With which the time will load him. Th'archbishop
Is the king's hand and tongue, and who dare speak
One syllable against him?

Gar.   Yes, yes, Sir Thomas,
There are that dare, and I myself have ventur'd   40
To speak my mind of him: and indeed this day,
Sir (I may tell it you), I think I have
Incens'd the lords o'th'council that he is

27. y'are] *F;* you're *Theobald.*   34. is] *F;* he's *Theobald;* he is *Capell.*
36. moe] *F;* more *Rowe.*   37. time] *F4;* Lime *F.*   42. Sir (I . . . you), I
think] *F;* Sir, I . . . you, I think, *Johnson;* Sir (I . . . you I think) *Staunton.*
43. Incens'd] Incenst *F;* Insens'd *Rann.*

28. *way*] i.e. of thinking, religious
belief; a biblical usage, cf. Acts, xix. 9,
where "the way of God" is glossed,
"By this word Way, the Hebrewes
understand any kind of life, and here
it is taken for Christianitie" (Geneva,
1615); see also I. iii. 61 above.

33. *remark'd*] noted; the earliest use
known to *O.E.D.*, but cf. "remarkable", *Ant.*, IV. xv. 67.

34–6. *Beside . . . preferments*] These
preferments were spread over several
years from 1530 onwards, and are
noted in Holinshed, pp. 913, 929, 940;
later he became Earl of Essex and
Lord Chamberlain. His career is
dramatized in the play *Thomas Lord
Cromwell* (1602; reprinted 1613 with
"W.S." on the title-page).

36. *gap and trade*] opening and
beaten path; "trade" is the road or
resort of trade, cf. *2 H 4*, I. i. 174 and
R 2, III. iii. 156, "the king's highway, /
Some way of common trade" (cited
Steevens).

moe] more, cf. III. ii. 5.

37. *time*] the course of events
(Pooler), cf. *Ham.*, I. v. 188; this emendation in F4 of "Lime" (F) is generally
accepted.

43. *Incens'd*] Malone explained, "I
have roused the lords of the council by
suggesting to them that . . .", and
Steevens glossed, "prompted, set on";
Nares and Onions read "insens'd"
(after Rann), meaning 'informed', a
verb current in literary use from the
15th to the 17th centuries. Although
the construction with "that" is not
otherwise known, Malone's reading is
preferable: "incense(d)" occurs twice
elsewhere in the play, cf. III. ii. 61, and
there is no other use of 'insense' in
Shakespeare.

(For so I know he is, they know he is)
A most arch-heretic, a pestilence   45
That does infect the land: with which they, mov'd,
Have broken with the king, who hath so far
Given ear to our complaint, of his great grace
And princely care foreseeing those fell mischiefs
Our reasons laid before him, 'hath commanded   50
To-morrow morning to the council board
He be convented. He's a rank weed Sir Thomas,
And we must root him out. From your affairs
I hinder you too long: good night, Sir Thomas.
                              Exit Gardiner and Page.

Lov. Many good nights, my lord; I rest your servant.   55

                    Enter KING *and* SUFFOLK.

King. Charles, I will play no more to-night,
      My mind's not on't, you are too hard for me.
Suf. Sir, I did never win of you before.
King. But little, Charles,
      Nor shall not when my fancy's on my play.   60
      Now Lovell, from the queen what is the news?

48-9. complaint, . . . grace / . . . care] *Camb. 1865;* Complaint, . . . Grace. /
. . . Care, *F;* complaint . . . Grace / . . . care, *Pope;* complaint, (. . . grace /
. . . care; *Var. 1773 (after Capell).*   50. 'hath] *Collier 2;* hath *F;* he hath *Pope.*
54. S.D. *Exit] F; Exeunt Johnson; after* servant, *l. 55, Capell.*   55. servant.] *F;*
servant. [S.D.] *Exit Lovell. Theobald.*   60. fancy's] *F4;* Fancies *F.*   play.]
play. [S.D.] *Re-enter* Lovel. *Theobald.*

44. *For*] Deighton conjectures "For,
. . .", interpreting "so" as meaning 'if';
i.e., 'if I know, they will take what I
say as true, and they will then know'.

45. *most*] very great, cf. *2 H 4,* IV. i.
71 (Abbott 17).

46. *mov'd*] made angry, cf. *Wint.,*
I. ii. 150.

47. *broken with*] disclosed their
opinions to; originally, to break one's
heart or mind with someone; cf. *Gent.,*
III. i. 59, "I am to break with thee of
some affairs / That touch me near"
(Steevens).

49. *fell*] cruel, terrible.

50. *'hath*] probably, as Malone conjectured, an abbreviation of "he

hath", comparable to "'has", I. iii. 59.
The omission of 'that', required after
"so far", l. 47, is not unusual, cf.
Abbott 281-2.

52. *convented*] summoned; especially
for trial or examination, cf. *Meas.,* v. i.
157, *Cor.,* II. ii. 58.

rank weed] cf. *Ham.,* III. iv. 151; *Oth.,*
IV. ii. 67.

55. *rest*] remain, cf. *Mac.,* I. vi. 20.
This line is spoken as Gardiner goes
off, which might take some time on the
wide stage of the Globe, and there is no
point in putting it before the S.D., as
did Capell.

57. *too hard*] more than I can manage, cf. *Oth.,* I. iii. 364.

Lov. I could not personally deliver to her
        What you commanded me, but by her woman
        I sent your message, who return'd her thanks
        In the great'st humbleness, and desir'd your highness 65
        Most heartily to pray for her.
King.   What say'st thou? Ha?
        To pray for her? what, is she crying out?
Lov. So said her woman, and that her suff'rance made
        Almost each pang a death.
King.   Alas good lady.
Suf. God safely quit her of her burthen, and   70
        With gentle travail, to the gladding of
        Your highness with an heir.
King.   'Tis midnight Charles;
        Prithee to bed, and in thy prayers remember
        Th'estate of my poor queen. Leave me alone,
        For I must think of that which company   75
        Would not be friendly to.
Suf.   I wish your highness
        A quiet night, and my good mistress will
        Remember in my prayers.
King.   Charles, good night.
                                        Exit Suffolk.

                Enter SIR ANTHONY DENNY.

        Well sir, what follows?
Den. Sir, I have brought my lord the archbishop,   80
        As you commanded me.
King.   Ha? Canterbury?
Den. Ay my good lord.

---

78. S.D. *Enter . . . Denny*] so Blair; *after* follows? *in* F.

62. *deliver*] make known, cf. I. ii. 143
above.
68. *suff'rance*] suffering, cf. II. iii. 15
above (Pooler).
70. *quit*] release.
71. *gladding*] making happy, cf. II. iv.
194 above.
72. *midnight*] a more general term
than it is now, which could refer to
one a.m. (cf. l. 1, "It's one a'clock

. . .") ; E. Honigmann compares *John a
Kent* (1590; M.S.R. 1923, l. 298),
"The houre is one at midnight".
74. *estate*] condition, cf. *Lr.*, v. iii.
209, "having seen me in my worst
estate" (Pooler).
78. S.D. Denny] Foxe says that
Denny was the messenger sent by the
king to fetch Cranmer; see Appendix
II, p. 212.

King.   'Tis true: where is he, Denny?
Den. He attends your highness' pleasure.
King.   Bring him to us.
                              [*Exit Denny.*]
Lov. [*Aside.*] This is about that which the bishop spake;
   I am happily come hither.   85

                Enter CRANMER *and* DENNY.

King. Avoid the gallery. *Lovell seems to stay.* Ha? I have said.
      Be gone.
   What?   *Exeunt Lovell and Denny.*
Cran. [*Aside.*] I am fearful: wherefore frowns he thus?
   'Tis his aspect of terror. All's not well.
King. How now my lord? You do desire to know
   Wherefore I sent for you.
Cran.   [*Kneeling.*] It is my duty   90
   T'attend your highness' pleasure.
King.   Pray you arise,
   My good and gracious Lord of Canterbury:
   Come, you and I must walk a turn together;
   I have news to tell you. Come, come give me your hand.
   Ah my good lord, I grieve at what I speak,   95
   And am right sorry to repeat what follows.
   I have, and most unwillingly, of late
   Heard many grievous, I do say my lord,

---

83. S.D. *Exit Denny*] *Rowe; not in F.*   84. S.D. *Aside*] *Rowe; not in F.*   85. S.D.
Enter . . . Denny] *so F; Re-enter Cranmer with Denny. Capell and Edd.*   86. Avoid
. . . gone] *so Capell; two lines in F, ending* Gallery. / . . . gone.   87. What?]
separate line in F; omitted F2.   S.D. *Aside*] *Dyce (after Capell); not in F.*   89–
90. How . . . duty] *so Rowe 3; four lines in F, ending* Lord? / . . . wherefore /
. . . you. / . . . dutie.   90, 108. S.D. *Kneeling*] *Johnson; not in F.*   94. I . . .
hand] *so Pope (reading* I've . . . you. Come, give . . . hand); *two lines in F, ending*
you. / . . . hand.

   85. *happily*] luckily, cf. IV. ii. 10.
   86. *Avoid*] leave, quit, cf. *Cor.*, IV. v.
25, "Pray you, avoid the house"
(Clarendon Ed.).
   gallery] Foxe, p. 1694, says that
Cranmer and the king met in "the
Galerie where the king walked", and
the word has been taken into the text
here. There is no need to suppose that
Lovell, who spoke to the king at l. 62,

is on the upper stage at this point.
   87. *fearful*] afraid.
   88. *aspect*] expression, cf. III. ii.
369.
   91. *arise*] the idea of Cranmer's
kneeling is borrowed from Foxe, who
says, "When the king had sayde his
minde, the Archbishop kneeled
downe . . .".
   98. *grievous*] serious.

Grievous complaints of you; which being consider'd,
Have mov'd us and our council, that you shall   100
This morning come before us, where I know
You cannot with such freedom purge yourself,
But that till further trial in those charges
Which will require your answer, you must take
Your patience to you, and be well contented   105
To make your house our Tower: you, a brother of us
It fits we thus proceed, or else no witness
Would come against you.

Cran. [*Kneeling.*]   I humbly thank your highness,
And am right glad to catch this good occasion
Most throughly to be winnow'd, where my chaff   110
And corn shall fly asunder. For I know
There's none stands under more calumnious tongues
Than I myself, poor man.

King.   Stand up, good Canterbury,
Thy truth and thy integrity is rooted
In us thy friend. Give me thy hand, stand up;   115
Prithee let's walk. Now by my holidame,
What manner of man are you? My lord, I look'd

---

106. you, a brother of us] *so F;* you a Brother of us, *F2;* you, a Brother of us, *F4;*
to a brother of us *Collier 3.*   116. holidame] *Camb. 1865;* Holydame *F;*
halidom *Hudson.*

---

100. *mov'd*] prompted, made us decide.

102. *purge*] clear of guilt, cf. v. ii. 186, *1 H 4*, III. ii. 20; a proper use of the word.

104–5. *take . . . you*] the same phrase appears in *Wint.*, III. ii. 232 (Clarendon Ed.).

106–7. *you . . . proceed*] The punctuation of F, kept here, suggests that the preposition 'against' has been omitted after the verb "proceed", in accordance with a fairly common practice in Shakespeare, cf. Abbott, 198–202. Most editors add a comma after "us", and interpret 'you, (being) a brother (i.e. a fellow-councillor) with us, it is necessary that we take action in this way': for the occasional omission of 'being', see Abbott 381. For "fits", cf.

Cym., III. v. 22. The line is difficult metrically, but no odder perhaps than several other long lines in the play, cf. below, l. 113, and II. iv. 86.

110. *throughly*] thoroughly, cf. *Wint.*, II. i. 99 (Pooler).

112. *stands under*] is subject to, cf. III. ii. 3 above.

114. *is*] where two singular nouns are the subject, the verb in Shakespeare is frequently singular, cf. *Cym.*, v. ii. 2 (Abbott 336).

116. *holidame*] originally 'haligdom', the state of being holy; the suffix 'dame' was due, it seems, to "popular etymology, the word being taken to denote 'Our Lady'" (*O.E.D.*). "Halidom" occurs in *Gent.*, IV. ii. 136.

117. *look'd*] expected, cf. *Wint.*, IV. iv. 369, "The gifts she looks from me".

You would have given me your petition, that
I should have ta'en some pains to bring together
Yourself and your accusers, and to have heard you   120
Without indurance further.

Cran.   Most dread liege,
The good I stand on is my truth and honesty:
If they shall fail, I with mine enemies
Will triumph o'er my person, which I weigh not,
Being of those virtues vacant. I fear nothing   125
What can be said against me.

King.   Know you not
How your state stands i'th'world, with the whole world?
Your enemies are many, and not small; their practices
Must bear the same proportion, and not ever
The justice and the truth o'th'question carries   130
The due o'th'verdict with it: at what ease
Might corrupt minds procure knaves as corrupt
To swear against you? such things have been done.
You are potently oppos'd, and with a malice

---

120. to have] *F;* t' have *Dyce 2.*   121. indurance further] *F;* indurance, further *Capell.*   122. good] *F;* ground *Rann (Johnson conj.).*   123. fail] *F;* fall *Rowe 2.*   131. due] dew *F.*   134. You are] *F;* you're *Pope.*

---

121. *indurance further*] usually taken as 'imprisonment in addition'; Foxe, pp. 1693–4, uses the word twice in connection with imprisonment, e.g. "if . . . they do commit you to the Tower, require of them . . . that you may have your accusers brought before them without any further indurance", but in both cases 'hardship' (the power of enduring, or what has been endured), would make as good sense. Since Shakespeare employed the word in this way in *Ado*. II. i. 246 and *Per.*, v. i. 137, "the thousandth part / Of my endurance", he may have meant 'further hardship' here; this would avoid the necessity of interpreting 'further' in the special sense of 'in addition'.

122. *good*] virtue, cf. IV. ii. 60 above and *Meas.*, v. i. 427; the Clarendon Ed. interprets as 'good defence'.

124. *weigh not*] do not value, cf. *Wint.*, III. ii. 44, "For life, I prize it /

As I weigh grief, which I would spare".

125. *nothing*] not at all, cf. *Cym.*, IV. iii. 14, "I nothing know where she remains".

128. *not small*] i.e. of great power or rank, cf. "little", IV. ii. 66 above.

128–9. *practices . . . proportion*] their plots (cf. I. ii. 127) must be correspondingly great and many (Pooler).

129–31. *not . . . with it*] the justice of a cause does not always ensure a just verdict. The "due" is the fit reward, cf. *Per.*, v. iii. Gower 86, "Of monstrous lust the due and just reward".

131. *at what ease*] how easily; perhaps an extension of the phrase 'at ease', meaning 'without anxiety', cf. *Cæs.*, I. ii. 208, "at heart's ease" (so Pooler).

132. *Might . . . corrupt*] cf. the proverb, 'Two false knaves need no broker', Tilley, K 147.

134. *potently*] powerfully, cf. *Ham.*,

Of as great size. Ween you of better luck,   135
I mean in perjur'd witness, than your master,
Whose minister you are, whiles here he liv'd
Upon this naughty earth? Go to, go to,
You take a precipice for no leap of danger,
And woo your own destruction.

Cran.   God and your majesty
Protect mine innocence, or I fall into   141
The trap is laid for me.

King.   Be of good cheer,
They shall no more prevail than we give way to:
Keep comfort to you, and this morning see
You do appear before them. If they shall chance   145
In charging you with matters to commit you,
The best persuasions to the contrary
Fail not to use, and with what vehemency
Th'occasion shall instruct you. If entreaties
Will render you no remedy, this ring   150
Deliver them, and your appeal to us
There make before them. Look, the good man weeps:

137. whiles] *F;* while *Pope.*   139. precipice] *F2;* Precepit *F.*   152. good man]
F3; goodman *F.*

ii. ii. 204, "I most powerfully and
potently believe".

135. *Ween you of*] do you look for;
elsewhere in Shakespeare only in
1 H 6, ii. v. 88; Foxe has, "Thinke you
to have …".

136. *witness*] evidence (Clarendon
Ed.), cf. *Wint.,* iv. iv. 288, "witnesses
more than my pack will hold".

137. *whiles*] adverbial genitive,
common in Shakespeare, cf. *Ant.,* ii. i.
4 (Abbott, 137).

138. *naughty*] wicked, cf. *Mer. V.,* v.
i. 91, "a good deed in a naughty
world". (Pooler).

139. *precipice*] "Precepit" (F) is recorded in *O.E.D.* as the only instance
of this form of 'precipice', and may be
what Shakespeare wrote: the word
seems to have been a recent introduction into English, first recorded in

1598, and the form, from French 'pre-
cipite', "A dangerous cliffe …", (Cotgrave's *Dictionary,* 1611), had perhaps
not become fixed. But one of the commonest confusions in print was between *t* and *c,* which were alike in secretary hand, cf. B. and F., *Bonduca*
(M.S.R. 1951), where the MS (*c.*
1625) has, l. 135, "my *fate.* he cryed
out nobly", and the Folio (1647), "my
face, he cri'd out nobly".

142. *trap is*] i.e. trap which is.

143. *give way to*] give them scope, cf.
iii. ii. 16.

144. *Keep … you*] cf. l. 105 above,
"take / Your patience to you".

146. *commit*] i.e. to the Tower, cf.
i. ii. 193.

148. *vehemency*] a common early
form of 'vehemence'; cf. "arrogancy",
ii. iv. 108.

He's honest on mine honour. God's blest mother,
I swear he is true-hearted, and a soul
None better in my kingdom. Get you gone,   155
And do as I have bid you. *Exit Cranmer*. He has strangled
His language in his tears.

Enter Old Lady [*;* LOVELL *following*].

Gent. Within.   Come back: what mean you?
Old L. I'll not come back, the tidings that I bring
Will make my boldness manners. Now good angels
Fly o'er thy royal head, and shade thy person   160
Under their blessed wings.

King.   Now by thy looks
I guess thy message. Is the queen deliver'd?
Say ay, and of a boy.

Old L.   Ay, ay my liege,
And of a lovely boy: the God of heaven
Both now and ever bless her: 'tis a girl   165
Promises boys hereafter. Sir, your queen
Desires your visitation, and to be
Acquainted with this stranger; 'tis as like you
As cherry is to cherry.

King.   Lovell!
Lov.   Sir.
King. Give her an hundred marks. I'll to the queen.   170

                                        Exit King.

156–7. He . . . tears] *so Hanmer (reading* All *for* His)*; one line in* F.   157. S.D.
Lovell following] Capell; *not in* F.   158 ff. S.H. Old L.] Lady. F.   170. Give
. . . queen] *so Pope; two lines in* F, *ending* Markes. / . . . Queene.

153. *God's . . . mother*] this oath, like
the similar one at v. ii. 32, is not in
Foxe.

156–7. *He . . . tears*] Foxe has merely,
"had much adoe to forbeare teares".

157. S.D. Old Lady] As Steevens
noted, she is presumably the character
who appeared in II. iii. It is the
dramatist's device to link the birth of
Elizabeth (1533), reported in Holinshed but not in Foxe, with the trial of
Cranmer, for which Foxe gives no
date.

157. S.D. Lovell following] F has no
entry for Lovell; possibly he should
rush on in answer to the king's summons, l. 169, where an entry for him
was placed in Var. 1773.

165. *her*] Anne, Elizabeth, or both;
Johnson noted the ambiguity.

167. *visitation*] you to visit her; cf.
I. i. 179 and n.

170. *marks*] originally a mark was
the measure of weight of 8 oz., hence
the sum of money equivalent to this
amount of silver; the rate was stan-

Old L. An hundred marks? By this light, I'll ha' more.
   An ordinary groom is for such payment.
   I will have more, or scold it out of him.
   Said I for this the girl was like to him?
   I'll have more, or else unsay't; and now, while 'tis hot,
   I'll put it to the issue.   [*Exeunt.*]   176

SCENE II—[*Anteroom and council-chamber.*]

Enter CRANMER, ARCHBISHOP OF CANTERBURY; [*pursuivants,
   pages &c. are in attendance at the door.*]

Cran. I hope I am not too late, and yet the gentleman

174–6. him?...put] him? Ile / Haue...now, while 'tis hot, / Ile put *F;* him?./
I will have ... now, / While it is hot, I'll put *Var. 1778 and Edd.*   176. S.D.
Exeunt] Capell; *Exit Ladie. F.*

Scene II

Scene II] *Scena Secunda. F.*   *Anteroom . . . council-chamber.*] *This Ed.; Before the*
Council-Chamber. *Theobald; The council-Chamber. Capell.*   *pursuivants . . . door*]
This Ed., after Var. 1778.   1. I am] *F; I'm Pope.*

dardized early at 20 pennies to the
ounce, so the 'mark' came to represent
13s. 4d., but there was no coin of this
value.

   171. *By this light*] a common oath,
originally 'by God's light' (the light of
day), or 'by this good light', cf. *Tp.,*
11.ii. 147.

   ha' more] A bearer of good news
would expect a handsome reward; so
Sir Robert Carey ignored the pro-
hibition of the Council to ride to Scot-
land and inform James in 1603 that
Elizabeth had died, and was made a
gentleman of the king's bedchamber.

   172. *groom*] as distinct from her rank
of lady-in-waiting; she is of gentle
birth.

   174. *like to him*] Pooler cites Rowley, *When You See Me* (1605; M.S.R.
1952), ll. 288–90, "shee that brings the
first tydings . . . let her be sure to say
the Childs like the father, or els shee
shall have nothing".

175–6.] It is hardly in keeping with
the Old Lady's manner of speech to
expand the contractions in these lines,
as most editors do; perhaps the
irregularity indicates a pause after
"unsay't".

   176. *put . . . issue*] bring it to the
point of decision.

Scene II

Scene II] This scene is developed
and considerably expanded, from
Foxe's account of Cranmer's trial, for
which see Appendix II, pp. 212 ff. Foxe
mentions Butts, but elsewhere speaks
of the lords in general, except for the
Earl of Bedford, whose speech, as he
gives it, is shared in the play between
Norfolk, the Chamberlain, and Cromwell (ll. 140–8). The development of
Gardiner and Cromwell is the dramatist's own, though Foxe elsewhere
notes their enmity.

   S.D. pursuivants] properly, mes-

That was sent to me from the council, pray'd me
To make great haste. All fast? What means this? Ho!
Who waits there? Sure you know me?

Enter Keeper.

Keep.   Yes my lord,
But yet I cannot help you.
Cran.   Why?
Keep.   Your grace   5
Must wait till you be call'd for.

Enter Doctor Butts.

Cran.   So.
Butts. [*Aside.*] This is a piece of malice: I am glad
I came this way so happily. The king
Shall understand it presently.   *Exit Butts.*
Cran. [*Aside.*]   'Tis Butts,
The king's physician; as he pass'd along   10
How earnestly he cast his eyes upon me:
Pray heaven he sound not my disgrace: for certain
This is of purpose laid by some that hate me
(God turn their hearts, I never sought their malice)
To quench mine honour; they would shame to
         make me   15
Wait else at door, a fellow-councillor,
'Mong boys, grooms and lackeys. But their pleasures
Must be fulfill'd, and I attend with patience.

5–6. But . . . So.] *This Ed.; four lines in F, ending* you. / Why? / . . . for. / . . . So.
6. S.D. *Enter . . . Butts] so F; after* Why?, *l. 5, Capell.*   7. S.D. *Aside] Dyce; not
in F.*   piece] *F2;* Peere *F.*   9. S.D. *Aside] Johnson; not in F.*   12. sound] *F;*
found *Rowe.*   17. 'Mong . . . pleasures] *so Rowe 3; two lines in F, ending*
Lackeyes. / . . . pleasures.

sengers of state, but often weakened to
mean simply 'servants'.

3. *fast*] shut; cf. *Mer. V.*, II. vi. 49,
"make fast the doors".

4. *Sure*] surely, cf. I. iii. 15 (Abbott
1).

8. *happily*] luckily, or fitly; cf. v. i.
85.

9. *presently*] at once.
12. *sound*] make known, cf. *Per.*, I. iv.

13, "Our tongues and sorrows do
sound deep / Our woes into the air";
Schmidt interprets as 'fathom', but the
disgrace is obvious.

13. *laid*] arranged, *sc.* as a trap, cf.
v. i. 142.

14. *turn . . . hearts*] change their feelings.

17–18. *pleasures . . . fulfill'd*] their
wishes must be carried out.

Enter the KING *and* BUTTS *at a window above.*

Butts. I'll show your grace the strangest sight—
King.   What's that, Butts?
Butts. I think your highness saw this many a day.   20
King. Body a' me; where is it?
Butts.   There my lord:
The high promotion of his grace of Canterbury,
Who holds his state at door 'mongst pursuivants,
Pages and footboys.
King.   Ha? 'tis he indeed.
Is this the honour they do one another?   25
'Tis well there's one above 'em yet; I had thought
They had parted so much honesty among 'em,
At least good manners, as not thus to suffer
A man of his place, and so near our favour
To dance attendance on their lordships' pleasures,   30
And at the door too, like a post with packets:
By holy Mary, Butts, there's knavery;
Let 'em alone, and draw the curtain close:
We shall hear more anon.

19. sight—] *Rowe;* sight. *F.*   21. Body a' me] *F;* Body o' me *Pope.*   23. pursuivants] Pursevants *F.*   27. They had] *F;* They'd *Pope.*   34.] *Scene III.* Camb. *1865.*

18. S.D. at . . . above] This is the only certain indication of the use of the upper stage in this play, and as commonly, it is in connection with action on the stage below; see Chambers, *E.S.*, III. 116, 119.

21. *Body a' me*] an exclamation used by Henry in Rowley's *When You See Me* (1605; M.S.R., 1952), ll. 2601, 2678, etc. (Clarendon Ed.).

23. *holds his state*] maintains his dignity, cf. I. iii. 10.

25. *honour . . . do*] respect they pay.

26. *one above 'em*] like "master", v. i. 136, this reference is ambiguous, and might be to God or to Henry. The effect is to create a partial identification of the two.

27. *parted . . . honesty*] shared so much decency; cf. *Wint.*, I. ii. 18.

29. *place*] rank, office.

near] cf. II. ii. 134.

31. *post . . . packets*] courier, stationed at stages along the roads, to carry the king's "packet" (cf. III. ii. 76) to the next stage; cf. Dekker, *News from Hell* (1606; Grosart, II. 104), "The Post . . . having put up his packet, blows his horne, and gallopes all the way".

32. *By . . . Mary*] cf. v. i. 153 and n.

33. *curtain*] The impression is thus left that the king overhears all that goes on before his re-entry at l. 147. There are few indications of the use of curtains on the upper stage at the first Globe theatre (see J. C. Adams, *The Globe Playhouse*, 1943, pp. 139–44, for evidence relating to various theatres); the second Globe, rebuilt after the fire in 1613, had upper-stage curtains as shown by S.D. "They drew the curtaines", Massinger, *Picture* (1630) L1ᵛ.

*A council-table brought in with chairs and stools, and placed under the
    state. Enter* LORD CHANCELLOR, *places himself at the upper
    end of the table, on the left hand; a seat being left void above him,
    as for Canterbury's seat.* DUKE OF SUFFOLK, DUKE OF NOR-
    FOLK, SURREY, LORD CHAMBERLAIN, GARDINER, *seat
    themselves in order on each side.* CROMWELL *at lower end, as
    secretary.*

Chan. Speak to the business, master secretary;   35
        Why are we met in council?
Crom.   Please your honours,
        The chief cause concerns his grace of Canterbury.
Gar. Has he had knowledge of it?
Crom.   Yes.
Nor.   Who waits there?
Keep. Without, my noble lords?
Gar.   Yes.
Keep.   My lord archbishop;
        And has done half an hour to know your pleasures.   40
Chan. Let him come in.
Keep.   Your grace may enter now.

Cranmer approaches the council-table.

34. S.D. *A council-table . . . state*] *so* F; *omitted Var. 1773 and Edd.   secretary.*]
F; *secretary. Keeper at the door. Camb. 1865.*   35. master] *Var. 1778;* M. F.

34. S.D.] Most editors alter the S.D.
as given in F and introduce a new
scene here, after adding an *Exeunt* for
the king, Butts, Cranmer, and attendants. The directions in F indicate that
Cranmer is on stage all the time, presumably kept waiting outside one of
the doors to the stage (cf. l. 4); the furniture for the council's session may
have been brought on through another. Thus when he is called before
the council, all he has to do is to
approach the table (l. 41). An
audience would readily accept the
presentation of Cranmer as on stage,
but *outside* the council-chamber.
    S.D. state] does the 'state' remain on
stage throughout the play?
    upper end] the end furthest re-
moved from the door, and occupied

by the officials of highest rank; cf.
Wint., IV. iv. 59.
    35–147.] As Pooler noted, the cita-
tion of Cranmer is here set between the
birth (7 September) and baptism
(11 September 1533) of Elizabeth,
though it probably took place as late
as 1544, long after Cromwell's death.
At III. ii. 393 Wolsey was told that
Sir Thomas More had been appointed Chancellor, though this official is left unidentified here, perhaps
to avoid the intrusion of a person-
ality.
    35. *Speak to*] discuss; cf. II. iv. 164
and n.
    38. *had knowledge*] been informed,
cf. *Wint.,* II. ii. 2, "Let him have knowledge who I am" (Pooler).
    39. *Without*] outside (cf. 'within').

Chan. My good lord archbishop, I'm very sorry
  To sit here at this present and behold
  That chair stand empty: but we all are men,
  In our own natures frail, and capable   45
  Of our flesh; few are angels; out of which frailty
  And want of wisdom, you that best should teach us
  Have misdemean'd yourself, and not a little;
  Toward the king first, then his laws, in filling
  The whole realm by your teaching and your
        chaplains'   50
  (For so we are inform'd) with new opinions
  Divers and dangerous; which are heresies,
  And not reform'd, may prove pernicious.
Gar. Which reformation must be sudden too,
  My noble lords; for those that tame wild horses   55
  Pace 'em not in their hands to make 'em gentle,
  But stop their mouths with stubborn bits and spur 'em,

45–6. frail, . . . angels] *so Capell;* fraile, and capable / Of our flesh, . . . Angels; *F;* frail and capable / Of frailty *Pope;* frail, incapable; / Of our flesh, . . . angels; *Malone;* frail, and culpable / Of our flesh; . . . angels *Collier 2.*   50. chaplains'] *Capell;* Chaplaines *F.*

43. *at . . . present*] sc. time (= modern 'at present'); cf. *Wint.,* i. ii. 192, "even at this present, / Now while I speak this" (Clarendon Ed.).

44–9. *but we . . . first*] This passage is borrowed from a speech of Stokesley, Bishop of London, to his clergy in 1530–1, as reported by Halle, ii. 200, "My frendes all, you knowe well that wee bee men frayle of condicion and no Angels, and by frayltie and lacke of wysedome we have misdemeaned our selfe toward the kyng our Soveraygne Lord and his lawes, so that all wee of the Cleargy were in the Premunire . . ." The speech is given in Foxe in identical words, see Appendix ii, p. 211, but over 700 pages from the main body of material used in this play. It does not appear in Holinshed.

45–6. *capable . . . flesh*] liable to be affected by bodily desires; the 'flesh', as often, is opposed to the 'spirit'. For "capable, cf. *All's W.,* i. i. 106, 223, "so thou wilt be capable of a courtier's

counsel", and *2 H 4,* i. i. 172 (so Clarendon Ed.). Malone emended to "incapable" because he wanted a correspondence with "want of wisdom" (l. 47) similar to that between "frail" and "frailty"; but the correspondence is there already, for it is lack of wisdom to give way to the flesh, even though, since the fall of man, all do so; cf. iii. ii. 378 and n.

50. *chaplains'*] F does not have apostrophes with possessive plurals, a use which did not become common until the 18th century, cf. i. iv. 93: Capell's reading is borne out by Foxe, who says, "you and your chaplains . . . have taught and preached".

52. *Divers*] possibly in the old sense of 'differing from the right', hence 'perverse', 'evil' (*O.E.D.* a. 2).

53. *pernicious*] disastrous; cf. ii. i. 50 and n.

56. *Pace*] exercise them in walking.

57. *stubborn*] hard, rigid, cf. *Troil.,* iii. i. 163, "his stubborn buckles".

Till they obey the manage. If we suffer
Out of our easiness and childish pity
To one man's honour, this contagious sickness,   60
Farewell all physic: and what follows then?
Commotions, uproars, with a general taint
Of the whole state, as of late days our neighbours,
The upper Germany, can dearly witness,
Yet freshly pitied in our memories.   65

Cran. My good lords; hitherto, in all the progress
Both of my life and office, I have labour'd,
And with no little study, that my teaching
And the strong course of my authority,
Might go one way, and safely; and the end   70
Was ever to do well: nor is there living
(I speak it with a single heart, my lords)
A man that more detests, more stirs against,
Both in his private conscience and his place,
Defacers of a public peace than I do: 75
Pray heaven the king may never find a heart
With less allegiance in it. Men that make
Envy and crooked malice nourishment,
Dare bite the best. I do beseech your lordships
That in this case, of justice, my accusers,   80

---

73. stirs] *F;* strives *Collier 2.*   75. of a] *F;* of the *Rowe.*   80. case, of] *This Ed.;* case of *F.*

58. *manage*] handling; 'manage' was the training, or the art of training horses, cf. *AYL.*, I. i. 13, "His horses . . . are taught their manage, and to that end riders dearly hired".

59. *easiness*] indulgence (Onions); or perhaps 'indifference', as at *Ham.*, V. i. 76.

62. *taint*] corruption.

63–5. *late . . . memories*] Foxe says, p. 1694, "thereby might spring horrible commotions and uprores, like as in some partes of Germanie it did not long agoe"; "upper" means 'inland', and the reference in Foxe may be to the peasants' revolt in Saxony in 1521–2.

68. *study*] effort, cf. III. i. 174.

72. *single*] free from guile (Malone);

cf. Haughton, *Englishmen for my Money* (1598–1616; M.S.R., 1912), l. 2487, "my love / Comes from a single heart unfaynedly". As Reed noted, the phrase "singleness of heart" is found in the Bible, cf. Acts ii. 46, Col. iii. 22.

73. *stirs against*] is active against; cf. *R 2*, I. ii. 3 (Clarendon Ed.).

74. *place*] office.

75. *Defacers*] destroyers, cf. *R 3*, IV. iv. 51.

77–9. *Men . . . best*] the idea is proverbial, cf. Tilley, D 432, F 107, 'He finds fault with others and does worse himself', etc.

80. *in . . . accusers*] F punctuates "in . . . justice, my accusers,"; "case" means 'judicial proceedings', and the phrase "case of justice" is pointless:

Be what they will, may stand forth face to face,
And freely urge against me.
Suf.   Nay, my lord,
That cannot be; you are a councillor,
And by that virtue no man dare accuse you.
Gar. My lord, because we have business of more moment,   85
We will be short with you. 'Tis his highness' pleasure
And our consent, for better trial of you,
From hence you be committed to the Tower,
Where being but a private man again,
You shall know many dare accuse you boldly,   90
More than (I fear) you are provided for.
Cran. Ah my good lord of Winchester: I thank you,
You are always my good friend; if your will pass,
I shall both find your lordship judge and juror,
You are so merciful. I see your end,   95
'Tis my undoing. Love and meekness, lord,
Become a churchman better than ambition:
Win straying souls with modesty again,
Cast none away: that I shall clear myself,
Lay all the weight ye can upon my patience,   100
I make as little doubt as you do conscience

---

85. we have] *F;* we've *Pope.*   90. know many] *F;* know, many *Theobald.*
92. Winchester: . . . you,] *F;* Winchester, . . . you, *Rowe;* Winchester, . . . you;
Collier.   93. You are] *F;* You're *Pope.*

the present punctuation gives "of
justice" = 'in fairness', 'according to
moral right', a common meaning.
    81. *Be . . . will*] whoever they are, cf.
II. i. 65 above.
    82. *urge*] press accusations, cf. *Cor.,*
IV. vii. 19, "he knows not / What I can
urge against him".
    84. *by . . . virtue*] by virtue of that, i.e.
your being a privy councillor (Pooler).
    85. *moment*] importance.
    89. *private*] i.e. having no public
office, cf. *Ant.,* III. xii. 15.
    93. *pass*] is allowed, cf. I. ii. 70 above.
    94. *judge and juror*] i.e. ready both to
try (as a judge) and to condemn (as a
juror). For the transposition of "both",
see Abbott 420–1.

96. *undoing*] ruin, cf. III. ii. 329.
    98. *modesty*] moderation, as "mod-
est", l. 103, means 'moderate'
(Pooler); cf. *Lr.,* II. iv. 25, "with all
modest haste", and IV. i. 82 above.
    100. *patience*] see Introduction, pp.
lvii ff., and III. ii. 388 and n. This is
the third reference to Cranmer's
"patience", cf. v. i. 105 and l. 18
above.
    101. *I . . . conscience*] I have as little
doubt as you have scruples. For "make
doubt", cf. *Cor.,* v. iv. 49, and for
"make conscience", cf. Nixon, *Strange
Foot-Post* (1613), D1r, "as though he
which maketh no scruple to breake the
seventh Commandement, will make
any conscience to keepe the third".

In doing daily wrongs. I could say more,
But reverence to your calling makes me modest.

Gar. My lord, my lord, you are a sectary,
That's the plain truth; your painted gloss discovers   105
To men that understand you, words and weakness.

Crom. My lord of Winchester, y'are a little,
By your good favour, too sharp; men so noble,
However faulty, yet should find respect
For what they have been: 'tis a cruelty   110
To load a falling man.

Gar.   Good master secretary,
I cry your honour mercy; you may worst
Of all this table say so.

Crom.   Why my lord?

Gar. Do not I know you for a favourer
Of this new sect? ye are not sound.

Crom.   Not sound?   115

Gar. Not sound I say.

Crom.   Would you were half so honest;
Men's prayers then would seek you, not their fears.

Gar. I shall remember this bold language.

Crom.   Do.
Remember your bold life too.

---

107. y'are] *F;* you are *Pope.*   111. master] *Var. 1778;* M. *F.*

104. *sectary*] adherent of a sect, cf.
l. 115; so in *Lr.*, I. ii. 164, a "sectary
astronomical" is a follower of astro-
logy (Pooler).

105. *painted gloss*] Perhaps two
senses are to be thought of, (*a*) false
show, cf. *Tim.*, I. ii. 16, "To set a gloss
on faint deeds"; (*b*) specious language,
cf. *LLL.*, IV. iii. 370, "Now to plain-
dealing; lay these glozes by". There
are two roots, the Greek giving 'gloss'
meaning 'comment', the German,
'gloss' meaning 'brightness', but the
words have always been liable to confusion with each other and with 'gloze',
the older form of *gloss* I. For "painted"
cf. "painted word" (i.e. deceit), in
Ham., III. i. 53.

discovers] reveals.

106. *words*] i.e. as opposed to
'matter' or meaning, cf. IV. ii. 38-9
and n.

110–11. *cruelty . . . man*] Steevens
compared III. ii. 333; the image of a
weight or burden and the idea of falling
run through the play, and Cranmer's
trial is expressed in terms similar to the
other trials, though its outcome is different. See Introduction, p. li.

112. *cry . . . mercy*] beg your honour's
pardon; the forms of address are of
course ironical here.

worst] i.e. you have the least right to
say so (Pooler); cf. *Per.*, IV. iii. 21.

115. *sound*] loyal, true, cf. III. ii. 274;
"honest", l. 116, has a similar meaning.

Chan.   This is too much;
    Forbear for shame my lords.
Gar.   I have done.
Crom.   And I.   120
Chan. Then thus for you my lord, it stands agreed
    I take it, by all voices; that forthwith
    You be convey'd to th'Tower a prisoner,
    There to remain till the king's further pleasure
    Be known unto us; are you all agreed, lords?   125
All. We are.
Cran.   Is there no other way of mercy
    But I must needs to th'Tower, my lords?
Gar.   What other
    Would you expect? You are strangely troublesome:
    Let some o' th' guard be ready there.

Enter the Guard.

Cran.   For me?
    Must I go like a traitor thither?
Gar.   Receive him,   130
    And see him safe i'th'Tower.
Cran.   Stay good my lords,
    I have a little yet to say. Look there my lords;
    By virtue of that ring, I take my cause
    Out of the gripes of cruel men, and give it
    To a most noble judge, the king my master.   135
Cham. This is the king's ring.
Sur.   'Tis no counterfeit.
Suf. 'Tis the right ring, by heaven: I told ye all,

119, 121. S.H. *Chan.*] Capell (*Theobald conj. for l. 121*); *Cham.* F.   120. I have]
F; I've *Pope.*   128. You are] F; you're *Pope.*   132. I have] F; I've *Dyce 2.*
136, 141. S.H. *Cham.*] F; *Cha. Capell*; *Chan. Var. 1821.*

119, 121. *Chan.*] Capell's emendation of *Cham.* (F) is surely right, for the
Chancellor is conducting the business;
minims were subject to much confusion in secretary hand, and the mistake might easily be made. Editors
have seen a similar confusion in the
speech-headings to ll. 136, 141, 181.

122. *voices*] votes, cf. I. ii. 70.

123. *convey'd*] escorted, cf. *R 3*, I. i.
45, "This conduct to convey me to the
Tower".

128. *strangely*] extremely, cf. IV. ii.
112.

130. *Receive*] take into custody, cf.
Cym., IV. iv. 5.

134. *gripes*] clutches, cf. II. ii. 135
and n.

When we first put this dangerous stone a-rolling,
'Twould fall upon ourselves.
Nor.   Do you think my lords
The king will suffer but the little finger   140
Of this man to be vex'd?
Cham.   'Tis now too certain;
How much more is his life in value with him?
Would I were fairly out on't.
Crom.   My mind gave me,
In seeking tales and informations
Against this man, whose honesty the devil   145
And his disciples only envy at,
Ye blew the fire that burns ye: now have at ye.

      Enter KING *frowning on them, takes his seat.*

Gar. Dread sovereign, how much are we bound to heaven
In daily thanks, that gave us such a prince,
Not only good and wise, but most religious: 150
One that, in all obedience, makes the church
The chief aim of his honour, and to strengthen
That holy duty out of dear respect,
His royal self in judgement comes to hear
The cause betwixt her and this great offender.   155

139. Do you] *F;* D'you *Pope.*   147.] S.D. *Enter Henry below* Sisson (*after* burns ye).   148. Dread . . . heaven] *so Pope; two lines in F, ending* Soveraigne, / . . . Heaven.

138–9. *stone . . . ourselves*] proverbial, cf. Prov. xxvi. 27, "he that rolleth up a stone, it will returne upon him" (cited Noble), and Tilley, S 889.

142. *in value with*] esteemed by, cf. *Cor.*, II. ii. 63, "remember / A kinder value of the people".

143. *gave me*] caused me to suspect, cf. *Cor.*, IV. v. 157, "my mind gave me his clothes made a false report of him" (Onions).

144. *tales . . . informations*] malicious gossip (cf. *Ant.*, II. ii. 136) and complaints that would enable proceedings to be taken. Jacob, *Law Dictionary*, says, "An *Information* hath somewhat in it of an Indictment, *viz.*, to alledge the Offence in particular, and also

something in Nature of an Action, to demand what is due . . .".

146. *envy at*] have a grudge against, cf. *John*, III. iv. 73.

147. *Ye . . . burns ye*] proverbial; Tilley cites under 'To blow the coals' (C 465), Edwards, *Paradise of Dainty Devices* (1576), L3ʳ, "I reape no other hire, / But burne my self, and I to blowe the fire".

have at ye] cf. II. ii. 84 and n.

151–2. *makes . . . honour*] i.e. makes it his main object to benefit the church.

153. *dear respect*] heartfelt regard (i.e. for the church); for "dear", cf. *Troil.*, v. iii. 9, "loud and dear petition".

King. You were ever good at sudden commendations,
      Bishop of Winchester. But know, I come not
      To hear such flattery now, and in my presence
      They are too thin and base to hide offences;
      To me you cannot reach. You play the spaniel,   160
      And think with wagging of your tongue to win me;
      But whatsoe'er thou tak'st me for, I'm sure
      Thou hast a cruel nature and a bloody.
      [*To Cranmer.*] Good man, sit down: now let me see the
            proudest
      He, that dares most, but wag his finger at thee,   165
      By all that's holy, he had better starve
      Than but once think his place becomes thee not.
Sur. May it please your grace—
King.   No sir, it does not please me;
      I had thought I had had men of some understanding
      And wisdom of my council; but I find none: 170
      Was it discretion lords, to let this man,
      This good man (few of you deserve that title)
      This honest man, wait like a lousy footboy
      At chamber-door? and one as great as you are?

158. flattery] *F; flatteries Rowe 3.*   presence] *F; presence, F2; presence;
Capell.*   159. base] *F; bare Singer 1 (Malone conj.).*   159–60. offences; / To me
... reach. You] offences, / To me ... reach. You *F; offences. / To me ... reach;
you Rowe; offences. / To me ... reach, you Johnson; offences. / To me ... reach
you Camb. 1865 (after Rann, who reads one for me); offences. / To me ... reach.
You Collier; offences. / To me, ... reach, you Hudson.*   164. S.D. *To Cranmer]
Rowe; not in F.*   164–5. proudest / He,] *so F;* proudest, / He *Collier.*   167. his]
F; this F4.   168. May it] *F; May't Pope.*   169. I ... had had] *F; I had
thought I had Rowe 2; I thought I had Pope; I thought, I had had Theobald.*

156. *sudden commendations*] impromp-
tu compliments, cf. IV. ii. 118.
   159. *base] bare* meaning 'threadbare'
(Onions), and perhaps 'unconcealed',
is a clever, if unnecessary, emendation
by Dyce.
   160. *spaniel*] a favourite image for
flatterers, cf. *Cæs.,* III. i. 43.
   161. *wagging*] cf. I. i. 33 above.
   164–5. *proudest He,*] so F; "he" is
frequently found meaning 'man', cf.
Shr., III. ii. 236, "the proudest he",
Cym., I. iii. 29, but here rhythm and
sense suggest that a comma after

"proudest" may have dropped out,
and Collier's reading, "proudest, / He
that . . ." may well be the correct
one.
   166. *starve*] die, as in *Lr.,* v. iii. 25,
"we'll see 'em starve first".
   167. *his place*] i.e. the office of privy
councillor (Malone). Many editors
follow F4 in reading "this", as a reference to the chair Cranmer occupies.
   169–70. *I . . . council*] The verbal
structure stems from Foxe, who has,
"I thought I had had wiser men of my
counsaile . . .".

Why, what a shame was this? Did my commission   175
Bid ye so far forget yourselves? I gave ye
Power as he was a councillor to try him,
Not as a groom: there's some of ye, I see,
More out of malice than integrity
Would try him to the utmost, had ye mean,   180
Which ye shall never have while I live.

Chan.   Thus far
My most dread sovereign, may it like your grace
To let my tongue excuse all. What was purpos'd
Concerning his imprisonment, was rather
(If there be faith in men) meant for his trial,   185
And fair purgation to the world than malice,
I'm sure, in me.

King.   Well, well my lords, respect him,
Take him and use him well; he's worthy of it.
I will say thus much for him, if a prince
May be beholding to a subject, I   190
Am for his love and service, so to him.
Make me no more ado, but all embrace him;
Be friends for shame my lords: my lord of Canterbury,
I have a suit which you must not deny me;
That is, a fair young maid that yet wants baptism;   195
You must be godfather, and answer for her.

---

180. mean] *F;* means *Pope.*   181. S.H. *Chan.*] *F; Cham. F3.*   190. beholding]
F; beholden *Rowe 2.*   192. him] *F; omitted Johnson.*

175. *shame*] infliction of disgrace, cf.
Ant., v. i. 62, "We purpose her no
shame".
176. *forget yourselves*] lose your sense
of propriety, cf. *Cæs.,* IV. iii. 29.
180–1. *try . . . live*] an allusion no
doubt to the martyrdom Cranmer was
to suffer in 1556, in the reign of
Henry's successor Mary.
180. *try*] quibbling on the senses,
'put on trial' and 'afflict'.
mean] opportunity; for the singular
form *mean,* cf. *Err.,* I. ii. 18 and *Oth.,*
III. i. 39.
182. *like*] please, cf. I. i. 100.
186. *purgation*] a normal law term
for "the Clearing a Man's Self of a

Crime" (Jacob, *Law Dictionary*); cf.
The King's Declarations (1613), B4^r,
"the obstinate shall not be admitted
his purgation, unlesse he pay the third
part of the fine . . .", and *Wint.,* III. ii.
7.
190. *beholding*] indebted, cf. I. iv. 41.
191. *so to him*] so F; it would be possible to punctuate "service. So to him,"
making the phrase an order to the
lords to go to Cranmer and embrace
him.
192. *Make . . . ado*] The same phrase
occurs in *Gent.,* IV. iv. 31 and *1 H 4,* II.
iv. 223; Foxe has, "well use him . . .
and make no more adoe".
196–202. *godfather . . . Dorset*] The

Cran. The greatest monarch now alive may glory
      In such an honour: how may I deserve it,
      That am a poor and humble subject to you?

King. Come, come my lord, you'ld spare your spoons; 200
      you shall have two noble partners with you; the old
      duchess of Norfolk, and Lady Marquess Dorset; will
      these please you?
      Once more my lord of Winchester, I charge you
      Embrace and love this man.

Gar.   With a true heart   205
      And brother-love I do it.

Cran.   And let heaven
      Witness how dear I hold this confirmation.

King. Good man, those joyful tears show thy true heart;
      The common voice I see is verified
      Of thee, which says thus: 'Do my lord of Canterbury 210
      A shrewd turn, and he's your friend for ever'.
      Come lords, we trifle time away: I long
      To have this young one made a Christian.
      As I have made ye one lords, one remain;
      So I grow stronger, you more honour gain.   *Exeunt.* 215

200–3. Come . . . you?] *so F; as verse Pope, omitting* will . . . you?   206. brother-love] *Var. 1793;* Brother; loue *F;* Brothers love *F2.*   208. heart] *F2;* hearts *F.*

information here comes from Holinshed, p. 934; the linkage of the baptism of Elizabeth with Cranmer's trial
is the author's own, cf. note on v. i.
Entry.

    200. *spare . . . spoons*] alluding to the
giving of 'apostle' spoons, twelve to a
set, with the figure of an apostle on the
handle, to godchildren at their
christening; cf. Jonson, *Bartholomew
Fair* (1614), i. iii. 100. The king joking-
ly suggests that Cranmer's modesty is
really niggardliness.

    201. *partners*] i.e. fellow-sponsors.
    202. *Lady Marquess*] i.e. "the old

marchionesse Dorset" (Holinshed, p.
934).

    206. *brother-love*] "Brother; loue I
doe it" (F) may be a version of
"brother, lo(w)e, I do it", and the
present reading a sophistication. For
a confusion of 'love' and 'low', see
Tourneur, *Revenger's Tragedy* (1607;
in *Works*, ed. Nicoll, 1929), II. i. 253,
"note the loue and deiected price of
it".

    209. *voice*] report, cf. III. ii. 405.

    211. *shrewd turn*] an act of malice, an
injury, cf. *All's W.*, III. v. 71; the phrase
is from Foxe, see Appendix II, p. 211.

SCENE III—[*An entrance to the court.*]

Noise and tumult within: enter Porter and his Man.

Port. You'll leave your noise anon ye rascals: do you take
the court for Parish-garden? ye rude slaves, leave
your gaping.

[*One*] *Within.* 'Good master porter, I belong to th'larder'.

Port. Belong to th' gallows, and be hang'd ye rogue; is   5
this a place to roar in? Fetch me a dozen crab-tree
staves, and strong ones; these are but switches to 'em:
I'll scratch your heads; you must be seeing christen-
ings? do you look for ale and cakes here, you rude
rascals?   10

Man. Pray sir, be patient; 'tis as much impossible
(Unless we sweep 'em from the door with cannons)
To scatter 'em, as 'tis to make 'em sleep
On may-day morning, which will never be:

Scene III

Scene III] *Scena Tertia. F; Scene IV. Camb. 1865.   An . . . court.*] *This Ed.; Court
of the Palace. Capell.*   1–10.] *so F; as verse Capell.*   2. Parish] *F;* Paris *F4.
4, 27.* S.H. *One*] *This Ed.; not in F.*   4. master] *Var. 1773;* M. F.   7. switches
to 'em:] *F;* switches.—To 'em *Warburton.*   11–12. impossible / (Unless . . .
cannons)] impossible, / Unlesse . . . Cannons, *F.*

Scene III] The material for this
scene is not provided by the sources,
but see l. 46 n.

1, 2. *leave*] cease, cf. III. i. 2.

2. *Parish-garden*] more often spelled
'Paris Garden', the great centre of
bear- and bull-baiting in London, and
notorious for the noise made by the
animals and spectators, cf. Jonson,
Epicoene (1609), where (IV. iv. 15),
Morose thinks of the noisiest places as
"*London*-bridge, *Paris*-garden, *Belins*-
gate, when the noises are at their
height and lowdest". For other references, see Sugden, *Top. Dict.*, p. 391.

rude] ignorant, barbarous, cf. *Ham.*,
v. i. 109.

3. *gaping*] shouting; *O.E.D.* cites
Middleton, *Family of Love* (1608;
Bullen, III. 17), "Peace, good Gud-
geon, gape not so loud".

4. *belong to*] i.e. am employed in.

6. *roar*] riot noisily; so bullying
swaggerers were called 'roarers', like
Val Cutting, the "Roarer, or Bully" of
Jonson's *Bartholomew Fair* (1614).

crab-tree] i.e. crab apple tree, the
wood of which is very hard; see
Tilley, C 787.

7. *switches*] thin shoots.

9. *ale and cakes*] traditional festival
fare, cf. *Tw. N.*, II. iii. 125, and
Nottingham Borough Records, IV (1889),
Chamberlain's Accounts, 1616–17,
"to the ringers of Saint Maries on
Michaelmas Daye . . . for cakes and ale
there as is auntiently used xiid.";
later, l. 68, the Chamberlain compares the gathering to a "fair".

14. *may-day*] a day of great festivity,
when men went early "into the sweete
meadowes and greene woods" to

We may as well push against Paul's as stir 'em.   15
Port. How got they in, and be hang'd?
Man. Alas I know not, how gets the tide in?
        As much as one sound cudgel of four foot
        (You see the poor remainder) could distribute,
        I made no spare, sir.
Port.   You did nothing, sir.   20
Man. I am not Samson, nor Sir Guy, nor Colbrand,
        To mow 'em down before me; but if I spar'd any
        That had a head to hit, either young or old,
        He or she, cuckold or cuckold-maker,
        Let me ne'er hope to see a chine again,   25
        And that I would not for a cow, God save her.
[One] Within. 'Do you hear master porter?'
Port. I shall be with you presently, good master puppy;
        Keep the door close sirrah.
Man. What would you have me do?   30
Port. What should you do, but knock 'em down by th'
        dozens? Is this Moorfields to muster in? Or have we

---

15. Paul's] *F4;* Powles *F.*   21–6.] *so F; as prose Pope.*   25. chine] *F;* queen
Collier 2.   26. a cow] *F;* a crow *Blair;* a crown *Collier 2;* my cow *Hudson*
(Staunton conj.).   27–8. master . . . master] *Var. 1773;* M. . . . M. *F.*   31–
65.] *so F; as verse Capell.*   31. What . . . do,] *separate line in F.*

---

gather dew, which was thought to
have medicinable properties; for a
description of May-day customs, see
Stow, *Survey of London* (1603), ed.
Kingsford, I. 98–9.

15. *Paul's*] St Paul's Cathedral;
Powles (F) was a common spelling and
form of reference; cf. Haughton, *Englishmen for my Money* (1598–1616;
M.S.R. 1912), l. 250, "his snoute, /
Able to shaddow *Powles,* it is so great";
and Sugden, *Top. Dict.,* pp. 395–8.

21. *Samson . . . Colbrand*] heroes of
legendary strength; as Pooler noted,
the slaying of Colbrand, a giant, by
Guy, Earl of Warwick, is celebrated
in Drayton's *Poly-Olbion* (1613), Song
xii.

24. *He or she*] cf. v. ii. 165.

25–6. *chine . . . her*] unexplained. The
"chine" is defined by Cotgrave
(*Dictionary,* 1611, cited *O.E.D.*), as

"*Eschinon,* the chyne, or upper part of
the backe betweene the shoulders",
and refers to the backs the Porter's
Man has been cudgelling: at the same
time it may mean the appropriate
joint of meat, or a 'crack or fissure',
and there may be a link with "cow" in
the idea of a joint of beef, or in some
bawdy sense if "cow" suggests
"woman" (cf. *Ado,* v. iv. 49). "Not for
a cow, God save her" may have been a
common phrase; it occurs in the MS
play *The Tell-tale,* p. 20, "*Victo*[*ria*]:
. . . rather then my bewty / should play
the villaine . . . / . . . / thus would I
mangle yt. *Julio:* not for a cow god
save her".

32. *Moorfields*] a holiday and summer resort of Londoners, reclaimed
from marshland and made into a park
in 1606; Herford and Simpson (Jonson's *Works,* x. 179) cite R. Johnson,

some strange Indian with the great tool come to
court, the women so besiege us? Bless me, what a fry
of fornication is at door! On my Christian conscience　35
this one christening will beget a thousand, here will
be father, godfather, and all together.

Man. The spoons will be the bigger sir: there is a fellow
somewhat near the door, he should be a brazier by
his face, for o' my conscience twenty of the dog-days　40
now reign in's nose; all that stand about him are
under the line, they need no other penance: that fire-
drake did I hit three times on the head, and three
times was his nose discharg'd against me; he stands
there like a mortar-piece to blow us. There was a　45
haberdasher's wife of small wit near him, that rail'd

---

45. blow us] *F;* blow us up *F3.*

Pleasant Walks of Moor-fields (1607), A3ᵛ, "But to what use are these Fieldes reserved? . . . Only for Cittizens to walke in to take the ayre . . ." Sugden, *Top. Dict.*, p. 353, says that Moorfields was used as a training ground "for the citizen forces", but shows no evidence.

33. *Indian . . . tool*] Many Indians were brought back from America and exhibited in England, cf. the similar reference in *Tp.*, II. ii. 34; the colonization of Virginia (Jamestown was founded in 1608) was very much in the news in 1612, when a lottery was held for it, and 1613, and there seems to be no specific allusion here to a particular man. For the bawdy significance of 'tool', cf. *Cym.*, II. v. 5, and *Two Noble Kinsmen*, III. v. 147 (Brooke, *Shakespeare Apocrypha*, p. 330).

34. *fry*] swarm of offspring, cf. *Mac.*, IV. ii. 84.

38. *spoons*] cf. v. ii. 200 and n.

39. *brazier*] one who makes brass; the sense "a reservoir for charcoal . . . heated to give warmth" (Var. 1778) is not recorded in *O.E.D.* before 1690.

40. *dog-days*] the days, usually reckoned as forty in number, preceding the rise of Sirius the Dog-star about 11 August, and regarded as the

hottest and most unwholesome in the year.

42. *under the line*] i.e. under the equator, cf. Rowlands, *Knave of Hearts* (1613), C1ʳ, "consorted / With such hot spirited fiery feminine; / That heate him more then underneath the line", and *Tp.*, IV. i. 235.

42–3. *fire-drake*] Malone cites Bullokar's *Expositor* (1616), "*Fire-drake.* A fire sometimes seen flying in the night like a dragon"; it is equivalent to "meteor", l. 49.

45. *mortar-piece*] i.e. gaping upwards; this high-angle weapon had a large bore.

blow us] blast us, blow us up; an odd usage.

46. *haberdasher's wife*] Malone cites Jonson's allusion to "all Haberdashers of small wit" in *Magnetic Lady* (1632), Induction, l. 12, and with this cf. the "haberdasher of lyes" of *1 Return from Parnassus* (1606; ed. Leishman, 1949, l. 1212); as Pooler noted, the passage may allude to the wife as silly, and as a dealer in cheap wit. Perhaps the "haberdasher" was suggested by Holinshed, who records that at Anne's coronation, "the companie of the haberdashers" played a prominent part, since the Mayor of

upon me till her pink'd porringer fell off her head, for
kindling such a combustion in the state. I miss'd the
meteor once, and hit that woman, who cried out
'Clubs', when I might see from far some forty trun-   50
cheoners draw to her succour, which were the hope
o'th'Strand where she was quarter'd; they fell on, I
made good my place; at length they came to th'
broomstaff to me, I defied 'em still, when suddenly a
file of boys behind 'em, loose shot, deliver'd such a   55
shower of pebbles, that I was fain to draw mine
honour in and let 'em win the work; the devil was
amongst 'em I think surely.

Port. These are the youths that thunder at a playhouse,
and fight for bitten apples, that no audience but the   60
tribulation of Tower-hill, or the limbs of Limehouse

52. Strand] Strond *F.*   56. pebbles] Pibbles *F.*   61. tribulation] *F;* Tribulation *Theobald.*   limbs] *F;* lambs *Steevens conj.*

London was one (p. 930). The phrase
seems to have remained current for
some time; it occurs in a letter of Pope,
10 April 1706 (*Works*, ed. Elwin and
Courthope, vi. 28).

46–7. *rail'd upon*] abused.

47. *pink'd porringer*] a round cap
resembling the upturned dish, cf.
Nashe, *Unfortunate Traveller* (1594;
McKerrow, ii. 300), "a scull crownd
hat of the fashion of an olde deepe
porringer", and *Shr.*, iv. iii. 65 ff.
M. Linthicum, *Costume in the Drama of
Shakespeare* (1936), cites other examples, and says such hats had gone
out of fashion by 1625 (p. 219).
"Pinked" means ornamented with
perforations, or scalloped.

48. *combustion*] commotion, cf. *Mac.*,
ii. iii. 63.

50. '*Clubs*'] the call that summoned
apprentices to join in a fight, cf.
Dekker, *Honest Whore* (1604; Pearson,
1873, ii. 64), "Sfoot, clubs clubs, pren-
tices, downe with em" (cited *O.E.D.*),
and *Tit.*, ii. i. 37.

50–1. *truncheoners*] cudgel-bearers; a
coinage apparently.

51–2. *hope . . . Strand*] i.e. belonged
to the shops in this street, which was

in the time of James I a fashionable
residential area; see Sugden, *Top.
Dict.*, pp. 488–9.

52–3. *fell on . . . place*] attacked; I defended my position; cf. *Cym.*, v. iii. 23.

34. *broomstaff*] i.e. they came to close
quarters, to fighting with staves; no
earlier use is known to *O.E.D.*

55. *loose shot*] "marksmen not attached to a company" (*O.E.D.*, loose a.
1k); cf. Sir J. Smyth, *Discourse concerning Weapons* (1590), p. 17, "Mos-
quettiers . . . are not to be imployed as
loose shot in skirmishes".

56. *fain*] obliged, cf. *Lr.*, iv. vii. 38.

57. *work*] fort, cf. *Oth.*, iii. ii. 3
(Clarendon Ed.).

59–60. *youths . . . apples*] i.e. the
apprentices; cf. R. Tailor, *The Hog
hath lost his Pearl* (1614), a play performed by apprentices, the prologue
to which says, "We may be pelted off
for all we know / With apples, egges, or
stones from thence below". For further
allusions to the behaviour of the audience, see Chambers, *E.S.*, ii. 548–50,
and *Shakespeare's England*, ii. 276–8.

61. *tribulation . . . Limehouse*] i.e. the
rough crowds who gathered to watch
executions on Tower Hill, where a

their dear brothers, are able to endure. I have some
of 'em in *Limbo Patrum*, and there they are like to
dance these three days; besides the running banquet
of two beadles that is to come.   65

Enter LORD CHAMBERLAIN.

Cham. Mercy o' me; what a multitude are here!
They grow still too; from all parts they are coming,
As if we kept a fair here: where are these porters,
These lazy knaves? Y'have made a fine hand, fellows!
There's a trim rabble let in; are all these   70
Your faithful friends o'th'suburbs? We shall have
Great store of room no doubt, left for the ladies,
When they pass back from the christening.

Port.   And't please your honour,

69. Y'have] *F;* Ye've *Rowe.*   73. And't] *F;* An't *Capell.*

gallows was kept for the punishment of
state prisoners, and the equally rough
population of the dockyard town
Limehouse, a little further eastwards
along the Thames. Limehouse is listed
with "*Shadwell, Wapping,* and other
Sea townes" as providing seamen for
England's merchant fleet by I. R., *The
Trade's Increase* (1615), E4ʳ. There is a
quibble on "limbs", "Lime", and
"Limbo", for which see next note, and
also an echo of the phrase "A limbe of
Sathan . . ." (Day, *Law Tricks,* 1608,
M.S.R., 1950, l. 1135), a popular term
for a rogue, an agent of the devil.

63. Limbo Patrum] properly a
region near hell where dwell the just
who died before the coming of
Christ; here, 'prison', as commonly,
cf. Sugden. *Top. Dict.,* p. 308, and
Parrot, *Mastive* (1615), G1ʳ, "Cap-
taine of the Roaring-boyes . . . now in
Limbo lowzy lies". The phrase perhaps repeats the sound of "limbs" and
"Lime", cf. Middleton, *Black Book*
(1604; Bullen, VIII. 12), "I had a warrant to search from the sherriff of
Limbo. How? from the sherriff of
Lime-street? replied mistress wimble-
chin (for she understood the word

Limbo, as if Limbo had been Latin for
Lime-street) ...".

64–5. *running . . . beadles*] a public
whipping (Johnson); literally a slight
refreshment, cf. I. iv. 12, and as the
Clarendon Ed. suggests, the dessert to
the 'feast' of being in prison. There is a
quibble in "running", for it was a
common punishment to whip offen-
ders through the streets, cf. *2 H 6,* II. i.
136, 158.

68. *fair*] see above, l. 9 and n.

69. *Y'have . . . hand*] i.e. you've made
a fine success of things; the adjective is
usually ironical in this phrase, cf. *Cor.,*
IV. vi. 117, "You have made fair
hands, / You and your crafts".

70. *trim*] fine; ironical, as at I. iii. 38.

71. *suburbs*] being outside the city
walls and jurisdiction, they contained
resorts of the lawless, and were noted
for crime and prostitution, cf. *Cæs.,* II.
i. 285; Nashe, *Christ's Tears over Jeru-
salem* (1593; McKerrow, II. 148),
"*London,* what are thy Suburbes but
licensed Stewes [brothels]?", and
Sugden, *Top. Dict.,* p. 491.

72. *store*] plenty, cf. *Cym.,* I. iv. 107,
"you have store of thieves".

73. *And't*] if it; cf. III. ii. 375.

We are but men, and what so many may do,
Not being torn a-pieces, we have done: 75
An army cannot rule 'em.
Cham.   As I live,
If the king blame me for't, I'll lay ye all
By th' heels, and suddenly; and on your heads
Clap round fines for neglect: y'are lazy knaves,
And here ye lie baiting of bombards when   80
Ye should do service. Hark, the trumpets sound,
Th'are come already from the christening;
Go break among the press, and find a way out
To let the troop pass fairly, or I'll find
A Marshalsea shall hold ye play these two months.   85
Port. Make way there for the princess.
Man.   You great fellow,
Stand close up, or I'll make your head ache.

79. y'are] *F;* you are *Var. 1773;* ye're *Dyce.*   82. Th'are] *F;* They're *Hanmer.*
83. press] preasse *F.*   86–9.] *so F; as prose Pope.*   87–9.] *so F; as two lines
ending* camblet / ... else *Keightley.*

76. *rule*] control.

77–8. *lay ... heels*] put you in fetters,
or in the stocks; cf. *2 H 4*, I. ii. 141.

78. *suddenly*] at once, without warning, cf. III. i. 70.

79. *Clap round fines*] impose heavy
fines, cf. *Mer. V.*, I. iii. 104 (Onions).

80. *baiting of bombards*] harassing
drunkards (as dogs bait a bear), instead of driving them out (doing service). Pooler, following Johnson, interprets as 'drinking', for the 'bombard',
a kind of cannon, had given its name
to a similarly shaped leather bottle, cf.
Tp., II. ii. 21, *1 H 4*, II. iv. 497, where
Falstaff is called "that huge bombard
of sack". "Baiting" may refer to eating, but is not used of drinking; it may
also indicate the action of fluttering
wings (*bating*), suggesting useless
action, or beating (*batting*); but the
chosen interpretation seems as good
as any, although the earliest use of
"bombard" to mean 'drunkard' cited
in *O.E.D.* is in 1617.

83. *press*] crowd, cf. IV. i. 78.

84. *fairly*] properly, cf. I. iv. 31.

85. *Marshalsea*] a prison in South-
wark, which dealt, amongst others,
with offenders belonging to the King's
household, of which the Porter and his
man are members.

86–9. *You ... else*] J. W. Saunders in
Shakespeare Survey 7 (1954), pp. 70–1,
argues strongly that the "great
fellow" here is a member of the
audience singled out at random, and
that the "rail" is the low railing that
certainly ran round the edge of some
Elizabethan stages. The existence of
this is known from the representations
of a stage on the title-page of W.
Alabaster's *Roxana* (1632), and of N.
Richards's *Messallina* (1640), and from
a few references; the most important,
not noticed by Saunders, is in W.
Smith's *Hector of Germany* (1615), H3ᵛ,
where an S.D. reads "Sit on the
Railes" (cited G. F. Reynolds, *Staging
of Elizabethan Plays*, 1940, p. 88). This
play was performed at the Red Bull
theatre, but it is likely, as the text here
suggests, that a stage-rail existed also
at the Globe.

Port. You i'th'chamblet, get up o'th'rail,

I'll peck you o'er the pales else.   *Exeunt.*

SCENE IV—[*The court.*]

Enter Trumpets sounding: then two Aldermen, LORD MAYOR, GARTER, CRANMER, DUKE OF NORFOLK *with his marshal's staff,* DUKE OF SUFFOLK, *two noblemen bearing great standing bowls for the christening gifts: then four noblemen bearing a canopy, under which the* DUCHESS OF NORFOLK, *godmother, bearing the child richly habited in a mantle, &c.; train borne by a lady: then follows the* MARCHIONESS DORSET, *the other god-mother, and ladies. The troop pass once about the stage, and* GARTER *speaks.*

88. chamblet] *F;* camblet *Pope;* camlet *Var. 1793.*   up o'] *F;* off *Rann;* up off *Hudson.*   89. peck] *F;* pick *Johnson.*   pales] *F;* poll *Collier conj. (Ed. 2);* pates *Knight 2.*

Scene IV

Scene IV] *Scena Quarta. F; Scene V. Camb. 1865.*   The court.] *this Ed.; The* Palace. *Theobald; Court of the Palace. Capell.*   Entry. Lord Mayor] *Rowe; L. Maior F.*

88. *chamblet*] camlet, a rich cloth made of silk and goat's hair; cf. G. Wither, *Abuses Stript* (1613), M7ʳ, "We are for *Serges* and *Perpetuanum*; / With other stuffe as *Crow-graine, Chamblets, Rash,* / And such like new devised for-raine trash"; perhaps it was in fashion when the play was written.

89. *peck . . . pales*] pitch you over the rails; for "peck", cf. *Cor.*, I. i. 204, "as high / As I could pick my lance", and for "pales", cf. *R 2*, III. iv. 40, "Why should we in the compass of a pale / Keep law . . .", where a quibbling allusion to stage-rails may be intended. If this interpretation is correct, the Porter must be addressing someone (an imaginary person?) who is on stage, and Saunders's theory would have to be modified; possibly "pales" is a misprint for "poles" (polls = heads), cf. Nixon, *Strange Foot-Post*

(1613), C2ʳ., "to claw men by the poles".

Scene IV

Scene IV] The christening is reported in Holinshed, p. 934 (see Appendix II, pp. 209 ff.), but Cranmer's prophecy, though it contains common-place material about kings in general and Elizabeth in particular, is not owed to the chronicles. For the probable topical significance of this scene, see Introduction, pp. xxix ff.

Entry. Garter] see note on IV. i. 36, Item 5.

marshal's staff]i.e. as Earl Marshal; cf. IV. i. 36, Item 7.

standing bowls] bowls with legs or a base on which they may be stood, cf. *Per.*, II. iii. 65; the gifts are as reported by Holinshed.

habited] clothed, cf. *Wint.*, IV. iv. 557.

Gart. Heaven, from thy endless goodness, send prosperous
　　life, long and ever happy, to the high and mighty
　　princess of England, Elizabeth.

　　　　　Flourish. Enter KING *and Guard.*

Cran. [*Kneeling.*] And to your royal grace, and the good
　　　queen,
　　My noble partners and myself thus pray,　　　　　　　　5
　　All comfort, joy in this most gracious lady,
　　Heaven ever laid up to make parents happy,
　　May hourly fall upon ye.
King.　　　　　　　Thank you good lord archbishop:
　　What is her name?
Cran.　　　　　　　Elizabeth.
King.　　　　　　　　　　　　Stand up lord;
　　　　　　　　　　　　[*The king kisses the child.*]
　　With this kiss take my blessing: God protect thee,　　10
　　Into whose hand I give thy life.
Cran.　　　　　　　Amen.
King. My noble gossips, y'have been too prodigal;
　　I thank ye heartily: so shall this lady,
　　When she has so much English.
Cran.　　　　　　　Let me speak sir,
　　For heaven now bids me; and the words I utter,　　15
　　Let none think flattery, for they'll find 'em truth.
　　This royal infant (heaven still move about her)

1-3. Heaven . . . Elizabeth] *as prose Capell; four lines in F, ending* Heaven /
. . . life, / . . . Mighty / . . . Elizabeth.　　4. S.D. *Kneeling*] *Johnson; not in F.*
9. S.D. *The . . . child*] *Johnson; not in F.*　　11. hand] *F;* hands *Var. 1821.*
12. y'have] *F;* you have *Hanmer;* ye have *Johnson;* ye've *Dyce.*　　17. infant
(heaven . . . her)] infant, Heaven . . . her; *F.*

1-3. *Heaven . . . Elizabeth*] the formula for such an occasion, more or
less as given in Holinshed, and similar
to the proclamation by Garter King of
Arms after the wedding of Princess
Elizabeth in 1613; see Introduction,
p. xxxi.

5. *partners*] fellow-sponsors, cf. v. ii.
201.

11. *Into . . . hand*] into whose charge.

12. *gossips*] godfather and god-
mother, originally 'god-sib', God-re-

lated, i.e. spiritually akin to child and
parents; cf. *Wint.*, II.iii.41 (Clarendon
Ed.).

prodigal] i.e. in gifts, the "standing
bowls" called for in the Entry above.

17. *heaven . . . her*] i.e. God be always
near her; cf. *2 H 6*, III.iii. 19, where
God is called, "thou eternal Mover of
the heavens", an allusion, as perhaps
here, to "the turning vault of heaven",
the dance of the spheres (Sir John
Davies, *Orchestra*, 1596, in ed. Bullett,

Though in her cradle, yet now promises
Upon this land a thousand thousand blessings,
Which time shall bring to ripeness: she shall be   20
(But few now living can behold that goodness)
A pattern to all princes living with her,
And all that shall succeed: Saba was never
More covetous of wisdom and fair virtue
Than this pure soul shall be. All princely graces   25
That mould up such a mighty piece as this is,
With all the virtues that attend the good,
Shall still be doubled on her. Truth shall nurse her,
Holy and heavenly thoughts still counsel her;
She shall be lov'd and fear'd: her own shall bless her;   30
Her foes shake like a field of beaten corn,
And hang their heads with sorrow: good grows with her;
In her days every man shall eat in safety
Under his own vine what he plants, and sing
The merry songs of peace to all his neighbours.   35
God shall be truly known, and those about her
From her shall read the perfect ways of honour,
And by those claim their greatness, not by blood.
Nor shall this peace sleep with her; but, as when
The bird of wonder dies, the maiden phoenix,   40

---

23. Saba] *F; Sheba Rowe 3.*   32. And . . . her] *so Rowe 3; two lines in F,*
ending sorrow: / . . . her.   37. read] *F; tread Collier conj. (Ed. 2).*   ways]
F4; way *F.*

Silver Poets of the Sixteenth Century,
p. 323).

23. *Saba*] the Queen of Sheba; so
spelt in bibles prior to the Authorized
Version of 1611, except the Geneva,
where "Saba" appears only in chapter
headings (Clarendon Ed.); see 1 Kings
x. 1 ff.

26. *mould . . . piece*] go to make such
a person; for "mould up", cf. Marston,
Antonio and Mellida (1602; Wood, I.
32), "earthly durt makes all things . . ./
Moulds me up honour" (cited
O.E.D.); for "piece", a favourite
word for the heroines of the last plays,
cf. *Tp.,* I. ii. 56, etc.

29. *still*] ever.

30. *own*] i.e. people; cf. *Cor.,* I. ix. 21.

33–5. *In . . . neighbours*] borrowed
from the vision of a golden age that
recurs throughout the Old Testament,
cf. 1 Kings iv. 25; 2 Kings xviii. 31;
Isaiah, xxxvi. 16–17; Micah, iv. 4
(cited Pooler), and a favourite reference in relation to the peace of the
reign of James I; see Introduction,
p. xxxii. This part of Cranmer's prophecy seems to be parodied, as
Steevens noted, in B. and F., *Beggar's
Bush* (1622?; *Works,* II. 223), II. i.

37. *read*] learn, cf. *Cym.,* III. iv. 17.

38. *greatness*] nobility.

40–1. *maiden . . . heir*] "She liveth
six hundred and sixtie yeares . . . And
feeling herself aged, she maketh her
nest with peeces of cynamon and in-

Her ashes new create another heir
As great in admiration as herself,
So shall she leave her blessedness to one
(When heaven shall call her from this cloud of darkness)
Who from the sacred ashes of her honour   45
Shall star-like rise, as great in fame as she was,
And so stand fix'd. Peace, plenty, love, truth, terror,
That were the servants to this chosen infant,
Shall then be his, and like a vine grow to him;
Wherever the bright sun of heaven shall shine,   50
His honour and the greatness of his name
Shall be, and make new nations. He shall flourish,
And like a mountain cedar, reach his branches
To all the plains about him: our children's children
Shall see this, and bless heaven.

King.   Thou speakest wonders.

Cran. She shall be, to the happiness of England,   56
An aged princess; many days shall see her,
And yet no day without a deed to crown it.
Would I had known no more; but she must die,
She must, the saints must have her; yet a virgin,   60
A most unspotted lily shall she pass
To th'ground, and all the world shall mourn her.

King. O lord archbishop,

60. her; yet a virgin,] *so F ;* her yet a Virgin; *Theobald.*

cense, and . . . she dieth thereupon.
And out of her marrow and bones
there commeth first a worme, which
afterward turneth to a little birde, that
in time prooveth an other Phenix" (La
Primaudaye, *Third Part of the French
Academy,* 1601, p. 241). This was a
common image of the royal succession;
for its possible reference to Princess
Elizabeth, daughter of James I, cf.
Introduction, p. xxxii.

42. *admiration*] ability to excite
wonder, cf. *Tp.,*iii.i. 38.

44. *cloud of darkness*] a phrase with
biblical echoes, cf. 2 Sam., xxii. 29,
"the Lord will lighten my darkness",
etc.

50–4. *Wherever . . . him*] These lines
are based on the prophecy in Genesis,

xvii. 4–6, ". . . a father of many nations
have I made thee . . . I will make thee
exceeding fruitfull, & will make
nations come of thee: yea, kings shall
proceed of thee" (Geneva), and cf.
Rom., iv. 17, etc. The passage was
frequently cited in reference to the
marriage of Princess Elizabeth in
1613, see Introduction, p. xxxi. Pooler,
following Malone, saw here an allusion to the colonization of Virginia (cf.
v. iii. 33 and n.), and a double compliment, to James and his daughter, is
probably intended.

58. *deed*] a good deed: the phrase
here has proverbial associations, cf.
iii.ii. 155 above, and Tilley, D 60, 'The
better day the better deed', etc.

61. *pass*] cf. iv. ii. 162.

Thou hast made me now a man; never before
This happy child did I get anything.   65
This oracle of comfort has so pleas'd me,
That when I am in heaven I shall desire
To see what this child does, and praise my maker.
I thank ye all. To you my good lord mayor,
And your good brethren, I am much beholding: 70
I have receiv'd much honour by your presence,
And ye shall find me thankful. Lead the way lords,
Ye must all see the queen, and she must thank ye,
She will be sick else. This day, no man think
'Has business at his house; for all shall stay: 75
This little one shall make it Holy-day.   *Exeunt.*

---

64. Thou hast] *F;* Thou'st *Pope.*   70. your] *Theobald (Thirlby conj.);* you *F.*
beholding] *F;* beholden *Pope.*   75. 'Has] *so F;* He has *Capell.*   76. Holy-
day] *F;* holy day *Johnson;* holiday *Var. 1778.*

64. *made . . . man*] ensured my prosperity (*O.E.D.* man, sb¹7.); cf. *Wint.*,
III.iii.124, "You're a made old man",
and *Tp.*, II.ii.32, "there would this
monster make a man" (an equivocal
use).

65. *get*] achieve, quibbling on
'beget'.

66. *oracle*] echoing Welsey's words
at III.ii.104.

70. *your*] Theobald's emendation of

"you" (F) is surely correct, cf. Holinshed, p. 934, "the maior . . . with his
brethren"; final *r* in secretary hand is
often so attenuated as almost to disappear.

beholding] indebted.

74. *sick*] unhappy; often used loosely
of emotional states, cf. *Cym.*, I.vi.119,
"pity, that doth make me sick".

76. *Holy-day*] the occasion is holy as
well as festal.

THE EPILOGUE

'Tis ten to one this play can never please
All that are here: some come to take their ease
And sleep an hour or two; but those we fear
W'have frighted with our trumpets, so 'tis clear
They'll say 'tis naught: others to hear the city   5
Abus'd extremely, and to cry 'That's witty',
Which we have not done neither; that I fear
All the expected good w'are like to hear
For this play at this time, is only in
The merciful construction of good women,   10
For such a one we show'd 'em: if they smile,
And say 'twill do, I know within a while
All the best men are ours; for 'tis ill hap
If they hold, when their ladies bid 'em clap.

Epilogue

4. W'have] *F;* We've *Rowe.*   8. w'are] *F;* we're *Johnson.*

5. *naught*] worthless, cf. *H 5,* I. ii. 73, "his title . . . was corrupt and naught".

5–6. *city . . . witty*] perhaps a glance at the private theatres, as distinct from public theatres like the Globe; abuse of citizens was a stock theme in the former, cf. Field, *Woman is a Weathercock* (1612; ed. W. Peery, 1950), II. i. 273, "Ile thinke / As abiectly of thee, as any Mongrill / Bred in the Citty; Such a Cittizen / As the Playes flout still" (this was a private theatre play); see A. Harbage, *Shakespeare and the Rival Traditions* (1952), p. 274 ff.

7. *that*] so that (Pooler).

8. *expected good*] the praise we looked for.

10. *construction*] interpretation, cf. *Cor.,* v. vi. 21. The appeal in this epilogue to the women first, and from them to the men, is very reminiscent, as Steevens noted, of the epilogues to *AYL.* and *2 H 4.*

Appendix I

HENRY VIII AND THE BURNING OF THE GLOBE THEATRE

There are several contemporary accounts of the burning of the Globe on 29 June 1613, which show that the play being performed then was called *Henry VIII* or *All is True* (see Introduction, pp. xxvi–xxviii). These are printed below, together with a ballad on the subject, first printed in 1816, the authenticity of which has not been proved or disproved.[1] It has, however, been accepted as genuine by Shakespearian scholars. Other contemporary references to the fire may be found, as in Ben Jonson's *Execration upon Vulcan* (1614?), which mentions the "two poor chambers" (guns) that started it. This, and others, are cited in full in E. K. Chambers, *Elizabethan Stage*, II. 419–23, and are not reprinted here.[2]

(1) MS Harleian 7002, folio 268 (British Museum).

The nearest in time is Thomas Lorkin's letter to Sir Thomas Puckering, dated "Lond. this last of June 1613. in great hast". In spite of the professed haste, the letter has many insertions and additions, and perhaps shows an attempt to provide a literary flavour. The account of the fire is sandwiched between a report of the Earl of Southampton's intention to travel to Spa, and a note of a controversy over a book. The pointed brackets indicate insertions; square brackets deletions.

No longer since then yesterday, while Bou^rbege his companie were acting at ye Globe the play of Hen: 8. and there shooting of certayne chambers in way of triumph; the fire ⟨catch'd &⟩ fastened vpon the thatch of ye house and ⟨there⟩ burned so

1. The collection of manuscripts which is said to have contained it was "recently . . . sold . . . to Mr. G. D. Smith of New York" (Chambers, *E.S.*, II. 420, writing in 1923). I have not been able to trace it further.

2. Perhaps it is worth quoting an epigram of John Taylor's not given by Chambers, from *The Nipping and Snipping of Abuses* (1614), Epigram 33, Sig. K3ᵛ, "Aspiring *Phaeton* with pride inspirde, / Misguiding *Phebus* Carre, the world he firde: / But *Ovid* did with fiction serve his turne, / And I in action saw the Globe to burne". The fire seems to have been something of a nine days' wonder.

furiously, as it consumed [the whole house] all in lesse then two houres [;] (the people hauing enough to doe to saue themselues.).

(2) *Reliquiae Wottonianae* (3rd edition, 1672), pp. 425–6; *The Life and Letters of Sir Henry Wotton*, ed. L. Pearsall Smith (2 vols., 1907), II. 32.

The letter is dated 2 July 1613 and is devoted to this account of the Globe fire, except for a brief introduction promising news of state affairs, and a briefer postscript.

Now, to let matters of State sleep, I will entertain you at the present with what hath happened this week at the Banks side. The Kings Players had a new Play called *All is True*, representing some principal pieces of the Reign of Henry 8. which was set forth with many extraordinary circumstances of Pomp and Majesty, even to the matting of the stage; the Knights of the Order, with their Georges and Garter, the Guards with their embroidered Coats, and the like: sufficient in truth within a while to make greatness very familiar, if not ridiculous. Now, King *Henry* making a Masque at Cardinal *Wolseys* House, and certain Canons being shot off at his entry, some of the Paper, or other stuff wherewith one of them was stopped, did light on the Thatch, where being thought at first but an idle smoak, and their eyes more attentive to the show, it kindled inwardly, and ran round like a train, consuming within less then an hour the whole House to the very grounds.

This was the fatal period of that vertuous Fabrique; wherein yet nothing did perish, but a few forsaken Cloaks; only one man had his Breeches set on fire, that would perhaps have broyled him, if he had not by the benefit of a provident wit put it out with bottle ale.

(3) *Letters of John Chamberlain*, I. 467.

From a letter dated 8 July 1613, which sends the latest news to Sir Ralph Winwood.

But the burning of the Globe or play-house on the banck-side on St. Peters day cannot scape you, which fell out by a peale of chambers (that I know not upon what occasion were to be used in the play) the tampin or stoppell of one of them lighting in the thatch that covered the house, burned yt downe to the ground in lesse then two howres with a dwelling house adjoyning: and yt was a great marvayle and fayre grace of God, that the people had so little harme, having but two narrow doores to get out.

(4) John Stow, *Annals or a General Chronicle of England*, continued

by Edmund Howes (1618). The citation is from the 1631 edition, pp. 1003–4.

For the reign of James, the continuation of Stow's chronicle provides something like a diary of important events, amongst which the burning of the Globe found a place.

> Also upon S. *Peters* day last, the Play-house or Theatre, called the *Globe*, upon the Banke-side neere *London*, by negligent discharging of a peale of Ordnance, close to the South side thereof, the Thatch tooke fire, and the wind sodainly disperst the flame round about, and in a very short space the whole building was quite consumed, and no man hurt: the house being filled with people, to behold the play, *viz.* of Henry the eight, And the next spring it was new builded in farre fairer maner then before.

(5) *Gentleman's Magazine*, lxxxvi (February 1816), 114; Chambers, *E.S.*, II. 420–22.

This ballad appeared in an article on the London theatres signed Eu. Hood; its title does not correspond with either of the titles of lost ballads on the fire recorded in the *Stationers' Register* (ed. E. Arber, III. 528), on the "sodayne Burninge of the Globe" and "a doleful ballad of the general overthrow of the famous theater . . ."; but it seems that ballads were not frequently entered in the Register, and its non-appearance there signifies little. However, Dr H. F. Brooks draws my attention to the association of "petition" and "abhor" in the last stanza; the use of "abhor" in this connection seems only to have arisen in the reign of Charles II when, in 1679–80, petitions were organized appealing for the assembling of parliament, which Charles had prorogued, and thereupon "a set of counter-petitions was promoted by the court, expressing an abhorrence of all seditious practices"; when parliament eventually met, in October 1680, the commons "voted these abhorrers to be betrayers of the liberties of the nation" (G. Burnet, *The History of My Own Time*, ed. O. Airy, 1900, II. 248, 262). This may be a clue to the real date of the ballad. The verse is very crude.

A Sonett upon the pittiful burneing of the Globe
Playhouse in London

Now sitt the downe, Melpomene,
Wrapt in a sea-cole robe;
And tell the dolefull tragedie,
That late was playd at Globe:
For noe man that can singe and saye,
Was scard on St. Peter's daye.
    Oh sorrow, pitifull sorrow, and yett all this is true.

All yo^w that please to understand,
Come listen to my storye;
To see Death with his rakeing brande,
Mongst such an auditorye:
Regarding neither Cardinall's might,
Nor yet the rugged face of Henry the eight.
   Oh sorrow &c.

This fearfull fire beganne above,
A wonder strange and true;
And to the stage-howse did remove
As round as Taylor's clewe;
And burnt downe both beam and snagge,
And did not spare the silken flagge.
   Oh sorrow &c.

Out runne the Knights, out runne the Lords,
And there was great adoe;
Some lost their hatts, and some their swords;
Then out runne Burbidge too;
The reprobates thoughe druncke on munday,
Pray'd for the Foole and Henry Condye.
   Oh sorrow &c.

The perry wiggs and drumme-heads frye,
Like to a butter firkin;
A wofull burneing did betide
To many a good buffe jerkin:
Then with swolne lipps, like druncken Flemmings,
Distressed stood old stuttering Heminges.
   Oh sorrow &c.

Noe shower his raine did there downe force,
In all that sunn-shine weather:
To save that great renowned howse,
Nor thou, O alehowse! neither:
Had it begunne belowe, sans doubte
Their wives for feare had p——d itt out.
   Oh sorrow, &c.

Bee warned you stage strutters all
Least yo^w againe be catched;
And such a burneing doe befall,
As to them whose howse was thatched:
Forbeare your whoreing breeding biles,
And lay up that expence for tiles.
   Oh sorrow, &c.

Goe drawe yo^w a petition
And doe yo^w not abhorr itt;
And gett with low submission,
A licence to begg for itt:
In churches, sans Churchwardens checks
In Surrey and in Middlesex.
    Oh sorrow, pittifull sorrow, and yett all this is true.

APPENDIX II

SOURCES

This appendix contains passages from Holinshed's *Chronicles* and Foxe's *Acts and Monuments* on which large sections of *Henry VIII* were certainly based. It includes some material not given in Boswell-Stone's *Shakespeare's Holinshed* and it is presented in a different, and it is hoped, more helpful arrangement. The sequence here is chronological, i.e. the passages are given in the order in which they appear in the chronicles; each quotation is preceded by the line references of the passage(s) in the play to which it relates, and by the year-date, where the historian has made it clear. It can thus be seen at a glance to what extent the dramatist foraged among Holinshed's pages in particular, jumping backwards and forwards, selecting, re-arranging, and compressing his material. The side-notes, which are especially common in Holinshed, are only given where they do not directly repeat what is in the main text, and have relevance to the play. Shakespeare's use of his sources is discussed in the Introduction, pp. xxxiii ff., and in the commentary throughout.

Raphael Holinshed, *Chronicles*, vol. III (1587).

    [III. ii. 120 ff.] 1508: pp. 796–7. This yeare was Thomas Ruthall made bishop of Durham . . . To whome . . . the king gave in charge to write a booke of the whole estate of the kingdome. . .

    . . . But see the mishap! that a man in all other things so provident, should now be so negligent. . . For this bishop having written two bookes (the one to answer the kings command, and the other intreating of his owne private affaires) did bind them both after one sort in vellame . . . as the one could not by anie especiall note be discerned from the other. . .

Now when the cardinall came to demand the booke due to the king: the bishop unadvisedlie commanded his servant to bring him the booke bound in white vellame... The servant ... brought foorth ... the booke intreating of the state of the bishop, and ... gave it to the cardinall to beare unto the king. The cardinall ... understanding the contents thereof, he greatlie rejoised, having now occasion ... to bring the bishop into the kings disgrace.

Wherefore he went foorthwith to the king, delivered the booke into his hands, and breefelie informed the king of the contents thereof; putting further into the kings head, that if at anie time he were destitute of a masse of monie, he should not need to seeke further therefore than to the cofers of the bishop, who by the tenor of his owne booke had accompted his proper riches and substance to the value of a hundred thousand pounds. Of all which when the bishop had intelligence ... he was striken with such greefe of the same. that he shortlie through extreame sorrow ended his life...

[II. i. 5–41] 1520: p. 850. During this time [of the handing over of Tournai to the French king] remained in the French court diverse yoong gentlemen of England, and they with the French king rode dailie disguised through Paris, throwing egges, stones, and other foolish trifles at the people, which light demeanour of a king was much discommended and jeasted at. And when these yoong gentlemen came againe into England, they were all French, in eating, drinking, and apparell, yea, and in French vices and brags, so that all the estates of England were by them laughed at: the ladies and gentlewomen were dispraised, so that nothing by them was praised, but if it were after the French turne, which after turned them to displesure, as you shall heare.

p. 852. Then the kings councell caused the lord chamberleine to call before them diverse of the privie chamber, which had beene in the French court, and banished them the court for diverse considerations, laieng nothing particularlie to their charges, & they that had offices were commanded to go to their offices. Which discharge out of court greeved sore the hearts of these yoong men, which were called the kings minions.

[I. ii. 189–92] 1520: p. 852–3. the king speciallie rebuked sir William Bulmer knight, bicause he being his servant sworne, refused the kings service, and became servant to the duke of Buckingham

[I. i. 1 ff.] 1520: p. 853. The French king desirous to continue the friendship latelie begun betwixt him and the king of England, made meanes unto the cardinall, that they might in some convenient place come to an interview togither... But the fame went that the cardinall desired greatlie, of himselfe, that the two kings might meet, who mesuring by his will what was convenient, thought it should make much with his glorie, if in France also at some high assemblie of noble men, he should be seene in his vaine pompe and shew of dignitie: hee therefore breaketh with the king of that matter . . . and thus with his persuasions the K. began to conceive an earnest desire to see the French king, and thereupon appointed to go over to Calis, and so in the marches of Guisnes to meet with him... Herewith were letters written to all such lords, ladies, gentlemen, and gentlewomen, which should give their attendance on the king and queene, which incontinentlie put themselves in a readinesse after the most sumptuous sort. Also it was appointed that the king of England, & the French king, in a campe betweene Ard and Guisnes, with eighteene aides, should in June next insuing abide all commers being gentlemen, at the tilt, at tourneie, and at barriers . . . both the kings committed the order and manner of their meeting, and how manie daies the same should continue, & what preheminence each should give to other, unto the cardinall of Yorke; which to set all things in a certeintie, made an instrument, conteining an order and direction concerning the premisses by him devised and appointed.

The whole maner of the interview committed to the cardinall.

[I. i. 72 ff., II. i. 40 ff., III. ii. 259–64.] 1520: p. 855.

The peeres of the realme receiving letters to prepare
themselves to attend the king in this journie, and no
apparant necessarie cause expressed, why nor
wherefore; seemed to grudge, that such a costlie
journie should be taken in hand to their importunate
charges and expenses, without consent of the whole
boord of the councell. But namelie the duke of Buckingham, being a man of a loftie courage, but not
most liberall, sore repined that he should be at so
great charges for his furniture foorth at this time,
saieng; that he knew not for what cause so much
monie should be spent about the sight of a vaine
talke to be had, and communication to be ministred
of things of no importance. Wherefore he sticked not
to saie, that it was an intollerable matter to obeie
such a vile and importunate person. . . Now such
greevous words as the duke thus uttered against him,
came to the cardinals eare; whereupon he cast before
hand all waies possible to have him in a trip, that he
might cause him to leape headlesse. But bicause he
doubted his freends, kinnesmen, and alies, and
cheeflie the earle of Surrie lord admerall, which had
married the dukes daughter, he thought good first to
send him some whither out of the waie. . .

At length there was occasion offered him to com-
passe his purpose, by occasion of the earle of Kildare
his comming out of Ireland. For the cardinall . . .
accused him to the king, of that he had not borne
himselfe uprightlie in his office in Ireland, where he
was the kings lieutenant . . . he was committed to
prison, and then by the cardinals good preferment
the earle of Surrie was sent into Ireland as the kings
deputie, in lieu of the said earle of Kildare, there to
remaine rather as an exile, than as lieutenant to the
king, even at the cardinals pleasure, as he himselfe
well perceived.

[i. ii. 171–6.] 1520: p. 856. Now it chanced that
the duke . . . went before into Kent unto a manor
place which he had there. And whilest he staid in
that countrie till the king set forward, greevous complaints were exhibited to him by his farmars and

tenants against Charles Knevet his surveiour, for such bribing as he had used there amongest them. Whereupon the duke tooke such displeasure against him, that he deprived him of his office, not knowing how that in so dooing he procured his owne destruction, as after appeared.

[I. i. 176–93.] 1529: p. 856. [On the visit of Charles V to England, May 1520] ... but speciallie to see the queene of England his aunt was the emperour his intent, of whome ye may be sure he was most joifullie received. . . . The chiefe cause that mooved the emperour to come thus on land at this time, was to persuade that by word of mouth, which he had before done most earnestlie by letters; which was, that the king should not meet with the French king at anie interview: for he doubted least if the king of England & the French king should grow into some great friendship and faithfull bond of amitie, it might turne him to displeasure. . . . And forsomuch as he knew the lord cardinall to be woone with rewards, as a fish with a bait: he bestowed on him great gifts, and promised him much more, so that hee would be his friend, and helpe to bring his purpose to passe. The cardinall ... promised to the emperour, that he would so use the matter, as his purpose should be sped.

[I. i. 6 ff.] 1520: p. 858. The daie of the meeting [of the Field of the Cloth of Gold] was appointed to be on the thursdaie the seaventh of June, upon which daie the two kings met in the vale of Andren, accompanied with such a number of the nobilitie of both realmes, so richly appointed in apparell, and costlie jewels ... that a woonder it was to behold and view them in their order and roomes, which everie man kept according to his appointment.

The two kings meeting in the field, either saluted other in most loving wise, first on horssebacke, and after alighting on foot eftsoones imbraced with courteous words, to the great rejoising of the beholders: and after they had thus saluted ech other,

they went both togither into a rich tent of cloath of
gold . . . and then departed for that night, the one to
Guisnes, the other to Ard.

[I. i. 33–8.] 1520: p. 859. [A long description of the
tilts, at which "the two kings surmounted all the rest
in prowesse and valiantnesse".]

[I. i. 89–94.] 1520: p. 860–1. On mondaie, the
eighteenth of June, was such an hideous storme of
wind and weather, that manie conjectured it did
prognosticate trouble and hatred shortlie after to
follow betweene princes.

[I. i. 212–22, I. ii. 129 ff.] 1521: p. 862–3. . . . the
cardinall boiling in hatred against the duke of Buckingham . . . devised to make Charles Knevet, that
had beene the dukes surveior . . . an instrument to
bring the duke to destruction. This Knevet being
had in examination before the cardinall, disclosed
all the dukes life. And first he uttered, that the duke
was accustomed by waie of talke, to saie, how he
meant so to use the matter, that he would atteine to
the crowne, if king Henrie chanced to die without
issue: & that he had talke and conference of that
matter on a time with George Nevill, lord of Aburgavennie, unto whome he had given his daughter in
marriage; and also that he threatned to punish the
cardinall for his manifold misdooings, being without
cause his mortall enimie.

The cardinall having gotten that which he sought
for . . . procured Knevet . . . that he should with a
bold spirit and countenance object and laie these
things to the dukes charge, with more if he knew it
when time required. Then Knevet partlie provoked
with desire to be revenged, and partlie mooved with
hope of reward, openlie confessed, that the duke had
once fullie determined to devise meanes how to make
the king away, being brought into a full hope that he
should be king, by a vaine prophesie which one
Nicholas Hopkins, a monke of an house of the Chartreux order beside Bristow, called Henton, sometime his confessor had opened unto him.

The cardinall having thus taken the examination of Knevet, went unto the king, and declared unto him, that his person was in danger by such traitorous purpose, as the duke of Buckingham had conceived in his heart . . . he exhorted the king to provide for his owne suertie with speed. The king hearing the accusation, inforced to the uttermost by the cardinall, made this answer; If the duke have deserved to be punished, let him have according to his deserts. The duke . . . was streightwaies attached, and brought to the Tower by sir Henrie Marneie, capteine of the gard. . . . There was also attached the foresaid Chartreux monke, maister John de la Car *aliàs* de la Court, the dukes confessor, and sir Gilbert Perke priest, the dukes chancellor.

. . . by the knights and gentlemen, he was indicted of high treason, for certeine words spoken . . . by the same duke . . . to the lord of Aburgavennie: and therewith was the same lord attached . . . and so likewise was the lord Montacute, and both led to the Tower.

[I. ii. 151–71, 178–210.] 1521: p. 864. . . . the same duke . . . said unto one Charles Knevet esquier, after that the king had reprooved the duke for reteining William Bulmer knight into his service, that if he had perceived that he should have beene committed to the Tower . . . he would have plaied the part which his father intended to have put in practise against king Richard the third at Salisburie, who made earnest sute to have come unto the presence of the same king Richard: which sute if he might have obteined, he having a knife secretlie about him, would have thrust it into the bodie of king Richard, as he had made semblance to kneele downe before him. And in speaking these words, he maliciouslie laid his hand upon his dagger, and said, that if he were so evill used, he would doo his best to accomplish his pretensed purpose, swearing to confirme his word by the bloud of our Lord.

Beside all this, the same duke . . . at London in a place called the Rose, within the parish of saint Laurence Poultnie . . . demanded of the said Charles

Knevet esquier, what was the talke amongest the
Londoners concerning the kings journeie beyond the
seas? And the said Charles told him, that manie
stood in doubt of that journie, least the Frenchmen
meant some deceit towards the king. Whereto the
duke answered, that it was to be feared, least it
would come to passe, according to the words of a
certeine holie moonke. For there is (saith he) a Chartreux moonke, that diverse times hath sent to me,
willing me to send unto him my chancellor: and I
did send unto him John de la Court my chapleine,
unto whome he would not declare anie thing, till de
la Court had sworne unto him to keepe all things
secret, and to tell no creature living what hee should
heare of him, except it were to me.

The duke dis-
covereth the
secrecie of all
the matter to
his owne
undooing.

And then the said moonke told de la Court, that
neither the king nor his heires should prosper, and
that I should indevour my selfe to purchase the good
wils of the communaltie of England [willed him in
anie wise to procure the love of the commons, p. 863];
for I the same duke and my bloud should prosper,
and have the rule of the realme of England. Then
said Charles Knevet; The moonke maie be deceived
through the divels illusion: and that it was evill to
meddle with such matters. Well (said the duke) it
cannot hurt me... And further, at the same time, the
duke told the said Charles, that if the king had miscarried now in his last sicknesse, he would have
chopped off the heads of the cardinall, of sir Thomas
Lovell knight, and of others; and also said, that he
had rather die for it, than to be used as he had beene.

[II. i. 1 ff.] 1521: pp. 864-5.... the cardinall chief-
lie procured the death of this noble man... Which
thing caused the dukes fall the more to be pitied and
lamented ... the duke ... was arreigned in Westminster hall, before the duke of Norffolke ... to dis-
cerne and judge the cause of the peeres ... the duke
was brought to the barre, and upon his arreigne-
ment pleaded not guiltie, and put himselfe upon his
peeres. Then was his indictment read, which the
duke denied to be true, and (as he was an eloquent
man) alledged reasons to falsifie the indictment;

pleading the matter for his owne justification verie
pithilie and earnestlie. The kings attourneie against
the dukes reasons alledged the examinations, confessions, and proofes of witnesses.

The duke desired that the witnesses might bee
brought foorth. And then came before him Charles
Knevet, Perke, de la Court, & Hopkins the monke
... which like a false hypocrite had induced the duke
to the treason with his false forged prophesies.
Diverse presumptions and accusations were laid
unto him by Charles Knevet, which he would faine
have covered. The depositions were read, & the
deponents delivered as prisoners to the officers of the
Tower... Thus was this prince duke of Buckingham
found giltie of high treason, by a duke, a marques,
seven earles, & twelve barons. The duke was brought
to the barre sore chafing, and swet marvellouslie; &
after he had made his reverence, he paused a while.
The duke of Norffolke as judge said; Sir Edward,
you have heard how you be indicted of high treason
... putting your selfe to the peeres of the realme,
which have found you giltie... You shall be led to
the kings prison, and there laid on a hardle, and so
drawne to the place of execution, and there be
hanged...

The duke of Buckingham said, My lord of Norffolke, you have said as a traitor should be said
unto, but I was never anie: but my lords I nothing
maligne for that you have doone to me, but the
eternall God forgive you my death, and I doo: I shall
never sue to the king for life, howbeit he is a gratious
prince, and more grace may come from him than I
desire. I desire you my lords and all my fellowes to
pray for me. Then was the edge of the axe turned
towards him, and he led into a barge. Sir Thomas
Lovell desired him to sit on the cushins and carpet
ordeined for him. He said nay; for when I went to
Westminster I was duke of Buckingham, now I am
but Edward Bohune the most caitife of the world.
Thus they landed at the Temple, where received
him sir Nicholas Vawse & sir William Sands baro-
nets, and led him through the citie, who desired ever
the people to pray for him, of whome some wept and

lamented, and said: This is the end of evill life, God
forgive him . . . it is pitie that hee behaved him so . . .
[the] shiriffes . . . led him to the scaffold on Tower
hill, where he said he had offended the kings grace
through negligence and lacke of grace, and desired
all noble men to beware by him, and all men to pray
for him, and that he trusted to die the kings true man.

[i. i. 200; ii. i. 53, 107 ff.] 1521 : pp. 869–70. Henrie
Stafford . . . duke of Buckingham . . . raising warre
against Richard the third usurping the crowne, was
in the first yeare of the reigne . . . betraied by his man
Humfrie Banaster (to whome being in distresse he
fled for succour) and . . . beheaded without arreigne-
ment or judgement . . .
    Edward Stafford soone to Henrie . . . being also
duke of Buckingham . . . was constable of England,
earle of Hereford, Stafford, and Northhampton. . .
He is tearmed in the books of the law . . . to be the
floure & mirror of all courtesie. This man . . . was by
Henrie the seventh restored to his fathers inheri-
tance, in recompense of the losse of his fathers life. . .

[ii. ii. 121 ff.] 1522: pp. 871–2. This Pace was a
right worthie man. . . Learned he was also, and in-
dued with many excellent good gifts. . . But . . . the
more was he misliked of the cardinall, who sought
onelie to beare all the rule himselfe . . . so that he procured that this doctor Pace under color of ambas-
sage, should be sent foorth of the realme. . .

[i. i. 94.] 1523: p. 872. . . . the French king commanded all Englishmens goods being in Burdeaux,
to be attached, and put under arrest. . .

[i. ii. 20 ff.] 1525: p. 891. The king being determined thus to make wars in France . . . by the cardinall there was devised strange commissions, and
sent . . . into everie shire . . . that the sixt part of
everie mans substance should be paid in monie or
plate to the king. . . Hereof followed such cursing,
weeping, and exclamation against both king & cardinall, that pitie it was to heare.

... The duke of Suffolke sitting in commission ... in Suffolke, persuaded ... the rich clothiers to assent therto: but when they came home, and went about to discharge and put from them their spinners, carders, fullers, weavers, and other artificers ... the people began to assemble in companies ... the rage of the people increased, railing openlie on the duke. ... And herewith there assembled togither after the maner of rebels foure thousand men. ..

A rebellion in
Suffolke by
the grievous-
nesse of the
subsidie.

[I. ii. 68 ff.] 1525: pp. 891–2. The king ... willed to know by whose meanes the commissions were so streictlie given foorth. .. The cardinall excused himselfe, and said ... the kings councell, and namelie the judges, said, that he might lawfullie demand anie summe by commission, and that by the consent of the whole councell it was doone. .. The king indeed was much offended. .. Therefore he ... caused letters to be sent into all shires, that the matter should no further be talked of: & he pardoned all them that had denied the demand. .. The cardinall, to deliver himselfe of the evill will of the commons ... caused it to be bruted abrode, that through his intercession the king had pardoned and released all things.

[II. i. 147 ff.] 1527: p. 897. There rose a secret brute in London that the kings confessor ... had told the king that the marriage betweene him and the ladie Katharine, late wife to his brother prince Arthur was not lawfull: whereupon the king should sue a divorse. .. The king was offended with those tales, and sent for sir Thomas Seimor maior of the citie of London, secretlie charging him to see that the people ceassed from such talke.

The kings
marriage
brought in
question.

[II. i. 154 ff.; II. ii. 90–107; III. ii. 85–6.] 1528: p. 906. The truth is, that ... the king ... determined to have the case examined. .. The cardinall verelie was put in most blame for this scruple now cast into the kings conscience, for the hate he bare to the emperor, bicause he would not grant to him the archbishoprike of Toledo, for the which he was a suter. And therefore he ... sought a divorse betwixt

the king and the queene, that the king might have
had in marriage the duchesse of Alanson, sister unto
the French king...

... the king ... thus troubled in conscience ...
thought to know the truth by indifferent judges,
least peradventure the Spaniards, and other also in
favour of the queene would saie, that his owne subjects were not indifferent judges in this behalfe. And
therefore he wrote his cause to Rome, and also sent
... to the great clearkes of all christendome, to know
their opinions, and desired the court of Rome to send
into his realme a legat, which should be indifferent,
and of a great and profound judgement, to heare the
cause debated. At whose request the whole consistorie of the college of Rome sent thither Laurence
Campeius, a preest cardinall, a man of great wit and
experience ... and with him was joined in commission the cardinall of Yorke...

[II. ii. 112–30.] 1528: p. 907. ... the king ... bad
hir [Katherine] choose the best clearks of his realme
to be of hir counsell, and licenced them to doo the
best on hir part that they could, according to the
truth...

... About this time the king received into favour
doctor Stephan Gardiner, whose service he used in
matters of great secrecie and weight, admitting him
in the roome of doctor Pace, the which being continuallie abroad in ambassages ... by the cardinals
appointment, at length he tooke such greefe therewith, that he fell out of his right wits.

[II. iv. Entry, 1–55, 119–239.] 1528: pp. 907–8.
The place where the cardinals should sit to heare the
cause of matrimonie ... was ordeined to be at the
Blacke friers... The court was platted in tables and
benches in manner of a consistorie, one seat raised
higher for the judges to sit in. Then as it were in the
midst of the said judges aloft above them ... was a
cloth of estate hanged, with a chaire roiall under the
same, wherein sat the king; and besides him, some
distance from him sat the queene, and under the
judges feet sat the scribes and other officers...

The king is
desirous to be
resolved by
the opinions
of the learned
touching his
marriage.

The maner of
the session, e-
verie perso-
nage of ac-
count in his
place.

Then before the king and the judges within the court sat the archbishop of Canturburie Warham, and all the other bishops... Thus was the court furnished. The judges commanded silence whilest their commission was read, both to the court and to the people assembled. That doone the scribes commanded the crier to call the king by the name of king Henrie of England, come into the court, &c. With that the king answered and said, Heere. Then called he the queene by the name of Katharine queene of England come into the court, &c. Who made no answer, but rose out of hir chaire.

And bicause shee could not come to the king directlie, for the distance severed betweene them, shee went about by the court, and came to the king, kneeling downe at his feet, to whome she said in effect as followeth: Sir (quoth she) I desire you to doo me justice and right, and take some pitie upon me, for I am a poore woman, and a stranger, borne out of your dominion, having heere no indifferent counsell, & lesse assurance of freendship. Alas sir, what have I offended you, or what occasion of displeasure have I shewed you, intending thus to put me from you after this sort? I take God to my judge, I have beene to you a true & humble wife, ever conformable to your will and pleasure, that never contraried or gainsaide any thing thereof, and being alwaies contented with all things wherein you had any delight, whether little or much, without grudge or displeasure, I loved for your sake all them whome you loved, whether they were my freends or enimies.

I have beene your wife these twentie yeares and more, & you have had by me diverse children. If there be anie just cause that you can alleage against me, either of dishonestie, or matter lawfull to put me from you; I am content to depart to my shame and rebuke: and if there be none, then I praie you to let me have justice at your hand. The king your father was in his time of excellent wit, and the king of Spaine my father Ferdinando was reckoned one of the wisest princes that reigned in Spaine manie yeares before. It is not to be doubted, but that they had gathered as wise counsellors unto them of everie

Queene Katharines lamentable and pithie speech in presence of the court.

realme, as to their wisedoms they thought meet, who deemed the marriage betweene you and me good and lawfull, &c. Wherefore, I humblie desire you to spare me, untill I may know what counsell my freends in Spaine will advertise me to take, and if you will not, then your pleasure be fulfilled. With that she arose up, making a lowe curtesie to the king, and departed from thence.

The queene departing out of the court is called againe.

The king being advertised that shee was readie to go out of the house, commanded the crier to call hir againe, who called hir by these words; Katharine queene of England, come into the court. With that (quoth maister Griffith) Madame, you be called againe. On on (quoth she) it maketh no matter, I will not tarrie, go on your waies. And thus she departed, without anie further answer at that time ... and never would appeare after in anie court. The king perceiving she was departed, said these words in effect: For as much (quoth he) as the queene is gone, I will in hir absence declare to you all, that shee hath beene to me as true, as obedient, and as conformable a wife, as I would wish or desire. She hath all the vertuous qualities that ought to be in a woman of hir dignitie ... she is also surelie a noble woman borne...

With that quoth Wolseie the cardinall: Sir, I most humblie require your highnesse, to declare before all this audience, whether I have beene the cheefe and first moover of this matter unto your maiestie or no, for I am greatlie suspected heerein. My lord cardinall (quoth the king) I can well excuse you in this matter, marrie (quoth he) you have beene rather against me in the tempting heereof, than a setter forward or moover of the same. The speciall cause that mooved me unto this matter, was a certeine scrupulositie that pricked my conscience, upon certeine words spoken at a time when it was, by the bishop of Baion the French ambassador, who had beene hither sent, upon the debating of a marriage to be concluded betweene our daughter the ladie Marie, and the duke of Orleance, second son to the king of France.

Upon the resolution and determination whereof, he desired respit to advertise the king his maister

thereof, whether our daughter Marie should be legitimate in respect of this my marriage with this
woman, being sometimes my brothers wife. Which
words once conceived within the secret bottome of
my conscience, ingendered such a scrupulous doubt,
that my conscience was incontinentlie accombred,
vexed, and disquieted; whereby I thought my selfe
to be greatlie in danger of Gods indignation. Which
appeared to be (as me seemed) the rather, for that he
sent us no issue male: and all such issues male as my
said wife had by me, died incontinent after they
came into the world, so that I doubted the great displeasure of God in that behalfe.

The king
confesseth that
the sting of
conscience
made him
mislike this
mariage.

Thus my conscience being tossed in the waves of a
scrupulous mind, and partlie in despaire to have
anie other issue than I had alredie by this ladie now
my wife, it behooved me further to consider the state
of this realme, and the danger it stood in for lacke of
a prince to succeed me, I thought it good in release
of the weightie burthen of my weake conscience, &
also the quiet estate of this worthie relme, to attempt
the law therin, whether I may lawfullie take another
wife . . . not for anie displeasure or misliking of the
queenes person and age, with whome I would be as
well contented to continue, if our mariage may stand
with the laws of God, as with anie woman alive.

In this point consisteth all this doubt that we go
about now to trie, by the learning, wisedome, and
judgement of you our prelats and pastors of all this
our realme . . . to whose conscience & learning I have
committed the charge and judgement. . . Wherein,
after that I perceived my conscience so doubtfull, I
mooved it in confession to you my lord of Lincolne
then ghostlie father. And for so much as then you
your selfe were in some doubt, you mooved me to
aske the counsell of all these my lords: whereupon I
mooved you my lord of Canturburie, first to have
your licence . . . to put this matter in question, and so
I did of all you my lords: to which you granted under
your seales, heere to be shewed. That is truth, quoth
the archbishop of Canturburie. After that the king
rose up, and the court was adjorned untill another
daie.

[II. iv. 72–119, 231–5.] 1529: p. 908. Heere is to
be noted, that the queene in presence of the whole
court most greevouslie accused the cardinall of untruth, deceit, wickednesse, & malice, which had
sowne dissention betwixt hir and the king hir husband; and therefore openlie protested, that she did
utterlie abhorre, refuse, and forsake such a judge, as
was not onelie a most malicious enimie to hir, but
also a manifest adversarie to all right and justice, and
therewith did she appeale unto the pope, committing hir whole cause to be judged of him. But notwithstanding this appeale, the legats sat weekelie . . .
and still they assaied if they could by anie meanes
procure the queene to call back hir appeale, which
she utterlie refused to doo. The king would gladlie
have had an end in the matter, but when the legats
drave time, and determined upon no certeine point,
he conceived a suspicion, that this was doone of purpose, that their dooings might draw to none effect or
conclusion.

The king
mistrusteth
the legats of
seeking de-
laies.

[III. i. 24–97, 177–84.] 1529: p. 908. . . . the king
sent the two cardinals to the queene . . . to persuade
with hir by their wisdoms, and to advise hir to surrender the whole matter into the kings hands by hir
owne consent & will, which should be much better
to hir honour, than to stand to the triall of law, and
thereby to be condemned, which should seeme
much to hir dishonour.

Queene Ka-
tharine and
the cardinals
have commu-
nication in
hir privie
chamber.

The cardinals being in the queenes chamber of
presence, the gentleman usher advertised the queene
that the cardinals were come to speake with hir.
With that she rose up, & with a skeine of white
thred about hir necke, came into hir chamber of
presence, where the cardinals were attending. At
whose comming, quoth she, What is your plesure
with me? If it please your grace (quoth cardinall
Wolseie) to go into your privie chamber, we will
shew you the cause of our comming. My lord (quoth
she) if yee have anie thing to saie, speake it openlie
before all these folke, for I feare nothing that yee can
saie against me, but that I would all the world

should heare and see it, and therefore speake your mind. Then began the cardinall to speake to hir in Latine. Naie good my lord (quoth she) speake to me in English.

Forsooth (quoth the cardinall) good madame, if it please you, we come both to know your mind how you are disposed to doo in this matter betweene the king and you, and also to declare secretlie our opinions and counsell unto you: which we doo onelie for verie zeale and obedience we beare unto your grace.

My lord (quoth she) I thanke you for your good will, but to make you answer in your request I cannot so suddenlie, for I was set among my maids at worke, thinking full little of anie such matter, wherein there needeth a longer deliberation, and a better head than mine to make answer: for I need counsell in this case which toucheth me so neere, & for anie counsell or freendship that I can find in England, they are not for my profit. What thinke you my lords, will anie Englishman counsell me, or be freend to me against the K. pleasure that is his subject? Naie forsooth. And as for my counsell in whom I will put my trust, they be not here, they be in Spaine in my owne countrie.

And my lords, I am a poore woman, lacking wit, to answer to anie such noble persons of wisedome as you be, in so weightie a matter, therefore I praie you be good to me poore woman, destitute of freends here in a forren region, and your counsell also I will be glad to heare. And therewith she tooke the cardinall by the hand, and led him into hir privie chamber with the other cardinall, where they tarried a season talking with the queene...

The queene refuseth to make sudden answer to so weightie a matter as the divorse.

[II. iv. 229–35.] 1529: p. 908. With that (quoth cardinall *Campeius*) ... I will adiourne this court for this time, according to the order of the court of Rome. ... This protracting of the conclusion of the matter, king Henrie tooke verie displeasantlie. Then cardinall *Campeius* tooke his leave of the king and nobilitie, and returned towards Rome.

[III. ii. 1–3, 30–6, 228–51, 336–49, 451–4.] 1529:
pp. 908–9. Whilest these things were thus in hand,
the cardinall of Yorke was advised that the king had
set his affection upon a yoong gentlewoman named
Anne, the daughter of sir Thomas Bullen vicount
Rochford, which did wait upon the queene. This
was a great griefe unto the cardinall, as he that perceived aforehand, that the king would marie the said
gentlewoman. . . Wherefore he began with all diligence to disappoint that match, which by reason of
the misliking that he had to the woman, he judged
ought to be avoided more than present death. While
the matter stood in this state . . . the cardinall required the pope by letters and secret messengers, that in
anie wise he should defer the judgement of the
divorse, till he might frame the kings mind to his
purpose.

The kings
affection and
goodwill to the
ladie Anne
Bullen.

Howbeit he went about nothing so secretlie, but
that the same came to the kings knowledge, who
tooke so high displeasure with such his cloked dissimulation, that he determined to abase his degree.
. . . When the nobles . . . perceived the cardinall to be
in displeasure, they began to accuse him of such
offenses as they knew might be proved against him,
and thereof they made a booke conteining certeine
articles, to which diverse of the kings councell set
their hands. The king understanding more plainlie
by those articles, the great pride, presumption, and
covetousnesse of the cardinall, was sore mooved
against him; but yet kept his purpose secret for a
while. . .

In the meane time the king, being informed that
all those things that the cardinall had doone by his
power legantine . . . were in the case of the premunire . . . caused his atturneie . . . to sue out a writ
of premunire against him. . . And further . . . the
king sent the two dukes of Norffolke and Suffolke to
the cardinals place at Westminster, who (went as
they were commanded) and finding the cardinall
there, they declared that the kings pleasure was that
he should surrender up the great seale into their
hands, and to depart simplie unto Asher, which was
an house situat nigh unto Hampton court, belonging

to the bishoprike of Winchester. The cardinall demanded of them their commission that gave them such authoritie, who answered againe, that they were sufficient commissioners, and had authoritie to doo no lesse by the kings mouth. Notwithstanding, he would in no wise agree in that behalfe, without further knowledge of their authoritie, saieng; that the great seale was delivered him by the kings person, to injoy the ministration thereof, with the roome of the chancellor for the terme of his life, whereof for his suertie he had the kings letters patents.

This matter was greatlie debated betweene them with manie great words, in so much that the dukes were faine to depart againe without their purpose, and rode to Windsore to the king, and made report accordinglie; but the next daie they returned againe, bringing with them the kings letters. Then the cardinall delivered unto them the great seale. . . Then the cardinall called all his officers before him, and tooke accompt of them for all such stuffe, whereof they had charge. And in his gallerie were set diverse tables, whereupon laie a great number of goodlie rich stuffe. . .

There was laid on everie table, bookes reporting the contents of the same, and so was there inventaries of all things in order against the kings comming. . . Then he had two chambers . . . wherein were set up two broad and long tables upon trestles, whereupon was set such a number of plate of all sorts, as was almost incredible. . .

After this, in the kings bench his matter for the premunire, being called upon, two atturneis, which he had authorised . . . confessed the action, and so had judgement to forfeit all his lands, tenements, goods, and cattels, and to be out of the kings protection. . .

[III. ii. 393-4.] 1529: p. 910. On the foure & twentith of November, was sir Thomas Moore made lord chancellor, & the next day led to the Chancerie . . .

[III. ii. 293-332.] 1529: p. 912. During this parlement was brought downe to the commons the booke of articles, which the lords had put to the king against the cardinall, the chiefe whereof were these.

1. First, that he without the kings assent had procured to be a legat, by reason whereof he tooke awaie the right of all bishops and spirituall persons.

2. Item, in all writings which he wrote to Rome, or anie other forren prince, he wrote *Ego & rex meus*, I and my king: as who would saie, that the king were his servant...

4. Item, he without the kings assent carried the kings great seale with him into Flanders, when he was sent ambassador to the emperour.

5. Item, he without the kings assent, sent a commission to sir Gregorie de Cassado, knight, to conclude a league betweene the king & the duke of Ferrar, without the kings knowledge...

7. Item, that he caused the cardinals hat to be put on the kings coine...

9. Item, that he had sent innumerable substance to Rome, for the obteining of his dignities, to the great impoverishment of the realme.

Thomas Crumwell advanced to the kings service.

[III. ii. 412 ff.] 1530: p. 913. But at this time diverse of his servants departed from him to the kings service, and in especiall Thomas Crumwell one of his chiefe counsell, and chiefe dooer for him in the suppression of abbeies.

[III. ii. 454–7; IV. ii. 12–30, 48–68.] 1530: pp. 916–17. Unto whom the cardinall said ... Sir, heere my lord of Northumberland hath arrested me... When night came, the cardinall waxed verie sicke... The next daie he rode to Notingham, and there lodged that night more sicke: and the next daie he rode to Leicester abbeie, and by the waie waxed so sicke that he was almost fallen from his mule; so that it was night before he came to the abbeie of Leicester, where at his comming in at the gates, the abbat with all his convent met him with diverse torches light, whom they honorablie received and welcomed.

To whom the cardinall said: Father abbat, I am

come hither to lay my bones among you, riding so
still untill he came to the staires of the chamber . . .
and as soone as he was in his chamber he went to bed.
This was on the saturday at night, and then increased he sicker and sicker, untill mondaie, that all men
thought he would have died: so on tuesdaie saint
Andrewes even, master Kingston came to him. . .
Well, well, master Kingston (quoth the cardinall) I
see the matter how it is framed: but if I had served
God as diligentlie as I have doone the king, he would
not have given me over in my greie haires. . . Then
they did put him in remembrance of Christ his passion, & caused the yeomen of the gard to stand by to
see him die . . . & incontinent the clocke stroke eight,
and then he gave up the ghost, and departed this
present life: which caused some to call to remembrance how he said the daie before, that at eight of
the clocke they should loose their master. . .

The cardinall ascribeth his fall to the just judgement of God.

This cardinall . . . was a man undoubtedly borne
to honor . . . exceeding wise, faire spoken, high
minded, full of revenge, vitious of his bodie, loftie to
his enimies, were they never so big, to those that
accepted and sought his freendship woonderfull
courteous, a ripe schooleman, thrall to affections,
brought a bed with flatterie, insatiable to get, and
more princelie in bestowing, as appeareth by his two
colleges at Ipswich and Oxenford, the one over-
throwne with his fall, the other unfinished, and yet
as it lieth for an house of students, considering all the
appurtenances incomparable thorough Christendome, whereof Henrie the eight is now called founder, bicause he let it stand. . . [Wolsey was] never
happie till this his overthrow. Wherein he shewed
such moderation, and ended so perfectlie, that the
houre of his death did him more honor, than all the
pompe of his life passed. . .

This Thomas Wolseie was a poore mans sonne of
Ipswich . . . & there borne, and being but a child,
verie apt to be learned . . . he was made bachellor of
art, when he passed not fifteene yeares of age, and
was called . . . the boie bachellor.

Example of
pride and ar-
rogancie.

[II. iv. 105–15.] 1530: p. 917. Here is the end and
fall of pride and arrogancie of men exalted by fortune to dignitie: for in his time he was the hautiest
man in all his proceedings alive, having more respect
to the honor of his person, than he had to his
spirituall profession, wherin should be shewed all
meekenes, humilitie, and charitie . . . his sudden
comming up from preferment to preferment; till he
was advanced to that step of honor, which making
him insolent, brought him to confusion.

[II. iv. Entry.] 1530: p. 920. Then had he his two
great crosses of silver, the one of his archbishoprike,
the other of his legacie, borne before him whither soever he went or rode, by two of the tallest priests that
he could get within the realme.

[II. iv. Entry.] 1530: p. 921. Now of his order in
going to Westminster hall. . . Before him was borne
first the broad seale of England, and his cardinals
hat, by a lord, or some gentleman of worship . . . & as
soone as he was once entered into his chamber of
presence, his two great crosses were there attending
to be borne before him: then cried the gentlemen
ushers, going before him bare headed, and said:
. . . make waie for my lords grace. Thus went he
downe through the hall with a sergeant of armes before him, bearing a great mace of silver, and two
gentlemen carieng two great pillers of silver.

[I. iv.] 1530: pp. 921–2. . . . when it pleased the
king for his recreation to repaire to the cardinals
house . . . there wanted no preparations. . .
On a time the king came suddenlie thither in a
maske with a dozen maskers all in garments like
sheepheards, made of fine cloth of gold . . . with
visards of good physnomie. . . And before his
entring into the hall, he came by water to the water
gate without anie noise, where were laid diverse
chambers and guns charged with shot, and at his
landing they were shot off . . . it made all the noblemen, gentlemen, ladies, and gentlewomen, to muse
what it should meane, comming so suddenlie, they

sitting quiet at a solemne banket, after this sort.

First yee shall understand, that the tables were set
in the chamber of presence . . . the lord cardinall
sitting under the cloth of estate, there having all his
service alone: and then there was set a ladie with a
noble man, or a gentleman and a gentlewoman
throughout all the tables in the chamber on the one
side . . . all which order and devise was doone by the
lord Sandes then lord chamberleine to the king and
by sir Henrie Gilford comptroller of the kings
majesties house. Then immediatlie after the great
chamberleine, and the said comptroller, sent to
looke what it should meane (as though they knew
nothing of the matter) who looking out of the win-
dowes . . . returned againe and shewed him, that it
seemed they were noblemen and strangers that arrived at his bridge, comming as ambassadours from
some forren prince.

With that (quoth the cardinall) I desire you, bicause you can speake French, to take the paines to go
into the hall, there to receive them according to their
estates, and to conduct them into this chamber,
where they shall see us, and all these noble personages being merie at our banket, desiring them to sit
downe with us, and to take part of our fare. Then . . .
they received them . . . and conveied them up into
the chamber. . . At their entring into the chamber
two and two togither, they went directlie before the
cardinall, where he sate and saluted him reverentlie.

The cardinall
reverentlie sa-
luted of the
maskers.

To whom the lord chamberleine for them said:
Sir, for as much as they be strangers, and can not
speake English, they have desired me to declare unto
you, that they having understanding of this your
triumphant banket, where was assembled such a
number of excellent dames, they could doo no lesse
under support of your grace, but to repaire hither, to
view as well their incomparable beautie, as for to
accompanie them at mum-chance, and then to
danse with them: and sir, they require of your grace
licence to accomplish the said cause of their coming.
To whom the cardinall said he was verie well content they should so doo. Then went the maskers, and
first saluted all the dames. . .

... Then quoth the cardinall to the lord chamberleine, I praie you (quoth he) that you would shew
them, that me seemeth there should be a nobleman
amongst them, who is more meet to occupie this seat
and place than I am, to whome I would most gladlie
surrender the same according to my dutie, if I knew
him.

Then spake the lord chamberleine to them in
French, and ... said to my lord cardinall: Sir (quoth
he) they confesse, that among them there is such a
noble personage, whome, if your grace can appoint
him out from the rest, he is content to disclose himselfe, and to accept your place. With that the cardinall taking good advisement among them, at the
last (quoth he) me seemeth the gentleman with the
blacke beard, should be even be [*sic*.]: and with that
he arose out of his chaire, and offered the same to the
gentleman in the blacke beard. . . The person to
whom he offered the chaire was sir Edward Nevill,
a comelie knight, that much more resembled the
kings person in that maske than anie other.

The king dis-
visardeth his
face and is ve-
rie pleasant.

The king perceiving the cardinall so deceived,
could not forbeare laughing, but pulled downe his
visar. . . The cardinall eftsoons desired his highnesse to take the place of estate. To whom the king
answered, that he would go first and shift his
apparell, and so departed into my lord cardinals
chamber...

Then the king tooke his seat under the cloth of
estate. . . Thus passed they foorth the night with
banketting, dansing, and other triumphs...

[IV. ii. 33–44.] 1530: p. 922. This cardinall ... was
of a great stomach, for he compted himselfe equall
with princes, & by craftie suggestion gat into his
hands innumerable treasure: he forced little on
simonie, and was not pittifull, and stood affectionate
in his owne opinion: in open presence he would lie
and saie untruth, and was double both in speach and
meaning: he would promise much & performe little:
he was vicious of his bodie, & gave the clergie evill
example...

[IV. i. 94–9.] 1532: p. 928. The king having purchased of the cardinall after his attendure . . . his
house at Westminster, called Yorke place . . . he
bestowed great cost in going forward with the building thereof, and changed the name, so that it was
after called the kings palace of Westminster.

[II. iii. 60–4.] 1532: p. 928. On the first of September . . . the K. being come to Windsor, created the
ladie Anne Bullongne marchionesse of Penbroke,
and gave to hir one thousand pounds land by the
year. . .

[III. ii. 41–2, 67–71, 400–6; IV. i. 22–33, 108–12.]
1533: pp. 929–30. And herewith upon his returne
[from France], he married privilie the ladie Anne
Bullongne the same daie, being the fourteenth daie
of November . . . which marriage was kept so secret,
that verie few knew it till Easter next insuing, when
it was perceived that she was with child. . . It was
also enacted . . . that queene Katharine should no
more be called queene, but princesse Dowager, as
the widow of prince Arthur. In the season of the last
summer died William Warham archbishop of Canturburie, and then was named to that sea Thomas
Cranmer the kings chapleine, a man of good learning, . . . which latelie before had beene ambassador
from the king to the pope.

After that the king perceived his new wife to be
with child, he caused all officers necessarie to be
appointed to hir, and so on Easter even she went to
hir closet openlie as queene; and then the king
appointed the daie of hir coronation to be kept on
Whitsundaie next following. . . The assesment of the
fine was appointed to Thomas Cromwell, maister of
the kings jewell house, & councellor to the king, a
man newlie received into high favour. . . The matter
of the queenes appeale whereunto she still sticked
. . . was communed of . . .

This matter was opened . . . to the ladie Katharine
Dowager . . . the which persisted still in hir former
opinion, and would revoke by no meanes hir appeale
to the court of Rome. Whereupon the archbishop of

Canturburie accompanied with the bishops of London, Winchester, Bath, Lincolne, and divers other learned men in great number, rode to Dunstable, which is six miles from Ampthill, where the princesse Dowager laie, and there . . . she was cited to appeare before the said archbishop in cause of matrimonie . . . and at the daie of appearance she appeared not, but made default, and so she was called . . . fifteene daies togither, and at the last, for lacke of appearance, by the assent of all the learned men there present, she was divorsed from the king, and the marriage declared to be void and of none effect.

[IV. i. 14–19.] 1533: p. 930. In the beginning of Maie, the king caused open proclamations to be made, that all men that claimed to doo anie service, or execute anie office at the . . . coronation . . . should put their grant . . . in the Starrechamber before Charles duke of Suffolke, for that time high steward of England, . . . and other commissioners. The duke of Norffolke claimed to be erle marshall. . .

[IV. i. 36–94.] 1533: p. 933. First went gentlemen . . . after them the judges in their mantels of scarlet and coiffes. Then followed the knights. . . After them came the lord chancellor in a robe of scarlet open before . . . after him came the kings chapell and the moonks solemnelie singing with procession, then came abbats . . . then after them went the maior of London with his mace and garter in his cote of armes, then went the marquesse Dorset in a robe of estate which bare the scepter of gold, and the earle of Arundell which bare the rod of ivorie with the dove both togither.

Then went alone the earle of Oxford . . . which bare the crowne, after him went the duke of Suffolke in his robe of estate also for that daie being high steward of England, having a long white rod in his hand, and the lord William Howard with the rod of the marshalship, and everie knight of the garter had on his collar of the order. Then proceeded foorth the queene in a circot and robe of purple velvet furred with ermine in hir here coiffe and circlet as she had the saturdaie [p. 931, hir haire hanged downe, but on hir head shee had a coife with a circlet about it full of rich stones], and over hir was borne the cano-pie by foure of the five ports, all crimsin with points of blue and red . . . and the bishops of London and Winchester bare up the laps of the queenes robe. The queenes traine which was verie long was borne by the old duches of Norffolke: after hir folowed ladies being lords wives, which had circots of scarlet. . .

The queene under a cano-pie borne by foure of the cinque ports.

When she was thus brought to the high place made in the middest of the church, betweene the queere and the high altar, she was set in a rich chaire. And after that she had rested a while, she descended downe to the high altar and there pro-strate hir selfe while the archbishop of Canturburie said certeine collects: then she rose, and the bishop annointed hir on the head and on the brest, and then she was led up againe, where . . . the archbishop set the crowne of saint Edward on hir head, and then delivered hir the scepter of gold in hir right hand, and the rod of ivorie with the dove in the left hand, and then all the queere soong *Te Deum*, &c. Which doone, the bishop tooke off the crowne of saint Edward. . .

Now in the meane season everie duches had put on their bonets a coronall of gold wrought with flowers, and everie marquesse put on a demie coron-all of gold, everie countesse a plaine circlet of gold without flowers, and everie king of armes put on a crowne of coper and guilt, all which were worne till night. When the queene had a little reposed hir, the companie returned in the same order that they set foorth . . . then she was brought to Westminster hall.

[v. i. 158 ff.; v. iv. Entry and 1 ff.] 1533: pp. 934-5. The seventh of September . . . the queene was delivered of a faire yoong ladie, on which daie the duke of Norffolke came home to the christening, which was appointed on the wednesdaie next follow-ing. . . The godfather at the font, was the lord arch-bishop of Canturburie, the godmothers, the old dutches of Norffolke, & the old marchionesse Dorset widow . . . the child was named Elizabeth.

. . . the child was brought to the hall, and then
everie man set forward; first the citizens two and
two . . . next after them the aldermen and the maior
alone: next the maior the kings councell . . . then
came the earle of Essex, bearing the covered basins
gilt . . . the marquesse Dorset bearing the salt.

Behind him . . . the old dutches of Norffolke bare
the child in a mantell of purple velvet, with a long
traine furred with ermine. The duke of Norffolke
with his marshall rod went on the right hand of the
said dutches, and the duke of Suffolke on the left
hand. . . The countesse of Kent bare the long traine
of the childs mantell . . . in the middest over the said
child was borne a canopie, by the lord Rochford, the
lord Husce, the lord William Howard, and by the
lord Thomas Howard . . . after the child followed
manie ladies. . .

When the ceremonies and christening were ended,
Garter cheefe king of armes cried alowd, God of his
infinite goodnesse, send prosperous life & long to the
high and mightie princesse of England Elizabeth: &
then the trumpets blew. Then the archbishop of
Canturburie gave to the princesse a standing cup of
gold: the dutches of Norffolke gave to hir a standing
cup of gold . . . the marchionesse of Dorset gave three
gilt bolles. . . Then they set forwards, the trumpets
going before. . .

In this order they brought the princesse to the Q.
chamber, & tarried there a while, with the maior &
his brethren the aldermen. . . From that time forward
(God himselfe undertaking the tuition of this yoong
princesse, having predestinated hir to the accomp-
lishment of his divine purpose) she prospered under
the lords hand, as a chosen plant of his watering, &
after the revolution of certeine yeares with great
felicitie and joy of all English hearts atteined to the
crowne of this realme, and now reigneth over the
same: whose heart the Lord direct in his waies, and
long preserve hir in life, to his godlie will and pleasure, and the comfort of all true and faithfull subjects.

[IV. ii. 108–54.] 1536: p. 939. The princesse

Dowager lieng at Kimbalton, fell into hir last sicknesse, whereof the king being advertised, appointed
the emperors ambassador . . . named Eustachius
Caputius, to go to visit hir, and to doo his commendations to hir, and will hir to be of good comfort.
The ambassador with all diligence did his duetie
therein, comforting hir the best he might: but she
within six daies after, perceiving hir selfe to wax
verie weake and feeble, and to feele death approch-
ing at hand, caused one of hir gentlewomen to write
a letter to the king, commending to him hir daughter
and his, beseeching him to stand good father unto
hir: and further desired him to have some consideration of hir gentlewomen that had served hir, and to
see them bestowed in marriage. Further, that it
would please him to appoint that hir servants
might have their due wages, and a yeeres wages
beside. This in effect was all that she requested,
and so immediatlie hereupon she departed this
life. . .

John Foxe, *Acts and Monuments* (1597). [Foxe assigns no date to the
following excerpts; they will be found in almost identical terms in the
1583 edition of *Acts and Monuments*, pp. 1052, 1863, 1866. The second
extract is from a report of Cranmer's life given among accounts of the
lives of martyrs of Queen Mary's reign; he died in 1556.]

[v. ii. 43–9.] p. 959. [from a speech of Stokesley,
Bishop of London to his clergy] My friendes all, you
knowe well that we be men fraile of condition and no
Aungels, and by frailtie and lacke of wisdome, we
have misdemeaned our selfe towarde the king our
soveraigne Lord and his lawes. . .

[v. ii. 210–13.] p. 1691. . . . it came into a common
proverbe: Doe unto my lord of Canturbury displeasure or a shrewd turne, and then you may bee
sure to have him your friend whiles he liveth.

[v. i. 40–54, 79–157; v. ii.] pp. 1693–4. Notwithstanding, not long after that, certaine of the Counsaile, whose names neede not to be repeated, by the

intisement & provocation of his ancient enemie the
Bishop of Winchester, and other of the same sect,
attempted the king against him, declaring plainely,
that the Realme was so infected with heresies and
heretickes, that it was daungerous to his highnesse,
farther to permit it unreformed, least peradventure
by long suffering, such contention should arise, and
ensue in the Realme among his subjects, that thereby might spring horrible commotions, and uprores,
like as in some partes of Germanie, it did not long
ago: The enormitie whereof they could not impute
to any so much, as to the Archbishop of Canturbury,
who by his own preaching, and his Chapleins had
filled the whole Realme full of divers pernicious
heresies. The king would needes knowe his accusers.
They answered that forasmuch as he was a Counseller no man durst take upon him to accuse him:
but if it would please his highnesse, to commit him to
the Tower for a time. . .

The king perceiving their importunate sute
against the archbishop (but yet not meaning to have
him wronged . . .) graunted unto them that they
should the next day, commit him to the Tower for
his triall. When night came, the king sent Sir
Anthonie Denie about midnight, to Lambeth to the
Archbishop, willing him forthwith to resort unto him
at the Court. The message done, the Archbishop
speedily addressed himselfe to the Court, and comming into the Galerie where the king walked, and
taried for him, his highnesse said: Ah my Lorde of
Canturbury, I can tell you newes. For divers waighty
considerations it is determined by me, and the
Counsaile, that you to morrowe at nine of the clocke
shall be committed to the Tower, for that you and
your Chaplaines . . . have taught and preached, and
thereby sowen . . . such . . . heresies, that it is feared,
the whole realme being infected with them no small
contention, and commotions will rise . . . as of late
daies the like was in divers parts of Germanie, and
therfore the Counsell have requested me, for the
triall of the matter, to suffer thē to commit you to the
tower, or else no man dare come forth, as witnesse in
these matters, you being a Counsellor.

When the king had said his mind, the Archb. kneeled downe and said: I am content if it please your grace, with al my hart, to go thither at your highnes commandement, and I most hũbly thank your majesty that I may come to my triall, for there be that have many waies slandered me, and nowe this way I hope to trie my selfe not worthy of such report.

The king perceiving the mans uprightnesse, joyned with such simplicitie, saide: Oh Lorde, what maner a man be you? What simplicitie is in you? I had thought that you would rather have sued to us to have taken the paines to have heard you, and your accusers together for your triall, without any such indurãce. Do not you know, what state you be in with the whole world, and how many great enemies you have? Do you not consider what an easie thing it is, to procure three or foure false knaves to witnesse against you? Thinke you to have better lucke that waie, then your maister Christ had? I see by it, you will run headlong to your undoing, if I would suffer you. Your enemies shall not so prevaile against you, for I have otherwise devised with my selfe to keepe you out of their handes. Yet notwithstanding to morrow when the Counsaile shall sit, and send for you, resort unto them, and if in charging you with this matter, they do commit you to the tower, require of them . . . that you may have your accusers brought before them without any further indurance, and use for your selfe as good perswasions that way as you may devise, and if no intreatie or reasonable request will serve, then deliver unto them this my ring . . . and saie unto them, if there be no remedie my Lords, but that I must needes go to the tower, then I revoke my cause from you, and appeale to the kinges owne person by this token unto you all, for . . . so soone as they shall see this my ryng, they knowe it so well that they shall understande that I have resumed the whole cause into mine owne handes. . .

The Archbishop perceiving the kinges benignity so much to him wards, had much ado to forbeare teares. Well, said the K. go your waies my Lord, and do as I have bidden you. My L. humbling himselfe with thankes, tooke his leave of the kinges highnesse for that night.

The archbishop being one of the Counsel, made to stand at the Counsel chāber doore waiting.

On the morrow about 9. of the clocke before noone, the counsaile sent a gentleman Usher for the Archbishop, who when hee came to the Counsaile chamber doore, could not be let in, but of purpose (as it seemed) was compelled there to waite among the Pages, Lackies, and serving men all alone. D. Buts the kings phisition resorting that way, and espying how my lord of Cant. was handled, went to the kings highnesse and said: My Lorde of Cant. if it please your grace is well promoted: for nowe he is become a Lackey or a serving man, for yonder hee standeth this halfe hower at the Counsaile Chamber doore amongste them. It is not so (quoth the king) I trowe, nor the Counsaile hath not so little discretion as to use the Metropolitane of the Realme in that sort, specially being one of their own number. But let them alone (saide the King) and wee shall heare more soone.

Anone the Archbishop was called into the Counsaile chamber, to whom was alleadged, as before is rehearsed. The Archb. aunswered in like sort, as the king had advised him: and in the end when he perceived that no maner of perswasion or intreatie could serve, he delivered them the kings ring, revoking his cause into the kings hands. The whole Counsaile being thereat somewhat amazed, the Earle of Bedford with a loud voice confirming his words with a solemne othe, said: when you first began the matter my Lordes, I told you what would come of it. Do you thinke that the king will suffer this mans finger to ake? Much more (I warrant you) will hee defend his life against brabling varlets. You doe but cumber your selves to heare tales and fables against him. And so incontinently upon the receipt of the kings token, they all rose, and caried to the K. his ring, surrendring that matter as the order and use was, into his own hands.

The coūsaile be ing set against the Archb he sheweth ye kings ring and appea leth from them.

When they were all come to the kings presence, his highnes with a severe countenance, said unto them: Ah my Lordes, I thought I had had wiser men of my counsaile then now I find you. What discretion was

this in you, thus to make the Primate of the realme
& one of you in office, to waite at the counsaile
chamber doore amongst serving men? You might
have considered that he was a counsellor as wel as
you, and you had no such commission of me so to
handle him. I was content that you should trie him
as a Counseller, and not as a meane subject. But now
I well perceive that things be done against him
maliciouslie, and if some of you might have had your
mindes, you would have tried him to the uttermost.
But I doe you all to wit, and protest, that if a Prince
may bee beholding unto his subject (and so solemnelie laying his hand upon his brest) said: by the faith
I owe to God, I take this man here my Lord of
Canturburie, to bee of all other a most faithfull subject unto us, and one to whome wee are much beholding, . . . And with that one or two of the chiefest
of the Counsaile, making their excuse, declared, that
in requesting his induraunce, it was rather ment for
his triall, and his purgation against the common
fame , and slander of the worlde, then for any malice
conceived against him. Well, well my Lordes (quoth
the king) take him and well use him, as hee is worthy
to be, and make no more adoe. And with that every
man caught him by the hand, and made faire
weather of altogethers, which might easilie bee done
with that man.

And it was much to be marveiled, that they would
go so far with him, thus to seeke his undoing, this
well understanding before, that the king most entirely loved him & alwaies would stand in his
defence . . . as many other times the kinges patience
was by sinister informations against him tried.

Absence of real villains;
Henry seems truly troubled

D'you mind if I open these windows

No, I don't...

It's very warm in here

Yes it is. Ah-hư.